THE GREEK PHILOSOPHERS

(The Founders of Western Civilization)

By

Harry G. Costis, Ph.D.
Professor Emeritus, CSU Fresno, California
Lecturer on Greek Philosophy; Elderhostel Program

An historical perspective on the Greek philosophers
as human beings, scholars, and concerned citizens;
summarizing their theories, research, and applications.
This is a comprehensive narrative of human intellectual
evolution affecting man's history--in the span of less than 600 years.

Fresno, California, 2004

WHAT OTHERS SAY........

"...The combination of history and philosophy is rare...."

Jack Pitt, Professor of Philosophy
California State University, Fresno

"...This is a "magnum opus." It is this kind of book that keeps the spirit of ancient Greece alive..."

Stephen Benko, Professor of Classical History
Sonoma, California

"...What a masterpiece! I am going to set it on the coffee table in my front room and try to read some everyday..."

Charles Weaver, Ph.D.
St. Mary's University; San Antonio, Texas.

"...In the Prologue of The Greek Philosophers, Dr. Costis writes that his work is designed to give in a concise manner for the layman, and in encyclopedic fashion, the salient points of the Greek philosophers in a manner devoid of complicated jargon, so that an initiate can understand. As one of these initiates, I can state unequivocally that Dr. Costis has succeeded not only in achieving his goal, but also in surpassing it. For me, reading his book proved to be a revelation—an epiphanic experience...."

Patricia Booras
Philoptochos Society; Fresno, California

"...The Greek Philosophers, a profound and unique book; a realistic account of life in ancient Greece....."

Aris Zavitzanos, President
The Hellenic Cultural Institute; Monterey, California.

"....I have always wanted to find such a comprehensive reference book that delineates Greek philosophy from its origins on through its influence on thought throughout the ancient world. I am certain that the poet Robinson Jeffers, who was himself a student of Greek philosophy and a translator of Euripides, would have been an enthusiastic reader of The Greek Philosophers ..."

Alex A.Vardamis, President
Robinson Tor House Foundation; Carmel, California

"...Good grounding of Plato's work in pre-Socratic thought...... Precise in bringing out the aims of the author, the meaning of the study of the Greek thinkers in his intellectual development, and the ideals which they inspire..."

Mariana Anagnostopoulos, Professor of Philosophy
California State University, Fresno.

**This Book is dedicated
to my wife**

Paula Ann (Kalypso)

The Greek cities in the Classical Age, Vth century BC

Classics Publishing Company
Damareos 185, Athens, Greece
B.O. Box 26854, Fresno, California, 93729-6854

Library of Congress Cataloguing–in-Publication Data
          Costis, Harry G.,
The Greek Philosophers (The Founders of Western Civilization).

ISBN 0-9748044-0-1

10 9 8 7 6 5 4 3 2 1

"…….Let me say that our system of government does
not copy the institutions of our neighbors. It
is more the case of ours being a model to others,
than of ours imitating anyone else. Our institution
is called a DEMOCRACY because power is in the hands
not of a minority, but of the whole population.
When it is a question of settling private disputes,
everyone is equal before the law. When it is
a question of putting one person before another in
positions of public responsibility, what counts is not
membership in a particular class, but
the actual ability the man possesses.

No one, as long as he has it in him to be of
service to the State, is kept in political obscurity
because of poverty. And just as our political life
is free and open, so is our day to day life
in our relations with each other…."

Pericles (Funeral Oration)

PROLOGUE

The achievements of the ancient Greeks, in all fields of human intellectual endeavor, have always held a fascination for me. Of course, living under the shadow of the Acropolis in a country where one is repeatedly faced with reminders of their civilization, and speaking, reading, and writing a language which, with some modern modifications, was the native language of these famous men, one cannot help but be impressed and fascinated.

I first became acquainted with the early Greek writers and thinkers while attending Greek High School studying ancient history and classical Greek. The subject that impressed me most, however, was ancient Greek drama. I still vividly recall the impression that I had when I once attended Sophocles' play, **"Oedipus the King,"** at the theater of **Herodus Atticus**, at the foot of the Acropolis. I was 17 years old then, and lived in a district of Athens which was about 5 kilometers (3 miles) from the theater. After the play that evening, well past midnight, I walked the distance home and my mind was absorbed completely by the images, emotion, drama, acting, and time span since it was written--as well as the language and the setting. I could not believe that this play, presented 2,397 years ago, could still be viewed with awe and admiration today.

This experience motivated me to seek out the school's library, where I read the plays that I could find of the ancient dramatic and comic writers; and my interest was increasing each time. Whenever the Athens Classical Festival would produce another play, either in Athens or Epidaurus theaters, I would disregard time and cost to attend.

During the fall semester of that same year, the textbook for the classical Greek language class was Plato's **Crito**. For the first time, I read and experienced the fascination of the Platonic works. I remember that I memorized the first page of the dialogue, in the original language, in which Crito visits Socrates in jail and tries to persuade him to escape. That was another opportunity to seek out the bookstores and libraries searching for Platonic works. Reading them was a pleasant experience because, as Aristotle stated, they are "poetry in prose"; but understanding them was a different matter, and I came to realize that it requires a lifetime pursuit. Plato made me aware of man's agony resulting from his efforts to "survive" and secure the elusive goal of "Happiness."

I experienced this awakening during the second phase of the Greek Civil War, which occurred from 1945 to 1949. It was during this period that I became aware and inquisitive about the events unfolding about me: the atrocities of the Civil War and the irrationality, hatred, and cruelty of the two parties involved--as well as the destruction that they caused. It was a time when the Latin motto: **"Homo Homini Lupus"** (**Man is a wolf to his fellow man**) could be applied. It also occurred to me that all this strife resulted from a difference of opinion regarding the administration of the political and economic system, and how one should live one's life.

It was then that I was first introduced to Plato's **<u>Republic</u>**. I discovered that Plato attempted to answer these same questions in his monumental work--over 2,300 years ago. He was concerned with **how people should live their lives and organize their societies.** In 1975, while in Athens as a visiting professor at Athens Economics University, I discovered that a Greek publishing firm, **"Papyrus,"** had just released 87 volumes of all existing works of ancient Greek authors. I purchased the entire series, and ever since have been studying these fascinating books.

I soon realized, while reading these books, that the ancients had an acute perception of societal problems and a deep understanding of cause and effect relationships. They had expressed their thoughts clearly and convincingly, and had conscientiously adhered to logical and scientific criteria of investigation in their research. While examining their recommendations for solving societal problems in ancient times, I would always find their conclusions pertinent to today's society as well. I believe that in several areas we are still addressing the same issues and have similar concerns.

Ten years ago the St. Nicholas Ranch and Retreat Center at Dunlap, California, as part of the Elderhostel program , invited me to lecture on the Greek philosophers, and ever since I have been involved with this institute teaching a Greek philosophy course. This has been an ideal setting for me to share with others what I have been researching for so many years. The Elderhostel program has been a unique opportunity and a very rewarding experience. The notes of these lectures, in an expanded version, constitute the basis of this book.

My primary objective in publishing this book, in addition to the need to communicate with the students at the Elderhostel, is to relate to others the great psychological and intellectual benefits that can be derived from studying ancient Greek philosophy: tranquility to the mind; maturity in understanding societal issues and problems; sobriety in the tendency to one-sided determinism, and realization of the Socratic principle: **"Γνωθι Σ' Αυτον"** (Know Thyself).

This book does not provide a deep analysis of Greek philosophical precepts, because there are thousands of volumes in our public and university libraries that offer appropriate coverage and are readily available for one who is interested in an in-depth analysis. There are references in the bibliography section for such treatises.

Instead, this work presents in a concise, encyclopedic, and historical fashion for the lay person, the salient points of the Greek philosophers--in a manner devoid of complicated jargon--so that an initiate can understand. An attempt is made, in this short study, to convey not only what these brilliant men said and believed, but, whenever possible, to present pertinent information about their lives and relationships. Also, the spirit and conditions of the period during which they lived are noted; because their ideas and concepts can be better understood when one envisions the political, economic, and social conditions that prevailed then[1]. Some anecdotes and popular sayings of the times are also included, in order to describe their personalities and idiosyncrasies.

The material in this book is divided into three chronological periods: (1) This period covers the pre-Socratic philosophers, known as the Naturalists or Cosmologists-- commencing with the inception of the Olympic Games (776 B.C.) and extending to the end of the Persian Wars (479 B.C.). (2) This period covers the moral and ethical philosophers-- including Socrates, Plato, and Aristotle--commencing with the end of the Persian Wars and ending with the death of Aristotle (322 B.C.). (3) This period covers the philosophers of the Hellenistic period--the Epicureans, Stoics, Cynics, Skeptics, the Academy, the Lyceum, et al.--commencing with the death of Alexander (323 B.C.) and ending with the complete subjugation of Greece by Rome (146 B.C.).

I would like to thank my wife, Polly, who edited the manuscript and helped immensely with her recommendations; and my daughter, Athena, and son, Alexander, for their support and interest. I would also like to thank Dr. Adriana Anagnostopoulos, professor of philosophy at California State University, Fresno, who read the manuscript and provided valuable suggestions. Sincere thanks are extended as well to the thousands of Elderhostel students who, with their inquisitive minds and dialectic discussions, in true Socratic fashion, made the completion of this work significantly easier.

Harry G. Costis
Fresno, California, 2004

---

[1] See a short review of Greek history at the conclusion of Chapter 1, and a full reference in the Bibliography for those interested in further study.

AEGIS

NO FOE CAN PENETRATE THE RANKS
WITH KNOWLEDGE AT THE FORE,
OR CONQUER NATIONS WITH RESOLVE
AND HONOR AT THEIR CORE.

KALYPSO

INTRODUCTION

The Greek thinkers, for a little over 500 years (from the 7th century B.C. to the 2nd century B.C.), approached the basic questions and problems affecting individuals and organized societies, in a way that opened new horizons in the development of human civilization. No doubt previous civilizations and cultures (those of the Middle-East and Egypt from 4500 B.C.) were also concerned with these matters, and certainly made a significant contribution. The difference is that the **Greeks** examined these issues with a free mind in a **scientific manner**, introducing logic and reason into their research. They were interested in the truth based on factual evidence, and scrutinized the results critically--not bound by dogmatic constraints.

The **Naturalists or (Cosmologists)** were primarily interested in answering questions and addressing problems that pertained to the phenomena of Nature and its reactions. They also explored the heavenly bodies such as the **stars**, the **sun**, the **moon,** and their apparent movements. They judged that the Earth was the center of the **Cosmos,** and that the sun, stars and moon revolved around it. Some did believe, however, that the **Earth was a sphere;** and they were successful in measuring its circumference within a very small margin of error. They never developed the telescope, and therefore never had the chance to scrutinize these heavenly bodies more closely. The movement of the planets, however, did not conform to the model of the Earth being the center of the universe, with all heavenly bodies revolving uniformly around it. Hence, the name **planet**, from the Greek word "Πλανητης" (wanderer). As a result of this observation, **Philolaus, the Pythagorean** (c.475 B.C.), first, and **Aristarchus** from Samos (c. 270 B.C.) proclaimed that the Earth is not the center of the universe, but instead revolves around its axis and a central **fire (Εστια).** They were ridiculed by their contemporaries with the assertion that, if indeed the Earth revolves around its axis, then on a cloudy day one would observe the clouds moving rapidly in the opposite direction. It was over 1800 years later that this issue was finally resolved, when **Copernicus**, in 1543 A.D., established that the Earth moves and that the sun is the center of our solar system *(the heliocentric vs. the geocentric system).* But apart from the question of the movement of the heavenly bodies, which the Greeks, incidentally, never considered to be "gods," these early philosophers were also concerned with other matters and phenomena of the physical world. Thus, **Heraclitus** from Ephesus proclaimed in c. 500 B.C.: "Τα παντα ρει και ουδεν μενει" (Everything is in a flux and nothing is stationary). He conceived the idea that everything evolves continuously. This type of thinking set the stage for further study, which eventually led to **Charles Darwin's "Theory of Evolution"** several centuries later. **Anaximander** (c. 550 B.C) and other scientists subsequently, proclaimed *that nothing is destroyed and nothing is created, but only changes state.* This led to the work of **Lavoisier,** several centuries later on the "**Indestructibility of Matter."** Democritus, in c. 450 B.C., stated that matter consists of infinitesimally small particles that cannot be divided any further, which he called *atoms* (ατομα). This advanced research, centuries later, and was the precursor for the development of **atomic physics. Zeno of Elea,** at about the same time, was concerned with the concept of continuity and change, from a mathematical perspective, and developed his famous paradoxes mocking Heraclitus' conception of change and continuity. Another brilliant mathematician who left his imprint on the path of progress was **Pythagoras,** known by every school child, even today, for his famous **Pythagorean Theorem.** This theorem states that *the square of the hypotenuse of a right triangle is equal to the sum of the squares of the other two sides,* and has been a significant tool in geometry for measurements and a number of practical applications. Pythagoras also introduced the theory of numbers, the idea of communal living, and sharing resources in order to develop friends rather than enemies. He refined the study of **mathematics** and **geometry,** and is the first to have introduced the **Theory of Music** and **musical modes and scales,** by observing the relationship (empirically, most likely) between length of string and pitch of sound. The **Naturalists** opened a new page in the history of human intellectual development. These early Greek scholars invented and introduced basic scientific concepts in many fields, and led the way for scientists during subsequent years, as well as during the **"Renaissance,"** to make the significant discoveries and inventions that propelled scientific investigation to today's levels.

After the **Naturalists,** the **Moral and Ethical Philosophers**--represented mainly by the **Sophists, Socrates, Plato, Aristotle,** and the Schools during Hellenistic times: **the Academy, the Lyceum, the Epicureans, the Stoics, the Skeptics, and the Cynics,** addressed questions concerning man and his society, These men were responsible for the development of **moral and ethical philosophy.** Not that they were the first to introduce these ideas, but they were the first to study these concepts in a scientific manner--known today as the **dialectic** or the **Socratic Method.** The basic question that Socrates posed was: *"What is the best way for one to lead his life"?* Such concepts as: *"restraint," "nothing in excess," "know thyself," "justice," "freedom," "free expression of one's opinion," "virtue," "prudence," "temperance," "bravery,"* et al., were the fundamental tenets of these philosophers. Serious concern was shown by these thinkers, particularly **"Plato" and "Aristotle,"** for the *"ideal system of government"* and for the *"ideal"* or *"virtuous man."* *Education, discipline, and knowledge* were deemed to be the fundamental prerequisites for the achievement of an ideal society and of the ideal, "perfect" man. While **Socrates** and **Plato** were the idealists who dreamed of a perfect society, and proclaimed that it is man's duty and obligation to strive for excellence, in order to understand not only himself, but his environment as well, **Aristotle** introduced a new pragmatic view. He was not as much interested in the "ideal man" and the "ideal society," as he was concerned with building the **foundation of modern science.** We may say that Aristotle, in a systematic manner, set the fundamental principles of such fields as: **political science, psychology, anthropology, botany, zoology, logic, the scientific method, et al.** From **322 B.C.,** when Aristotle died, until the Renaissance in the Italian city-states in the **14th and 15th centuries A.D. (over 1500 years),** Aristotle's books constituted the **"textbooks"** and **"handbooks"** of the civilized world. Two individuals, **Zeno** from Citium (the "father" of the Stoic philosophy), and **Epicurus** from Athens (the "father" of the Epicurean philosophy), were the proponents of a new brand of philosophy that flourished during the **Hellenistic period.** Zeno was concerned with the burdens of life and wanted man to return to a simple existence--the **life of Nature**--in order to eliminate unnecessary complications and inbred problems. He taught that **apathy** and complete eradication of emotion are the necessary ingredients for a **simple, complete, and productive life. Epicurus** wanted to emancipate man from fear, and particularly: **the fear of Death.** The pursuit of moderate pleasure usually leads to happiness, but this must be accompanied by reason and restraint. Death, he asserted, is something that one should not be afraid of, because: **"When death comes, we do not exist; and when we exist, death does not come."** All is conditioned by the senses. These two philosophers and their students had a strong influence on their contemporaries and on future philosophers up until our time. They also had an influence on the **Christian scholars** who formulated and established Christian ethics. While the achievements of the ancient Greeks in the area of philosophy, science, and abstract thinking progressed significantly, one would wonder how much they involved themselves with the practical applications and aspects of their theoretical conceptions. **Plato** was concerned with creating the **"Idea Society,"** and tried during his repeated trips to Sicily and Southern Italy, to test some of the tenets of his political philosophy on the Greek city-states there. Plato concluded, after his attempted experiments, that only when men become **"Sons of God"** (perfect) would an ideal society be achieved. He set up in **Νομοι** (Laws) a prototype based on the doctrine of the separation of authority, as well as ones for education, and discipline. After the death of **Alexander** and the dissemination of the Greek way of thinking throughout the known world, new Greek scientists and experimenters advanced the applications of the Aristotelian and Natural Philosophers' theories. A major center of practical research flourished in Alexandria, where a number of scientists introduced new methods and techniques; some of these were:

EUCLID (c. 280 B.C.) advanced the subject of **geometry.** In 13 books he developed the entire field of plane geometry that is used today.

APOLLONIUS (c. 280 B.C.) developed an approach to the subject of **analytic geometry,** and in his book **Conics** gave us such terms as: **"parabola", "hyperbola", "ellipse," etc.**

KTESIBIUS (c. 200 B.C.) was known for his water clocks and water organs.

HERO (c. 150 B.C.) was a versatile, practical scientist; an engineer we would say today. He combined work in physics and mechanics with the construction of various tools powered by steam or compressed air, including a model **steam engine.**

He devised a system that automatically opened and closed the doors of the Palace of Ptolemy, by heating water and directing steam through a pipe, which activated a lever that opened or closed the doors by increasing or reducing the flow of steam.

He also developed the principle of the first **jet engine** by directing steam inside a sphere (see p. 77) which, in diametrically opposite exterior spots on the circumference, had two small pipe openings leading to the opposite direction at 90 degree angles. The steam escaped from the small pipes and in the process caused the sphere to rotate. The more steam applied, the faster the sphere would rotate.[2]

HEROPHILUS (c. 280 B.C.) known as the father of anatomy, identified the brain as the center of the nervous system and set the stage for the study of different kinds of nerves and their functions.

"Μη μου τους κυκλους ταραττε"
(Do not damage my drawings)

ERASISTRATUS (c. 150 B.C.) anatomically analyzed and plotted the subdivisions of the **heart**; and more impressively, realized that the heartbeat causes the pulse.

ERATOSTHENES (c. 230 B.C.) was a well-known geographer and Director of the famous Library of Alexandria. He plotted a map of the world and, using geometry, **measured the circumference of the Earth to within approximately 800 kilometers of the true figure.** He knew the distance between Aswan (a city in south Egypt) and Alexandria was approximately 800 kilometers. He also knew that the sun casts no shadow at Aswan at midday; while in Alexandria, at the same time, it casts a shadow of 7 degrees. He divided 7 into 360, multiplied by 800, and came up with the figure 41,142 kilometers. The true figure of the circumference of the Earth at the poles is 40,260.

ARCHIMEDES (c. 250 B.C.) was from **Syracuse, Sicily,** and is credited with a number of inventions and **mechanical advances.** First, he developed the well-known **Archimedes screw**--a water pump, by which water could be pumped up from the river, and which is still used today in Egypt and other parts of the world. He was the first to introduce the concept of **hydrostatics,** and studied properties of **solids** and **liquids.** The story of the discovery of the **"specific weight,"** while he was in the bathtub, is well known. Contemplating whether the crown of the king was composed of solid gold or mixed, he shouted **"Eureka!"(I have found (it)!)** and ran nude into the street when the idea of the "specific weight" occurred to him. **Archimedes** developed several proofs in mechanics and he is well known for his invention of the **lever and the pulley.** When he realized the potential of this invention, he proclaimed: **"Δος μοι πας τω και ταν γαν κινησω" (Give me a place to stand and I will move the Earth).** Using his mechanical devices, he delayed the capture of Syracuse by the Romans for two years, and is known to have said to an intruder: **"Μη μου τους κυκλους ταραττε"** (Do not disturb my drawings!), being so preoccupied with his studies that he did not notice the presence of an enemy soldier in his studio, who subsequently stabbed him to death[3] (See picture above).

---

[2] For the achievements of Hero in devising instruments with hot water and steam, see Marie Boas Hall. The Pneumatics of Hero of Alexandria (1971: New York, MacDonald-London and American Elsevier Inc.); on pp 55- 65 she describes the two examples presented above.

[3] For more detailed information about scientific developments at the time of the Greeks and their contributions, see reference #3, chapter two, and p.21 ff.

The **Phoenicians** developed the first alphabet, which consisted of 21 consonants and no vowels. The Greeks added vowels and created a new alphabet by the beginning of the first millennium. On the basis of this alphabet they developed a language which structurally, grammatically, syntactically, and etymologically surpassed any system of language that existed up to their time. It was an inflected language with a sophisticated system of endings, declensions, tenses, moods, and syntax that enabled them to express the most sophisticated and complicated abstract meanings and shades of meanings and thoughts. The structure of the language and the alphabet developed by the Greeks was taken up later by the Etruscans and subsequently by the Romans who developed the Latin alphabet on the basis of which the European Romance languages evolved. During Roman time and subsequently, scientists borrowed words from the Greek language to express new ideas pertaining to the Arts and Sciences. Most terms used today in certain fields of research are of Greek origin, and researchers still refer to Greek whenever a new **term** is needed. For example, in the field of computer science the emerging impact of the computer and the effect that it was expected to have in the area of communications necessitated the invention of new words and terminology, e.g.; the term **Cybernetics** was coined from the Greek word "governor" **(Κυβερνητης).**

If you open a daily newspaper at any section, you will most likely encounter many Greek words, such as: **school (Σχολειον), athletics (Αθλητισμος), mathematics (Μαθηματικα), history (Ιστορια), geography (Γεωγραφια), telephone (Τηλεφωνον), grammar (Γραμματικη), politics (Πολιτικα), democracy(Δημοκατια), diplomacy (Διπλοματια), chemistry (Χημεια), airplane (Αεροπλανο), music (Μουσικη), architecture (Αρχιτεκτονικη), poetry (Ποιησις), theater (Θεατρον), stomach (Στομαχι), nerves (Νευρα), character (Χαρακτηρ), diet (Διαιτα), bulimia (βουλιμια), anorexia (Ανορεξια), graphic (Γραφικος), basic (Βασικος), etc.** These are words of Greek origin which represent a discipline, an art, or a name with a host of other related words derived from Greek. Sometimes in a discipline, such as Medicine or Theater Arts, an extensive vocabulary in Greek is used. Note the word **"Theatre" (Θεατρον),** and you will encounter the following derivatives of Greek: **lyric, drama, tragedy, comedy, musical, scene, prologue, dialogue, characters, meter, choir, chorus, orchestra, symphony, melody, euphony, cacophony, etc.** You will find these words not only in English, but in all other European languages (*Romance, Anglo Saxon or Slavic root*) which were heavily influenced by Greek via the Latin language.

Intellectually, the Greeks surfaced about the turn of the first millennium. Prior to the Greeks, as mentioned earlier, there existed significant civilizations that flourished in the area of the Middle East and Egypt, dating back to c. 5,000 B.C. These early civilizations established the foundations of mathematics, geometry, architecture, building, medicine, astronomy, and others. Two of the **Seven Wonders** of the ancient world were located in that part of the world: *the Pyramids and the Suspended Gardens of Babylon* are evidence of the skills and scientific acumen of these civilizations at a time when the Greeks were still in a primitive state. It is documented that most of the Greek scholars traveled to Egypt and surrounding areas, and were familiar with the achievements of those civilizations; as for example--**Thales, Pythagoras, Democritus, Plato,** and others. On the basis of this information, in the last few years a drive has been generated to challenge the established acceptance that the roots of Western civilization date back to the Greeks. This drive proposes that the contribution of Egypt is of paramount importance, and suggests that the Greeks borrowed most of their knowledge from the Egyptians; therefore Western civilization is rooted in the civilization of Egypt and is Afro-Centric rather than Greco-Centric.[4] While the contribution of these earlier cultures is noted (see chapters 15 and 16), one has to accept that the progress of world civilization is not measured by the contribution of a specific group, person, or nation, but rather is a cumulative contributive process; and each group contributes piecemeal slowly through time to ultimate breakthroughs and advancements. In this sense, then, one could say that the **Egyptians** set the stage in such fields as *geometry, medicine, building, and astronomy; while* the **Sumerians, Phoenicians, and Babylonians** contributed to the fields of *law, mathematics, development of the language and the alphabet, navigation and building*. The Greeks advanced these fields and developed them into scientific disciplines which, through contributions of subsequent groups through the centuries, reached the levels known today.

There are certain areas, however, that the Greeks pioneered themselves and which came to constitute the foundations of Western Civilization. These were the *products of their own ingenuity, without recourse to earlier achievements*. These unique contributions of the Greeks would include:

1. **THE SCIENTIFIC METHOD.** The Greeks invented and practiced this method in their efforts to unearth the truth and establish theories. This method consists of the process whereby one has a problem in any field of the physical or social world, and sets up a hypothesis, which is the suggested solution to the problem. On the basis of an experiment (logical, empirical, mathematical), the validity of the hypothesis is determined. If the hypothesis is accepted, a theory is established[5]. If the hypothesis is rejected, new research will have to be initiated. The Greeks were the first to initiate this process of scientific inquiry while for almost five thousand years previous civilizations never considered it.

2. **LOGIC.** This field was developed by the Greeks. Aristotle wrote 5 books (**The Organon**) enunciating the subject succinctly, and these books have constituted the primer on the subject until today. It was this principle embedded in Thales' mind that made him reject the theocratic interpretation of the inundation of the Nile, and led him to search for a more **logical** physical explanation of the phenomenon (see p. 3).

3. **PHILOSOPHY.** This term literally means "**friend of wisdom**" and was coined later than the term **wisdom (Σοφια),** which implies that one is knowledgeable. The Greeks used this word with a different connotation; it did not only imply that a philosopher is wise, but also that he is interested in acquiring the Ultimate Truth. Philosophy then, for the Greeks, was the antithesis of dogmatism and theocratism. They were interested in searching to find the Ultimate Truth, based on logic and experimentation, regardless of whether the research concerned the physical or social sciences or whether higher authority would sanction it.

---

[4] For a comprehensive discussion on the controversy of Afro-Centrism, see Mary Lefkovitz's **Not Out of Africa,** (New York: A New Republic Book, Basic Books, 1996)
[5] Proper care should be applied so that a type II error may not be committed (accepting a false hypothesis).

4. DEMOCRACY. The political system in which the public makes decisions concerning matters of policy and the administration and management of the affairs of the State, developed and flourished in the ancient Πολεις (City-States). Solon, an Athenian law maker, first introduced the concept during the middle of the sixth century B.C., and by 508 B.C. **Cleisthenes** adopted it permanently. The Athenians and other city-states practiced this system until the time of the Romans.

5. FREE CHOICE AND FREE WILL. Pericles stated in his funeral oration delivered to the Athenians in 430 B.C.: *"We are free and tolerant in our private lives. We do not get into a "state" with our next door neighbor if he enjoys himself in his own way."* The concept of diversity, the dignity of man, and the free choice to practice whatever lifestyle one chooses was embedded in the system.

6. THE OLYMPIC GAMES. The spirit of competition and the recognition of excellence were exemplified in the Olympic Games, practiced continuously from the year of its inception (776 B.C.) until Theodosius, in 393 A.D., discontinued them. This spirit of competion extended into their commercial activities reaping success and economic progress. In contrast, the entire state of Egypt was owned by the Pharaoh and the Priests, and the public was the sharecropper.

7. HISTORY. The collection, analysis, and classification of data of past events, published in an impartial manner, interested only in revealing the truth, is a scientific discipline introduced by Herodotus--known as the Father of History--for the first time during the 5th century B.C. Thucydides, Xenophon, Polybius, and others established the standards for this discipline.

8. THE THEATER. Theatrical plays exhibiting the vicissitudes of life presented in an open theatre as a means of education and entertainment was a Greek invention, and developed into an art of immense significance for ancient as well as modern times. It presented the tragic, as well as the comic aspect of life, and thousands of tragedies and comedies were written by the dramatic playwrights of the ancients.

9. PERFECTION IN ART AND ADHERENCE TO DETAIL. If one observes a sculpture made by an Egyptian artist in the third millennium B.C., and another one made a thousand years later, the difference will be minimal. But if you observe a sculpture made by a Greek artist in the 6th century B.C., and another made 100 years later, the difference will be substantial. The Greeks were always seeking to perfect their art and adhered to detailed representation.

10. THE THEORY OF MUSIC. The **Pythagoreans** first discovered that there is a mathematical (ratio) relationship between the pitch of a note and the length of a string. Pythagoras was the first musical numerologist, and laid the foundations of acoustics. **Aristoxenus**, a pupil of Aristotle, set up the Theory of Music and analyzed the emotional nature of music, for which both the hearing and the intellect of the listener are essential.

The **Romans** inherited the Greek achievements; and it is said that the Romans conquered the Greeks militarily, but the Greeks conquered the Romans culturally. In the area of literature, for example, all of the themes and forms of literary style: **epic, tragedy, comedy, biography, history, lyric poetry and oratory** were fashioned after the Greek originals. The works of **Cicero, Lucretius, Virgil, Horace, Ovid, Seneca, Tacitus, et al.** were strongly influenced by the Greek masterpieces. And as a consequence of this, modern literary men such as: **Dante, Chaucer, Milton, Shakespeare, Goethe, Moliere, Racine, Rousseau, Shelley, and Byron (who fought in the War of Greek Independence and died in Greece)**, were significantly affected by the Greeks. This influence occurred after the Renaissance, when Greek achievements were recognized after the **lethargic** period **of over 1400 years** during the **Middle Ages,** Democracy came into existence again following the American and the French Revolution. There was a suggestion that the Founding Fathers of the American Constitution discovered the system of **federal government** practiced by the **Achaean League** during Hellenistic times, before the Roman conquest (as described by **Polibius),** and then modified and adopted it as a unique democratic system--with great success.[6] The **Socratic philosophers** reached a depth of understanding of human society and man himself, unprecedented for their and our times. They were the first who attempted to understand the **vicissitudes of human nature,** and explored man as another being on the planet with his **shortcomings, intelligence, and potential** for creation and destruction. They were the first to consider the possibility of peaceful, democratic, happy, and prosperous societies; and the first to look into the **role of women** in society and accord them equal status with men (**Plato's** **The Republic, Laws**). On the question of **political systems**, both **Plato** and **Aristotle** weighed the advantages and disadvantages of various forms of government which were in practice then. Plato conceived the ideal system as enunciated in **The Republic** and modified in the **Laws;** and Aristotle, in **Politics**, suggests that the ideal system would be feasible only when the citizens achieve *"maturity and understanding of their rights and their responsibilities."* It would be counterproductive to establish democratic institutions to govern people who are immature or ignorant of the Socratic and Platonic **"Γνωθι Σ'Αυτον"** (Know Thyself). It would also be counterproductive to impose tyranny on an advanced, equitable, just, and mature society of citizens.

WHY THE GREEKS?

The question naturally comes to mind: *Why are the ancient Greeks still viewed in awe after over 25 centuries, and what is the secret of their success?* There may be several reasons for this and perhaps several variables functionally related. But if one is to express an opinion, I think basically the following factors could be considered as having contributed to this event: The Greeks conceived the concept of the democratic system where the entire population participated in the administrative process of the State. Also, their capability to

---

[6] See an excellent book on the subject of federal systems of government, by Freeman, E.A. History of Federal Government, Macmillan and Co, Ltd., London, 1893. Freeman deals extensively with the ancient Greek experience with federalism, devoting two thirds of his book to the Achaean, Aetolian, and Acarnanian Leagues.

emancipate themselves from theocratic dogma, and their freedom of choice and free will in choosing among alternatives, presented an advantage to freely investigate their environment. The relatively poor land of mainland Greece (over sixty percent of the land is mountainous and arid) provided the incentive to experiment, be inventive, and develop the maritime arts. These factors, along with a certain inherent characteristic of curiosity and spirit of adventure, slowly developed a culture quite different from the rigid, dogmatic, and fatalistic traits of earlier civilizations which had not succeeded in rejecting the theocratic dogmatism of over five millennia.

The study of ancient peoples' achievements and experiences, concerning all matters related to the social, physical, and behavioral sciences, can produce beneficial effects in understanding society's problems and concerns of today. Their rigorous thinking and disciplined minds in researching the problems of man, offer an understanding of the complexities and frustrations we face today: crime, abuse, injustice, inequality, poverty, etc. The fact that they were confronted with these problems and had the courage and the ingenuity to attempt to understand and suggest solutions, may provide to the present citizen an awareness and appreciation of the gravity of today's problems as well; creating more mature citizens--impervious to demagogues, crafty charlatans, or vested interests camouflaged under false pretenses and protected by democratic institutions. These mature, educated, and informed citizens will then be able to vote rationally on issues and evaluate candidates' true credentials and qualifications for an ideal implementation of the democratic process.

CHRONOLOGICAL CHART

4,500 B.C.	First Organized Societies in the **Tigris-Euphrates** and **Nile** River Valleys
3,000 B.C.	Migrations into and out of Greece from Asia Minor, Eastern Mediterranean and Northern Europe.
2,200-1,400 B.C.	**Crete, Mycenae, Tyrins, Orhomenos, Thebes, Pylos.** Thriving Civilizations and Great Kingdoms at **Knossos, Phaestos,** and **Mycenae.**
c. 1500	Eruption of Volcano at **Thera.**
1400-1200 B.C.	Power of Mycenae and Other States grows. The **Trojan War** (1118 B.C.)
1100 B.C.	Greek Elements from the North invade Southern Greece. Destruction of Mycenae.
1000 B.C.	Dark Ages of Greece. **Dorians** invade Peloponnesus, Crete and Rhodes. **Aeolians** invade Thessaly and Boeotia. **Ionians** from Attica cross to Western Shores of Asia Minor.
800-700 B.C.	Formation of City-States and Rise of Aristocracy.
c. 800.	Homer writes the **Iliad** and **Odyssey**
776. B.C.	First **Olympic Games** held at Olympia.
750-500 B.C.	Greek Migrations and Establishment of Colonies in Sicily, Southern Italy, Euxenus Pontus (Black Sea), North Africa and other Parts of the Mediterranean.
c. 580 B.C.	**Solon** introduces the System of **Democracy** in Athens.
508 B.C.	**Cleisthenes** solidifies the Democratic system in Athens.

600-495 B.C.	Persians complete their expansion westwards and subjugate the Greek city-states of Asia Minor (**Miletus, Colofon, Alicarnassus, and others).**
490-479 B.C.	Greco-Persian Wars. **Marathon, Thermopylae, Artemision, Salamis, Plataea.**
479-431 B.C.	**The Golden Age of Greece**. Pericles builds the Parthenon. Unparalled Artistic and Intellectual Creativity.
469 B.C.	Birth of **Socrates.**
427 B.C.	Birth of **Plato.**
431-404 B.C.	The **Peloponnesian War** between Athens and Sparta and Defeat of Athens.
399 B.C.	Death of **Socrates.**
387 B.C.	**Plato** Builds the **Academy** at Colonos, Athens.
400-357 B.C.	Quarreling between the Greek City-States. Continuous Warfare. Rise of **Thebes, Corinth** and **Pella** as Powerful Centers.
335 B.C.	**Aristotle** Establishes the **Lyceum** in Athens.
357-336 B.C.	Rise of Macedonia and Control of All Greece. **King Philip II** of Macedonia New Political and Military Force in Greece.
334-322 B.C.	**Alexander III** (the Great). Campaign to Asia and Dissolution of the Persian Empire.
322 B.C.	Death of Alexander at Babylon. The beginning of the Era of the **Hellenistic World**. Hellenic Culture spreads roots throughout the Conquered World of Alexander.
323 B.C.	Death of **Aristotle.**
c. 300-200 B.C.	Macedonian Rule of All Greece.
306 B.C.	Establishment of the **Stoic School** of Philosophy.
304 B.C.	Establishment of the **Epicurean School** of Philosophy.

197-146 B.C.   Expansion of Rome. The **Achaean**, **Acarnanean** and **Aetolean** Leagues.

146. B.C.   Fall of Athens and Corinth to the Romans. End of Greek Freedom.

1828 A.D.   Establishment of the **First Free Modern Greek State**

LIST OF MAPS

TABLE OF CONTENTS

ALPHABETICAL LIST OF PROMINENT PEOPLE REFERRED TO IN THIS WORK

A

Aeschylus, 12
Alexander, 13
Anacharsis, 26
Anaxagoras, 8, 25, 56, 64, 84, 100
Anaximander, 27, 32
Anaximenes, 27, 35
Antisthenes, 10, 186, 268, 269
Anyutus, 87, 102
Archimedes, 9, 142
Aritarchus, 47
Aristides, 104, 106
Aristophanes, 85, 141
Aristotle, 8, 10, 26, 198

B

Basil the Great, 228
Bias, 26
Bion, 224
Bryson, 8
Buddha, 293

C

Carneades, 8, 225
Cephalus, 132
Cicero, 16
Chilon, 26
Chrysippus, 8, 252
Cleanthes, 149, 251
Cleisthenes, 137
Cleobulus, 26
Clitomachus, 225
Cranto, 224
Crates, 224
Critias, 10, 76, 107, 175
Crito, 103
Copernicus, 40

D

Da Vinci, Leonardo, 7
Demetrius Falirefs, 230
Democritus, 8, 10, 25, 36, 66
Diogenes (The Cynic), 268, 271
Diogenes Laertius, 8

E

Ekfantus, 42
Empedocles, 10, 25, 62
Epictetus, 238,259
Epicurus, 238, 259
Epimenides, 26
Eratosthenes, 9
Eryxias, 179
Eryximachus, 140
Euclid, 9, 116
Eudoxus, 127, 199
Euripides, 12, 46
Eurytus, 91
Euthedemus, 177
Euthephro, 111
Evritus, 116

G

Galileo, 29
Gorgias, 10, 76, 79, 113

H

Hamurabi, 280, 294
Harmides, 182
Hecateus, 264
Heraclides, 231
Heraclitus, 55, 100, 185
Hero, 9
Herodotus, 2, 8, 276, 278
Hesiod, 13

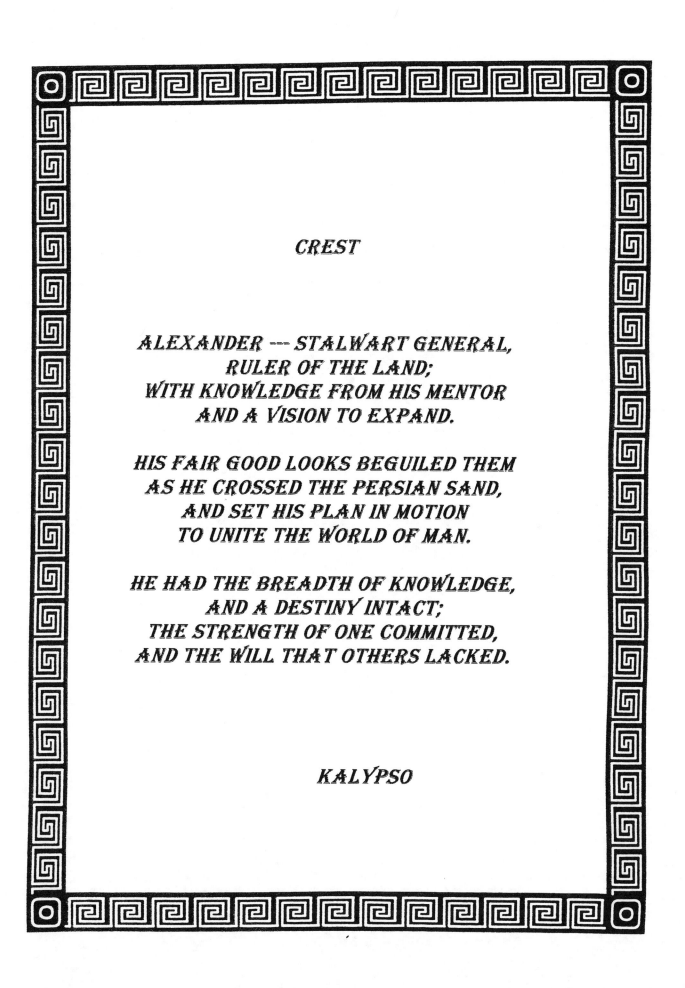

CREST

ALEXANDER --- STALWART GENERAL,
RULER OF THE LAND;
WITH KNOWLEDGE FROM HIS MENTOR
AND A VISION TO EXPAND.

HIS FAIR GOOD LOOKS BEGUILED THEM
AS HE CROSSED THE PERSIAN SAND,
AND SET HIS PLAN IN MOTION
TO UNITE THE WORLD OF MAN.

HE HAD THE BREADTH OF KNOWLEDGE,
AND A DESTINY INTACT;
THE STRENGTH OF ONE COMMITTED,
AND THE WILL THAT OTHERS LACKED.

KALYPSO

CHAPTER 1

THE GREEK WORLD AND ITS HISTORY

*"We regard wealth as something to be properly
enjoyed, rather than as something to boast about"*
Pericles

INTRODUCTION

The people who lived in the lower part of the Balkan peninsula and who eventually migrated to the western shores of Asia Minor and to Southern Italy and Sicily, known in history as the **Hellenes,** renamed later by the Romans as **"Graeci,"**[1] and finally referred to as **"Greeks"** in English and other European languages, were comprised of various migrating tribes, mixed with local elements of unknown origin who had arrived to mainland Greece in prehistoric times.

The migrating elements, all of the same Hellenic stock, were the **Achaeans, Dorians, Aeolians and Ionians,** and did not appear until about the second half of the second millennium B.C. The native populations who lived in the region before the immigrants arrived were the **Mycenaean's** (in Peloponnesus), the **Minoans** (on the island of Crete), the **Pelasgians** (native populations at such known ancient towns as: **Tiryns, Thebes, Orhomenos, Pylos, and other places)**, and the Cycladic elements in the Aegean islands. Their civilizations appear to have been influenced by the Middle Eastern cultures from 4500 B.C. **(See map 1).**[2]

Thus, the Hellenes did not make their appearance on the world scene until about 1500 to l300 B.C., but they established their presence very quickly and changed things dramatically, introducing a new era in a very short period of time. The achievements of the Hellenes in the physical and social sciences, in the span of less than 500 years (during the latter part of the B.C. era)

---

[1]There was a small Greek community in Western Peloponnesus that migrated to Southern Italy during the 8th century B.C., whose members were known as **"Γραικοί."** After they came in contact with the early Romans, the Romans used this name, transliterated in the Roman alphabet as **"Graeci,"** to refer to all immigrants to Southern Italy from Greece. When the Romans conquered Greece in the 2nd century B.C., they maintained this name, and even though the Greeks called themselves **"Hellenes,"** the world came to know them as **"Greeks."**

[2] See Chronological Chart, after Table of Contents, which lists the various periods of the Hellenes from the beginning until the end of the time period of concern to this work.

is regarded with awe, even today.

It can be inferred that the Greeks benefited from the achievements of the earlier Middle Eastern civilizations, as repeated references were made by ancient writers about prominent individuals of ancient Greece who visited Egypt and other Middle Eastern civilizations. But there are no references that survived in the writings of the ancient scholars describing the accomplishments of these early civilizations or the extent of their learning from them, with the exception of **Herodotus**. In his **Histories**, the **Father of History** describes some aspects of the civilizations and achievements of the Egyptians, the Babylonians, the Assyrians, Persians and others. The Greeks were successful merchants and curious travelers who had connections with the Phoenicians and traveled to the Middle Eastern regions as traders, where they came in contact with **the Assyrians, Babylonians, Egyptians, et al.,** and had the opportunity to observe their progress, returning to relate their experiences to their fellow citizens in the city-states.

It should be noted that the Greek civilization did not flourish along the banks of rivers and fertile lands as earlier civilizations did, but developed in a relatively arid, unproductive soil, on rugged and mountainous land. Because they were poor, they had to be inventive; and the incentives and the motivation must have been significantly greater as compared with those inhabitants of the **Nile and the Tigris-Euphrates** river valleys. It was perhaps because of these conditions that they had to innovate and search for other sources of income besides agriculture. Trade was by necessity a **sine qua non** condition for survival, and seafaring important for communication; thus, the maritime arts must have developed very early, and the association with other people with its concomitant benefits was enhanced significantly.

Around **1200 B.C.**, and perhaps later, the legendary **Trojan War** occurred. The cause of the conflict and the myth of **Helen of Troy** was most likely an invention by **Homer** to romanticize a war fought for the control of the Dardanelles to secure the sea lanes to the Black Sea and the grain trade from the Danube and the Ukraine. A similar legend is referred to during the same period concerning the **Argonauts and the Golden Fleece**, which was most probably a revengeful war against the Scythians.

By the turn of the millennium (10th and 9th centuries B.C.), the Greeks advanced very rapidly. They adopted the Phoenician alphabet, modified it, and developed a language unparalled in detail and ability to express the most abstract thoughts and reflection, which influenced Western languages and civilization dramatically. It is extraordinary that the Greeks were successful in constructing a language with such wealth of abstract concepts, such as: freedom, will, determination, justice, love, hope, etc., which is characteristic of advanced civilizations. Even today some cultures in the developing world do not have equivalent words in their vocabulary. By 776 B.C., the Greeks introduced the **Olympic Games** and established for the first time the free athletic competition and peaceful co-existence of people, at least during the year of the **Games**, even if they were warring at that point and would resume hostilities after they ended.

The contribution of the Greeks is not to be found in the construction of extraordinary buildings like the **Pyramids, the temple at Karnak,** or the **Suspended Gardens of Babylon**, but rather in a change of attitude--in a **free spirit of inquiry**--an obsession with detail in art and the demonstration of expression in prose and poetry. But above all, they are the ones who introduced and practiced the **"scientific method"** and the use of **logic** and observation in scientific inquiry. The foundation of modern science was laid in the short span of Greek dominance and extended from approximately **650 B.C. to 146 B.C.**, which is the period from the beginning of the Persian wars (the threat of the Ionian city-states by the Persians) during the time of **Thales and other natural philosophers** to the fall of Athens to the Romans.

The small Goddess with the Snakes, Crete

An incident which is referred to by Herodotus in his Book II of **Histories,** and also by Diogenes Laertius, a Greek biographer, in the **Life of Thales,** exemplifies this adherence to the notion of the scientific inquiry and pursuance of knowledge through experimentation and application of logical criteria. When Thales visited Egypt, sometime during the 7th century B.C., he observed that the river Nile was inundating its banks every year from the summer solstice to the fall equinox for over 90 days. He questioned the priests at Thebes about this phenomenon and the answer given was that the Nile is a god, and therefore the explanation of the event was beyond the jurisdiction of human inquiry; implying, given the theocratic nature of the Egyptian system, that it was not the domain of mortals to challenge or question God's behavior.

But Thales' inquisitive mind did not accept this explanation: as it did not seem appropriate and logical to him that a god would continuously cause this phenomenon. By then the Greek thinkers, starting with Thales and Pharecydes, were freeing themselves from the bonds of theocratic dogma and mysticism in the area of natural philosophy. This was the difference in approach that separated Greek thinkers from those of previous civilizations and cultures, who were acting often within the constraints of the theocratic bounds of their system. If any phenomenon would be attributed to the will of the gods, the inquiry would be terminated and the priest would attempt to explain the nature of the cause of the phenomenon within the religious context. But Thales was concerned about the **truth** of the matter and investigated further.

Diogenes Laertius relates that **Thales**[3] by not accepting the theocratic interpretation of the phenomenon as explained by the priests, attempted to give a scientific, physical interpretation by observation. He concluded, after he noted that the etesian Mediterranean winds were blowing towards the land at the same time with the overflow of the river, that these winds were responsible for the inundation. This approach, albeit wrong, is an application of the scientific method (experiment by observation) that Thales applied for the first time, as far as we know, in the history of human scientific inquiry.

Sometime later Herodotus visited Egypt and considered the hypothesis that was proposed by Thales and describes how he carried out an experiment himself, by applying a basic scientific test to the hypothesis. He relates that he observed other rivers in Syria, Lebanon, and in Libya, where the etesian winds blow from the sea to the shores and did not

The Interior of the Palace of Nestor, Pylos [14]

observe any inundation in these rivers. The conclusion was then: that the Nile was not overflowing its banks because of the etesian winds, nor from the will of the gods; and therefore, the problem was unresolved and the hypothesis proposed, that the winds caused the inundation of the river, was rejected. The ancient people, the Egyptians as well as the Greeks, had never been able to establish that the Nile overflowed its banks because of the monsoon rains in Central Africa in late

---

[3] **Thales** was considered by the ancients as the Father of Greek philosophy, and was highly respected for his contributions to geometry, astronomy, and physical philosophy (see Chapter 2).

winter and spring each year. The reason for this was that crossing the great Sudan desert was an insurmountable obstacle; and therefore, they never explored Africa, even though Herodotus relates an incident that describes a group that did cross the desert and supposedly came in contact with the Pygmies.

As is true with all human civilizations, as well as with individual scholars, there are those who lay the foundations and advance the basic concepts and set fundamental principles for further progress, and then there are those who build from there. It is extraordinary that from about 700 B.C. to about the second century B.C., the Greeks produced some brilliant minds who introduced a new era which was destined to change the course of history. Such names as: **Thales, Anaximander, Heraclitus, Pythagoras, Xenophanes, Zeno, Plato, Democritus, Aristotle, Socrates, Epicurus, Archimedes, Aristarchus, Euclid, Ptolemy, Hero, and many more,** are associated with establishing the foundations of Western civilization.

The Kore with the Almond Eyes,

The growth of a group or a nation in the field of scientific inquiry is always associated with economic power and wealth. There is no incidence in the history of the world when a people or a nation has achieved distinction while in poverty and deprivation. So it is the case with the Greeks, who even though, as we have seen, started out poor, subsequently, through trade, advanced significantly and achieved comfortable wealth. The first steps toward serious thinking in natural philosophy, in investigation of natural phenomena and the plight of man, appeared among the Greeks in the city-states of Ionia, in Asia Minor, which had achieved distinction in trade and wealth, and most of these scholars were members of well-off aristocratic families. It is not always true, however, that prosperous people will exhibit progress in scientific fields. The case in point is the Persian experience. About the same time that the Greeks were studying and investigating the phenomena of Nature and seeking answers and explanations, the Persians had all the wealth of the world; but their scientific progress was stagnant, as had been the case with other groups prior to them and subsequently. However, the point can be made that: scientific distinction is always associated with robust and thriving economies, but such economies do not always guarantee scientific progress.

Of course, the political system is important and the prevailing mentality and general attitude toward education, freedom, and intellectual curiosity are predisposing factors. The social environment that

cultivates free thinking and provides the individual with the freedom necessary to pursue research and attempt to answer questions, sets the stage for intellectual, artistic, and scientific achievements. It is also important, I believe, that the climate of the land and the weather conditions must be favorable to the disposition of critical thinking. In the case of Greece, the climate has always been mild, with ample sunshine and brilliant light; devoid of foggy and cloudy conditions that foster depression and desperation. The temperature has always been very temperate and the dryness of the atmosphere and the lack of excesses in upper and lower climatic limits are conditions conducive to activity for a long period of time during the year. If we judge from the climate today, and of course one has to make allowances for the changes throughout the millennia, the mild weather of Greece and the plethora of islands with open spaces and wide horizons have always developed a spirit

Olympias, Alexander's Mother

of: **boldness, adventure, and dynamism.**

But above all, the spirit of freedom and free choice, which whet the desire for achievement and distinction, are the basic fundamental prerequisites for peaceful competition, progress, and innovation. These elements in ancient Greece appeared to be flourishing very early. Most of the Greek city-states that experienced democratic rule, where the public was participating in the affairs of the city-states, debating the favorable and unfavorable points of issues concerning the daily affairs and activities of the State in the Assembly, were the true incubators for this free spirit. In the ancient states of Persia, Assyria, Babylonia, Egypt, and others, this spirit of freedom did not exist; and most of the decisions were made by the kings or priests. Thus literature, art, architecture, and other activities of the population, had to pass through the censorship of higher authorities.

THE PERIODS OF GREEK PHILOSOPHY AND SOURCES OF DATA

One of the cruelest and most bitter scientific crimes which adversely affected the evolution of human intellectual achievements through the centuries was the destruction of thousands and thousands of books and scientific treatises written by ancient Greek scholars. With the exception of

Battle at Issus, Alexander Vs. Darius

all works by Plato, a small portion of the works of Aristotle, some books relating to Plotinus (a Neo-platonic philosopher), and some fragments of works of hundreds of other writers in the area of natural and social philosophy, most of the other thousands of volumes have perished. These books were destroyed intentionally or unintentionally. Unintentionally, due to neglect,the material that they were written on--most of them on papyrus, animal skins, or other perishable substances--could not withstand atmospheric conditions without proper care and preservation. Intentionally, some of these books were destroyed by setting fires to the libraries where they were housed; as for example, the Library of Alexandria and the Library of Pergamum were set ablaze by disgruntled citizens motivated by religious convictions. The books that perished in the libraries or the ones destroyed by weather conditions perished forever, because there were few or no copies available elsewhere to replace them. Of over 700 books produced by the Stoic philosophers, nothing remains, with the exception of some fragments; and over 600 treatises written by Chrysippus perished. Of over 300 books that Epicurus had written, particularly 27 books on Nature and on Atomic Theory, nothing exists--with the exception of three letters. Of over 1000 dramatic works and comedies written by the dramatic poets, only 37 remain. All of the works of the pre-Socratic philosophers have not survived the test of time, and particularly neglect.

A decline is observed in intellectual curiosity, and scientific conscience and inquiry of the caliber and levels achieved by the Greeks, in non-theologian matters, by the beginning of the new era (A.D.). This atrophy seems to have intensified by the beginning of the fourth century A.D. From the death of Jesus Christ (33 A.D.) until 313 A.D., when the Roman Emperor, Constantine, converted to Christianity and declared freedom of religion for all Roman citizens, Christians suffered considerably in the hands of the Romans. They were used as fodder for wild animals at the Coliseum during public entertainment spectacles, or were burned alive, crucified, or accused of crimes committed by others so as to find excuses to persecute them. Most of the early Christian saints were individuals who were tortured, ridiculed, and subjected to disgrace to compel them to change their religious beliefs. When the Christians came to power in 325 A.D., their last concern was to preserve the writings and intellectual achievements of the pagans. Unfortunately, what they destroyed, or let be destroyed, was the legacy of the world civilization produced by the Greeks--also persecuted by the Romans at the same time. This state of affairs did not change throughout the medieval times until the Renaissance in the 15th century A.D. In other words, the neglect of the writings of these Greek scholars, with the exception of Plato and some of Aristotle, lasted for over seventeen hundred years. Plato, because of his moral and ethical philosophy, which parallels that of the Christian ethic--was considered a **"Christian before Christ,"** and his intellectual work has survived.

When describing the achievements of the early Greek philosophers **(the Naturalists)**, the availability of original data is very poor. Whatever information is available about these men comes from fragments left or from quotations and references by subsequent writers, such as **Aristotle, Plato, Plutarch, et al.** But unfortunately, quotations and references cannot be trusted very much as some may have chosen their references to substantiate their beliefs. Some information survived in the writings of early Christian theologians such as: **Clement, Origen, and Hippolitus of Rome;** and some later Roman writers preserved considerable information: **Cicero, Seneca, Tacitus, Marcus Aurelius, Lucretius, et al.**—as well as **Diogenes Laertius,** a mid-third century A.D. writer who wrote about the lives and theories **(Lives of Eminent Philosophers)** of eighty- two scholars. But unfortunately, Diogenes Laertius does not give sufficient information about the philosophy and depth of the work of these early Hellenes.

The number of Greeks who distinguished themselves in the relatively short span of the Greek presence in world history is indeed remarkable. There are hundreds of individuals who flourished in their various fields of expertise, such as: **physical philosophy, theoretical physics, dialectics, logic, Skepticism, Cynicism, ethics, politics, theoretical mathematics, geometry, and others.** It would have been an extraordinary treasure-trove if the total writings of these individuals had survived. With regard to writing and recording their thoughts and research findings in scientific treatises, some left writings behind them; while others wrote nothing at all. An example of philosophers who wrote nothing, but whose ideas were presented by their students, would include: **Thales, Socrates, Stilpon, Phillippus, Menedemnus, Theodorus, Carneades, Bryson, and Ariston of Chios** (who wrote only a few letters). Some philosophers wrote no more than one treatise each, and some examples would include: **Anaximander, Anaximenes, Melissus,**

Heraclitus, Parmenides, Anaxagoras, et al.; while examples of philosophers who wrote extensively would include: **Zeno, Xenophanes, Democritus, Plato, Epicurus, Chrysippus, Aristotle, et al.**

In the area of physical sciences research flourished extensively during Hellenistic times, but the fruition of this research was hampered due to lack of experimentation and tools necessary for measurement. The lack of advanced mathematics in this field also was a serious impediment. However, by the time of the Roman Era, beginning of the first century B.C., they had made substantial progress--if we consider the accomplishments of **Archimedes, Hero, Euclid, Eratosthenes, and others,** in the area of **mechanics, applied geometry, geography, and other** practical fields.[4] As pointed out earlier, most of the books deposited in libraries, as for example, in the Library of Alexandria[5] and the Library of Pergamum, perished during the big fires; the one at Alexandria set by Christian zealots—inadvertently; the one at Pergamum also by Christian zealots--deliberately.

In this short essay on Greek philosophy, the chronological sequence of philosophers or schools of philosophy is employed, because in this way one can associate historical events with the changes in politics and philosophy and better understand the views of the various scholars. Thus, strictly in chronological sequence, the three periods of Greek philosophy that are presented here are:

Miltiades

The pre-Socratic Period. This is the period that spans for approximately 250 years, from about the beginning of the Olympic Games at Olympia, in

---

[4] Refer to the **"Introduction"** for further information about accomplishments of Greek scholars in practical applications, during the Hellenistic period (300 -146 B.C.).

[5] The Library of Alexandria was the greatest and largest library of the ancient world, and had a collection of over 700,000 books (rolls); it was not only a library but also a museum and a university. The Library of Pergamum was also a large library; and both libraries, either by neglect, fire, or deliberate intent, were destroyed by the beginning of the 5th century A.D., along with their entire collection of books--a crime of extraordinary dimension. The Library of Alexandria was built by Ptolemy Soter with the help of Demetrius of Phaleron during the Hellenistic Era. Thousands of rolls were burned in 47 B.C. by Julius Caesar, and a great fire in 391 A.D., which was set deliberately by the Christians in their quest to destroy the statue of the god Serapis, destroyed a large part of the library completely. (For the Alexandrian Library see: **Edward Alexander Parsons, The Alexandrian Library (Amsterdam: 1952, The Elsevier Press),** Chap XIX, p. 273.

Peloponnesus (776 B.C.), to the end of the Persian wars (approximately 479 B.C.). This period is identified with such names as: **Thales, Anaximander, Heraclitus, Pythagoras, et al.,** who were known as **"physical philosophers"** because they were mostly concerned with questions related to the natural environment.

The Ethical and Moral Philosophy Period. This period spans approximately 170 years, and runs from the end of the Persian wars (479 B.C.) to the death of Alexander (323 B.C.). It is dominated by such names as: **Protagoras, Gorgias, Prodicus, Critias, Thrasymachus** (known as the Sophists), **Socrates, Plato, Aristotle, Leucippus, Democritus, and others** who set the foundation of the dialectic method and logic, and introduced ethical and moral philosophy at a scientific level.

The Hellenistic Period. This period started with the end of Alexander's campaign to Asia (Alexander's death 323 B.C.) and lasted until the subjugation of Greece by the Romans in 146 B.C. It is identified with such names as: **Zeno, Epicurus, Theophrastus, Pyrrhon, Antisthenes, and others** who established the well known schools of the: **Stoics, Skeptics and Epicureans (The Garden),** as well as the **Academy and the Lyceum.** In these philosophies one will find influences from the expanded world of the Greeks during the Hellenistic Era.

It is preferable to consider an exposition of the thoughts and developments of these brilliant men with reference to time, in order to compare the various sects and doctrines of philosophy with the political and social phenomena throughout history. The changes and the evolution of philosophy through the years can be better understood if the political events are juxtaposed. For this reason, a short historical perspective on ancient Greece is given below.

A BRIEF OVERVIEW OF ANCIENT GREEK HISTORY

EARLY EVENTS.

By the turn of the millennium, the Greeks had established themselves in mainland Greece, stretching from **Macedonia to Crete,** and from the **Aegean to the Ionian Islands.** With time, they expanded to the shores of Asia Minor and established settlements and built cities there, such as: **Allicarnassus, Miletus, Ephesus, Klazoemenae, Colofon, Priene, Phocaea, Lamsacus, and others.** But the Persians were expanding westward at the same time and a clash of civilizations was in the making. By 600 B.C., they had pushed close to the above Greek Ionian cities of Asia Minor and were threatening them. Some were subjugated by the Persians who, by 550 B.C., were demanding tribute and taxes **(See Map 2 at end of this chapter).** It was at that time that the Greeks from these cities, fleeing the Persians, started emigrating to Southern Italy and Sicily and established cities there. Such cities as: **Syracuse, Elea, Agrigentum, Messina, Croton, and others**, were built by immigrants from the Ionian shores of Asia Minor. These cities flourished for many years and established a culture of their own which produced some very outstanding individuals, such as: **Pythagoras, Xenophanes, Empedocles, Parmenides, Zeno, and others**, who contributed significantly to the development of scientific thinking. These cities eventually fell to the Romans and lost their past glory under the ruthless Roman military rule.

THE PERSIAN WARS (MARATHON, THERMOPYLAE, SALAMIS.)

The Persians, after taking over all of the Greek cities in Ionia, pushed westward, and by 490 B.C. demanded complete subjugation from mainland Greece. For this purpose they sent envoys to all Greek city-states demanding **earth and water** which meant complete capitulation. Most

Philip II, King of Macedonia

of the Greek city-states, afraid of the might of the Persians, relinquished **earth and water--** with the exception of the city-states of Athens and Sparta. The Spartans specifically, dropped the envoys in a well, telling them that it was there that they would find both!

In 490 B.C., the Persian King, **Darius,** sent two generals, **Datis and Artafernis**, with over 40,000 troops and cavalry, with the purpose of subjugating the Greeks. At the battle of **Marathon,** 26 miles north-east of Athens, the Athenians and their allies defeated the stronger Persian army and pushed them into the sea. According to the ancient historian, **Herodotus,** the Athenians (who were less than 10,000) defeated the army of Datis and Artafernis due to the superior strategy devised by the Athenian general, **Miltiades.**

The defeat bewildered Darius, as it was a humiliating insult that his great and invincible army was crushed by such a small and impoverished group after he had successfully taken over all of the cities and countries of the Middle East and Egypt. According to Herodotus, he prepared a large army of over one million men, cavalry, and a large fleet--ready to attack again--but he died in the meantime and his son **Xerxes** undertook to carry out his father's plans. Xerxes invaded Greece in **480 B.C.** from the north, after he had crossed the Dardanelles and conquered all of Macedonia, Thrace, and Thessaly, and met the Greeks at **Thermopylae.** Most of the Greek city-states were intimidated by the numerical superiority of the Persian army and pledged obedience to Xerxes; but the Spartans, led by their king, **Leonidas,** fought the Persians at the narrow crossing of **Thermopylae** until all the Spartans died in battle.

The Athenian general, **Themistocles,** had realized that it would be difficult for the Greeks to defeat the Persians in an open land battle and decided to fight them at sea instead. In a sea battle at **Salamis,** a small island southwest of Athens, in the Saronic Gulf, the Athenian navy aided by the allied ships of Corinth and other naval city-states, defeated the Persians decisively and forced Xerxes to flee Greece in disgrace. But the threat was not over yet, because Xerxes left behind his entire army under the command of **General Mardonius,** to continue the warfare. The Greeks united, and under the joint leadership of Sparta and Athens met the Persians at **Plataea,** a small city 40 miles northwest of Athens, near **Thebes**. After a cruel and lengthy battle, the Greeks defeated and killed Mardonius in the year 479 B.C., the beginning of the period known as **The Golden Age of Greece.**

THE GOLDEN AGE OF GREECE.

The Persian threat temporarily ceased and the Greek city-states resumed their life, free from the danger from the East. Athens was now the emerging superpower of this conflict, because it was the Athenian efforts first at Marathon, and later at Salamis and at Plataea, that contained the Persian invasion. Sparta was also a winner, because it was the Spartan King's sacrifice at Thermopylae and their decisive participation toward the defeat of Mardonius at Plataea that contributed to the overall victory. The monarchical and rigid system of government in Sparta did not take advantage of the opportunities that presented themselves after the defeat of the Persians, but instead remained committed to its isolation and maintained their existing practices without change.

The Lion of Chaeronia

Athens, however, created alliances **(The Delian League)** and established colonies in the entire region, becoming a force that was superior to whatever existed before. She was now the undisputed power, and influenced the political, economic, and intellectual affairs of the entire country. The city of Athens became the intellectual and trade center for the Greek world, and learned men were coming there to teach and be taught new ideas, theories, and methods. The famous dramatic playwright poets (**Aeschylus, Sophocles, Euripides, and the comic poet Aristophanes)** distinguished themselves and flourished at that time; and philosophers such as **Socrates, Anaxagoras, Empedocles, Democritus. et al.** advanced the intellectual and scholarly life. The democratic system of Athens encouraged a free exchange of ideas and products, which

resulted in considerable economic growth. **Pericles,** the elected leader of Athens, commissioned the construction of the **Parthenon** on the **Acropolis,** and famous artists and architects: **Phidias, Praxiteles, Iktinus, and Kallicrates** advanced art and erected beautiful buildings and statues which are still admired today.

Animosities, jealousies, trade disputes, and above all the interference of the King of Persia, broke down Greek solidarity, and by 431 B.C. a war broke out between Athens and Sparta--known as the **Peloponnesian War.** This civil war lasted for 30 years and destroyed the Athenian power and considerably diminished its influence. By the year 404 B.C., Athens was run by a dictatorship of 30 Tyrants--but democracy returned following the collapse of the tyranny. This, and the loss of her colonies, caused the power of Athens to diminish significantly, allowing the Spartans to assume leadership over Greece.

Between 400 B.C. and 340 B.C., for sixty years, the Greek city-states engaged in continuous warfare quarreling among each other and fighting bloody battles as new city-states developed prominence, such as: **Corinth, Thebes, Argos, Megalopolis, Pella** (in Macedonia), and others, changing the configuration of alliances and power centers. By the middle of the 4th century B.C., the center of military influence was **Pella**, the capital of Macedonia, where by 340 B.C. **King Philip II** had succeeded in establishing his control over most of Greece. The Persians, however, after their defeat at Salamis and Plataea, continued to occupy the Greek cities in Ionia, and the Persian kings became very influential in the political affairs of the Greek city-states by bribing unscrupulous politicians and subsidizing and encouraging internecine warfare. **(See map 3)**

THE MACEDONIANS AND ALEXANDER THE GREAT

King Philip conceived a plan to unite all Greeks and lead an expedition to destroy the Persian Empire. But before he completed his preparations he was assassinated in Pella in **337 B.C.,** and his son **Alexander III**, who became known as **Alexander the Great**, undertook the completion of his father's plans. He reorganized the army, crushed the Athenians and the Thebans who rose against the Macedonians when they heard of Philip's death, and forced an alliance among all Greeks. He was declared Supreme Commander and led the army against the Persians in order to liberate the Greek city-sates in Ionia and avenge the destruction inflicted on Greece when they invaded the country in 490 and 480 B.C. and continued to subjugate the Greek city-states of Ionia.

Alexander left Greece in the spring of **334 B.C.** with **30,000 troops** and **6,000 cavalry**, intending with this small army to destroy an empire which extended for over 3,000 miles and could amass an army of over one million troops--with chariots, elephants, war machines, and a great cavalry. He crossed the Hellespont and came face to face with the Persians at the **Granicus River** in northwest Asia Minor, near the city of Troy. The defeat of the Persians was total, raising the morale of the Greek Army, and within a short period of time, in the summer of 334 B.C., Alexander liberated all of the Greek city-states of Ionia and moved eastward. In **333 B.C.**, a decisive battle was fought near the city of Issus, where the Persian King, Darius, had placed his army of over one million soldiers. The battle was won due to the bravery and courage of the Macedonians and the rest of the Greeks, as well as the strategy of Alexander and the effective use of the Macedonian **Phalanx**. The victory shifted to the Greek side after Darius saw Alexander advancing through the center of his **Guard** and fled the battlefield.

King Darius was not discouraged, and another decisive battle was fought in **331 B.C.** near the city of Gaugamela, close to Persia, and resulted in another defeat for Darius, who then fled north where soon afterward he was assassinated by his own rivals. Thus, Alexander conquered the entire Persian Empire in the span of less than eight years. He completed his conquests and his empire finally by **323 B.C.** included: **Persia, Egypt, part of India (known today as Pakistan and Afghanistan), areas as far north as Armenia, and the entire region of Asia Minor. (See Map 4).**

The Greek influence had spread to the entire known world, and the Greek language and

Alexander the Great

culture were the dominant forces that affected the intellectual, political, and social life of all the groups under Alexander's Empire. Alexander, even though he was a military personality, was also a gifted political leader who wanted to unite the entire then known world in a **confederation**--envisioning full cooperation of the various ethnic groups; and his plan may have caused his demise. He encouraged intermarriages between the Greeks and the **"barbarians,"** and he himself married Roxanne, the daughter of King Darius. Throughout his campaign he invited scientists from Greece to study the physical world of the new region (the fauna and the flora), and by 324 B.C. he consolidated his power and returned to Babylon from India, the most eastern border of the empire. A year later he fell ill and in a few weeks died on June 23, 323 B.C. The historian Arian, who described his campaign in detail in a book that survived, wrote that Alexander developed a high fever and soon thereafter weakened considerably and died. Before he died he was asked to whom he would leave the command of his empire and he responded: **"Τω Καλλίστω"** **(To the Best).** Alexander's generals: **Seleucus, Ptolemy, Antigonus, Antipater, Antiochus, and Perdicas** split the Empire among themselves and ruled for almost two centuries. The year of

Alexander's death constitutes the next milestone of a new era which came to be known as **The Hellenistic Period,** when new philosophies and ideas flourished, different from previous ones. We discuss these new philosophies in chapters 12 thought 14 of this work.

THE HELLENISTIC PERIOD AND THE DECLINE OF GREECE

Mainland Greece was now included in the part of Alexander's empire which had its capital in **Pella,** and was ruled by **Antipater, Antigonus, Perdicas, and others**. They ruled for several years, but the democratic Greek city-states, headed by Athens, never accepted the Macedonian rule and revolted immediately after Alexander's death, and the civil war started all over again. Bloody battles were fought during most of the years of the third century B.C., and this brought a gradual decline, not only of the military power of Greece, but also of the intellectual, political, and social values and institutions. The shadow of **Rome** was now spreading eastward and the Greek city-states felt the threat from the **West** after they eliminated the threat from the **East.** New political alliances and political schemes were devised, such as the idea of federation, practiced by the **Achaean, Acarnanian** and other **Leagues**, which were the last bastions of Greek solidarity intended to fight the Romans. Eventually, by 146 B.C., the Romans conquered Greece when finally Athens and Corinth fell. For the conclusion of this chapter, a very short outline of the Roman world is given, along with a short description of the achievement of four Roman intellectuals during the period of the first and second centuries A.D.--identifying the conditions and political considerations that led to the fall of Rome.

THE ROMANS

From the middle of the 2nd century B.C., when the Romans subdued the city-states of Greece—Athens, Corinth, and the Macedonian state in the north--until approximately the middle of the 1st century B.C. -- the assassination of Julius Caesar--the Romans experienced a military expansion and solidified their control of the known world. They benefited immensely from the experience of the Greeks, whose achievements in the cultural and scientific fields they copied and adapted into their culture. But in the areas of science and philosophy they did not advance beyond the levels that the Greeks reached, even though they had been very successful in the field of building—roads, aqueducts, bridges, etc.--and in the field of administration where they kept their vast empire under control. They were slow to adapt to the advances of the scientists who had introduced breakthroughs in many areas, most significantly in the areas of transportation and distribution. The Romans were satisfied to continue use of the horse and the barge to transport merchandise in their immense empire, and did not take advantage of the potentials of Hero's steam engine experiments. In the area of art, literature, and the theater, they copied the Greeks; and in philosophy they were influenced primarily by the Stoics and the Epicureans. Even though they developed a reputation as pragmatists, they never took advantage of the achievements and potential of the early Greek physical philosophers--**Anaximander, Anaximenis, Thales, Pythagoras, etc.--** so that the fields of the physical sciences and mathematics did not advance beyond the basic roots that the Naturalists had planted. The Republic lasted until about the time of Caesar--a quasi-democratic system-- but after the completion of the conquests and the assassination of Caesar, a cruel oligarchic rule was established by Augustus. This system was a tyrannical one and worked well enough throughout the Empire—since in the provinces the system had always been tyrannical—but the exception was the city of Rome, which experienced tremendous misfortunes during the rule of the emperors. From about that time the most ruthless, bloody, corrupt, and unjust system was practiced by a group of inept emperors who exceeded in cruelty and corruption any in the history of man. Such names as **Tiberius, Caligula, Nero, Domitian, Nerva, and Trajan** are synonymous with suppression, madness, and injustice. During that period four names (**Lucretius, Cicero, Seneca, Tacitus**) were distinguished in the literary and intellectual world.

These individuals attempted to bring some semblance of justice and civilized life at a time when the empire was taken hostage by the emperors. They translated and studied the Greeks, and made significant contributions in the area of philosophy, literature, law, and the theater. A short summary of their work and their lives is presented below so as to give a sense of continuity and a bird's eye view of the spirit of Rome.

Julius Caesar

LUCRETIUS (96 – 55 B.C.)

Lucretius was born in the year 96 B.C., and died 55 B.C. He wrote a poem, in the Xenophanes pattern, titled "On the Nature of Things" (**De Rerum Natura),** which contained many different ideas on a number of subjects; for example*: physics, human life, pleasure.* He elaborated extensively on atomic theory by discussing Epicurus' book, **"On Nature" (Περι Φυσεως)**—the only existing evidence of the Atomists' doctrines on the atom-- and advanced his conviction that happiness is produced by the virtue of moderation. He was a follower of Epicurus and was also significantly influenced by the Stoics. His doctrines combined Stoicism and Epicureanism in a way that advanced practical living at the time, and still today. Lucretius wanted ordinary people, like himself, to understand and appreciate philosophical thought. He tried to simplify the philosophies of Zeno, Socrates, and Epicurus, and endeavored to instill in his philosophy a high degree of humanism. Lucretius had a strong influence on Virgil, who was born near the time when he died.

CICERO (106 – 43 B.C.)

Cicero lived in the middle of the most tumultuous era of Roman life--mid first century B.C.--when Caesar and Pompeii were competing for the rule of Rome. In 63 B.C. he was elected one of two consuls--a great honor for a man who did not have aristocratic senatorial lineage. In the dispute between Caesar and Pompeii, he sided with Pompeii, which was a mistake, because he was not only defeated, but Caesar was more of a man to understand Cicero. He criticized Anthony and Octavian for illegally encroaching on ancient Roman freedoms, and finally Anthony had him killed in 43 B.C., by having his hands cut and nailed to the Senate Post Rum as a warning to others who might wish to express the truth and oppose the Emperor. Cicero was modest and claimed that he was merely a popularizer who had taken up the task of translating Greek thought, so that it could be easily understood by his countrymen. He made no original discoveries, yet he helped discover the brilliant and original insights of his great predecessors. He applied the ethical principles of the Greeks to the uncultivated life of the Roman businessman and politician, and advocated that one should always do the right thing because, if not, in the long run he will lose and never gain an advantage. He wrote a book, **"On Duty,"** in which he prescribed simple rules of virtuous action by giving direct advice on how to be **"good"**, and elaborated on what really constitutes a prudent life. He stated that *"people should always know what the right way is,"* and encouraged them to always strive to achieve virtue and prudence, even if it meant that they would be poorer in material possessions. Cicero provided guidance to

Augustus, the Roman Emperor

the simple Roman regarding principles that one would find in Plato's **Republic** or Aristotle's **Ethics** or **Politics**, with subtle analysis and high intellectual content. The assassination of Cicero significantly diminished any vestige of intellectualism in **Roman life,** and tyranny and subjugation of the masses began with the ascent of Augustus to power. Cicero failed to persuade enough of his fellow citizens to save the Roman Republic.

LUCIUS ANNAEUS SENECA. (4 B.C. – 65 A.D.)

Seneca lived in an era when the two most despicable Roman emperors (Caligula 12-41 A.D., and Nero 37-68 A.D.) ruled the Roman world. He was one of the few intellectuals in Rome at the time and served as a tutor to Nero when the future Emperor was young. During the early years of Nero's rule, before he became mad, Seneca was counseling him, and for over 10 years was influential in the governance of the Roman Empire. He fell in disfavor with the Emperor and eventually became a victim of Nero's madness. Even though Seneca was indirectly responsible for some of Nero's crimes, he was an honest man of integrity who adhered to the Stoic doctrine and tried to instill integrity and justice in Nero. He wrote works on philosophy and some dramatic plays, but they lacked the psychological depth of his mentors and predecessors (**Aeschylus, Sophocles, and Euripides**) whom he tried to emulate. Strangely, Seneca's plays were popular during the Renaissance and even during Shakespearean times, but most likely Shakespeare was not influenced by his writings. Audiences were fascinated by the cruel, violent, dramatic, and realistic plays that Seneca wrote. He was a man of great accomplishments, but was always in poor health, and when he fell in disfavor with the Emperor he was saved from immediate execution because advisors informed Nero that he did not have much longer to live. Even though he was not a brilliant writer, he tried to keep alive the great tradition of his Greek predecessors in philosophy and drama within the bounds of his talent and understanding. He also made a sincere effort, though unsuccessful, to guide the mad young man, who had graduated from his tutorship, to become an honest ruler of the Roman world.

PUBLIUS CORNELIUS TACITUS (56-120 A.D.)

Tacitus was born in Gaul (today's France) when it was a Roman province. He studied law and politics, and ascended to the position of Consul, a very distinguished office in Roman government. He was appointed to positions of imperial bureaucracy, and, as a good lawyer, he upheld the law. He wrote biographies and histories that cover a long period of Roman dominance; and also the **Annals** which cover the beginning of Tiberius' reign to the end of Nero's: all together the first 100 years of the Empire--but much of this work is lost. As a historian, Tacitus tried to emulate **Thucidides**; but even though his work was notable, he did not possess the depth and intellectual integrity of Thucidides. His works have been very popular for many centuries, and people appreciated his descriptive style chronicling the intrigues, violence, persecutions, murders, and orgies of the Emperors Tiberius, Caligula, and Nero.

This then is, in summary, the history of ancient Greece for over 600 years which is of concern to us here in understanding the various political and social influences that affected the **spirit of the times,** and eventually the minds that formulated the various philosophies presented in the following pages. The last few comments on the Romans show the influence that the Greek thinkers had on Romans who played an intermediate force that brought about the Middle Ages and ultimate the Renaissance. After this short historical review, the examination of the thoughts and contributions of the various Greek philosophers will proceed on the basis of the chronological classification made earlier in this chapter. We shall consider first the period that spans from the beginning of the Greek intellectual era (about 776 B.C.) to the end of the Persian wars (479 B.C.). We shall continue with the second period which ends with the death of Alexander (323 B.C.), and conclude the discussion with the Hellenistic Period to the emergence of Rome as a new world power.

MAP 1
THE PREHISTORIC GREEK CITIES IN MAINLAND GREECE
AND THE SHORES OF ASIA MINOR
(3,000 TO 1000 B.C.)

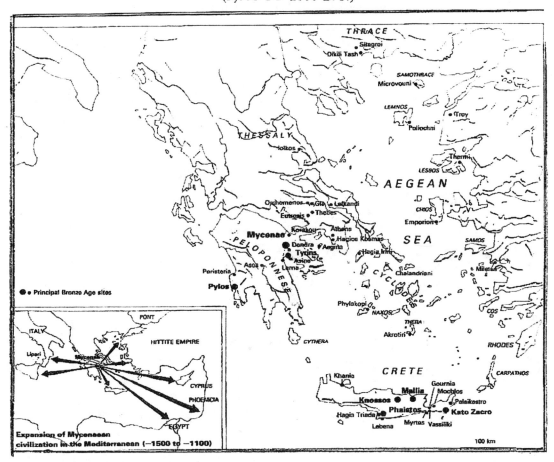

This map shows the early people who lived in the area of Greece from the 3rd millennium B.C. These were: the Minoan civilization in Crete, the Mycenaean civilization in the Peloponnese and the Cycladic civilization in the islands of the Aegean. Note the cities of Phaistos, Mallia, Kato Zacro and Gournia in Crete, and the cities of Tiryns, Pylos, Orhomenos, et.al. in mainland Greece. The cities in Asia Minor, with the exception of Miletus, had not yet developed.

MAP 2
THE HELLENIC EXPANSION TO THE MEDITERRANEAN SHORES,
BLACK SEA AND NORTH AFRICA
(1000 - 450 B.C.)

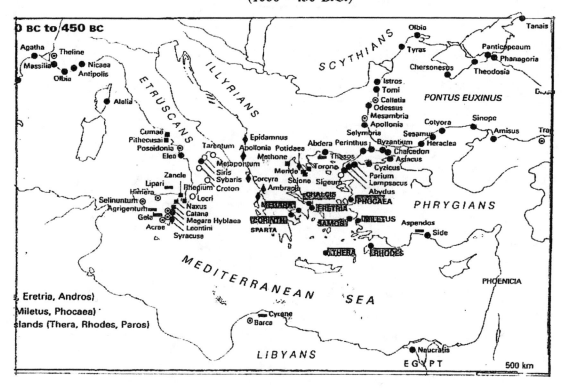

This map shows the expansion and colonization of the Hellenic civilization in all directions. Primary expansion was concentrated on the shores of Asia Minor, where such cities as: Miletus, Abydus, Lampsacus, etc. were built. Another destination was Sicily and Southern Italy, where such cities as: Syracuse, Catana, Croton, Metapontum, Elea, Agrigentum, Poseidonia et.al., were established, as well as several colonies on the shores on the Black Sea, such as: Byzantium, Sinope, Trapezus, Odessa and others were built. The Greek expansion was also directed to Northern Africa where Cyrene, Naucratis and Barca were built, and also to Spain and Southern France, where Hemeroscopion, Molaca, Massillia, Nicaea and other cities were established.

MAP 3
THE GREEK-CITY STATES DURING THE 5TH AND 4TH CENTURIES B.C., INCLUDING GREATER GREECE AND IONIA

This is the Greece of the Golden Age and prior to the appearance of the Macedonians and Alexander the Great.

MAP 4
THE EXPANSION OF THE GREEK CIVILIZATION UNDER
ALEXANDER THE GREAT
(334 TO 323 B.C.)

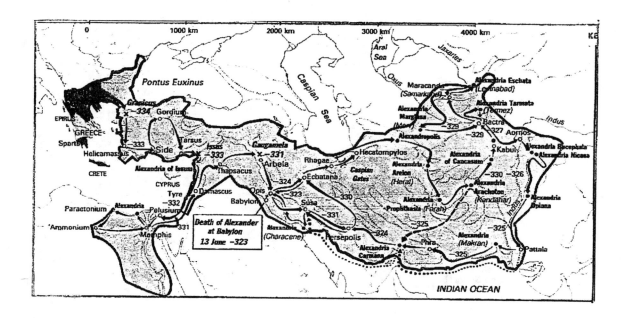

This map shows the borders of the empire built by Alexander in the span of 12 years. Alexander fought three decisive battles against the Persian king, Darius: at Granicus River in 334 B.C., at Issus, in 333 B.C., and at Gaugamela in 331 B.C. In 331 B.C., Darius died and the Persian Empire collapsed. Alexander then conquered Egypt after he captured the Phoenician cities of Tyre and Sidon. Afterwards he continued his campaign to India and Afghanistan, but returned to Babylon in 324 and died a year later on June 13, 323 B.C., at the age of 32.

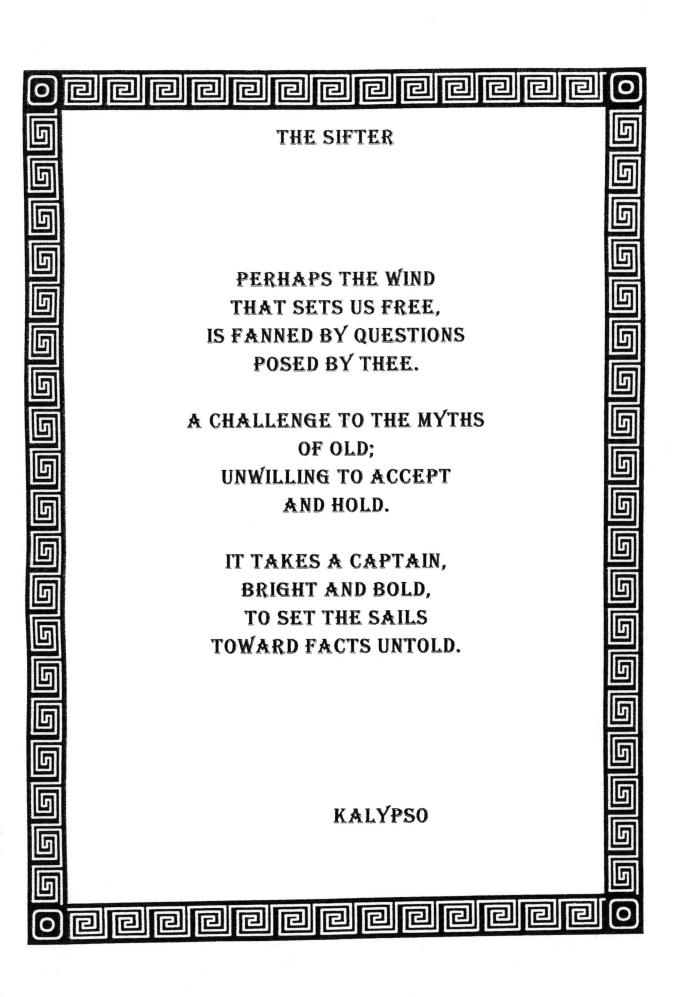

THE SIFTER

PERHAPS THE WIND
THAT SETS US FREE,
IS FANNED BY QUESTIONS
POSED BY THEE.

A CHALLENGE TO THE MYTHS
OF OLD;
UNWILLING TO ACCEPT
AND HOLD.

IT TAKES A CAPTAIN,
BRIGHT AND BOLD,
TO SET THE SAILS
TOWARD FACTS UNTOLD.

KALYPSO

CHAPTER 2

THE EARLY PERIOD OF GREEK PHILOSOPHY (THE IONIANS)

INTRODUCTION

During this period (776-479 B.C.), as noted earlier, the foundation of Greek philosophy and Greek scientific thinking was established. The individuals, who distinguished themselves in these areas and other fields of scientific inquiry, came mainly from the Greek city-states of Ionia or the city-states of Sicily and Southern Italy. By the beginning of the 8th century B.C, the Greek language had developed into a very expressive, detailed language with a vocabulary to suit the most abstract thinking. By then, the Homeric poems were circulated widely; while some city-states were using the democratic system of government, and the people were successfully involved in agriculture and maritime trade. The intellectuals/scholars initiated traveling outside the Greek world and came in contact with the peoples of earlier civilizations--such as the **Egyptians**, the **Babylonians and others.** They discovered that these people had made considerable progress in

The Ionian Island of Lefkada

architecture, mathematics, medicine, and other fields. But they also discovered, as we pointed out in the previous chapter, in the case of Thales and the inundation of the Nile, that the priests or the

Magi had the last word on practically all matters, such as education, art, administration, and they controlled the political system for millennia. When it concerned issues of natural phenomena, the theocratic system was highly rigid.   The pressing questions that these Greek scholars were interested in addressing were related to the understanding and explanation of the world around them.   They wanted to know why Nature behaved the way it did, and they were interested in establishing **"universal truths."**   Thus, the logical explanation, by observation, experiment, and establishment of cause and effect relationships on matters of physical phenomena, had started. This was the beginning of the departure from the dependence on myth and theology. We could call these

The Island of Poros

scholars **"Cosmologists"** or **"Naturalists,"** because they were focusing on Nature. The word "Nature" in Greek is **"Φυσις,"** and because of the emphasis of their research on **Nature,** they came to be known by their contemporaries as **"Physiocrats"** (**Φυσιοκρατες**), which was another word for **"Naturalists."** We use this term frequently in this work, even though the word **"Cosmologists"** could be equally appropriate, since they were also concerned with the universe (**κοσμος**).[1]

One of them, **Thales**, the father of Greek philosophy and one of the **Seven Wise Men of Antiquity (Σοφος)**, rejected the mythological and theological explanations of the creation of the world and its phenomena. He gave a natural explanation for its origin: declaring that everything originated from water. Two individuals, who were students and contemporaries of **Thales (Anaximander and Anaximenes)**, advanced new concepts, such as: **the Boundless (Απειρον=Infinity),** and the theory that **"Nothing originates from nothing and nothing is destroyed."**   One important question that arose and caused considerable consternation among these early philosophers, was the idea of a single, solid, indivisible matter (**Monistic Theory**)--as opposed to one composed of continuous change (**Pluralistic Theory**). **Parmenides** argued that

---

[1] One has to be careful not to confuse this term with the same term, **"physiocrat,"** which was coined during the 18th century A.D. to denote a group of thinkers in economics who claimed that Nature is the only source of income, and therefore the most important entity to consider in the theory of economics. Their school was against the policies of the *mercantilists.*

matter is solid, unchanging, and stationary; while **Heraclitus** and the **Atomists (Leucippus and Democritus)** postulated that everything is in a **"continuous flux,** and that the world and matter consist of **"void"** and **"atoms."** The mathematical concepts of **"continuity"** and **"change"** become a heated topic of discussion, and **Zeno** embarks on an extensive intellectual diatribe to discredit the idea by developing his famous **"Paradoxes."**

Empedocles, a contemporary of **Parmenides** (5th century), postulates that the world consists of four elements: **Earth, Air, Fire and Water,** which can come together or disassociate under the influence of **Love** and **Hate,** and introduces the concept of the **"Survival of the Fittest."** A very important thinker of the **Naturalists** was **Pythagoras from Samos.** He stressed that all things are **"numbers,"** meaning that the essence and structure of all objects in the world can be

Hippocrates

determined by finding the numerical relationship contained within them. **Anaxagoras**, another 5th century philosopher, postulates that the world consists of two parts: the one that we can perceive; and the one that we cannot. He developed this theory from the observation that in the animal world, and including the human, some species have a better sensory development than others. Some animals can see better at night than others, and some others hear better; as, for example: the cat has a more acute sense of hearing than other animals or humans. He suggests that the **Mind** is the powerful force that positioned everything in order. By the latter part of the 5th century B.C., these philosophers, particularly the Atomist **Democritus**, were addressing questions of ethics and human behavior. It was the beginning of this period that we classify as: *the Period of the Moral and Ethical Philosophers* **Socrates,Plato).** **Democritus** claimed that a sound and cheerful man, useful to his fellow men, is literally **"well composed."** Although destructive passions involve violent long-distance atomic reactions, education can help to contain them--creating a better composure. According to **Democritus,** civilizations are produced as a result of the **necessities of life,** which compel men to work and to make inventions and discoveries. When life becomes too easy, because all needs are satisfied, there is a danger that civilizations will decay as men become unruly and negligent. In this, and the next two chapters, we shall discuss in more detail these basic concepts that were the focus and concern of the Naturalists and also give some additional information about these individuals as human

25

beings and citizens of the ancient Greek Πολεις (city-states.) We have classified them into five Schools of Thought:

1.   **The Miletus School**
2.   **The Pythagorean School**
3.   **The Eleatic School**
4.   **The Ephesus School**
5.   **The Atomic School**

In this period seven[2] individuals distinguished themselves and were identified by their contemporaries as the **"Seven Wise Men"** of ancient times, in a fashion similar to the **Seven Wonders of the Ancient World.** There is not much information available about them, with the exception of **Solon** and **Thales**. In addition to these men, several other individuals also have been identified by ancient biographers as influential in their time, and, with the exception of Pharecydes, there is little additional information about them either.[3] Whatever information is available about the individuals identified in the footnotes, who distinguished themselves in the field of philosophy, comes to us through second-hand sources, because none of the books that these individuals wrote survived, with the exception of some fragments.

Some of the information about their lives and their theories is also found in the writings of other ancient authors such as **Aristotle ("Metaphysics;" Book 1, and Plato),** who referred to them in their treatises; and some information has been preserved by **Diogenes Laertius** (see ref. 8), who has written about their lives and their philosophies. Diogenes Laertius, however, was a biographer and did not elaborate extensively on the theories and views of these men. Also, a significant amount of information about them is provided by the **Suidas Lexicon;** but again, as the title implies, the information appears in the form of a biographical dictionary.

---

[2] These individuals lived in various parts of Greece. They were by place of birth, name, and age: **Periander** 625-585 B.C. (ruler- "tyrant" of Corinth); **Pittacus**, c. 600 B.C. (a native of Mitylene); **Cleobulus**, c. 600 B.C. (a native of Lindos); **Solon**, c. 594 B.C. (a native of Athens and Archon); **Thales**, 625-546 B.C. (a native of Miletus); **Bias**, c. 570 B.C. (a native of Priene); and **Chilon**, c. 560 B.C. (a native of Lacadaemony).

[3]The following four individuals also distinguished themselves in ancient times, and references about them by biographers and in fragments are available--but none of their works survived: **Anacharsis**, c. 590 B.C. (He was a Scythian whose mother was Greek); **Myson**, c. 600 B.C. (a native of Laconia); **Epimenides**, c.600 B.C. (a native of Crete; and **Pharecydes**, c. 540 B.C. (a native of the island of Syros), for whom a reference is made in the text of a letter that he sent to Thales, which was preserved by Diogenes Laertius.

THE MILETUS SCHOOL

The Greek city-states of Asia Minor: *Ephesus, Miletus, Alikarnassus, Klazomenae, Colofon, et al.,* proved to be the breeding ground for independent thinkers because of the prosperous economic conditions that prevailed in this area, and also due to their proximity to the Eastern cultures and civilizations of Mesopotamia and Egypt. The individuals who are identified with this school are: **Thales** (637-546 B.C.); **Anaximander** (610-547 B.C.); **Anaximenes** (585-525 B.C.); and **Pharecydes** (c. mid 6th century B.C.).

Thales

THALES (ΘΑΛΗΣ)

The Man. By far **Thales (Θαλής)** was one of the first among the Ionians who primarily investigated matters of Nature, mathematics, geometry and astronomy. He never wrote anything, or at least we do not know of anything that he wrote, that either survived or was referred to by subsequent ancient writers. He was one of the **Seven Sages** of the ancient world, and was born in Miletus in the 1st year of the 35th Olympiad (636 B.C.)[4], and died 90 years later in Miletus. We know that he traveled to Egypt and discussed various matters with the priests concerning the Egyptian civilization. There was some controversy about his place of origin, and there were some references that he was of Phoenician patronage, even though it has been asserted by Diogenes Laertius that he was a native Miletian and of a distinguished family.[5]

Thales was also known for his wise counsel and short apothegms. According to some

---

[4] The ancient Greeks used the **Olympiads** to keep record of time. The time span between Olympiads was four years, and the beginning was the year 776 B.C., as far as our calendar (which begins with the birth of Jesus Christ) is concerned. The year "1," for their calendar, was the first year of the first Olympiad, and an event that took place 44 years later would be referred to as the last year of the 11th Olympiad. **For example, the death of Socrates that took place in the year 399 B.C., by our calendar, would be referred to by the ancient Greeks as the first year of the 95th Olympiad {(776-399)/4=95}. As an alternate way of counting time, they referred to the time in office of heads of state: in the case of Athens, the third year of Pericles' rule.**

[5] See reference #8, where Diogenes Laertius, in Volume 2, p. 22, "Thales," discusses the background of Thales and the controversy surrounding his alleged Phoenician descent.

writers, he was the one who coined the term **"Know Thyself."** Responding to the question: **"Which is older, day or night"? he replied: "Night is the older by one day."** Someone asked him whether a man should hide an evil deed from the gods: **"No," he replied, "Nor yet an evil thought."** To the adulterer who inquired if he should deny the charge upon oath, he replied: **"Perjury is not worse than adultery."** Being asked what is difficult, he replied: **"To know oneself."** What is easy? **"To give advice to another."** What is most pleasant? **"Success."** What is divine? **"That which has neither beginning nor end."** Thales maintained that the universe contains a creative force that he called **"Physis"** (Φύσις)--which became the word for Nature-- from which the word physics originated. He was known also as a political consultant, and saved his city once by providing counsel on a policy matter. He advised his compatriots in an anticipated battle between Croesus (Lydian) and Cyrus (Persian), not to ally with Croesus, because he sensed that Cyrus would be the winner; and on the basis of his advice, the city of Miletus was spared by the Persians, who were victorious. Thales was also known to have been a good speculator and weather forecaster, and once profited by renting all the olive oil mills in the district--anticipating a big crop of olives.[6]

He used to say that there is no difference between life and death, and when someone inquired: **"Why don't you die then?"** he replied, **"Just because there is no difference."** Some stories about Thales include: He never married, and his mother was nagging him to marry; when he

Hippocrates Clinic

was young he used to say that it was **too early,** and when he became old he said that it was **too late.** When asked what were his three blessings, he answered: **he was grateful that he was born a human and not an animal; a man and not a woman; and a Greek, not a barbarian.** Some of his apothegms (sayings) include: **The Greatest is Space** because it holds all things. **The Swiftest is the Mind** because it speeds everywhere. **The Strongest is Necessity,** for it masters all; and **The Wisest is Time** because it eventually illuminates everything." The following story, related by Diogenes Laertius, is indicative of his modesty, humility, and the respect that he commanded among his compatriots in Miletus. The story goes that some fishermen in the Aegean found a tripod entangled in their nets and sold it to some youths from Ionia. The youths, in turn, not being able to decide what to do with the tripod, reached a decision to ask the Oracle at Delphi to render a judgment as to the disposition of it. The Oracle stated that **"The tripod should be given to whomever is most wise."** They decided that they should offer it to Thales. But Thales

---

[6] **Aristotle** discusses this incident of the olive oil mills and elaborates on the alertness of Thales, in Pol.i,1259 (6-18)

did not accept it, saying that certainly he was not "most wise." The story concludes when the tripod was finally sent to Delphi and dedicated to the "god" because they could not find anyone wiser than Thales.

He believed in democracy and supported the institution, even though his city-state experienced tyranny at times. When asked **what is the strangest thing he had ever seen,** he replied: **"An aged tyrant."** When asked how to bear adversity, he said: **"Identify worse plight in your enemies."** When queried on the best and righteous life, he advised to **"refrain from doing to others what you do not want others to do to you."** When asked which man is happy, he said: **"The one who is healthy, of resourceful mind, and docile character."** He advised not to be proud of outward appearances, but to concentrate on beauty of character instead. As with all early Greek philosophers and scientists, he also believed that the Earth was the fixed center of the universe, and that the sun, stars, and the moon revolved around it in cyclical orbits. He died in an unfortunate accident. While he was out walking in the countryside with his servant at night, gazing at the stars, as was his habit, he did not pay attention to a steep precipice, stepped over and was killed. The servant is reported to have said: **"It would be wiser to look more in front of your feet and less upon the stars."**

The Goddess Athena

His work; Thales was one of those extraordinary historical figures who merits placement in the same category as **Leibniz, da Vinci,** and **Galileo** of Renaissance Europe. He was the individual who introduced logical propositions in geometry and mathematics and proved them, thus advancing the cause of science and research to significant levels for subsequent scholars to pursue. His work was a diversion from the empirical and theocratic mode of thinking that prevailed up until his time. From Diogenes Laertius we know (see Letter to Pharecydes) that he traveled to the Middle East and came in contact with Egyptian mathematicians and astronomers, and no doubt profited from the advances they made in these fields up until that time. We also know that he was the first to organize the findings of his research in the field of geometry--in the form of logical propositions or "theorems." He hypothesized and proved that:

(1) a circle is bisected by its diameter.
(2) angles at the base of a triangle having two sides of equal length are equal.
(3) opposite angles of intersecting straight lines are equal.
(4) the angle inscribed in a semi-circle is a right angle.
(5) a triangle is determined if its base and the angles relative to the base are given. He excelled in astronomy and is known to have been the first to have predicted an eclipse of the sun in the year 585 B.C. He discovered and named the constellation of Ursa Minor, engaged in considerable research on the solstice and equinox, identified the four seasons, and divided the year

into 365 days. He studied geometry and mathematics, and is known to have been the first to inscribe a right triangle into a circle, and on the basis of similar triangles and a ratio equation, measured the height of the Great Pyramid of Cheops while he was in Egypt. He accomplished this by using the length of the shadow of the pyramid and the length of the shadow of his body as the first ratio (known quantities) and the vertical axis of the height of the pyramid (an unknown quantity) and his height (known quantity), as the other ratio--and solved a ratio equation of one unknown. He studied magnets and the properties of amber, and set the stage for the study and discovery of electricity--which later received its name from amber (**"Ηλεκτον-Electron"**). He postulated that water was the primary matter from which all life derived--and also believed in the immortality of the human soul. Diogenes Laertius preserved two letters that Thales sent, one to *Pharecydes in Syros* (one of the Cycladic islands in the Aegean), and one to Solon in Athens. The letter to Pharecydes reads as follows:

"I hear that you intend to be the first Ionian to expound theology to the Greeks. And perhaps it was a wise decision to make the book common property without taking advice, rather than entrusting it to any particular persons--a course which has no advantages. However, if it would give you any pleasure, I am quite willing to discuss the subject of your book with you; and if you bid me to come to Syros, I will do so. For surely, Solon of Athens and I would scarcely be sane if, after having sailed to Crete to pursue our inquiries there, and to Egypt to confer with the priests and astronomers, we hesitate to come to you. For Solon too will come-- with your permission. You, however, are so fond of home that you seldom visit Ionia and have no longing to see strangers, but, as I hope, apply yourself to one thing, namely writing, while we, who never write anything, travel all over Hellas and Asia."[7]

The letter to Solon reads as follows:

"If you leave Athens, it seems to me that you could most conveniently set up your abode in Miletus, which is an Athenian colony, for there you incur no risk. If you are vexed at the thought that we are governed by a tyrant, hating as you do all absolute rulers, you would at least enjoy the society of your friends. Bias[8] wrote inviting you to Priene; and if you prefer the town of Priene for a residence, I myself will come and live with you."[9]

---

[7] See reference #8, Volume I, p.45.

[8] **Bias** was another scholar of ancient times, known also as one of the Seven Wise Men of antiquity, and lived in Priene, another Ionian city near Miletus.

[9] See Reference #8, Volume I, p. 47

PHARECYDES (ΦΑΡΕΚΥΔΗΣ, 7th Century B.C.)

Because **Pharecydes** lived around the time of Thales and had a great influence on his contemporaries, it is appropriate to relate some interesting stories written about him by the ancient biographers. He is supposed to have been the first to write in Greek about Nature and the gods, and his name and actions were associated with supernatural powers similar to the Chaldean Magi and the priests of the Assyrians and the Babylonians. He supposedly predicted the sinking of a ship, an earthquake, and the outcome of the Messinian War. He spent his entire life in Syros and died in the year 540 B.C. during the 59th Olympiad. Diogenes Laertius, in his reference on Pharecydes, refers

The Kapodistrian University of Athens

to a letter that Pharecydes wrote to Thales, which reads as follows:[10]

> *"May yours be a happy death when your time comes. Since I received your letter, I have been attacked by disease. I am infested with vermin and subject to a violent fever with shivering fits. I have therefore given instructions to my servants to carry my writing to you after they have buried me. I would like you to publish it, provided that you and the other sages approve of it, and not otherwise, for I myself am not yet satisfied with it. The facts are not absolutely correct, nor do I claim to have discovered the Truth, but merely such things as one who inquires about the gods picks up. The rest must be thought out, for mine is all guesswork. As I was more and more weighted down with my malady, I did not permit any of the physicians or my friends to come into the room where I was, but as they stood before the door and inquired how I was, I thrust my finger through the keyhole and showed them how plague-stricken I was; and I told them to come tomorrow and bury Pharecydes."*

Pharecydes was the first to write about the phenomena of Nature. One should consider that up until that point, the Homeric poems (written a century or so prior to the time of the Ionian sages)

---

[10] For this letter see Reference #8, Diogenes Laertius, Volume I, p.127.

had a very clear and mythological view of the gods to whom they attributed human characteristics. Obviously then, the writings that he refers to, in his letter to Thales, relate to the gods and their influence on people. It was not very far ahead in time that Xenophanes, from the city of Elea, formally questioned the practices and characteristics attributed to the Olympic gods; and Anaxagoras, another Ionian during the 5th century, was condemned in Athens for impiety and atheism because of his disdain of qualities and characteristics attributed to gods.

ANAXIMANDER (Αναξιμανδρος)-(611-547 B.C.)

Anaximander--a prominent thinker, philosopher, and student of Thales--who later wrote about him-- was born in the city of Miletus in c.611 B.C., but it is not clear when he died; some speculate that he lived more than 64 years. Anaximander followed closely in the footsteps of Thales and was knowledgeable on quite a number of subjects, and had the reputation of a **"pansophist"** [11]
He drew maps—the first in existence in the Western world--illustrating the descriptions of the Aegean as well as the Mediterranean coastlines of his fellow-townsman, the geographer **Hecateus**.

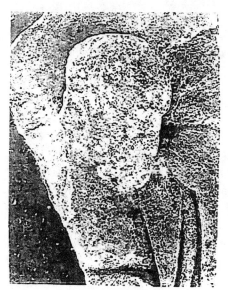
Anaximander

Anaximander seemed unsure of Thales' view that everything came from water, and that water was the main substance--the **"basic principle"** of the world. Apparently he found water too specific, too bound to its own nature; in a word, too essentially liquid to be transformed into the myriad things which water, for all intents and purposes--save those of theory--is not suitable. These early scholars were interested in interpreting their environment, and understandably Thales concluded that water was the basic substance because it was ubiquitous. For us today, knowing that there are over 100 basic elements, and that water is a compound of two of these elements, we would consider it naive for one to claim that water is the main substance. Similarly perhaps, but within his frame of thinking, Anaximander thought that the *"Stuff"* of which all things are made must be something more versatile, more adaptable, and more capable of transforming itself into an infinite variety of objects and parts. Indeed, that one specific kind of thing should be the substance of which all other things are made of, might well seem unreasonable. Only something that was no one thing in particular could turn itself with equal facility into anything and everything. And perhaps too, he was struck with the way in which *the conglomerate may be sorted out into pairs of opposites*, and thought that Thales gave undue prominence to the **"wet,"** and unduly discouraged the importance of the **"dry."** However

---

[11] What was meant by this term was that the philosopher was also: an astronomer, a geographer, a physicist, a political analyst, a mathematician, etc.

that may be, Anaximander refused to specify the nature of the substance of the world. It was simply considered to be something to which no particular character or limitation of any sort could be assigned. His speculation was that the ***Boundless—Infinite (Απειρον)--Indeterminate--*** was the origin of **"All"** in an evolutionary process. It should be noted that the concept of *"evolutionary process"*--a fundamental principle of the doctrine of evolution--preoccupied Anaximander as well as his successor, Anaximenes, and the Miletus School in all of their research. The Boundless, being undefined and unbounded, could be imagined without difficulty as assuming any shape whatsoever. Out of it all things arose and again into it all things were resolved without any alteration of their essential character. Instead of asking, *"What is the world made of?"*, he asks: *"What is the process by which the world is formed?"* He explains: "There is

an eternal motion in the Boundless, in the course of which pairs of opposites--hot and cold, wet and dry, light and darkness--become separated out from the Indefinite Substance. These opposites conflict with and suppress one another, and then continuously resolve again into the **Boundless."**

Another concept introduced by Anaximander, in the context of his research or speculation, is the principle of the whirling motion; and that the Earth was the center or vortex of this motion. If one observes a whirling motion in air or water, it is apparent that the heavier objects gravitate toward the center of the vortex, while lighter ones tend to move to the periphery. Thus, because he thought that the Earth was the center of the world, it followed logically that the Earth was the vortex and that the world whirled around it. Also, one is tempted to think that perhaps because of his concentration on the relationships of the opposites,

Plaka

his speculation on the creation of the world, through the force of the opposites, may have been influenced by the need to explain the changing seasons during the year. There must be an explanation and understanding of the force that is responsible for the seasons, and particularly how to account for the dominance of hot and dry in the summer and wet and cold in the winter. An elementary astronomy course student today would certainly know that this is because of the 23 degree tilt of the axis of the Earth's rotation on the plane of the ecliptic; Anaximander, however, attempted to explain this phenomenon by the introduction of the counter-balancing force of the "opposites," and introduced the idea that they continuously interact. Later this concept was elaborated on far more extensively by Heraclitus, another Ionian philosopher from the city of Ephesus, a few miles northeast of Miletus, and Plato used it in **Phaedo** *to prove!* the **Immortality of the Soul**. According to Anaximander, there is a continuous conflict between hot and dry on the

33

one hand, and cold and wet on the other, but this process is self-regulating and neither of the two forces is allowed to dominate--otherwise we would all drown in water or burn in fire. Anaximander postulated that the Earth is a cylinder floating in air, stationary due to its equidistant position from everything in the Heavens, and has no reason to move in one direction or another. This is the principle of "*Insufficient Reason*" that dominated the thinking of Christian theologians who believed that God should have no "sufficient reason" to place the Earth anywhere other than in the center of the Heavens.[12]

After Anaximander rejected Thales' thesis that the main substance on Earth was water, and that everything evolved from water, he initiated an evolutionary theory of development of the various living species on Earth. Thus, Anaximander's account of the origin of man and other animals is even more interesting: "Living creatures arose from the wet element; as it was evaporated by the sun, each enclosed into a spiny cell. As they advanced in age, they came out upon the drier cell. When the cell broke off, they survived for a short time. Man himself was born from animals of another species and was like a fish in the beginning. It seems astonishing to find at the very onset of Greek thought, a theory anticipating some of the most important arguments and conclusions of the modern doctrine of evolution--but it should be remembered that the idea of the development of all things out of a less organized beginning was natural to the Greek mind, while the idea or doctrine of the special creation, by theocratic dogmatism, was quite foreign to Hellenic thinking."(Ref 24, Ch.III, pp.89 ff.) Apparently, Anaximander believed in the existence of other worlds besides our own, but it is questionable if he meant an infinite succession of such world systems by the process of separation into opposites--an evolutionary process--or believed rather in an infinite succession of such systems--one after another. Anaximander wrote extensively, even though nothing survives today, most probably on matters of astronomy, physics, evolution, and Nature. He conceived the idea of infinity for the first time, and held that parts undergo change; but the whole remains unchangeable. He believed that the moon (which he thought was as big as the Earth!) shines from the sun's borrowed light, and that it consists of the **purest fire**. He was the inventor of the **gnomon** (an instrument that measures the width of an angle in degrees), and set up a sundial in Lacedaemon (Sparta) in order to mark the solstice and the equinox.

ANAXIMENES (ΑΝΑΞΙΜΕΝΗΣ) (c. 550 B.C.)

Anaximenes was the third of the Miletians who left his imprint on the development of physical philosophy and theoretical physics. He was a very intelligent man--unassuming, talented,

---

[12] During the middle Ages scholars used to quarrel about this concept of "Insufficient Reason," and famous was the joke: If a donkey is positioned between two bales of hay, the donkey will starve to death because it would have no "sufficient reason" to start eating from the bale on the left rather than from the bale on the right.

and with a vivid imagination. It is known that he flourished, circa 550 B.C., but it is not clear when he was born. Diogenes Laertius reports that he died during the 63rd Olympiad, which would mark the year of his death at 524 B.C. Nothing that he wrote survived, with the exception of some phrases and fragments. Therefore, most of the information about him comes from subsequent writers and biographers. His writings survived during the Hellenistic Era, until the advent of Christianity. Diogenes Laertius, who wrote a few lines about Anaximenes, states that Apollodorus wrote extensively about him--but even his writings perished. Anaximenes lived during a period when the Ionian League of the Ionian city-states was heavily pressed by the Persian expansion westward. By the year 495 B.C., the conquest of these cities had been completed and all serious philosophical work came to a standstill. A Miletian general, **Ermogenes,** attempted to save the city-states and organized a revolt against the Persians, soliciting the help of the Athenians and the Eritrean, but this effort failed and the Persian take-over was completed. Miletus and the other city-state's philosophical pre-eminence vanished, along with the rest of their strength and splendor. Though the teachings of the Miletus School still continued to inspire and influence philosophical speculation in Ionia, the succession of Great Thinkers came to an end. Like all his predecessors, Anaximenes asked what the **"material"** was of which all things are composed; and like Anaximander, he sought to discover the process by which the Substance turns into the variety of things that make up our sensory world. Anaximenes believed that the process by which our world arose from the original World-Material was *one of condensation and rarefaction.* When air is dilated so as to be rarefied, it becomes fire; while wind, on the other hand, is condensed air. Clouds are formed from compressed air by compression, and this, still further condensed, becomes water. Water condensed still more turns to earth; and when condensed as far as it can be, to

Knossos, reconstructed

stone. The cosmic system, thus evolved, floats in the infinite air from which it breathes in and draws its life cohesion and organization, just as we are held together as organic beings by the air which, inhaled by us, provides life. Anaximenes, unlike Anaximander, did not pursue his research and imagination into the biological world of how human beings and animals were created, but instead tried to strike a balance between the **"Boundless"** of Anaximander and **"Water"** of Thales. He found in air both the Boundlessness and transformation of water into vapor and ice. Air, then, was something that could be named and described, and yet was capable, as it seemed to sense and imagination, of turning quickly and easily, without resistance or friction, into other things.

He came very close to discovering an important principle of modern science: that science, searching for the truth, reduces all differences and abstractions of the quality and nature of things to a mere variance of atoms and particles. Anaximenes was on the verge of discovering this principle when he stated that the diverse properties and characters of objects were nothing more than different degrees of compression of one simple thing, which had a single unalterable character and constant and unchanging properties. Eventually (almost 100 years later) **Leucippus** and **Democritu**s, the Atomists, discovered this important principle (see p.66). While Anaximader conceived the Earth as a cylinder with depth, and explained that other heavenly bodies go under the Earth when we have day and night, Anaximenes maintained that the Earth is flat--like a leaf-- and that other heavenly bodies move on a plane horizontal to its position, so that night occurs due to the differences in the elevations of the Earth. Yet Anaximenes made the distinction and recognized the difference between the planets and the stars. He, along with the Miletians, raised these two questions, which they answered in their own way: *(1) What is the real nature of things? (2) How does this nature manage to become the object of our sensory observations?* These two questions constitute the alpha and omega of natural Greek philosophy. They answered these questions succinctly, within their own understanding of the problem, but with latitude of generalization quite equal to our own. Today, however, when we think of the simplicity of their perceptions, it may seem at first thought rather odd and primitive even to have supposed that the universe could be reduced to Water, Air, or the Boundless, and re-extracted by a simple process of separation into opposites or rarefaction and condensation. But a moment's reflection will convince us that in relation to the data upon which their speculation was founded, these guesses were quite as reasonable as our own. One also should not lose sight of the fact that these men were bold and courageous enough to contradict the theocratic dogma of their time and take the first baby steps of this discipline which we call today "**physics.**" We should be careful not to criticize them, lest two and one-half thousand years from now our systems and our achievements may seem as immature and as unsophisticated as the speculations of the Miletians. Upon reflection, we may temper our view of the Miletians if we consider that, in the span of only a few centuries, we partially modified Newtonian physics. It is better for us not to judge the past, lest we too be judged by the future.

Characteristic of Anaximenes' total commitment to scientific inquiry and emancipation of his mind from mystic and theological dogma, is his explanation of the rainbow. His contemporaries, buttressed by the religious establishment, believed that the rainbow was a goddess- -appearing at will here and there. He, however, pointed out that the rainbow is formed by the rays of the sun going through condensed air (moisture). Also of interest, concerning Anaximenes, are the two letters that Diogenes Laertius published, both sent to Pythagoras in Southern Italy, which dealt with matters pertaining to Thales' death and the specter of the Medes' (Persian) threat to the Ionian city-states. These are:[13]

---

[13] For these two letters see Reference #8, Diogenes Laertius, Volume I, p. 133.

Anaximenes to Pythagoras:

"Thales, the son of Examyas, has met an unkind fate in his old age. He went out from the court of his house at night, as was his custom, with his maid-servant to view the stars, and forgetting where he was as he gazed, he reached the edge of a steep slope and fell over. In such a way have the Miletians lost their astronomer. Let us who were his pupils cherish his memory, and let it be cherished by our children and his pupils; and let us not cease to entertain one another with his words. Let all our discourse begin with a reference to Thales.

Anaximenes to Pythagoras:

"You were better advised than the rest of us when you left Samos for Croton, where you live in peace. For the sons of "Aeacus" (a mythological figure, referred to by Hesiod as the Father of all Greeks) work incessant mischief and Miletus is never without tyrants. The

king of the Medes is another terror for us, not indeed so long as we are willing to pay tribute; but the Ionians are at the point of going to war with the Medes to secure their common freedom, and once we are at war we have no more hope for safety. How then can Anaximenes any longer think of studying the heavens when threatened with destruction or slavery? Meanwhile, you find favor with the people of Croton and with the other Greeks in Italy; and pupils come to you even from Sicily."

Pythagoras

PYTHAGORAS

The Man; Pythagoras (Πυθαγόρας) was born in Samos in the year 570 B.C., and died in Croton, Southern Italy, in the year 496 B.C. He emigrated to Croton when he was young, after he returned from an extended trip to Egypt and other states in Mesopotamia, where he had studied the cultures and achievements of these ancient people. He was accepted by the Egyptian priests to the extent that they allowed him to visit the sacred alters, and he even learned the Egyptian language. He also visited the Chaldean Magi and was exposed to their mysteries and religious rites. When he returned to Samos from this extended trip to the Middle East, he discovered that the government of his city-state had changed to a tyrannical dictatorship. For this reason, he and his friends and students emigrated to Croton, Italy. But most likely the main reason which motivated him to leave Samos was the threat of the Persian king and his army, which was steadfastly creeping westward capturing the Greek city-states one by one, as Anaximenis pointed out above.

In Croton the immigrants joined other Greeks who were there before them and developed into a sizable and prosperous community. The Pythagoreans had been advocating and practicing communal living when they established themselves in Croton, where they had chosen to settle permanently, finding it conducive to growth and development. They were, however, concerned and interested not only in the development of the material wealth of the new inhabitants, but also in their intellectual, spiritual, ethical, and moral life as well. Pythagoras believed that in life some people develop servile natures, and some greedy for fame and gain; but the philosopher seeks the **Truth.** He taught that people should not pray for themselves because they do not know what really benefits them. **Drinking,** he referred to as a **malaise,** and advised against all excesses--saying that no one should go beyond moderation either in drinking or eating. He divided life into four quarters and compared it with the seasons: 20 years a **Boy** (spring); 20 years a **Youth** (summer); 20 years a **Young Man** (fall); and 20 years an **Old Man** (winter). According to ancient biographers, Pythagoras' father was a gem-engraver, and when Pythagoras left to visit Egypt, he carried with him three engraved cups which he took as gifts for the priests. He was a student of Pharecydes, and after his death he left Syros and returned to Samos. While still very young, so eager was he for knowledge, that he left his own country and had himself initiated into all the mysteries and rites, not only of Greece, but also of foreign countries. It is said about him that Hermes promised to grant him any two wishes except immortality: He requested to retain throughout his life and after death a **"memory"** of his experiences. Pythagoras' students were organized in groups whose sole objective was to improve the lives of all people: men and women equally. Their basic concentration, however, was on scientific matters. They acquired strength and political power, but were faced with strong opposition, and by the 3rd century B.C. they were dispersed by the expanding Romans who finally conquered all of Greece.

His Work; Pythagoras sought to find solutions to problems through **order and harmony.** He was as interested in the problems of Nature investigated by prior philosophers as he was with where **"things"** came from--as well as with what things **"are"** in their substance and how they behave. According to Aristotle, the Pythagoreans were looking for solutions through the harmony of numbers and interrelationships, which was the mathematical approach to solving problems; and one should expect so, since they **all were mathematicians.** Pythagoreans suggested a different way of interpreting the world, unlike their predecessors (**Thales, Anaximander and Anaximenes)** and contemporaries (**Heraclitus),** by introducing the harmony of numbers and the relationships of mathematics. They advanced geometry, and one of their practical discoveries in this field was the "Pythagorean Theorem." Numbers were assigned to spatial linear dimensions in the same way one would assign dots on a die or on dominoes. By doing so they correlated geometry and arithmetic, which eventually evolved into the field known as **"analytic geometry."** The way they developed the "Pythagorean Theorem" must have derived from this arithmetic-geometric relationship. If you assign numbers to all sides of a triangle in the order of 3:4:5, and then draw a square on each side of the triangle, as in the following diagram (Figure 1), and then calculate the area of these squares by squaring each side of the triangle, you will find that the area of the square of the hypotenuse (5) is equal to the sum of the areas of the squares of the other sides (3 and 4) of the triangle. They proved, geometrically, the validity of the observation and thus the theorem was established (the triangle in the diagram is a right triangle because the relationship of the numbers 3:4:5 as the lengths of the sides produces a right triangle axiomatically). The concept of the **"square root"** derives from this analysis, as the concept "root" is the side of the triangle on the basis of which the square was built. If, in Figure 1, where the side of the hypotenuse is 5 units in length, the area of the square thus constructed is 25 units and the square root of 25 is 5. Five is the root or the base length of the square.

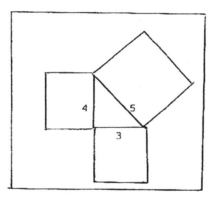

Figure 1

Pythagoras was credited with having discovered the musical intervals on the monochord scale, and he developed the musical scales and modes. He had a strong influence on the development of the theory of music, and it was Pythagòras and his School that associated numbers (ratios) with the musical tones and string intervals. For example, they discovered, most likely empirically, that if you hold the chord of a stringed instrument at one half (1/2) distance, the sound produced, if the string is plucked, will be one octave higher. If you hold the string at two-thirds (2/3) distance, the sound produced will be 1/5 higher; while when you hold the string at 3/4 distance, the tone produced will be 1/4 higher. In subsequent years the Pythagoreans (the scholars who followed Pythagoras in the School) developed a full set of ratios of distances and musical tones, and by dividing and multiplying these ratios they were in a position to develop a variety of tones and melodies. The basic musical instrument of the Greeks was the lyre, a seven-stringed instrument which was taught in schools. The Pythagoreans had an interest, as all Greeks, in teaching their children to sing, play the lyre, and memorize and recite the poems of the dramatic and epic poets.

The Pythagoreans (particularly the latter scholars) differed significantly from the Miletians in the area of astronomy. In some sense the Pythagoreans had a more realistic approach to the position and movement of the Earth in the firmament, which significantly influenced Copernicus to develop the heliocentric system in the 16th century A.D., almost two thousand years later. They could not accept that the Earth was flat or that it was a cylinder--motionless and stationary--as their contemporaries and predecessors claimed. They believed instead that the Earth was a sphere, judging from the shape of its shadow on the moon during a lunar eclipse, and that it revolved around its axis. They also stated that the Earth could not be the center of the world; but that it moved along with other heavenly bodies around a **"Central Fire=Εστία"** (but did not clarify whether this "Central Fire" was the sun, or some other celestial center.) The Pythagoreans did not accept that the Earth was the center of the world, because they observed that sometimes the planets appeared closer to Earth and sometimes farther away, and occasionally followed a course uncharacteristic of a body orbiting the Earth. Nicholas **Copernicus**, in his treatise **"On Revolutions of Celestial Spheres,"** states the following:

"....As a matter of fact the Pythagoreans, Heraclides, and Ekfantus were of this opinion" (that the earth revolves), *"and so was Nicetas the Syracusan: they made the Earth to revolve at the midpoint of the world. For they believed that the stars set by reason of the interposition of the Earth, and that with cessation of that they rose again."*

And further down Copernicus writes:

"....And so it would not be very surprising if someone attributed some other movement of the Earth in addition to the daily revolution. As a matter of fact, Philolaus, the Pythagorean, a mathematician of no ordinary ability, whom Plato's biographers say Plato went to Italy for the sake of seeing, is supposed to have held that the Earth moved in a circle and wandered in some other movements, and was one of the stars"[14]

The Chair of the High Priest

The Pythagoreans were impressed with the harmony of numbers and by the relationships of the laws of mathematics. They contributed a significant portion of their time to develop laws and theorems concerning geometry; and they were precise and demanding accuracy and practical use of what they were studying. One mathematical concept, however, that they were unable to comprehend or explain, was the concept of the **"irrational number."** According to the Pythagorean theorem, if in a right triangle the two sides are of a distance of one (1), then the distance of the hypotenuse would be the square root of two (2), which would be an irrational number(1.414213....). Applying this fact to a practical use, they could not comprehend why the distance of one side of a real field, whose shape is a right triangle, should be an approximate number, while the object has a real precise physical distance. They had not yet

---

[14] Commings Saxe and Linscott Robert N. (Editors), **Man and the Universe: The Philosophers of Science** (New York: Random House Inc, 1947, pp.52 ff)

advanced the concepts of: *approximate numbers, various scales of measurement, and the idea of continuity and limits.*

Pythagoras encouraged people to respect one another and not to turn friends into enemies: but rather enemies into friends. He admonished them to deem nothing their own **(the concept of communal living)**; to support the **Law;** and to wage war on lawlessness. He preached never to kill or harm trees that are not wild, or any animal that does not injure man. The communal mode of life that the Pythagoreans suggested and lived by was an extension of the belief that **the good life is a simple life,** and that communal interrelationships establish bonds that develop friendships and everlasting cooperation. Pythagoras' lifestyle and philosophy were received well by a number of people in ancient times, but he also created many enemies. It is not clear how Pythagoras died or how old he actually was. Some say that he died in a house fire set by disgruntled would-be

Dionyssus Theatre and Sophocles

attendants who were denied admission; others say that he died in a war between the city-states of Syracuse and Agrigentum; and by some accounts he was older than 74, reported by Diogenes Laertius. There were a number of books written about Pythagoras in ancient times, as he was considered one of the most brilliant minds of ancient Greece; but unfortunately none survive today. There is an extensive reference to a number of books describing him, written by his contemporaries and later writers. He encouraged **vegetarianism** and urged people to develop a **simple life** so that they could live on things easily procurable--spreading their tables with uncooked foods and drinking pure water only. For this was the way he proposed to achieve: **"A healthy mind in a healthy body"** (Νούς υγιής εν σώματι υγιή). He believed in the **Immortality of the Soul,** and this was probably the result of his Oriental travels and discussions with the priests of Egypt and the Magi of the Chaldeans; since most of the philosophers during his time believed that the soul perishes with the body. He was the first to have introduced weights and measures in Greece, and the first to declare the evening and the morning star **(Venus)** to be one and the same. Pythagoras wrote seven books, but none of them have survived: **(1) On Education, (2) On Statesmanship, (3) On Nature, (4) On the Soul, (5) On Piety, (6) Helothales (the father of Epicharmus of Cos), (7) Croton,** and other secondary treatises. He compared life to the Great Games: Some went to compete for the prize, others with wares to sell; but the best he judged to be the **spectators.**

By the time of the Pythagoreans the distinction between "Greek" and "Barbarian" had already been established, and one important feature of that distinction was that the Greek child would have to be educated in all encyclopedic subjects, including music and gymnastics. The Greeks were the first to introduce physical education as part of the curriculum of the educational system. The culture of the Gymnasium (the place of exercise and training) is one of the Greek legacies to world civilization. Athletics was also responsible for the advancement of a medical discipline, as the trainers developed an expertise in healing injuries and treating traumas. In addition, students were required to study music, play an instrument, sing songs, and recite poems of the epic writers. The Pythagoreans built their society on these principles and developed a more advanced and philosophic curriculum for adults. They emphasized a method of mental training which stressed retention of information, and children and adults were required to record the events that took place the previous day. The

Herodus Atticus Theatre

6

life of the Pythagorean commune was based on an ascetic system (Ασκησις = **training),** and personal discipline was one of its primary features. The members were taught that the world, including human society, is held together by the orderly arrangement of its parts (what we call today the **ecological balance**); therefore, it is a duty to cultivate order and beauty in one's own life. The word **"Κόσμος,"** which means **"Beauty"** and **"Order,"** was developed by the Pythagoreans: It also means the **"world."**

The Pythagorean philosophy of life, that of the communal style which encouraged friendships and shared resources, as well as helping to satisfy each other's needs, lasted for over 400 years.   The philosophies that followed, those of Socrates, Zeno, and Epicurus, were strongly influenced by the philosophy of the Pythagoreans. A number of thinkers developed out of the Pythagorean School, and contributed significantly to the development of Greek philosophy and science.   They were: **Ipassus, Petro, Ippon, Philolaus, Evritus, Iketas** and **Ekfantus.** Pythagoras died before Socrates and his students were born.

CYPHER

THERE ARE MANY SIDES
OF NOTHING;
WE STORE OUR SENSES THERE.
THEY NOW APPEAR
AS SOMETHING,
UNLESS WE STRIP THEM BARE.

THERE ARE MANY SIDES
OF NOTHING,
BUT ONLY ONE TRUE VIEW
OF WHAT APPEARS
AS SOMETHING,
DISTINGUISHED FROM THE TWO.

KALYPSO

CHAPTER 3

THE EARLY PERIOD OF GREEK PHILOSOPHY (THE ELEATS)

As for poverty, no one needs be ashamed to admit it;
the real shame is in not taking practical measures to escape from it.
Pericles

THE ELEATIC SCHOOL

The thinkers that we discuss in this chapter, the Eleats (primarily **Xenophanes, Parmenides and Zeno of Elea),** were the ones who challenged the validity of the assertions of their contemporaries and predecessors by claiming that the world is: **solid, one, unchanging** and **stationary (Monism),** denying altogether the concept of *"change and evolution."* The impact that

the Eleats had on the development of Greek philosophy was significant, as it brought forth arguments against existing principles and traditions. But the Eleats distinguished themselves with other innovations for their time as well. **Xenophanes** introduces the idea of **Monotheism,** and attacks the conception of many gods (**Polytheism**) and their influence on humans--as introduced by Hesiod and praised by Homer, Pindar, and the dramatic poets. In the case of Monistic theory (the unchanging and solid "world--matter"--from the Greek word **"Μονος"** (which means "single"--"one"), that Parmenides introduced, a new interpretation of the world is advanced which differs from the world of the Miletians, Pythagoreans, and Ephesians (**Pluralism**). We are addressing now an unchanging world; a world that is "solid," as contrasted with a world of *"change" and evolution*-- in spite of

Erehthion and Karyaties

apparent change. Furthermore, Parmenides presents doubts as to the capability of our senses to correctly perceive the world. In other words, if we depend entirely on our senses to discern our environment, we will most likely have a distorted view.

We discuss briefly below the establishment of the Greek Community of Elea, in Southern

43

Italy (where most of these thinkers came from), and its people, and then generally discuss the points that the Eleats made and the impact that they had on their contemporaries and subsequent thinkers. As we noted earlier, the Persian kings were advancing westward rapidly, and by 495 B.C. most of the Ionian city-states were under Persian control or were paying tribute to the Persian king. We have already seen that Pythagoras left Samos and established the **Commune** in Croton, and his example was followed by others. One of these scholars was **Xenophanes** who, fleeing the Persian pressures, left the city of Colofon with his family and a number of followers and settled in Italy. Quite a number of other immigrants had left their cities in Asia Minor earlier, such as the Phocaeans, who established colonies further north on the southern tip of Italy, and one of them was the community of Elea. Xenophanes must have been one of the original immigrants to Elea because, according to Diogenes Laertius, he wrote a poem of 2000 lines praising the bold adventures of the Phocaeans in their efforts to find refuge in Elea.

According to some writers, Xenophanes established in Elea a new and special school of thought, known as the **Eleatic School**, and introduced a different approach to philosophical research and thinking related to the problems of Nature and man, which differed significantly from his predecessors and contemporaries. There were four renowned scholars who were associated with the **Eleatic School** during this period, even though two--**Zeno** and **Melissus**--lived well into the period of the "Golden Age" (5th century), and these were:

ʌ Teacher and Young Student

Xenophanes	:	**570 to 470 B.C.**
Parmenides	:	**c. 515-450 B.C.**
Zeno of Elea	:	**c. 460 B.C.**
Melissus	:	**c. 456 B.C.**

We do not know the actual year of birth and death of the latter two; but, according to Diogenes Laertius, they flourished during a period identified with a certain Olympiad: Parmenides with the

69th Olympiad; Zeno with the 79th Olympiad; and Melissus with the 80th Olympiad. In other words, they were all contemporaries within 44 years (11 Olympiads). The figure given above is the period when they were most renowned. They initiated investigation of *matter* with the purpose of establishing that sensory perceptions do not necessarily identify the **Truth.** The concepts of **Change** and **Evolution** come under attack, and Zeno--the logician and dialectician of the Eleats-- develops the famous **Zeno Paradoxes** to discredit these concepts. The notion of motion, time, and change is addressed and analyzed extensively. Actually, these men ushered in a new dimension of philosophical thinking that bordered on metaphysics, which motivated Aristotle to investigate the subject further and write extensively on it. Two books on metaphysics by Aristotle deal partially with these concepts that the Eleats introduced. We could say, however, that the Eleats, as well as the **Pluralists (Ionians)**, established theories and speculation that constitute the system and the philosophy of physics. These ideas and concepts: *matter, power, numbers, size, movement, creation, evolution, being, continuity, discreteness, space, time, atom, and change*, were clearly formulated by these early Greek thinkers. These individuals were students of one another and followed the philosophies and doctrines of the School; certainly there were quite a number of others who were involved, but we have no record of their contributions. Let's now provide more detailed information that is available about **Xenophanes, Parmenides, Zeno** and **Melissus.**

XENOPHANES (Ξενοφάνης)

Xenophanes was a citizen of the city of Colofon, in Asia Minor, where he was born in the year 570 B.C. He felt uncomfortable with the pressure of the impending Persian invasion, and in 536 B.C. he left with his family and other citizens of Colofon who sought freedom, for Southern Italy. They settled in the town of Elea, where they established themselves and flourished through the years, until they were taken over by the Romans several centuries later. Xenophanes actually was a poet and musician, and he was traveling from place to place singing his songs and teaching philosophy and other subjects throughout the Elea area, Sicily (Syracuse), and surrounding communities. His total philosophical views and convictions appeared in a treatise (poem) titled **"On Nature,"** of which only some fragments survived. What he did not like most about the established religion at the time, was the polytheistic nature of the ancient Greek religion and the human behavior of the gods as exemplified by Homer, Hesiod, and the playwrights. He did not accept this kind of behavior which gave license to humans to behave likewise. The following passage illustrates Xenophanes' view of the gods and what he thought of the way his compatriots regarded the deities:

"Αλλ' οι βροτοί δοκέουσι θεούς γεννάσθαι
Την σφετέρην δ' εσθήτα τ'εχειν φωνήν τε δεμας
Είς Θεός εν Τε Θεοίσοι και Ανθρώποις Μέγιστος
Ούτε δέμας θνητοίσιν ομοιον ούτε νόημα
Αλλ' απάνευθε πόνοιο νοου, φρενί παντα κραδαίνει
Ούλος ορά, ούλος δε νοεί, ούλος δέ τ'ακούει"[1]

*(But the mortals want to create gods
And have Gods' dress, voice and body.
There is one Almighty God for both humans and gods,
Who resembles neither in body nor in mind to the mortals;
Who from afar controls the pain and shakes the mind,
He sees all; he understands all; and hears all.)*[2]

---

[1] See Plato's Dialogues, "Parmenides" (Reference 11, Book 6, pp 8-9)

[2] Translation by the author

In this passage we see that Xenophanes wanted to emancipate his compatriots from the prejudices of the past and from these kinds of relationships with the gods. He disliked the idea of gods given human images, and strove to disregard the concept of polytheism by saying that God is: **One, Omniscient, and Omnipotent.** God, he argued, resembles humans neither in form nor in thought. His reasoning for this was that he noticed that the various ethnicities would present gods according to their images. For example, the Ethiopians would paint their gods with dark skin and full lips; while the Scythians would present their gods with blue eyes and blond hair. If the cow or the lion could paint, he argued, they too would paint their gods according to their images--and most likely four-legged.

It might be appropriate, at this time, to comment briefly on the nature and the relationship between gods and humans. When humans would be faced with a dilemma or an unfortunate circumstance they would resort to the gods, either through the soothsayers or the oracles, and ask what they should do. It should be noted, however, that the gods' response was dependent on the extent of animal sacrifice, and of material offerings such as statues, temples, and outright monetary donations to the priests of the specific god. If it would be perceived that the god would favorably respond to the offering, then that was a sign that the request was accepted and the god was pleased. From the poet **Euripides,** we know of the request of the priest of **Artemis** at **Aulis** that **Agamemnon** sacrifice his first-born daughter, **Iphigenia,** so that the god Apollo would be pleased and allow the winds to blow and the ships to sail to Troy. Also of interest is the case referred to by Sophocles--where **Teiresias,** the soothsayer, inspired by god, demanded that Oedipus should find and punish the killers of Laius so that the disease that was destroying the crops of the Thebans would cease. *This then was a give and take relationship.* The following passage from Herodotus illustrates how the Athenians used the gods to serve their interests when Themistocles, the Athenian general, asked the city-states and islands for contributions to the Athenian treasury:

> *"From the islanders, the Adrians did not contribute money to Athens when Themistocles asked, even though he submitted the following reasons with his request: that the Athenians have the support of two important deities named* **Persuasion** *and* **Need,** *and for this reason money should be forthcoming to them. The Adrians responded that they understood the Athenian greatness and prosperity, and also that they are in possession of good deities. They further stated that they are very poor, and they too have two miserable deities who do not seem to want to leave their island, but insist on living there: Their names are* **Poverty** *and* **Distress.** *With these deities the Adrians were unable to give money to Athens; because as great as the Athenian might was, it could not be greater than the Adrian weakness."*[3] [4]

---

[3] **Herodotus, <u>Histories</u>, Ourania, 111, (Ref 6, Book 3)**

[4] Translation by the author

Aristophanes relates another incident when a god was reduced to mockery. The god Dionyssus is portrayed in the **"Frogs"** as a coward, glutton, and lecher. And this play was not only produced at the Great Dionyssia in Athens (a festival in honor of Dionyssus), but won the first prize; so clearly, most Athenians did not consider such mockery as blasphemous. What was important was to make: the **right sacrifices** to the **right god** at the **right place** with the **right words.** Religion was concerned more with ritual practices than morals and ethics. The reason for these sacrifices is clear from Hesiod's admonition: **"You give to the gods so that they may give to you in return."** An inscription found in the Acropolis of Athens, where an Athenian was making sacrifices to the goddess Athena with the request that she respond to his request in kind, reinforces this **"quid-pro-quo"** (this for that) relationship between men and gods. Among the Greeks in ancient times, the relationship between gods and humans differed significantly from practices followed among all other religions and cultures of the same period.

Difillus, Dramatic playwright

As far as Xenophanes' other views of the world are concerned, he still believed the same doctrines pronounced by Anaximander and Anaximenes concerning astronomy: that the Earth was the center of the world and that the sun revolved around the Earth in cyclical orbit. But he disregarded the idea of change and the concept of evolution through which the world was created. He adhered to monotheism and espoused democratic doctrines. Diogenes Laertius reports that the ancient philosophers and scholars considered him to be one proud **"accuser"** of Homer, since he did not want to accept the man/god relationship in the *Iliad* and the *Odyssey*, which, of course, was not a popular position, as these two epic poems were well received. He did not seem to be anyone's student, but rather had quite a number of students himself; the most famous of those were Parmenides and Zeno.

When once asked how old he was, he replied in a poetic form: **"Seven and sixty are now the years that have tossed my cares up and down the land of Greece, and there were twenty and five years more from my birth up, if I know to speak truly about these things."** (In other words, he was over 90 years old.) Empedocles, who was his contemporary, once remarked to him that it is impossible to find a wise man: **"Naturally,"** Xenophanes replied, **"for it takes a wise man to recognize one."** Xenophanes, along with the other Eleats, was one of those philosophers who did not trust the human senses. He felt that they would mislead us. A stick in the water, for example, looks bent; it is the mind that corrects what the eye sees. He took issue with the idea that we can gain real knowledge through our senses alone. He proposed that things are not always as they seem; and sometimes they do not appear as they are.[5] When once he noticed a seashell embedded in a rock in the quarries of Syracuse, he inferred that land and sea masses were not always as they are today. This most rational and straightforward approach to thinking led the early Greeks into logical experimentation, observation, and measurement, because he could have said: *"How interesting, God planted a seashell in this rock."* This thinking allowed these early scholars to advance the physical sciences for the first time; their progress, however, was hampered by the fact that they could not prove their assertions, and the doubts about their validity precipitated continuous argumentation and skepticism. A new school of philosophy (**The Skeptics**) developed later on during Hellenistic times, and had a counterproductive influence on the development of the physical sciences. But from a scientific point of view, these individuals introduced the seeds of scientific inquiry which germinated later.

PARMENIDES (ΠΑΡΜΕΝΙΔΗΣ)

Another important representative of the Eleatic School was **Parmenides.** Parmenides was a student of Xenophanes, even though, according to Diogenes Laertius, it was another philosopher-- the Pythagorean **Ameinias**--who influenced him more than **Xenophanes.** He was born in **Elea** in 515 B.C., and we know that he flourished at the beginning of the 5th century B.C. (69th Olympiad), and that he died around the middle of the 5th century (c. 450 B.C.). Parmenides stated his theory of monism in a poem, of which some fragments have survived, and in the following verses one can discern his thoughts about the "world" (The Greek word **"εον"**=Being):

> "Πολλα μαλ'ως αγένητον εόν και ανώλεθρον έστιν
> ούλον μονογενές τε και ατρεμές ηδ' ατέλεστον
> ουδεποτ' ην ουδ' έσται, επεί νυν εστίν ομόν παν
> ουδέν διαιρετέον εστί, επεί παν εστίν όμοιον"[6]

(Being was not born and cannot be destroyed
It is homogeneous, unswerving and unending
It has no beginning and no end as It always exists the same
It cannot be divided and is of uniform substance)[7]

The above passage is only a small portion of a large narrative in poetic style of hundreds of

---

[5] This is comparable in our modern court system to the following: A man is accused of a crime and goes to trial. He is guilty and is convicted or acquitted; or he is innocent and is acquitted or convicted. This is also known in the field of statistics as the "hypothesis testing decision matrix."

[6] See Plato's dialogue "Parmenides" (Reference 11, p.11)

[7] Translation is by the author

verses. In it one notes Parmenides' conception of the **"world"**: homogeneous, undivided, eternal, unending; with no beginning and no end. It is an attack against the Ephesian (Heraclitus) idea that everything is in flux, and that the world is changing in an evolutionary process (Anaximander) in motion. The Eleats based this assertion on the assumption that what we see is not always true. In

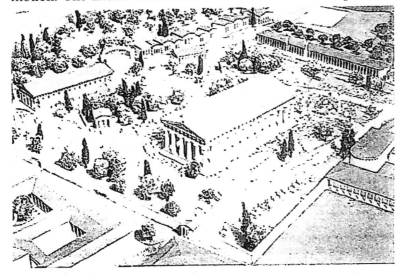

Ancient Olympia

some ways this approach was intended to counter the atomist conception of the world consisting of atoms and void. One can say that this disparate view resembles today's assertion by the creationists that the world was **created** (*the religious version*) -- as contrasted with the doctrine that the world **evolved** (*the evolutionists' version*). The Greek verb used in this case, as it appears in the first line of the above quotation, is **"Εστιν"** (It Is), meaning that the world **"is,"** exists; and that it is solid. It is of

importance in this context to ask what Parmenides meant by these words. **"It"** should be: *"whatever can be thought about or delved into"* ("the world"); while **"Is"** *is the meaning of the verb "to be,"* *in the context of "the house Is" (exists)--rather than "the house is white." By this Eleatic view, when one says that* **"the house is,"** *does not imply change or that the house can be divided into smaller houses or evolve into something else, because then you do not refer to the house anymore.* This view that the "world" can evolve and change was accepted by the Pluralists because they believed that all things are subject to change (evolution). The Miletians' view of Pluralism was that they conceived of some original substance to be the primary **"Matter,"** and from it they derived a multiplicity of objects and identified change as a natural process of modification of the first **"Matter"** (the effect of the opposites--or the process of condensation and rarefaction). The pre-Parmenides thinkers trusted their senses to supply the basic data to interpret the world. Parmenides' rigid system made it difficult to advance a clear, rational explanation. Most of the thinkers after Parmenides, including Aristotle, took notice of this stringent logic, and all attempted, in one way or another, to point out various ways in which his objections to multiplicity and change could be mollified.

In a fashion similar to Xenophanes', Parmenides recorded his beliefs and convictions in poetic form. His main work, **"On Nature,"** was a philosophical treatise with great emphasis on logic and truth--which differentiated between the mind and the senses. All of his writings were based, not only on **Nature** or **God,** but also on the pursuit of Truth and Knowledge. He is considered the only pre-Socratic philosopher to have initiated discussion on matters of Ethics,

Logic, Justice, and Truth, in addition to his concerns on matters of physics. He was interested in searching for the **"soul"** of man and addressing the problems of society as a functioning entity, while also searching for ways which would lead to the well-being and happiness of his fellow men.

Truth, according to Parmenides, comes from clear understanding and mental conception and not by observation only. He introduces the idea of "ontology" (the nature and existence of Being), and methodically and passionately concerns himself with the idea of **"Being,"** as well as what is **"Right" and "Wrong."** He stands for the God that Xenophanes created after he destroyed the gods of Homer and Hesiod. The meaning of life assumes a different dimension with Parmenides-- followed by Zeno and finally Plato. He provides new approaches to the concepts of idealism and pragmatism, even though he is not considered the father of either. He separates the idea **(the theoretical)** from the tangible **(the practical).** This distinction is very important for the evolution of Greek philosophy, because highly theoretical concepts were approached, and the mind and the speculative conception of things played a pivotal role in research during Hellenistic times.

Homer

Plato wrote a special dialogue named **"Parmenides"**--or **"Concerning Ideas,"**--in which he describes a discussion that took place among Parmenides, Zeno, and Socrates, 50 years prior to Plato's time. This dialogue examines primarily the notion of what is **True;** what is **Right;** what is **Existence;** and the **Socratic Theory of Ideas or Forms**--as well as man's capability of learning and understanding his universe. In this dialogue, the influence that the Eleatic School had on Plato and subsequent ethical philosophers is obvious.

ZENO OF ELEA (Ζήνων ό Ελεάτης)

Zeno was a pupil of Parmenides, and both lived and were prominent during the **Golden Age of Athens,** in the middle 5th century, under the rule of Pericles. Zeno was what we would call today a technician, and was concerned with solidifying Parmenides' conception of the idea of "Being." He is mostly known for his famous **"Paradoxes."** We do not have any of his writings-- with the exception of some fragments--and references about him by subsequent writers who wrote only about his **"Paradoxes."** In the development of his **"Paradoxes"** Zeno significantly refined the dialectic method, and in some ways he is considered the father of this method of reasoning. This is a strict logician's approach to solving problems by advancing a proposition and applying the method of **"reductio ad absurdum"** in order to accept or refute it. Zeno adhered to Parmenides' rejection of infinity, continuity, and change, as well as his belief that the world is Solid, One, and

Unchanging. He also attempted to prove those who held an opposite view wrong by refuting the notion that the world changes. He argued that if we consider any basic "Matter," then we can make one of three statements about **It**: **"It** is"; **"It** is not"; or **"It** both is and is not." The third statement is false because it is a contradiction or an oxymoron;[8] the second statement is also false because you cannot speak of something that does not exist (the ancient Greeks, who did not accept the existence of "nothingness,"[9] never developed the concept of zero.) Therefore; the first statement is valid. Thus--**"It** is." There can be no change; for otherwise this would imply that **It** was not everywhere equally dense, and that there is no empty space or **"void,"** as the Atomists argued, for this would imply that at such a space **It** is not.

Hesiod

can be described as follows.[10]

This leads then to the conclusion that the universe is motionless, unchanging, solid; a uniform sphere and not in the continuous **"flux"** that Heraclitus postulated: The **All** is **One.** This judgment reached by Parmenides and Zeno was based on logic alone. If the conclusion conflicts with the senses, it is because appearances can be deceptive. Zeno's logical attempt to refute the positions of his opponents is unique; and it was from these early steps that the dialectic method was developed.

Zeno presented his "Paradoxes," most likely in a book that perished, and we know of them only through the writings of Aristotle in **Metaphysics,** and of **Simplisius** and **Philoponus**—well known writers of the Roman Era. These paradoxes are: **(1) The Paradox of Plurality; (2) the Paradox of Dichotomy; (3) The Paradox of Achilles; (4) The "Paradox of the Arrow; and (5) the Paradox of the Stadium;** and others. Some of these **paradoxes** are difficult to interpret, particularly the last one--**The Paradox of the Stadium.** But in a brief summary, four of these paradoxes

---

[8] An oxymoron is a paradox in two words. For example: "cruel kindness," "laborious idleness," "loud silence."

[9] The Greeks did not develop the concept of zero, which was first conceived by the Hindus and was put into practice by the Arabs. But zero did not gain prominence as part of the real number system until much later (during the Renaissance).

[10] For Zeno's **Paradoxes,** see Wesley C. Salmon (editor), Zeno's Paradoxes, (1970: Indianapolis and New York, The Bobbs-Merrill Co, Inc.) and H.D.P. Lee, **Zeno of Elea,** (Amsterdam, Adolf M. Hakkert Publisher). In this book the original Greek wording of the **Paradoxes** is presented as written by **Simplisius, Philoponus, and Aristotle.**

1) The Paradox of Plurality: This paradox addresses the Pythagorean and Ionian concept that the "world" is in a constant flux, and consequently matter continuously evolves into smaller particles, according to the Atomists; in other words, Zeno wanted to discredit the idea of "plurality" of matter (matter consisting of small, infinite parts). His argument essentially, in a **"reductio ad absurdum"** approach, is: Let the process of subdivision of matter be assumed to have been completed. Then there will remain either certain infinitesimal parts or magnitudes that are indivisible but infinite in number, or parts that have no magnitude--have vanished into nothing. But both conclusions are absurd; the first because so long as any part having magnitude is left, the process of division is not complete; the second because if the part vanished, then the initial whole is composed of nothing.

2) The Paradox of Dichotomy. This paradox explores the concepts of time and space. If we subdivide space into points of finite size, but infinite in number, for a particular distance, and subdivide time into instants but finite, then it would be impossible to travel the particular space of infinite points in finite time. This paradox is referred to as the **"Dichotomy Paradox,"** named so by Aristotle because of dichotomizing space. Viewed in a different context, this paradox can be described as follows: A runner can never get to the end of a racecourse, because before he can cover the whole distance he must cover the first half of it. Then he must cover the first half of the remaining distance and so on *ad infinitum.* In other words, he must first run one-half, then an additional one-fourth, then an additional one-eighth, etc.--always remaining somewhat short of his goal.

3) The Paradox of Achilles. This paradox deals with the idea that in a finite space of infinite points, a runner, Achilles (known in antiquity as a very fast runner), will never overtake a tortoise that has had a head start, because **one cannot traverse an infinite number of points in finite time instants.** Achilles can never catch up with the tortoise, no matter how fast he runs, because in order to overtake the tortoise Achilles must run from his starting point A to the tortoise's original starting point B; meanwhile, the tortoise will continue to point C. Now Achilles must reach point C, and while Achilles is covering this new distance, the tortoise has moved still further to point D. Thus, whenever Achilles arrives at a point where the tortoise was, the tortoise has already moved further ahead. Achilles can narrow the gap between him and the tortoise, but he can never actually catch up with the tortoise.

4) The Paradox of the Arrow. This paradox investigates the concept of motion. Actually, the question is whether motion is continuous or discrete. The argument starts with the flying arrow. Zeno argues that something permanent either moves or stands still; but **nothing is in motion while it is in a space of its own length.** At a definite moment the moving body, in this case the arrow, is always at one spot. Therefore the moving arrow is not in motion. To phrase it differently: An object in flight always occupies a space equal to itself. But what always occupies a space equal to itself is not in motion; it is therefore at rest. One could compare this example with the process of motion pictures. There are a great number of pictures sequentially positioned on a film, and when the film passes through a light it gives the appearance of motion.

Concepts of infinity, continuity, and change, as well as the application of irrational numbers, resulted in numerous hurdles for the early thinkers; as for example, in the case of the famous **"Delian Problem"** for the Athenians, which was a real challenge that presented difficulties during the Peloponnesian War. They could not comprehend how they could double the contents of their sacrificial containers. The Oracle was advising them to double the volume of the containers, which meant that they had to increase the dimensions by an irrational number; for example, the cubic root of two,[11] if the container is a cube with unity dimensions.

According to ancient biographers, Zeno was of a liberal mind and hated tyranny. He fought against it and plotted to overthrow the tyrant **Nearchus of Elea**, and was arrested. During cross-examination he requested that the tyrant approach so that he could whisper something in his ear; instead, he grabbed it with his teeth and did not let go until he was stabbed to death. There are other versions of this incident, and one of them recounts that the ones present were so appalled by the treatment Nearchus was affording Zeno, that they stoned the tyrant to death.

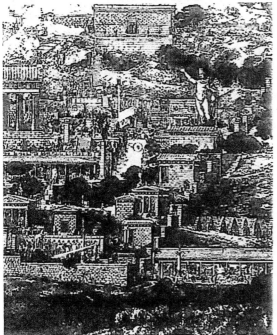

The Delphic Sanctuary of Apollo

MELISSUS (Μέλισσος)

Melissus lived from about 480 to 420 B.C., and was most renowned around the time of the 79th Olympiad (about 460 B.C.). He was a native of the island of Samos, and was introduced at an early age to the Monist theory of the Eleats, which he embraced totally throughout his life, becoming their chief representative in Greece proper. It was Melissus who brought Eleatic principles to the Aegean Island states. He disagreed strongly with Anaxagoras and Empedocles, who were his contemporaries, on philosophical matters concerning **change, evolution, and motion.** Anaxagoras and Empedocles endeavored rigorously to establish the concepts of motion and change, contrary to the Monists' position. Melissus wrote extensively on the subject, and judging from some fragments of his writings that have survived, and from writings of later scholars, he caused considerable intellectual discussion on the matter of **change and motion,** contradicting

---

[11] If a cubed vessel contains one unit of some liquid, the volme is $X^3=1$. In order to double this volume then from $X^3=1$, will change to $X^3 = 2$. Solving this equation for X, we get, $X= 2^{1/3}$ (the third root of 2), which is equal to $X=1.59920759\ldots\ldots$Thus, the Athenians were asked to increase the dimensions of the vessel to 1.259920759 from 1.000, which is an irrational (approximate) number. To the Athenians, who were concerned with precision and accuracy, it meant an impossible act.

the Monists' approach. This discussion must have had an effect on the development of the atomic theory by **Leucippus and Democritus,** who were also his contemporaries. The Atomists established the existence of **"void,"** which Melissus rejected outright, thus precluding the possibility of motion. The idea of change and evolution was uniformly accepted prior to the appearance of the Eleats--at least among intellectuals. Melissus labored diligently to prove, in a fashion similar to Zeno's paradoxes, that **plurality** cannot exist with a unified **being.** It was from this point that Leucippus and Democritus formulated the basic elements of their atomic theory, by positing: "Why not?" Plurality could exist with a unified being: Thus, they developed the idea of the **atom** and **void.**

Melissus was involved in the administration of the affairs of his island state, and while serving as a general in the Samian navy, he fought the Athenian fleet in the year 441 B.C. His philosophic doctrines were further refined, and he is credited with advancing the dialectic method of reasoning by introducing the concept of **"time"** as another important variable of the idea of **"being."** He advanced some very esoteric concepts about the notion of infinity, motion, time, and change, and represented the island of Samos as an intellectual torch bearer s of his time--heading a long tradition of scholars such as Pythagoras, Aristarchus, and others that Samos contributed to the world.

CHAPTER 4

THE EARLY PERIOD OF GREEK PHILOSOPHY (THE EPHESIANS AND THE ATOMISTS)

> "We do not say that a man who takes no
> interest in politics is a man who minds
> his own business; we say that he has no
> business here at all."
>
> Pericles

INTRODUCTION

In this chapter we discuss the contributions to Greek philosophy of five important men who distinguished themselves during the 5th century B.C., with the exception of one, (Heraclitus) who also lived during the 6th century B.C. (540-480). These thinkers were: (1) **Heraclitus**--from the city of Ephesus in Ionia; (2) **Anaxagoras**--from the city of Clazomenae in Ionia; (3) **Empedocles**--from the city of Agrigentum in Sicily; (4) **Leucippus;** and (5) **Democritus**--from the city of Abdera in eastern Macedonia. These were the individuals who postulated, among other things, that the world is in a constant transformation--clashing with the Eleats who believed that the world is **Solid, One, and Stationary.** By the beginning of the 5th century B.C., rigorous thinking on matters of physics was rapidly advancing, introducing new ideas and new conceptions of the world. These individuals introduced some theories (hypotheses) which, even though speculative, indicate that a fertile, progressive, scholarly, and inquisitive environment--emancipated from mystical and theological bounds--prevailed. **Heraclitus** introduces the idea of continuous flux, the viewing of opposites as one, the concept of **"logos,"** the tension of opposites, speculation on intelligent control of the world; and finally, new and significant perceptions regarding the human soul. Empedocles introduces the notion that *Love (Φιλοτης) and Strife (Νεικος)* are the two powerful forces responsible for motion and change, as well as for the cosmic equilibrium. He discusses the four basic **roots** of matter (*Earth, Water, Air, and Fire*), and accepts an original multiplicity of basic elements, contradicting Parmenides with whom he agreed in some other areas of speculation. **Anaxagoras** was the first scholar to assign a major role to the **Mind** in the formation of the world, and stated that it initiated motion, which then took over as the driving force by which an ordered

Apollo Sanctuary at Delphi

55

world was created. Finally, **Leucippus** and **Democritus** conceived the idea that the world consists of *atoms and void* in a continuous motion, and their theory closely approximates our current conception of the creation of the world today (**The Big Bang**). The first three of these scholars were considered as constituting the **School of Ephesus** because they approached matters in a similar fashion, but Heraclitus was the dominant personality; the older one who came from the city of **Ephesus,** in **Asia Minor.**

Also, these thinkers, particularly Democritus, concerned themselves with questions and problems that affected man and his society during their time, in addition to questions relating to the origin of the world and its destination. Their world was experiencing rapid changes while the structure of the theocratic system was coming under attack, and Greek thinkers were trying to solve the problems of their societies, weighing the advantages and disadvantages of various political forms in their search for the best societal system, and evaluating the political experiences of the systems prevailing throughout the Greek city-states at the time. The culmination of their research and investigation was to create a new philosophy which was concerned with: *justice, ethics, morality, political forms of government, the distribution of wealth, law and order, psychology, and sociology.* Socrates, who was a contemporary of Empedocles and Anaxagoras, was to be the individual who made this philosophy the purpose of his life, and actually died for it in his efforts to disseminate this new brand of thinking. Anaxagoras was the scholar who had close ties with Pericles, for he served as his advisor and supporter in managing the Athenian democracy. In addition to the Ephesians' concerns about the social issues, examined mostly by **Anaxagoras** and **Empedocles**, the main thrust and influence of the Ephesians resulted from the tenets and philosophy of **Heraclitus**--the main representative of the School.

HERACLITUS:

THE MAN: Heraclitus was born in the city of Ephesus in Ionia, in the year 540 B.C., and died there in 480 B.C. There are conflicting references as to the year of his death, and there are some indications that he lived over 60 years. He was a serious thinker, stark and demanding, what we would call today a **law and order** man. He noticed weaknesses in the democratic system of government and wanted to provide reformation and modification. Because of his serious thinking and sharp criticism of the inefficiencies in the society, he used to say that: "**As the laws of Nature are unyielding and demanding compliance, so should the laws of society dictate an unyielding ethical and moral code.**" Heraclitus enunciated his entire philosophy in a book which did not survive, but which had been given several titles. According to some it was titled ***The Muses,*** by others, ***Concerning Nature,*** and still others, ***A Helm Unerring for the Rule of Life.*** This book was very difficult to understand and had been the subject of discussion in several treatises, none of which exist today. It appears that it was written in an enigmatic oracular style, similar to the Delphic oracle which neither revealed nor concealed--but intimated. Thus, Heraclitus' book was noted for obscurity.[1]

---

[1] An example of an oracular statement of the Delphic Priestess, **Pythia**, which would cause consternation in its interpretation, was the one given to Achilles when he asked whether he should go to war and if he would survive. Pythia responded as follows: *"Ηξεις Αφιξες Ου θνηξεις Εν Πολεμω."* This means: "You will Go You will Return not

We have information about the book from other writers who referred to Heraclitus' doctrines--such as **Plato, Aristotle,** and several **Roman writers.** For example, the difficulty of

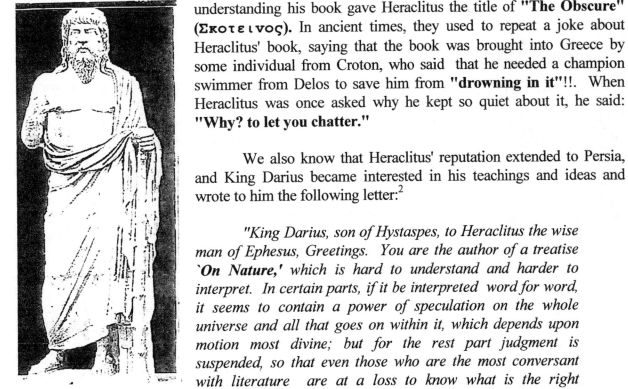

Heraclitus

understanding his book gave Heraclitus the title of **"The Obscure"** (Σκοτεινος). In ancient times, they used to repeat a joke about Heraclitus' book, saying that the book was brought into Greece by some individual from Croton, who said that he needed a champion swimmer from Delos to save him from **"drowning in it"**!!. When Heraclitus was once asked why he kept so quiet about it, he said: **"Why? to let you chatter."**

We also know that Heraclitus' reputation extended to Persia, and King Darius became interested in his teachings and ideas and wrote to him the following letter:[2]

"King Darius, son of Hystaspes, to Heraclitus the wise man of Ephesus, Greetings. You are the author of a treatise `On Nature,' which is hard to understand and harder to interpret. In certain parts, if it be interpreted word for word, it seems to contain a power of speculation on the whole universe and all that goes on within it, which depends upon motion most divine; but for the rest part judgment is suspended, so that even those who are the most conversant with literature are at a loss to know what is the right interpretation of your work. Accordingly, King Darius, son of Hystapses, wishes to enjoy your instruction and your Greek culture. Come then with all speed to see me at my palace. For the Greeks, as a rule, are not prone to mark their wise men and they neglect their excellent precepts which make for good living and learning. But at my court there is secured for you every privilege and daily conversation of a good and worthy kind, and a life in keeping with your counsels."

Heraclitus responded to this invitation from Darius with the following letter:

"Heraclitus of Ephesus to King Darius, son of Hystapses, Greetings: All men upon Earth hold aloof from Truth and Justice; by reason of wicked folly, they devote themselves to avarice and thirst for popularity. But I, being forgetful of all

---

Die in the War." The question is where you place the coma; if after "Ου," then the oracle means you will die in the war. But if the coma is placed before "Ου," then the oracle means that you will return safe from the war.

[2] See Reference #8, where Diogenes Laertius, in Volume I, presents these letters.

wickedness, shunning the general satiety which is closely joined with envy, and because I have a horror of splendor, could not come to Persia, being content with little, when that little is to my mind."

Hermes

This correspondence reveals Heraclitus' distaste for glory, splendor, and good living, and indicates that he was dedicated to a simple and relatively poor life--free to pursue his endeavors and research. Most of the scholars at his time held him in high esteem, even though he was of a rebellious character and was coming in conflict with them. It is also true that he preferred to stay in his hometown all his life, did not travel abroad, and did not have good relations with his compatriots in Ephesus. There were quite a number of treatises written by ancient writers about Heraclitus and his book, but unfortunately very few survived. The grammarian scholar, **Diodotus**, stated that Heraclitus' book was not a treatise upon Nature but upon government, the physical part serving merely for illustration. **Schythinos**, a satirical poet, undertook to translate the discourse of Heraclitus into verses, and he is credited with the following epigram:

"Heraclitus am I; why do you drag me up and down, you illiterate? It was not for you I toiled, but for those who understand me. One man in my sight is a match for thirty thousand, but the countless hosts do not make a single one. This I proclaim you in the hall of Hades."

Another epigram runs as follows:

"Do not be in too great a hurry to get to the end of Heraclitus the Ephesian's book. The path is hard to travel. Gloom is there and darkness, devoid of light. But if an initiate be your guide, the path shines brighter than sunlight."

Heraclitus exerted a strong influence on ancient thinkers, and his views on continuous change in the universe, as well as his support of the concept of the *Indestructibility of Matter,* were fundamental doctrines that directed thinking in the area of physical philosophy. The notion also of the juxtaposition of opposites led later thinkers to explore the concepts of **"thesis," "antithesis," and "synthesis"** during the modern era.

HIS WORK. Heraclitus conceived of the world as being dominated by **Logos (Λογος),** which could be seen as a superior divine force--a **godlike** rational power. Heraclitus was searching for the omnipotent power that created all these marvels that surrounded him, and sought answers to ever-present questions such as: Where do things come from and what is their destination--since he believed that everything changes. He popularized the idea that the only unchanging feature of the universe is its mutability, which, as we saw in the previous chapter, was the major disagreement that the Eleats had with previous philosophers: This disagreement culminated in the development of *Zeno's Paradoxes.*

He proposed that the basic material that everything is composed of is **fire,** as contrasted with **water,** which was Thales' postulate. He maintained that individual opinions of people regarding their environment diverge--and sensory impressions are relative. For example, an object

may appear hot or cold to different observers, but there must be an underlying unity beneath the ever vanishing multiplicity of phenomena. He considered the way up and the way down *to be the same.*[3] For Heraclitus, even more than his contemporaries (**The Miletians**), the physical world are a place of change--but change that is regulated by the **Super Power (Logos).** He envisaged most of these changes between opposites. These opposites, however, which Heraclitus referred to as differentiations, really contained an **Inner Unity;** for example, night and day, which superficially appear to be separate and opposed, in fact form a single underlying continuum by virtue of their unbroken succession. This resembles strife, but this strife is not "unnatural," since it is regulated by the **Logos;** rather it is inherent in all natural objects, and if it ceased, the measured interaction--and consequently the unity, the very *existence* of the world order--would be destroyed.

Athena

Heraclitus was concerned that men should learn physical philosophy, because he connected "Logos" with the soul of man, and this concept actually became the basis of the Platonic "Theory of the Soul." According to Heraclitus, the soul is made of fire, which can be diminished and extinguished by the flooding caused by **vice and immorality.** When active, the soul makes physical contact with the fiery element in things outside and is nurtured by it; indeed, if the soul resists vice and immorality it can survive death for a time as **Divine Fire.** Thus Heraclitus, by emphasizing the structure of things rather than their mere material substance, and by showing how man's soul and behavior were essentially connected with the world as a whole, made philosophical advances of the greatest importance. All information available about Heraclitus comes from secondary sources and from fragments of his book. It is also presented through the eyes, perceptions, and prejudices of those who studied his book and were interpreting it in a way that they saw fit within their scheme of things. But if we judge by the philosophies of the subsequent thinkers, we can see that Heraclitus had a significant impact on **Socrates, Plato,** and **Aristotle.** Thus, Heraclitus' notion that *universal reason* is accessible to man, through his soul may have inspired Socrates in his quest to find the **"Ideal Man."** Heraclitus' contrast between an apparent realm and a realm of more persistent reality influenced Plato in his **"Theory of Ideas"** and **"Theory of the Soul,"** in achieving the *Ideal Man*

---

[3] This idea of the relative position of things was one of the "Modes of Contradiction" in the theory of the Skeptics (see chapter 13).

and "*The Ideal State*" (see chapters 8, 9). Heraclitus' contribution to the problem of "Uniqueness" of matter (Parmenides) and "Plurality" (Ionians) -- universal and particular--most likely influenced Aristotle in his work on metaphysics. Heraclitus' conception of the doctrine of "Logos," was further developed among the Stoics (chapter 15), the Neoplatonists (chapter 13), and the Christians *Εν Αρχη Ην Ο Λογος (At the beginning was the Word): the Gospel by St John.*

We have already seen how the Eleatic School satisfied the need to understand and solve problems by reflection and contemplation of the inner relationships of things, instead of depending solely on the senses. With the Ephesus School the direction in the area of **"Logos"** and the conceptual understanding of the real world, and the world of man, reached a higher level of sophistication than earlier thinkers had achieved. By introducing the metaphysical concept of **"Logos,"** the notion of **being,** and the truth of existence, Heraclitus elevates the understanding of the problems of the world to a higher plateau. This type of logical analysis of phenomena does not apply only to the realm of Nature, but also to societal structures, political systems,

The West Metope of the Parthenon (Poseidon and Athena)

and the mode of functioning of an organized society. He claimed that "**Logos,**" *the Universal Truth,* is eternal, and has been set up **neither by a god nor by a man**[4], but exists and will continue to exist forever. [5] This order in the world, this internal structure with its indispensable rules, i.e., with its rhythm, applies equally to man as well as to Nature. In other words, Heraclitus speculates about a unified theory that keeps the universe functioning, and is not willing to accept that the Doer that keeps it so is one God. He accepts that it is an entity that cannot be perceived, but must be embraced and studied--and he named it **Logos.** Heraclitus' philosophy tries to emancipate itself from the need to determine the parameters of the world marked by the beginning and end of things. Heraclitus acknowledged that the explanations provided by the philosophers prior to him did not address the mysteries and the problems of the physical world, but he could neither solve nor disprove them experimentally.

He was interested in understanding relationships between elements, the internal structure and the rules and rhythms, according to which the world moves and adjusts. It made no sense to Heraclitus to look for the beginning and end of things, because these concepts are senseless-- since

---

[4]"Κοσμον τονδε τον αυτον απαντων ουτε τις θεων ουτε ανθρωπων εποιησεν" (**Heraclitus**)

[5] The word "Logos" has different meanings in Greek: in mathematics it means a "ratio" of two variables; in accounting it means an "account"; and in theology it means "Divine Reason."

the world is eternal. The world has its reasons. It moves according to its **Logos,** and no being can exceed this internal structure or boundary, because it would contradict the eternal **Logos.** But for Heraclitus, the world also "moves"; it is in a continuous flux with an infinite number of variations

The Island of Spetses

and contradictions. He expressed this with the well-known dictum: "**Everything is in a flux and nothing is stationary (Τα Παντα Ρει Και Ουδεν Μενει).**" He believed that humans cannot understand that *that which contradicts itself also agrees with itself.* The world is a harmony that combats itself; and things are never stable, but represent forces inside them that continuously change. Each phase receives significance not from its own existence, but because of the relationship of the preceding and proceeding events. Consequently, in order to characterize a phase of "being," we ought to contrast it with the preceding one. Thus, if the phase of "being" is **Life** itself, then we must contrast it with its opposite phase--which is **Death.** In order to understand what occurs in this world and how it happens, we must mentally combine it with the opposite. This concept constitutes a fundamental premise and philosophy.[6]

But we cannot understand with our senses that the world is a combination of opposites. The world apparently is harmonious and yet it opposes itself; where there is joy there is sorrow; where there is black there is white; and where there is light there is darkness. The world, then, is found in a continuous flux--dominated by the ever-present *unity.* This concept of *continuous flux* is illustrated in the dialogue **KRATYLUS** by Plato. In referring to this idea of Heraclitus, Kratylus compared the world to a river that continuously flows and changes. We cannot say that we are **in it** if we enter, because the very moment we enter, the river moves, and thus we may say we are **in the river,** but not in the **same** river. This example further illustrates the influence that Heraclitus had on Plato.

EMPEDOCLES
THE MAN. Empedocles was born in Agrigentum, Sicily, in the year 492 B.C., and he was two years old when the Persians invaded Greece for the first time, and twelve years old when the Greeks decisively defeated the Persians at Salamis. He was a contemporary of Socrates, Protagoras (the Sophist), Anaxagoras, and Zeno; and from an aristocratic background. Agrigentum, in the southwestern coast of Sicily, was a prosperous Greek city after it was successful in two wars against

---

[6] This idea of conflicting opposites was the basis of the Marxian-Hegelian doctrine: **Thesis, Antithesis** and **Synthesis**--according to which **Capital** is Thesis; **Labor** is Antithesis; and the **Class Struggle** is the Synthesis, which eventually leads to revolution. This theory was based upon a philosophical analysis by Schopenhauer, who was perhaps influenced by Heraclitus.

the Carthaginians, and Pindar, the famous poet, praised it as an idyllic city with a picturesque landscape, beautiful buildings (some still exist today), and pleasing architecture.

He was a multifaceted personality, talented in engineering, medicine, poetry, biology; the first to elevate rhetoric to a scientific level, a mystic theologian, and above all: a philosopher. He commanded high esteem on the part of his compatriots, even though in the eyes of some sober thinkers of his time, such as Xenophanes, he appeared flamboyant. Being a mystic and a theologian was of interest, because by that time, as we have pointed out earlier, the religious convictions of the intellectuals were changing to monotheism of an unknown god, beginning with Xenophanes' disregard of the Olympic gods. Xenophanes was a philosopher who influenced Empedocles by his religious convictions; but most likely, due to political animosities, he was exiled to Peloponnesus-- and it is stated by some writers that he died there. He was involved in politics and had come in conflict with the Tyrant of Agrigentum, whom he conspired to oust, which was most likely the reason for his banishment. Empedocles studied the Pythagorean philosophy, but it appears that he was banned from the Pythagorean enclave because he recorded notes of the school lectures and made them public--which was a violation of their rules. (Plato, too, was banished from Croton when he publicly revealed the lectures of the School). At the beginning, Empedocles was an admirer of Xenophanes, and lived with him for some time and imitated his poetry before meeting the Pythagoreans, who influenced him immensely.

He wrote two basic books that we know of, **On Nature** and **Purifications,** of which only a few lines (450) are extant. Also, he wrote tragedies, political speeches, and poetry--of which nothing remains; **On Nature** reflects upon scientific and philosophical matters; while **Purifications** relates to the nature and destiny of the soul. Being a medical doctor, he had a legendary reputation, and it is alleged that he revived a woman from certain death after all other physicians had failed; and as a result, people believed that he was immortal and a son of God. It was not unusual for some to consider themselves as sons of gods,[7] because the ancient Greeks were fond of mythology. It is certainly not known how or when he died. By some accounts he died when he reached old age, by jumping into the crater of the volcano Aetna. Some other accounts indicate that he died in Peloponnesus after he was banished from Agrigentum; and still some others claim that he was traveling from Agrigentum to Messina by carriage when he fell and broke his leg, and as a result of the accident became ill and died.

HIS WORK. Empedocles was a contemporary of Zeno's, and his basic philosophy was an attempt to reconcile the postulates of Parmenides and Zeno that "Matter" is: **eternal, indivisible, and unchanging**--as contrasted with the philosophy of the Miletians and Heraclitus: that the world undergoes **constant motion and change**. The Eleatic School's belief, as we learned in the previous chapter, is contrasted with the evident data of sensory experiences that indicate that our world is one of plurality and change. Empedocles assumes the existence of four distinct elements or roots: **Earth, Water, Air, and Fire**, and two distinct primal forces: **Love. (Φιλοτης)** and **Strife**

---

[7] Consider, for example, **Alexander** and **Hercules**, who both regarded themselves as sons of "God."

(Νειϰος). "Existing" and "perishing" are nothing but mixing and separation under the influence of **"Love"** and **"Strife"** respectively. Minerals, plants, and animals (all entities of the familiar world) are compounds of the four basic roots (Earth, Fire, Air, and Water) in fixed proportions. **Empedocles' Chart (at left),** shows two superimposed squares--one representing the basic four roots (*Earth, Fire, Water, and Air)* and the other the forces *(Hot, Cold, Wet, and Dry)*--which result from the influence of **"Love" and "Strife." The determination** of the nature of any specific **"thing"** on Earth is a multifunctional coordinate point plotted on the diagram.

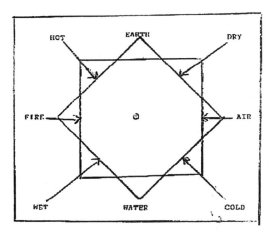

Empedocles' Chart

The philosophy of Empedocles concerning the physical world had a significant impact, indirectly, through the refinements of subsequent scholars who studied his ideas and carried them through the centuries to the Renaissance period. First, his conception of the world consisting of the four basic elements, and all material objects of this world consisting of these basic elements or "roots," as he used to refer to them, is the first step of a formal study of chemistry. Second, the distinction between matter and mechanical force, in fixed proportions in chemical interactions, and the observation that light is matter that travels at a finite speed, as well as the theory that in perception we receive film like influences emitted by bodies, are fundamental concepts of physics. Empedocles was especially influential on the ancient atomists, **Leucippus and Democritus** (see next section), as well as Plato. All previous thinkers did not feel the need to explain how things came together, with the exception of the Miletians, and how various objects, humans, and animals appeared on this Earth. They did not give a reason or an explanation for motion; and of course Parmenides denied motion altogether. By introducing "Love" and "Strife," two non-material elements, Empedocles established the basic sources of motion. These were cosmic forces which function much as "attraction" and "repulsion" in modern scientific theory; and "change" occurs as a result of Love and Strife. Love, he wrote, attracts objects together into a single whole; but Strife accentuates basic differences, and so disassociates the elements by mutual repulsion. Obviously, this destroys unity--but also creates new multiplicity, and enables individual objects such as man, animals, and plants to come into existence. There are various stages of the world, depending on the presence or absence of **Love and Strife**, or a combination thereof.

The second book of Empedocles', **Purifications**, essentially examines the soul of man. He believed that the human soul, being a fundamental component of life, operates through perception and thought. It is composed of the four "roots" and also contains the forces of Love and Strife. The soul is an **Immortal Spirit** that can be corrupted into sin by Strife; and if this happens it will be exiled from the heavenly regions. According to Empedocles, the exiled or "banished" soul is re-incarnated in all forms of life, including animals and plants--and this constitutes punishment. But the soul can be influenced by Love to achieve happiness in the **Elysian Fields**. If you replace "Strife" with the human senses you arrive at the Platonic view of the human soul, with several modifications, to account for almost 100 years that separated Empedocles' early life until the time Plato wrote **Phaedo,** in which he enunciated his "**Theory of the Soul.**" Empedocles disliked the gods of Hesiod and believed that people should use their senses to acquire knowledge, even though he found the narrowness of the senses in conceiving abstract concepts a mitigating factor. He introduced the idea that "good cheers" and prudence would reach the **Truth**.

ANAXAGORAS (500-428 B.C)

Guitar player

THE MAN. Another individual from the Ionian city of Clazomenae, who distinguished himself as a philosopher and reformer, was **Anaxagoras**. He was one of those thinkers who set **Mind** above matter, and considered "**Mind**" as the instrument of Order.[8] The Greek word for **Mind** is **Νους** and he became known as "**The Nous.**" He was from a rich family, but he relinquished his inheritance to his brothers and sisters and moved to Athens when he was 20 years old, and is known to have introduced natural philosophy to the Athenians. He spent all of his adult life there, and must have arrived probably when conscripted into the Persian Army, as at that time Clazomenae was under Persian domination. He was a friend of Pericles and helped raise rhetoric to perfection. The following story, related by **Plutarch**, illustrates the man's adherence to scientific principles and his desire to explain phenomena by scientific speculation rather than mystical and superstitious means: Plutarch relates that in the countryside of Attica, a human skull was discovered that had a horn in the center of the forehead. It was considered an omen, and the skull was brought to Pericles who asked a local soothsayer to interpret the meaning. The soothsayer said that the abnormality meant that Pericles would defeat one of his political opponents. Anaxagoras opened the skull and observed that there was an abnormality in the configuration of the brain inside the skull, in that the brain was positioned near the front of the cavity pointing toward the horn. He suggested that it was this abnormality in the brain that caused the horn. It was a far different explanation from the one offered by the soothsayer. Yet, because the political opponent of Pericles lost shortly afterwards, the public accepted the soothsayer's explanation of a divine omen rather than Anaxagoras' opinion based on visual and physical analysis of this aberration.

During the Peloponnesian War the Athenians were looking for scapegoats for an unpopular

---

[8] "All things were together; then came Mind and set them in order."

war, and he was accused of being instrumental in changing a law passed by the Assembly, according to which it was forbidden for anyone to disregard the supernatural or give instruction about the heavenly bodies. During the time that he lived in Athens he was influential in the intellectual life of the city, and helped to introduce Ionian scientific speculation. He considered himself a **citizen of the world** and wrote a book, in prose, titled **"Nature of the World,"** of which only a few fragments survived. One of his students, **Archelaus**, is said to have been **Socrates'** teacher. When he was once asked if he was concerned about his native land, Clazomenae, he replied: **I am greatly concerned with my fatherland**--and pointed to the sky. He stated that the sun is molten iron, and that there are valleys and ravines in the moon; he also held that winds arise when the air is rarefied by the sun's heat; that thunder is the collision of clouds, and lightning is their violent friction. When he was once asked the purpose of his life, he answered: to **study the sun, the moon, and the heavens.** In analyzing the Homeric poems, he emphasized the matter of ethics and morality, rather than the heroism and quarreling among the heroes (**Achilles, Agamemnon, Odysseus, Menelaus, etc.),** or among the gods (**Aphrodite, Athena, Apollo, Hera, Zeus, Artemis, etc.).** Anaxagoras was tried for impiety in Athens because he made statements contradicting the established religion and was accused of violating the laws passed by the Assembly. He was fined five talents and banished, and that only because he was a friend and protégé of Pericles; otherwise he could have lost his life, as was the case with Socrates 30 years later. He left Athens, after 30 years there, and went to **Lampsacus** where he died soon thereafter. The people of Lampsacus honored him, as well as the people of **Clazomenae**, his birthplace. Anaxagoras was a great influence on Socrates, the Sophists, and the other Athenian thinkers, and Plato refers to him often in his dialogues. Ethics, that was introduced by Socrates as the main subject of his philosophy, and analyzed by the dialectic method, was first posed by Anaxagoras.

HIS WORK. He attached major importance to the role of the mind in the formation of the world, and Aristotle felt that this was a decisive philosophical advance. He considered that everything is mingled with everything else, and that substance is part of things in a certain proportion of basic material. But the mind is pure, not mixed with anything else, and it is fundamentally a powerful force in all living things of any size or substance. Therefore **Mind** is the originating force in the universe. As we have said repeatedly, all of these thinkers were concerned with the origin of the world, and Anaxagoras offered the following cosmogony: He considers the Hesiodic chaos existing, but proposes that the mind, placed in this chaotic primal material, forced a whirling motion in a circular direction with a vortex, and as the motion spread and accelerated, "things" started to separate out from the primordial mixture; the dense separated from the rare; the hot from the cold; the bright from the dark, and the dry from the moist. An ordered world appeared, whose main components are earth, sky, sea, and dry land, and whose most striking objects are the heavenly bodies that circle constantly overhead. It is of interest, in this instance, to compare Anaxagoras' theory of the creation of the world by the motion set forth by the **Mind** in this vortex of the chaos, where the whirling motion separated the land from the sea, the cold from the hot, etc., with the interpretation of the creation of the world in **Genesis** of **The Old Testament,** where God, starting with an amorphous (chaotic) world, separated day from night, waters from the land, and hot from cold. There is a striking similarity here, but the mechanism and motivation are different. This conception must have influenced the Atomists in their research of the creation of the world (read on). Anaxagoras lived and proposed his theories over 100 years before Aristotle, and must have been the only scientist prior to Aristotle (with the exception of the Miletians) who showed an interest in the biological sciences as well. He discussed the function and purpose of the plant's seed. Based on the principle that was dominant at his time: *"Nothing is destroyed and nothing is created from nothing,"* he had to explain why one should not interpret the creation of the leaves and the branches of the trees as something just created "new" from nothing, in violation of this principle of *nothing being created from nothing.* Obviously, if one trusts his senses, it would seem that something new is created. He explains that nothing new is created, but rather the tree grows and flourishes by assimilating similar constituent substances from the soil that it is rooted in, or the water and air which it comes in contact with during its life span, and that this accounts for the transformation.

Democritus

THE ATOMISTS: LEUCIPPUS AND DEMOCRITUS. In examining the physical world around them and the phenomena manifested daily, ancient scientists were concerned with what this universe consists of, and what are its constituent parts. The position of the Eleats that "things" are unique, undivided, and solid was one approach, but, on the other hand, the existence of multiplicity of matter as viewed by the senses, caused by motion and change, was another view. It should be clear that both cannot be correct, and one cannot discount either theory without some logical explanation. It was natural to consider the multiplicity of matter because one can see that it can be subdivided. There was a need to find some method or theory to circumvent this obvious contradiction. Two individuals, who were contemporaries, introduced a new theory reconciling the two views, and in the process developed the atomic theory. These were the physical philosophers: **Leucippus and Democritus.**

THE MEN. **Leucippus** was a student of Zeno from Elea, but very little is known about his life. We do know, however, that it was Leucippus who coined the term **"atom" (Ατομον)** implying that at some point matter cannot be divided any further. Even though ancient biographers had a lot to say about **Democritus**, the next thinker who speculated about this subject, they relate very little about Leucippus. Leucippus was most probably born in the city of **Miletus**, in Asia Minor, and was active during the period from **450 B.C. to 420 B.C.,** and emigrated to Abdera, in Macedonia, which was a colony of Miletus. We know that he wrote two books: **The System of the Universe** and **On the Mind;** only a few lines have survived from the first and nothing from the second. We also know nothing of his whereabouts or when he died. But if there is very little known about Leucippus, there is quite a lot of material available about **Democritus**. He is considered to have been the main proponent of the ancient atomic theory, and we know more about him, as a man, than about **Leucippus,** because of information that ancient biographers left behind. **Democritus** was from **Abdera**, **Macedonia,** and was born in **460 B.C**--and died 103 years later in **357 B.C**. He traveled extensively throughout the entire known world, and spent his parental inheritance on his trips, visiting the **priests in Egypt,** the **Chaldean Magi** in Babylon, and the **Gymnosophists** (fakirs) in India.

He was well-rounded in **philosophy, general education, art, physics, and ethics.** His theory about atoms and the universe parallels very closely with that of Leucippus, and it may be that the atomic theory developed and attributed to Leucippus is Democritus', given the fact that they were contemporaries. Yet, there are some who claim that Democritus' main work, **The "Great Diacosmos,** in which he states his atomic theory, is **Leucippus,'** even though the most likely scenario is that they developed this theory together; after all, they were 10 years apart in age. Democritus may have received more attention from future writers because he lived much longer than Leucippus. It is related by Diogenes Laertius that Democritus wrote, in total, 52 books--none of which have survived today--with the exception of approximately 600 fragments. Four of his books, referred to collectively as his **Physical Works** and individually as **The Great Diacosmos,** are believed to have contained a comprehensive exposition of the origin of the world, the genesis of animals, and the cultural history of mankind. In **The Lesser Diacosmos, Description of the World,** and **On the Planets,** Democritus enunciated his theories on "atomic physics," astronomy, stars, and planets. Since none of these books survived, the only sources available are from the writings of **Epicurus,** the Roman philosopher **Lucretius**, later writers, and fragments. **Epicurus** and **Anaxarchus** were philosophers who espoused Democritus' atomic theory; particularly **Epicurus,** who wrote extensively on the subject, but of course nothing has survived today, except a letter from Epicurus on the general subject of physics to one of his students, **Herodotus. Plato** is known to have been against Democritus' atomic theory, and reportedly said all books by Democritus should be burned!

THEIR WORK The atomic hypothesis originated out of the need, as pointed out above, to reconcile Melissus' denial of the existence of change and motion and the acceptance of change and motion by **Empedocles, Anaxagoras,** the **Pythagoreans,** the **Miletians,** and others. The next question that needed to be addressed was the existence of "void." **Melissus** had shown that there is no void; therefore, by necessity, such a thing as plurality does not exist. In other words, he was not willing to accept that some being can be subdivided into parts, because there is no room and motion to cause this separation: plurality cannot exist with unified "beings." The atomic theory was born when Leucippus/Democritus retorted to Melissus' doctrines by asserting that "being" consists of an infinite plurality of entities that they called "atoms," each too small to be seen, but each possessing some bulk, and each endowed with the salient characteristics of the Eleatic **One**--especially **indestructibility.** This attribute of indestructibility was an Ionian idea; therefore, the atom so created by Democritus and Leucippus satisfied the Eleatic premise of uniqueness. The next question that Atomists had to answer was: **"How does change come about?"** They give the following explanation of *change and motion*, as well as of the creation of the world: Diogenes Laertius gives us the following account, attributed to Leucippus, of the creation of the world through the interaction of atoms and void:

> *"...The sum of all things is unlimited and they all change into one another. The All includes the empty as well as the full. The worlds are formed when atoms fall into the void and are entangled with one another; and from their motion, as they increase in bulk, arises the substance of the stars. The sun revolves in a larger circle around the earth. The Earth rides steadily, being whirled about the center; its shape is that of a drum." ....*

> And........*"Leucippus was the first to set up atoms as first principles. The above is a general summary of his views; on particular points they are as follows. "He declares the All to be unlimited, as already stated; but of the All part is full (matter, atoms) and part is empty, and these he calls elements. Out of these arise the worlds unlimited in number and into them they are dissolved. This is how the worlds are formed. In a given section many atoms of all manner of shapes are carried from the unlimited into the vast empty space. These collect together and form a single vortex, in which they jostle against each other and, circling around in every possible way, separate off, by like atoms joining like. And, the atoms being so numerous that they can no longer revolve in equilibrium, the light ones pass into the empty space outside, as if they were being winnowed; the remainder keep together and, becoming entangled, go on their circuit together, and form a primary spherical system. This parts off like a shell, enclosing within it atoms of all kinds; and as these are whirled around by virtue of the resistance of the center, the enclosing shell becomes thinner, the adjacent atoms continually combining when they touch the vortex. In this way the Earth is formed by portions brought to the center coalescing. And again, even the outer shell grows larger by the influx of atoms from outside, and, as it is carried around in the vortex, adds to itself whatever atoms it touches. And of these some portions are locked together and form a mass, at first damp and miry, but when they have dried and revolve with the universal vortex, they afterwards take fire and form the substance of the stars......As the world is born, so, too, it grows, decays and perishes, in virtue of some necessity, the virtue of which he does not specify."[9]*

What we garner from the above is that when atoms join together, they create "things" (the substances of the universe), and when these "things" break up and dissolve back into the void, the "thing" is destroyed; but no individual atom is destroyed in the process. This particular aspect of the

---

[9] Reference 8, Volume II, p. 439.

atomic theory of these two philosophers is indeed ingenious, in that, first, it gives us a glimpse of the theory of the evolution of the world, and second, it brings together the Monist theory of **One**, which in this case is the atom--and the "plurality" view of atoms coalescing into "things." This theory must have developed while Leucippus was in Abdera as a director of the school that he established, and Democritus was there as a student. The cosmos, the "universe," is unlimited and consists of **"atoms"** and **"void."** For all Atomists, matter consisted of an unlimited (infinite) number of atoms; but unlike other thinkers at their time, they believed that atoms, even unlimited in number, cannot be subdivided any further, and this conviction lasted until about the twentieth century when Albert Einstein, in 1905, published his "**Theory of Relativity**" doctrine stating that the atom can be split, and if so emits energy. The worlds **(the stars and the planets)** are formed, according to **Leucippus/Democritus,** when atoms fall into the void and are entangled with one another, creating motion as they increase in bulk; resulting in **matter and substance.** If one looks through the fragments left of the writings of these two men, no evidence will be found stating the purpose of the creation of this universe. There is no "Mind" or "Love and Strife," or God that Anaxagoras and Empedocles speculated was behind their theory. Leucippus/Democritus postulated that "nothing is created at random," but there is an explanation for everything--and everything is brought into being by **necessity.** They were criticized viciously, and Plato and Aristotle never accepted their theory, which in later years did not fare any better, and was denigrated by Christians and Neo-Platonists. It was not until after the Renaissance, over 1900 years later that French philosophers revived the system and wrote comments about it, and it was not rejuvenated until recently--during the 19th and 20th centuries.

Democritus conceived of the soul as being composed of the finest, roundest atoms; mobile, like those of fire, and distributed throughout the body-- alternating with the others. The Mind, he regarded as a concentration of unmixed soul-atoms located in the breast. He worked out an elaborate theory of vision, according to which an impression is made on the intervening air by the shapes of things, and is conveyed to the pupils of the eyes in a distorted form.

Democritus was also influential as an ethical and moral philosopher, and is credited with the dictum: **"He who does wrong is more unfortunate than the one wronged."** He cannot be compared, in his moral and ethical philosophy, with Socrates and Plato; fragments mostly contain commonplace maxims concerning the virtues of **justice, temperance, and moderation**. His ideal for cheerfulness, tranquility, and well-being is refined--though somewhat self-centered--and not based, as with Epicurus, on a hedonistic foundation. The evidence is not enough to determine whether Democritus believed in the existence of gods; but he was contemptuous of orthodox religious theories and practices, and of the value of prayer. It is clear that he paved the way for the Epicurean philosophy.

With this discussion on Democritus and the Atomists, we conclude the area of Greek philosophical thinking classified as Pre-Socratic or Physical Philosophy. The following chapters introduce the **Golden Age of Greece** and the philosophies of **Socrates, Plato,** and **Aristotle.**

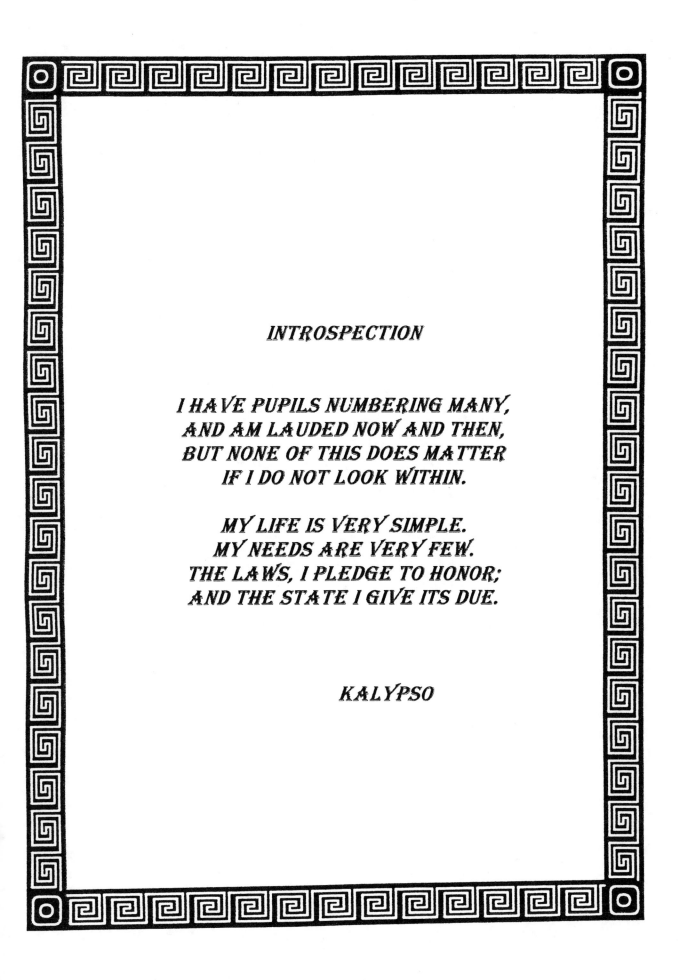

INTROSPECTION

I HAVE PUPILS NUMBERING MANY,
AND AM LAUDED NOW AND THEN,
BUT NONE OF THIS DOES MATTER
IF I DO NOT LOOK WITHIN.

MY LIFE IS VERY SIMPLE.
MY NEEDS ARE VERY FEW.
THE LAWS, I PLEDGE TO HONOR;
AND THE STATE I GIVE ITS DUE.

KALYPSO

CHAPTER 5

THE GOLDEN AGE OF GREECE
(THE SOPHISTS)

"Our love of what is beautiful does not lead
to extravagance; our love of things of the
mind does not make us soft."
Pericles

After the defeat of the Persians at **Salamis** in 480 B.C., and after the decisive battle at **Plataea** a year later, when it became evident that the almighty Persian Empire with its large army and navy, and abundance of resources and wealth, could not defeat a few small, impoverished, and quarrelling Greek city-states, the Greek spirit was buoyant; and the prospect of the future was looking bright--as the threat of the menacing East seemed to subside. For over two hundred years the Persians were slowly advancing westward, subjugating the Greek city-states of Ionia and adversely influencing the political life of Greece. The idea was now accepted that the future could be different, and that their status could improve and their standard of living change for the better if the threat of war with Persia would diminish (even though the city-states of Ionia were still under Persian domination). The defeats of the Persians opened up new perspectives. The Athenians solidified their strength and created alliances, while expanding their influence by extending trade with the **North, South, East and West.**

Solon

Of all the Greek city-states, Athens was the first to adopt a democratic system of government and practice it for centuries. **Solon,**[1] one of the seven wise-men of ancient times, initiated a

---

[1] Solon, at the beginning of the sixth century B.C.(c. 580 B.C.), is known to have introduced the very basic principles of democracy: abolishing the enslavement of people for debts; creating a 400 member Assembly; establishing a council of advisors to guide the Assembly; and dividing the people into 4 classes--according to their income (Πεντακοσιομεδιμνοι, Ιππεις, Ζευγιτες, Θητες), reforming agricultural exports, trade, and generally setting the foundations of the democratic system that followed. **Peisistratus** and his sons, tyrants, abolished Solon's system for several years (561 B.C to 545 B.C.), but **Cleisthenis,** a gifted leader, eventually established and refined the democratic process by the latter part of the sixth century (518-508 B.C.).

71

system of democracy after he rejected the repressive constitution that an earlier legislator, **Dracon,** had enacted. Under this democratic rule the impetus for growth, progress, and seeking alternative ways of doing things was encouraged. By the time of Pericles, over 40 years after the Persian wars, this open exchange of ideas and inquiry in a free society created an environment where a variety of people from throughout the Hellenic world were drawn to Athens, which was rapidly developing into a center of intellectual, commercial, and scholarly pursuits. All other free Greek city-states, not only those of the mainland, but those of the "Diaspora" in Ionia, Southern Italy, Sicily, and elsewhere, were progressing and developing power and influence. This was the period when all the famous scholars representing the schools of thought that we have discussed earlier, were coming to Athens to exchange ideas, visit with other scholars, and keep up with recent developments. It was a time when famous names in philosophy, such as: **Parmenides, Anaxagoras, Democritus, Zeno of Elea, Empedocles, et al.,** exercised a great influence on the molding of the scientific activities of the intellectual elite centered in the city-state of Athens. This period of enlightenment, creativity, and progress, came to be known as the **Golden Age of Greece.** It was an era of progress and significant changes and advancement in all areas of research and knowledge. The expansion of domestic, as well as foreign trade, and the free movement of people and ideas during this period, created a climate of hope and a tendency to experiment with other methods and practices in the social environment. But before we proceed further to explore the changes that were the consequences of this new climate, let **Pericles,** the **Archon-General** of Athens, through Thucidides, give us a glimpse of how the Athenian democracy was working. Thucidides describes the prevailing environment in Athens, circa 430's B.C. in a speech that he delivered (431 B.C.) at the burial of the dead soldiers after the first year of the Peloponnesian War; we learn of the institutions, practices, and laws of the Athenian democracy, and of the way people were conducting their private affairs. A segment of that speech follows:

PERICLES' FUNERAL ORATION (By Thucidides)

.........*"Let me say that our system of government does not copy the institutions of our neighbors. It is more the case of ours being a model to others, than of ours imitating anyone else. Our institution is called a* **DEMOCRACY** *because power is in the hands, not of a minority, but of the whole people. When it is a question of settling private disputes, everyone is equal before the law; when it is a question of putting one person before another in positions of public responsibility, what counts is not membership in a particular class, but the actual ability which the man possesses.*

No one, so long as he has it in him to be of service to the State, is kept in political obscurity because of poverty. And just as our political life is free and open, so is our day to day life in our relations with each other. We do not get into a "state" with our next-door neighbor if he enjoys himself in his own way, nor do we give him the kind of black looks which, though they do no real harm, still do hurt peoples' feelings. We are free and tolerant in our private lives; but in public affairs we keep to the Law. This is because it commands our deep respect. We give our obedience to those whom we put in positions of authority, and we obey the laws themselves, especially those

72

which are for the protection of the oppressed, and those unwritten laws which is an acknowledged shame to break.

And there is another point. When our work is over, we are in a position to enjoy all kinds of recreation of our spirits. There are various kinds of contests and sacrifices regularly throughout the year; in our own homes we find beauty and good taste which delight us every day and drive away our cares. Then the greatness of our city brings it about that all the good things from all over the world flow into us, so that to us it seems just as natural to enjoy foreign goods as our own local products.

Our love of what is beautiful does not lead to extravagance; our love of things of the mind does not make us soft. We regard wealth as something to be properly enjoyed, rather than as something to boast about. As for poverty, no one need be ashamed to admit it; the real shame is in not taking practical measures to escape from it.

Here each individual is interested not only in his own affairs, but in the affairs of the State as well; even those who are mostly occupied with their own business are extremely well-informed on general politics, this is a peculiarity of ours; we do not say that a man who takes no interest in politics is a man who minds his own business; we say that he has no business here at all.

We Athenians, in our persons, take our decisions on policy or submit them to proper discussions: for we do not think that there is an incompatibility between words and deeds; the worst thing is to rush into action before the consequences have been properly debated. And this is another point where we differ from other people.

Pericles

We are capable at the same time of taking risks and of estimating them beforehand. Others are brave out of ignorance; and when they stop to think, they begin to fear. But the man who can most truly be accounted brave is he who best knows the meaning of what is sweet in life and of what is terrible, and then goes undeterred to meet what is to come.

Again, in questions of general good feeling there is a great contrast between us and most other people. We make friends by doing good to others, not by receiving good from them. This makes our friendship all the most reliable, since we want to keep alive the gratitude of those who are in our debt by showing continued goodwill to them; whereas the feelings of one who owes us

73

something lack the same enthusiasm, since he knows that when he repays our kindness, it will be more like paying back a debt than giving something spontaneously.

We are unique in this. When we exhibit kindness to others, we do so not out of any

Thucydides

calculating of profit or loss: but rather without afterthought, relying on our free liberality. Taking everything together then, I declare that our city is an education to Greece, and I declare that, in my opinion, each single one of our citizens, in all manifold aspects of life, is able to show himself the rightful lord and owner of his own person, and do this moreover, with exceptional grace and exceptional versatility.

*And to show that this is not empty boasting for the present occasion, but real tangible fact, you have only to consider the power which our city possesses and which has been won by those very qualities which I have mentioned. **Athens,** alone of the states we know, comes to her testing time in a greatness that surpasses what was imagined of her. In her case, and in her case alone, no invading enemy is ashamed at being defeated, and no subject can complain of being governed by people unfit for their responsibilities. Mighty indeed are the marks and monuments of our empire which we have left. Future ages will wonder at us, as the present age wonders at us now..............."*

Thucydides is considered by modern scholars of history as an unbiased, impartial and reliable historian; and even though he was an Athenian, he described the events of the Peloponnesian War impartially and brought forth an abundance of information concerning political developments during the period. Thucydides, when writing Pericles' speech, must have omitted the political boasting that Pericles probably delivered to lift the spirits of his compatriots in the first year of the War. We have no reason, therefore, to doubt the veracity of what Pericles is saying in the above passage when describing the conditions of the Athenian State. Among other things, we note the freedom that the individual was accorded in carrying out his own lifestyle; the equality of all people before the law; the election of the competent to public office; the extent of international trade; the free and open political and private life; an element of humanism--by enacting special laws for the protection of the oppressed; a desire for and practice of free artistic expression; the

74

involvement of the individual in the political process; the possibility of anyone ascending to a position of authority--regardless of class or income-- and the political might of Athens as a city-state.

The victorious general of the battle of Salamis, Themistocles, had perceived after the Battle of Marathon in 490 B.C., that the salvation of Athens and all of Greece from the Persian threat would be achieved only through the creation of a strong naval power. Thus, in the years that ensued

Bias

from 490 B.C. to 480 B.C., when the sea battle at Salamis was fought, the Athenians created a strong navy--which not only provided the means to defeat the Persians, but also built the military and commercial might of the city-state of Athens for the years to come. Immediately after the hostilities with the Persians ended, Athens established the **Delian League,** which was an alliance of several city-states for the purpose of providing mutual support and protection. This alliance was very successful. It provided wealth to the treasury of Athens; it opened up trade—and, as Pericles states in his speech, the products of the city-states were freely exchanged while Athens played the role of the central power. Wealth, then, was accumulating quickly, and wherever prosperity exists all activities grow--including the arts and the sciences. In this receptive environment new views and new philosophies tend to prevail. In the previous chapters we noted that the **physical philosophers** were concerned with Nature and matters related to theoretical physics and mathematics. Some kind of skepticism is developing now, and the new thinkers seem to be more interested in areas that we would classify today as

the *social and behavioral sciences*; while the physical philosophers were mostly concerned with matters relating to the origin of the world: what we would call today **physics, chemistry, biology, mathematics, etc.--**This new environment also provided an impetus to investigate man and his society and acknowledged the need for improving education and the dissemination of knowledge. The city-states never developed a public system of education, as we know it today, and therefore a curriculum of study had to be provided by the private sector. A new breed of professionals emerged, and the most famous of them traveled from city to city to provide education in the form of lectures and tutoring sessions; many were local teacher-scholars who also offered lectures and private lessons to local students and those coming from far away to attend their classes. These individuals were paid well for their services and most of them acquired wealth, prestige, and power.

Another important development during this period, particularly as a result of Pericles' influence on the expansion of democracy, was the need for advocates on behalf of individuals who would address the courts, the Assembly, or other institutions when petitioning the State or defending themselves in courts. Most of the people were farmers and did not have the skills to handle the language effectively in public. The need for advocates who could write these speeches, so that the plaintiff or the defendant could address the court had become a necessity. These same individuals who provided most of the education, and who could handle the language most effectively, availed their services to the litigants for a handsome fee. In a comedy by Aristophanes, **"Wasps,"** we learn of the insatiable desire for litigation under the open court system of Athens. Aristophanes portrays an old man so obsessed with serving as a juror, that he was neglecting all his other activities and duties. Finally, his son barricaded the house to discourage him from going to the courts. These advocates developed influence and power by writing the speeches that the plaintiffs or defendants would deliver in open court--prosecuting or defending their cases. From these speeches we now know some of the private life of the ancient Athenians, as well as the morals, ethics, traditions, and social practices at the time, because the speeches were addressing disputes of the civil, criminal, or commercial code. There were a number of famous and not so famous men who flourished in this field in Athens and other places at that time, and who later left some outstanding pieces of writing. Just to mention a few: **Gorgias, Protagoras, Lysias, Prodicus, Critias, Thrasymachus, Isocrates,**

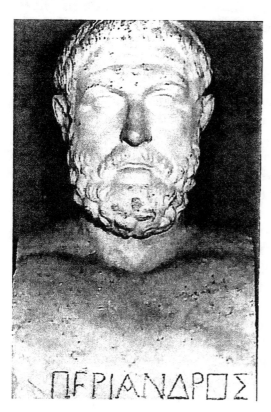

Periandrus

et al., were men who were either defending or prosecuting cases in court, or writing political speeches to be delivered at the **Assembly (Εκκλησια του Δημου)** or the **Parliament (Βουλη)** debating political matters; and the speeches that they wrote constituted outstanding pieces of literary art.

Wealth breeds power; and power sometimes corrupts. The moral and ethical standards in the world of Greece were changing. The perception of objectivity, justice, and "right" and "wrong" was distorted. The roving teachers appeared to provide an education based upon skilled rhetoric and apparent logical percepts, but were accused of distorting values by stressing skills which would enable students to achieve their goals of acquiring wealth, power, and privilege. These individuals, particularly those concerned with education, some of them possessing outstanding intellectual capability, were indeed considered as "Σοφοί"--"Wise Men." The word "Φιλόσοφος" **(Philosopher)** that denotes an individual who is a **"Friend of Wisdom,"** was not yet used extensively, but the word **"Sophos" (Wise**) was commonplace to denote a person who has accumulated knowledge and special skills. There is a significant difference in the meaning of these two words. A philosopher came to be known as a person interested not only in knowledge and wisdom, but also in *objective truth*. These "teachers" were known as **"Σοφιστές"** (Sophists); but they were not entirely devoted to the **ultimate Truth.**

The word **sophist** and **sophistry** connotes, even today, a derogatory attribute, implying that one who is a **sophist** or one who uses **sophistry** attempts to distort real values and introduces falsehoods. The Sophists' external appearance was pompous, and their attire

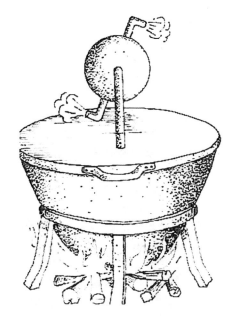

ostentatious. They regarded themselves as the carriers of enlightenment and progress. Even though they claimed that they followed the traditions, they nevertheless, according to some critics, acted in a self-serving way; and therefore, the ultimate result was that they bypassed traditions. They cultivated an environment of doubt; challenging established practices, ethics, and the State. Old philosophy had drawn a distinction between natural and human law, but the Sophists now encouraged emphasis on **Nature** rather than the notion of the **Law.** For them: **Nature** equaled **"Truth;"** and **Law** equaled **"Convention,"** which one should or could adjust according to personal pursuits and interests. In spite of the criticism directed against the Sophists, by ancient and modern writers, the fact should be considered that they introduced an element of humanism and enlightenment; developed the art/science of rhetoric; refined the language; and uplifted the educational level of the people through their tutoring schools and lectures. The reason that the word **"sophist"** has such a degrading connotation, is that one of the greatest critics of the Sophists was **Socrates** who, even though he himself was considered a Sophist, criticized their methods and teachings as being injurious to the society because, he argued, they were neglecting ethical and moral values, and embracing mostly materialistic and false standards.

Hero's Steam Experiment

It was this criticism by Socrates against the Sophists' methods, during the latter half of the 5th century that fostered a debate on moral and ethical issues and ultimately created the new era that we defined above as: the **Era of Ethical and Moral Philosophy**, as initiated and developed by Plato and Socrates. We discuss the influence of Socrates and Plato in developing moral and ethical philosophy in the following chapters (chapters 6-9). But let us further explore the class of the "Sophists," because indeed some of them were outstanding minds who contributed significantly to the development of research and interest in what we would call today the social and behavioral sciences. There were quite a number of individuals who distinguished themselves in the art of rhetoric and education during ancient times and who fit into the classification of "Sophists;" but we shall briefly identify only the most famous and discuss the work of two of them, **Protagoras** and **Gorgias.** Other names that appear in the literature as Sophists are: **Prodicus, Hippias, Antiphon, and others** (associated with the school of **Protagoras**); and **Polos, Kallicles, Thrasymachus, Critias, and others** (associated with the school of **Gorgias**).

PROTAGORAS: Protagoras was born in **490 B.C.** in Thrace, and died in **420 B.C.** in Athens. He wrote extensively, but the only references that we have of his writings are the titles of his works as recorded by Diogenes Laertius. These are:

The Art of Controversy
On Wrestling
On Mathematics

On the State
On Ambition
On Virtues
On the Ancient Order of Things
On the Dwellers in Hades
On the Misdeeds of Mankind
On Precepts
On Forensic Speech for a Fee (two books)

Hero's Continuous Altar Fire Caused by Hot Air

None of these books survived, even though Diogenes Laertius mentions that the above books existed during his time (probably about 250 A.D.). But even though we do not know much about his books, except the titles, we know a great deal about him, his beliefs, and his teachings from Plato who, in **Theaetetus** and **Protagoras,** discusses Protagoras and his philosophy extensively.

Plato accused Protagoras of distorting the truth and regaling his listeners with illogical arguments. Aristotle stated that the teachings of Protagoras do not contain truth, but apparent probabilities of truth, and have no place in other professions except that of the orator. Protagoras, however, was the first who created and completed Greek grammar and introduced the declension of the tenses, types of sentences, and the variation of the three genders of the nouns. These, of course, were significant contributions toward the completion and perfection of the Greek language.

GORGIAS. He was born in Southern Italy in the year **483 B.C.,** and died in **376 B.C.** at the age of 107. We know a great deal about his views from the Platonic dialogues: **Gorgias**, and **Meno**. He apparently made himself rich in Southern Italy, because when he came to Athens in the year 427 B.C. as an ambassador from his city-state, at the age of 56, he was living a very opulent life, and impressed the Athenians at the Assembly with his expertise in rhetoric. Even though he attended philosophy courses presented by pre-Socratic philosophers, mainly Parmenides, he nevertheless devoted himself to teaching the youth and became the most distinguished Sophist. He wrote a book titled **On Nature**, a sequence to similar works of pre-Socratic thinkers (**Empedocles and Parmenides**), in which he postulated a negative view toward knowledge and the capability of the human being in understanding his environment and being able to communicate this knowledge to others. This pessimistic and Skeptic view of Gorgias', coupled with Protagoras' belief that *man is the only standard of measurement for all things*, created an intellectual environment filled with doubt. As a result of this viewpoint, the efforts of the thinkers at this time were directed toward identifying the relationship between *knowledge and being, and between knowledge and rhetorical expression*--rather than toward the paths that the physical philosophers had introduced. Nevertheless, Gorgias perfected the art of oratory and devoted his time to educating the youth and preparing them to become great orators.

The Island of Lefkada

THE PHILOSOPHY OF THE SOPHISTS.

Most of the information that we have available about the Sophists, and their influence on Greek philosophy and society, comes to us from the Platonic dialogues, in which Socrates is shown to criticize some of the practices which were apparently advocated by the Sophists. Some modern writers, however, consider the Sophists as having had a positive influence in the fields of education, language, and the art of rhetoric; and view them as important scholars who introduced elements of humanism into Greek society prior to Socrates. The four main doctrines of the Sophist philosophy can be summarized as follows:

(1) **SUBJECTIVITY VS. OBJECTIVITY**. The fundamental and important difference between "objectivity" and "subjectivity," which was the essence of Greek scholarship up to that time, was blurred by the Sophists. Protagoras claimed that: ***"Man is the measure of all things; of those existing that they exist, and of those non-existing that they do not exist."*** In this statement there is an element of humanism by placing emphasis on: man as an individual and as a member of society. It directs attention toward the "human being," (male and female) and gives it stature in life; and, as a result, promotes a system of egalitarianism within democratic institutions, which advanced human rights and questioned the validity of the deep-rooted institution of slavery. However, this principle had a profound impact on the validity of knowledge and the objective pursuit of **Ultimate Truth**. By emphasizing man as the measure of all things, implies also that man's subjective perception, conception, and understanding of basic values or matters pertaining to Man, Nature, and Society, represents the **truth**. This ushered a novel approach to the search for objective truth, and ultimately emphasized subjectivity and individual judgment: which was not in any way scientific. If two different people view the same object and disagree in their assessment of its characteristics, by this principle: *both are right*. This also places emphasis on sensory perceptions and mitigates intellectual conceptions, and transcendentalism. The impact of this principle on scientific research and objective inquiry, which was the main purpose of previous thinkers who introduced the doctrine of the Scientific Method, was detrimental.

(2) **VALIDITY OF KNOWLEDGE**. The Sophists introduce doubt about the validity of knowledge by denying that man can learn the secrets of Nature. Gorgias promotes the doctrine that: **"Nothing exists; and if it exists it is difficult to understand; and if understood it is difficult to communicate to others."** The Sophists realized that all efforts of the Ionian and Eleatic sages toward understanding Nature had been reduced to a series of arguments and counter-arguments that brought a heavy dosage of skepticism regarding man's capacity to understand his environment. The detrimental effect that this principle had on scientific inquiry was not only the element of skepticism that it introduced, but also the undermining of the principle of previous scholars who recognized the difficultly of unearthing the secrets of Nature, but insisted that the efforts of true research should be continued until ultimate success is achieved.

(3) **RELATIVISM**. Things look that they are, but are not; and are not, and yet look that they are. Also, things look that they are and are; and look that they are not and are not. In this sense then, it is difficult for one to know if he is facing the true nature of things or rather an alternate view. This principle convinced the Sophists that things are relative; and what we conceive as the ultimate truth may only be an image or a shadow of truth. They came to accept natural law because Nature does not deceive, and discard human law as dubious and possibly incorrect. An area in which the Sophists had a detrimental effect on the society, based upon their conviction of relativism, was their tendency to undermine traditions. Traditions are established through time, tested by practice, validated by experience, and often constitute fundamental pillars that uphold moral and ethical standards in

80

society. During their travels the Sophists had noticed that various peoples observed different customs and traditions relating to a similar purpose. From Herodotus' **Histories** they noted that the Persians cremated their dead, while the Greeks buried them; some tribes in India ate their dead; the Phoenicians spread their remains over a sacred lake; and the Egyptians mummified their dead. Therefore, they challenged the validity of customs and questioned whether custom is dictated by Nature, or is a convention set up by humans to accommodate specific needs at a particular place and time. To Socrates, it seemed that the Sophists were undermining custom and tradition: subverting the standards of morality and ethics.

(4) **AGNOSTICISM.** As we noted in the previous chapter, the idea of questioning the religious polytheistic system had been advanced by Xenophanes. But now the Sophists probed further into this question and Protagoras proclaims:" **I am unable to reach knowledge about the gods, either that they exist, or that they do not exist, or of their essential nature"; for many are the obstacles that impede knowledge: both the obscurity of the question and the shortness of life."** This is a view of agnosticism that goes beyond Xenophanes' views. As we pointed out in previous chapters, the ancient Greeks were deeply religious people, but they had a certain freedom to view religion independently and it was not unusual for the poets to present an image of the gods as human. There are quite a number of cases where a god could be ridiculed; as for example, in the case of Aristophanes in **Clouds**-- where **Socrates** states that there is no **Zeus**, and that all talk about him is rubbish. But Protagoras' element of agnosticism angered people because Protagoras, as teacher and renowned rhetorician, had an impact on the society

The Island of Lefkada

and the youth. As time progressed, however, this professed doubt--as to the existence of gods-- developed into atheism, for which Socrates was accused and lost his life; which of course was a travesty, since Socrates was a pious, religious individual.

It was along these lines of thinking, on the part of the Sophists, that invited the wrath of Socrates against them. The Sophists resemble, in some measure, the European philosophers of the 18th century who brought the Enlightenment to Europe. When making comparisons one must bear in mind the period when the Sophists lived and the needs that they were called upon to fulfill. They were the teachers; the tutors who came in to provide education, and in that sense, they can be viewed as the men who introduced educational methods, teaching styles, and objectives of education. In that capacity, they also expanded the horizons of education and addressed the new generation's needs for training and advancement. As teachers, the Sophists promoted: rhetoric, grammar, dialectics, sociology, cultural anthropology, and political reform. They were the first who

Ionic style.

raised their voice against slavery and recognized the value of the individual in a free society. Their interest in man was certainly a positive one; but of course they did not continue further toward the development of a general theory or definition, instead they concerned themselves with the "**special**" man and his passions, problems, and interests. As masters of rhetoric, they succeeded in changing the meaning of things through linguistic tricks. To some critics, the Sophists distorted the established order without distinguishing the worthy from the unworthy. They equated man's freedom with arbitrary choice (free license to act), and clouded the notion of justice. Protagoras correctly noted the subjectivity of personal sentiments and feelings, as well as psychological characteristics; but the fact that he gave them the stature of general truth angered the Socratics, who felt that it was a crime to ignore the laws of logic--and above all: the laws of Justice, Ethics and Morality. They were considered proponents of **pure materialism.** [2]

Socrates questioned the ultimate consequence of the road molded by the Sophists and followed by the society at his time. He preached, taught, and died for Justice and the Ethical and Moral law that he thought society should follow, based upon: *Temperance, (Πραοτης), Justice, (Δικαιοσυνη), Bravery (Ανδρεια), and Prudence (Σωφροσυνη)*--rather than personal gratification and pursuit of excessive possessions which ultimately lead to the disintegration of societal, ethical, and moral values.

In time, the intellectual core of Athenian democracy showed signs of erosion under the influence of the Sophists, who emphasized the acquisition of material possessions and the pursuit of wealth--above the development of the mind and the pursuit of knowledge. The State under the Delian

---

[2] See Chapter 16 for information about some similar developments in India by the turn of the millennium, before the advent of Jainism and Buddhism.

League, was acquiring wealth also, and the free enterprise system—which promoted enrichment and power, when it was corrupted, became a mitigating factor in the advancement of intellectual and scholarly pursuits. The Sophists were the by-product of this system and exhibited their influence by disregarding the Naturalists' emphasis on research for the sake of research and discovery of the truth, but rather accumulating wealth so as to acquire power. This kind of phenomenon one could easily identify with the societies of the post World War II era, in our times, where the pursuit of material possessions, power, and pleasure predominate. For the ancient Athenians, Socrates appeared in the marketplace and attempted to awake them from an erroneous course, but failed, and by the end of the 5th century the Athenian society collapsed.

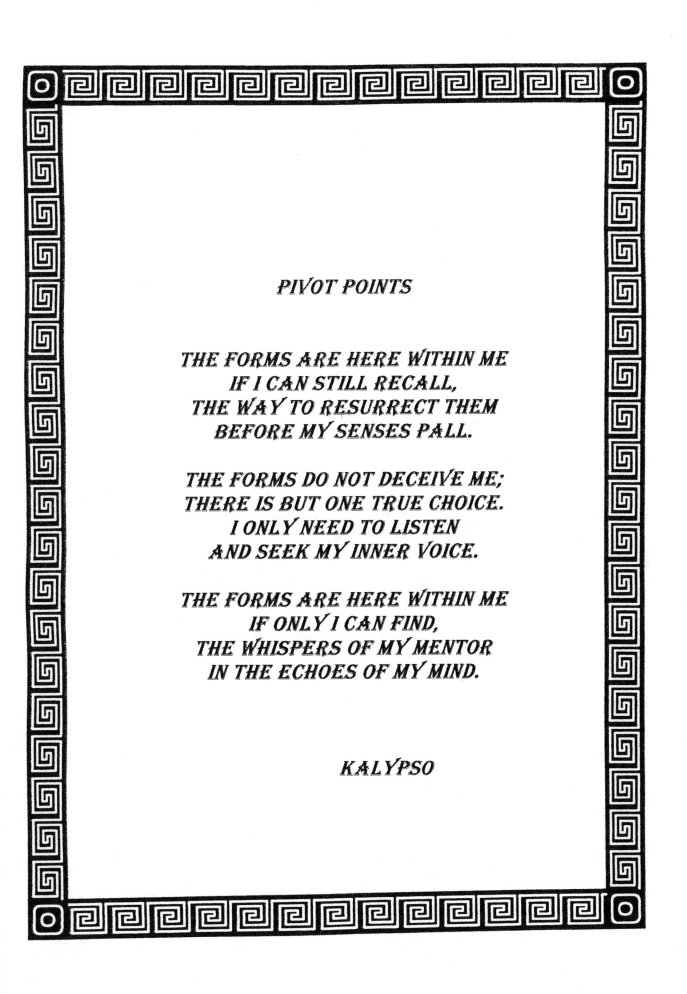

PIVOT POINTS

THE FORMS ARE HERE WITHIN ME
IF I CAN STILL RECALL,
THE WAY TO RESURRECT THEM
BEFORE MY SENSES PALL.

THE FORMS DO NOT DECEIVE ME;
THERE IS BUT ONE TRUE CHOICE.
I ONLY NEED TO LISTEN
AND SEEK MY INNER VOICE.

THE FORMS ARE HERE WITHIN ME
IF ONLY I CAN FIND,
THE WHISPERS OF MY MENTOR
IN THE ECHOES OF MY MIND.

KALYPSO

CHAPTER 6

THE LIFE OF SOCRATES AND PLATO (AS MEN AND PHILOSOPHERS)

"Future ages will wonder at us, as the
present age wonders at us now."

Pericles

SOCRATES

THE MAN   Socrates was born in Athens, in 469 B.C., and died there in 399 B.C. He lived in Athens all his life, with the exception of two trips to **Amphipolis and Potidea**, in Northern Greece,

Socrates

where he exhibited heroism in battle while he was in the army. His father, **Sophroniscus,** was a sculptor; and his mother, **Phaenarete,** was a midwife. From his early life he showed signs of intellectual interest, and in spite of the attempts of his father to make him a sculptor, he joined the intellectual elite of the city, became a student of **Anaxagoras and Archelaus** (not the tyrant), and spent his time studying the early Greek philosophers. He was an accomplished public speaker, and during the period of the 30 Tyrants (a short-lived dictatorship after the Athenian defeat in the Peloponnesian War) he was forbidden to engage in rhetoric. He was so skillful in presenting his arguments that he was antagonizing his opponents and was hated, despised, and laughed at; but he endured it all patiently and goodnaturedly. His arguments sometimes would incite violent acts by his irritated opponents, but he would never resort to violence himself. He was witty, cynical, and demonstrated a degree of humor and irony in his argumentation. When once he was kicked by someone, his friends expressed surprise at his composure; he responded: **"What do you do when you are kicked by a donkey, do you take the donkey to court?"** He liked to argue with anyone who would

listen, but his objective was not to convince others of his ideas and his beliefs--but rather to unearth the *truth*. He showed feelings of dedication and devotion, and once during battle he saved **Xenophon at Amphipolis,** by carrying his wounded body off the battlefield. He cherished[1] the

---

[1] Both Socrates and Plato were disillusioned with the methods and practices of the democratic parties in Athens during the years of the Peloponnesian War; and Plato, particularly, held them responsible for causing the defeat of

benefits of the Athenian democracy of freedom of expression, free speech, and political choice—to the extent that once, while in the army, he disobeyed the generals when he was ordered to bring a prisoner from Salamis for execution, because he felt it was an unjust decision.

On another occasion, he was offered a site by Alcibiades, one of his students, to build a house for himself. He refused and said: **"Would I not look ridiculous if I needed a pair of shoes**

Ancient Agora and Stoa of Attalus

and someone offered me a full hide and I accepted it?" This incident exemplified the man's superior dignity of character, independence, and realization of the vanity of material things. Also, going though the marketplace and seeing things exhibited for sale, he would say: **"How many things I can do without!. . . ."** He was so contemptuous of rich tyrants that he once refused gifts and favors from the dictators **Archelaus of Macedonia and Scopas of Larissa.** He also refused invitations from them to visit their court. He was so fastidious in his way of life that he managed to escape infection during the plague that hit Athens in 429 B.C. Aristophanes, the great Athenian comic-poet, ridiculed Socrates in his play, **The Clouds**, in the following passage:

> *"Oh, man that justly desires great wisdom, how blessed will be your life among Athenians and Greeks, being retentive of memory and thinker that you are, with endurance of toil for your character; never you are weary whether standing or walking, never numb with cold, never hungry for breakfast: from wine and overeating and all other frivolities you do turn away."*

He was capable of representing opposing sides of an argument equally, because he had the skill to draw his conclusions from the facts. When his son was once angry with his mother, Socrates made him feel ashamed of himself. He was very respectful of human dignity, and when one of his students, **Charmides,** offered him some servants to derive some income from, he refused-- even though he was poor and his family was deprived of a good living standard. He was

---

Athens by engaging in incessant quarrelling.

repeating his favorite saying: **There is only one "good" in life--and that is "knowledge." And there is only one "evil" in life--and that is "ignorance."** He used to say that **wealth and noble lineage bring their possessor no dignity; but on the contrary, evil.** He was keeping himself occupied at all times, because he believed that **"Idleness is the Mother of all Evil" (Αργια Μητηρ Πασης Κακιας).** He used to scoff at those who criticized him because he learned to play the lyre (harp) in his old age, by saying that he found nothing wrong or absurd in acquiring a new skill **"at any age."** He liked to dance, thinking that such exercise helped to keep the body in good condition. He said that a supernatural force or "Sign" **(Δαιμονιον)** warned him beforehand of the future, and that he knew nothing except the fact of his own ignorance: "I *know one thing that I know nothing*" **(Εν Οιδα Οτι Ουδεν Οιδα).** Once he was asked to comment on what would constitute a virtue for a young man, and he replied: **"Among Other Things, Doing Nothing in Excess" (Μηδεν Αγαν).** Virtue was one of the cornerstones of his philosophy; and once, when he attended a play by Euripides, in which the following statement concerning virtue was uttered by the actor:

"It is best to let Her roam at will,"

he got up and left the theater, because he could not stand to see Virtue assailed. When someone once asked Socrates whether he should marry or not, he responded that he would "regret" whatever

The Road to Dionyssus Theatre

he would decide. Concerning the youth, he would say that the young should continuously look themselves in the mirror, because in this way the handsome might acquire soon a corresponding behavior; and the ugly conceal their defects by education. Once he invited some people to dinner, and Xanthippe (his wife) was worrying about the quality of the meal; he said to her: **"Don't worry, because if they are reasonable men they will put up with it; but if they are not, we shall not trouble ourselves with them."** He used to say that the rest of the world lived to eat, while he himself ate to live. After the trial, when he was in prison, his wife told him: **You suffer unjustly;** he replied: **Why, you would have me suffer justly?** He had continuous quarrels with his wife, sometimes in the marketplace, as she accused him of not charging a fee to his rich students. Once, when Xanthippe first scolded him and then drenched him with water, his rejoinder was: **"Did I not say that Xanthippe's thunder would end in rain?"** When someone told him that Xanthippe's scolding of him was intolerable, he said: **"I have gotten used to it."** When she tore his coat off his back in the marketplace and his friends advised him to hit back, he answered: **"Yes, by Zeus, in order that while we are sparring, each of you may join in with: 'Go, Socrates!, 'Well done, Xanthippe!"**

His quarrels with his wife emanated from the fact that he was so preoccupied with his public engagements, that she was accusing him of neglecting his family by not accepting gifts and donations from his rich students, as well as fees for his tutoring--as was the prevailing practice with the Sophists. He used to say that he lived with a **"shrew;"** but just as horsemen are fond of breaking spirited horses, so he too could cope with the rest, if he adjusted to the society of Xanthippe. The event that most incensed his enemies was the dictum from Delphi that declared:

"Of all men living, Socrates is the most wise,"
(Ανδρων Απαντων Σωκρατης Σοφωτατος)

For this he was envied; but he was resented and hated primarily by various groups because he would take to task those who thought highly of themselves--proving them to be fools. But, overall, he was developing enemies *among the rhetoricians (Sophists), the Business Establishment, and the dramatic poets.* The rhetoricians were incensed because, through his dialectic method, he was successful in proving their arguments unsound. The Business Establishment was angered at him for advising his young students of the vanity of excessive material possessions, and the poets were unhappy with his criticism of their plays as distracting from the purpose of the Deity. Thus, **Anytus,** on behalf of the Business Establishment; **Melitus,** on behalf of the poets; and **Lycon,** on behalf of the rhetoricians, brought accusations against him which read as follows:(Ref.#8, Vol2, p.170)

> *"This indictment and affidavit is sworn by Meletus, the son of Meletus of Pithos, against Socrates, the son of Sophroniscus of Alopece: Socrates is guilty of refusing to recognize the gods recognized by the State, and of introducing other new divinities. He is also guilty of corrupting the youth. The penalty demanded is death."*

A trial was held and, after both views were heard, a vote was taken by the jurors; and by a small margin he was found guilty. When he was asked by the judge what should be the penalty that he would suggest[2], he offered to pay a penalty of 25 drachmas (a small amount). When this caused an uproar among the jurors, he added: "Considering my services, I assess the penalty to be my maintenance in the **Prytaneun** (Public Treasury) at public expense." This increased the votes

---

[2] In ancient times when the accuser wrote the affidavit of his suit, he had to state the penalty that he sought. The penalty could be: (1) Death, (2) Exile, or (3) Confiscation of property. Before the judge would determine the final penalty, the accused had the right to counterpropose a penalty of his own, from the above three.

against him in a second balloting by 81, and a sentence of death was passed. A month later he drank the hemlock and died. Later the Athenians felt such remorse that they shut down the training grounds and the gymnasia in mourning, exiled the other accusers (Lykon and Anytus), and put **Meletus** to death. They honored Socrates with a bronze statue made by the famous sculptor at the time, **Leucippus,** and placed it on the road of the **Panathenaic** procession. When Anytus visited the city of Heraclia, the place of his exile, the inhabitants expelled him forever.

Aphrodite and the Satyr

HIS WORK Socrates constitutes a milestone in Greek philosophy because he left his imprint in such a decisive way that all philosophers preceding him are known as **"pre-Socratic,"** and those following as **"post-Socratic."** His impact at the time was significant, and his influence continued in the Academy that Plato founded at "Colonos" (a suburb of Athens) well into the Christian Era. Socrates shared a certain humanistic approach similar to that of the Sophists, but he did not share other aspects of the Sophist philosophy. He was not interested in material possessions or worldly things. He advocated education--and particularly self-education--which would lead to self-discovery: **"Know Thyself."** He believed that people could learn to improve themselves, and wanted to help them achieve this goal: because through self-education they would understand and appreciate **"Good," "Justice," "Truth," and "Prudence."** He also thought that a person benefits more from improving his moral and ethical standing--rather than from increasing his worldly possessions.

His approach was the "Dialectic Method" in conversation and discussion about a subject, and consisted mainly of having individuals express their views--rather than imposing his own on them. He would proceed by asking them to define what they thought about such terms as: **temperance, justice, truth, and bravery, etc.,** and then discuss and analyze their positions. In the course of the conversation, original definitions or hypotheses would lead to acceptable or unacceptable conclusions; and therefore, the original proposition would be either accepted or rejected. Sometimes the conclusion would be a negative proof; for example, *what justice is not* rather than *what justice is.* At other times the conversation would lead to definitions of terms acceptable or unacceptable to all. He held firm to his conception of an Absolute Truth defining moral standards, and in no way could he be classified as a Skeptic in the area of ethics and morality--which was the case with most of the Sophists.

Basically, he was convinced that virtue and morality were connected with intelligence/knowledge, because he accepted that one must understand the **"what" and "why"** of his actions. He was not a dogmatist because no course toward virtue was dictated; rather he left it to the individual to judge it for himself. In other words: he was relying heavily on human intelligence and education. *In terms of "goods," he classified them into three classes: material goods (money and possessions) ranked as the least important; followed next by goods of the body (health and strength); and goods of the soul (ethical integrity and moral insight) at the top of the scale.* He preferred to lose material possessions and live in poverty and deprivation rather than lose his moral integrity. The basic core of his philosophy was that one should examine himself and measure his potential, talents, and limitations; recognizing that the human being is basically good in nature and that knowledge and virtue are important because they enable one to **"know"** himself. If we act immorally or unethically, it is because of ignorance rather than design. He defined ignorance as: being the state of not knowing the nature of **"good"** or what is ultimately desirable and beneficial to

the individual. He believed that people have a rational insight into what constitutes good conduct, and that they will inevitably do what is "**right**" and **"good"**--*both for them and for others.* Socrates was exhorting his fellow citizens to develop rational insight and care for their soul. This kind of exhortation one would view today within a religious context, as a command for good and virtuous living. He was ahead of his time; and the fact that he was, as Xenophanes before him, critical of the Greek polytheistic system of religion, created a hostile relationship with the Establishment. This, coupled with his **"divine sign"** (**Daemonion**) that came to him as an inner voice directing his actions and decisions, led to accusations of atheism by his enemies: which most certainly was not true.

Socrates and the Academy of Athens

        The purpose of his life was to exhort his fellow citizens to examine and *reflect upon the way in which they were leading their lives.* He stressed "Conduct" as a central issue of his philosophical thought, and the schools of philosophy established after him emphasized ethics and
morality as the pivotal core of their philosophies **(Stoics, Epicureans, Cynics, Neo-Platonics, et al.)** Several Christian messages, which appeared three hundred years later, have a distinctive Socratic flavor inherent in them. Unfortunately, his message was not heeded, as the moral and ethical standards of the latter part of the Hellenistic and upcoming Roman world deteriorated dramatically, by the second and third centuries A.D., under corrupt Roman emperors. With the advent of Christianity, these Socratic tenets were again recognized and reintroduced, forming the foundation of the religious dogma that influenced the moral and ethical standards of what came to be known as the *Western culture.*

Thus ended the life of an important man of ancient times, who, even though he may have had no significant influence on his immediate contemporaries--apart from the philosophers and intellectuals--was the person who introduced ethical and moral philosophy and searched for the **"virtuous man"** and **"the virtuous society."** He fought for compassion, justice, truth, ethics, morality, and virtue; and during the 70 years that he lived in Athens and taught his philosophy, influenced quite a number of people--above all: Plato. Plato, a young man of 28 at the time of Socrates' death, passed the torch forward and became a prolific dramatic, philosophical writer, who expounded and enhanced these ideas on moral and ethical philosophy: first proposed by Socrates.

PLATO (ΠΛΑΤΩΝ)

Plato

THE MAN Plato was an Athenian citizen, born on the island of Aegina, a few miles southwest of Athens, in the year 427 B.C., and died in Athens in the year 347 B.C. He lived for 80 years, even though there are some writers who contend that he lived longer. His original name was **ARISTOCLES,** but his gymnastics teacher named him **Plato (Πλατων)**, from the word **"Πλατυς=wide,"** because of his robust constitution; and according to some writers a reference to his wide forehead. He was an athlete and it is said that he wrestled at the Isthmian Games. At the age of 20 he joined Socrates' school and followed him around in the marketplace, shops, and the houses of friends, where they would discuss issues among themselves or with famous visitors. It should be noted that Athens, at that time, was the center of the intellectual world, and quite a number of thinkers from various parts of the Greek world converged there. Immediately after the death of Socrates, the political climate in Athens was not very favorable for his pupils, and naturally most of Plato's companions left for various parts of Greece. Plato went to **Megara** first, and there he joined **Euclides,** another of Socrates' pupils, but older than Plato, who had opened a school of philosophy. Most of these people feared for their lives because, after the return of the Democrats-- following the short reign of the Thirty Tyrants-- revenge was sought in order to placate the angry public who was seeking scapegoats for the defeat by the Spartans and the atrocities of the Tyrants. Since several of Socrates' pupils were involved in the War, particularly his friend **Alcibiades**, who was considered responsible for the earlier defeat of the Athenian expeditionary force in Syracuse, Sicily, the wrath of the Democrats turned against Socrates first, and his pupils later.

He did not stay long in Megara and soon left for **Cyrene, in Lybia,** where his friend Theodorus, a mathematician, had a school of mathematics. He stayed in Cyrene and studied mathematics for awhile, and later traveled to Italy, in Croton, to meet the Pythagorean philosophers, **Philolaus and Eurytus**. After leaving Italy, he traveled to Egypt and the Orient to acquaint himself with the practices of the Egyptians and other people of the Middle Eastern areas. While he was in Egypt he fell ill, and the Egyptian priests treated him; later in his writings he stated: **"Above all men, the Egyptians were best skilled in medicine."** He did not remain in Egypt long, and did not benefit very much from that expedition due to a war that was going on between the Persians and the Egyptians, and soon thereafter he left for Athens after several (13) years of wandering. When he returned to Athens he established **"The Academy"**--where he taught until the end of his life--with the exception of three trips to Italy and Sicily in-between. The academy was located in a suburb, southwest of Athens, and received its name from a mythological hero, "Academus"; it was the

center of learning where hundreds of scholars studied, including Aristotle, until several centuries later when it ceased to exist in the sixth century A.D. Apart from the influence that Socrates had on Plato, as far as his political philosophy is concerned, Plato was also influenced deeply by the writings of **Heraclitus**, the **Pythagoreans,** and the **Eleats.**

Stoa of Attalus, reconstructed

Altogether he made three trips to Italy[3]. During his first trip he visited Dionysius, the Tyrant of Syracuse, and when he insisted that a good ruler must also be virtuous, Dionyssius considered this admonition an insult, had him arrested and condemned him--but finally spared his life, and sold him as a slave. During ancient times anyone could become a slave, either as a prisoner of war or because of some unfortunate event in his life, resulting in disgrace or loss of fortune. But a slave could pay the ransom or have someone else pay for him and gain his independence. **Aesop,** for example, was a slave who bought back his freedom. Plato was brought to Salamis by his owner, who put him up for sale, and he was bought by a friend from Cyrene; his friends from Athens paid the ransom and secured his freedom. Dionysius regretted causing him such misfortune and wrote to Plato while he was in Athens, begging for forgiveness. Plato wrote back: **"I do not have the leisure to keep Dionysius in my mind."**

Plato also exhibited dedication to friends and devotion to the laws of the land and to the institutions of Athenian democracy, even though he had some doubts as to the efficacy of the institution as a political system. Once, when a general of the Athenian army was accused of neglect, no one wanted to represent him in court, but Plato stepped forward and decided to defend him. One

---

[3] See chapter 9 *"Laws," where* extensive discussion ensues about Plato's trips to Sicily.

day when Plato was walking up to the Acropolis, the accuser of the general met him on the way up; he stopped and told Plato: *"Plato, the hemlock of Socrates is waiting for you."* Plato replied: *"As I faced dangers when serving in the cause of my country, so I will face these dangers now in the cause of duty for a friend."* Plato never mentions his name in the dialogues--except in the case of

105. *Tl*   **Roman Agora, Athens**

Phaedo and the **Apology.** Aristotle was a devoted student in his early years of the Academy, and once remarked that Plato's dialogues are something between **prose and poetry;** on one occasion Plato was reading his dialogue, **Phaedo,** when the audience got up and left--but Aristotle stayed until the very end. When he died, Philip of Macedonia paid him honors at his funeral. He was buried at the Academy where he had spent most of his life in philosophical studies, and all the students joined in the funeral procession. He had many students at the time, including two female: **Lasthenia and Axiothea.**

Even though others have been credited for having used the dialectic method--such as Zeno from Elea and the Miletians--Plato is credited with its perfection, and for its establishment as an acceptable tool of research. **Dialectic** is the art of discourse by which we either refute or establish some proposition by means of questions and answers exchanged on the part of the persons involved. Plato's method of arriving at conclusions is the inductive method, using the dialectic approach, and adheres approximately to the following format:

My father is either other than or the same as your father. If then your father is other than my father, by being other than my father, he will not be my father. But if he is the same as my father, then by being the same as my father, he will be my father.

This is the kind of induction that proceeds by contradiction; and Plato used it not only to identify positive doctrines, but also for the purpose of refutation. Plato, next to Aristotle and Plutarch, was one of the most prolific writers of antiquity--at least as far as we know today, from what has been saved of the ancient texts.   There are quite a number of publications (**dialogues**) by Plato, whose authenticity is questioned by modern scholars. There are, however, 27 dialogues that are accepted as original works. Diogenes Laertius, who lived 500 years or more after Plato, presents the Platonic works in 9 tetralogies (groups of 4 dialogues dealing with related subjects), even though he himself mentions that some of the works and almost all of his 13 epistles (letters) were considered, even then, as suspicious in origin. We present the titles of the dialogues below as published by Diogenes Laertius c. 250 A.D.:

1st Tetralogy:	EUTHYPHRO--On Reverence. APOLOGY-- On Life After Death. CRITO--On the Laws. PHAEDO--On the Soul and Ethics.
2nd Tetralogy:	CRATYLUS--On Correctness of Names. THAEAETETUS--On Knowledge. SOPHIST-- On Being. POLITICOS--On Political Systems.
3rd Tetralogy:	PARMENIDES--On the Theory of "Ideas." PHILEBUS--On Pleasure. SYMPOSIUM--On Love. PHAEDRUS--On Platonic and Erotic Love.
4th Tetralogy:	ALCIBIADES--On the Nature of a Good Ruler. ALCIBIADES II--On Prayer. HIPPARCHUS--On the Love of Gain. THE RIVALS--On Philosophy.
5th Tetralogy:	THEAGES--On Philosophy. CHARMIDES--On Temperance. LAHES--On Courage. LYSIS--On Friendship.
6th Tetralogy:	EUTHEDEMUS--On Eristic Dialectic. PROTAGORAS--On Sophists. GORGIAS--On Rhetoric and Virtue. MENO--On Virtue and Theory of Recollection..
7th Tetralogy:	HIPPIAS MAJOR--On Beauty.

HIPPIAS MINOR--On Falsehood.
ION--On the Iliad.
MENEXENUS--On the Funeral Oration

8th Tetralogy: CLITOPHON--On Introduction.
REPUBLIC--On Ideal Political   System
CRITIAS--On the Atlantis.
TIMAEUS--On the Creation of the World.

9th Tetralogy: MINOS--On Law.
LAWS--On Political Systems.
EPINOMIS--On Philosophy versus Science.
EPISTLES--(13 in total)

In reference to the physical sciences, Plato presented a **"Theory of Creation"** of the universe by God; similar to that of the **Christian Genesis.** He defines "God" and "Matter" as the

*D*o*t*ic *style.*

Superpowers that dominate the physical world. He does not mean the Olympic gods and does not mention them by name; but he refers simply to "God" and defines "Matter" as: "Air, Water, Earth and Fire." He considered the Earth as the center of the universe--with the sun, moon, and the planets revolving around it--which is, of course, the apparent movement of the heavenly bodies. On "Good" and "Evil," he maintained that one should aspire to unite with God, but that virtue is in itself sufficient for happiness; although it needs, in addition, as instruments to use: ***Intrinsic advantages***, *such as: health, strength, and sound senses; and* ***Extrinsic advantages,*** *such as: wealth, good birth, and reputation.* He maintained, however, that: *"The wise man should be no less happy, even if he is without these things."* He lectured that one should partake in public affairs, marry, and refrain from breaking societal laws.   He believed that God takes note of human life and that He is a supernatural being. He was the first to define **"Good"** (Αγαθον) as that which is: *Praiseworthy, Useful, Proper,* and *Becoming.* These characteristics are interwoven with that which is consistent and in harmony with Nature.

94

HIS WORK   At the time of the death of Socrates in 399 B.C., Plato was 28 years old. He was growing up in an environment which was dominated by the Sophist principle that: **nothing exists; and nothing can be learned**. He did not accept this negative view of knowledge, but defended "real" knowledge and suggested two conditions necessary to attain it: (1) The unchanging nature of the subject for which knowledge was sought; and (2) The mind must have a clear conception and understanding of the subject. At the same time, the Heraclitean principle: **"Everything is in a Continuous Flux,"** was advocated by his contemporary **Kratylus,** which made it difficult to substantiate his points; since Kratylus believed that it is impossible to have a permanent grasp of things that continuously change. This principle--that nothing is stationary--embraced by the Sophists in order to deny the reality and validity of knowledge, was rejected by Plato--who believed that values, ethics, and morality are *Constants* in society. He felt compelled to find non-sensory **tenets** which could be of a permanent nature and accessible to the mind. These were the values and principles: *temperance, justice, bravery, prudence, compassion, and other virtues,* that Socrates was interested in defining in order to convince his audience of their permanent validity.

The Youth of Kythera

Plato believed that nothing can be more permanent than ideal *Justice, Beauty,* and *Compassion;* and therefore he attempted to focus on knowledge of these and find permanent valid truth through scientific, rigorous thinking. He believed that these principles provide the controlling patterns that lie behind the changing face of the visible world: the world of the senses, whose knowledge is possible. This point constitutes a departure of the Platonic-Socratic philosophy from the points of view of his contemporaries and previous theorists; he named these tenets **"Ideas" or "Forms":** the unchanging parts of a structure of reality. Plato was an idealist who believed that things have a substance beyond their apparent sensible substance, and felt that this concept applied not only in the area of ethics and morality, but also in the realm of Nature. If, for example, we can develop a formula to determine a relationship, as the Pythagoreans believed, then this can be viewed as the objective of his research. This concept is similar to that of a "parameter" that statisticians refer to when making estimations of population means, variances, ratios etc. Plato approached reality, in degrees, and attempted to discover why people form opinions on things and have varied perceptions of reality. Opinions are shaped by sensory perceptions and can be flawed by contradictions and illusions. People may be pressured to change their mind, and even if their opinions are correct: they cannot be proved. Knowledge, on the other hand, is the result of reasoning: it can be proved, demonstrated, and substantiated by data. Knowledge is not only based on sensory perception, but results from the mind's direct contact with the *Ultimate Reality or "Ideas."* According to Plato, the human being is a spirit that has an Immortal Soul. In **Phaedo** he extensively discusses the "concept" of the Soul. His philosophy can be summarized in three theories: (1) The "**Theory of Ideas or Forms**;" (2) The "**Theory of the Soul**;" and (3) The "**Theory of Recollection**." In the following three chapters the essence of these three theories is discussed, and a summary is given of those dialogues which are considered genuine.

CHAPTER 7

THE PLATONIC WORKS
(Theory of Ideas and the Soul)

> "Truth, O stranger, is a fair and durable
> thing. But it is a thing of which it is hard to
> persuade men."
>
> **Plato**

PLATO'S THEORY OF IDEAS OR FORMS (Ειδη).

The "**Theory of Ideas**" gives us a hint of how deeply the Eleatic philosophy influenced Plato. The Eleats asserted that the senses can deceive, and that it is only the intellect that can identify the true nature of visible or invisible entities. They also believed that beyond our sensory perceptions there exists another world; a metaphysical, highly transcendental world that can be conceived only through our mind and imagination. Therefore, reality, or truth, is an elusive concept because what is perceived as reality by one may differ from another's interpretation; distortions occur because one sees only images, or shadows of reality. Plato expounds on this concept by claiming that indeed any sensory or physical entity that we recognize is but a shadow of the true such entity; and there exists an ultimate reality--an ultimate truth--and named it "**IDEA**" or Form (Ειδος). This "**IDEA**" truly represents these entities, but it is beyond our sensory perceptions. He recognizes that "**IDEAS**" exist not only of the physical entities, but of such abstract concepts as justice, friendship, bravery, etc., as well. Another important influence on Plato was probably the Ephesians' doctrine that the world is in a continuous flux. Plato could not accept, however, that this doctrine could be applicable to moral and ethical values. He believed that these values are *constant*, as are Universal Truths, and not in continuous flux. But he endorsed the Eleatic premise that the "mind" plays an important role in comprehending our environment, social or physical, and it is the mind, not the senses, that can understand the properties of the powers involved in any evolutionary process. The **IDEAS** are independent of the sensory world, have their own substance, exist by themselves, and constitute the *Ultimate Truth--Ultimate Perfection, True Reality*--and can be recognized by our intellect only. If we analyze, for example, the abstract concept "justice," we may find that there are many different definitions of justice; one may be right and another wrong, and vice versa; or all may be wrong--but all cannot be right. The **IDEA** of justice in this case would be the true definition of justice, and may be elusive and difficult to obtain; as different people have dissimilar perceptions of the real nature of justice. Therefore, the **IDEA** can be discovered and identified only through intensive analysis, research, and intellectual determination. To arrive at the **IDEA** of justice, for example, as Plato does in the first book of **THE REPUBLIC**, one has to examine a number of alternative definitions in order to gain an understanding of the nature of the concept. The theory of

Ideas is essentially the means by which Plato encourages man to reach the ultimate reality, *the state of virtue.* This can be achieved by education and recognizing the difference between good and evil. If man strives to reach the Idea of "good," which can be seen as the goal and purpose of every human being, then he will reach a state of *happiness, benevolence and harmony.* Plato and Aristotle believed that a human being is born with certain talents and inclinations and noted also, from history and experience, that man is a wolf to his fellow man. Achieving these talents and inclinations is a struggle that requires great preparation and determination. Plato provides hope that reaching for the **Ideas** through education and learning is tantamount to reaching perfection-- which will ultimately bring harmony, peace, and happiness.   Plato uses a dramatic example, the allegory of the cave (See **The Republic, p. 136**), to illustrate the struggle and the goal of reaching the **"IDEA"** of **"Agathon"**--the ultimate **"Good."**. It is because of this kind of intellectual conception that Plato is considered a highly idealistic and, in some ways, a utopian philosopher. But the importance of this theory is that it promotes hope, an optimism to search for the truth--the Ultimate Reality--because in this way humans will improve their lives and achieve happiness by becoming perfect. *This promotes and values education and knowledge for the achievement of harmony, peace, and ultimately happiness--and not the material possessions and enrichment that the Sophists vigorously promoted.* The purpose of most Platonic dialogues is to define and reach the **IDEA** of the subject discussed; and in some cases he proves, or establishes through the dialectic method, *what the Truth (IDEA)* **is not**, *rather than what* **it is**. Plato encountered difficulties and opposition to this concept, and for a time the Academy was split over it. **Aristotle**, an important member of the Academy, broke off relations with Plato in 354 B.C., due to this controversy, and left the Academy for **Assos,** in Asia Minor, soon thereafter.

PLATO'S THEORY OF THE SOUL

The island of Lefkada

Philosophers through the centuries have always been interested in providing answers, among other things, to the pressing questions about man as a human being and as an entity of the society--regarding his/her origin, life, purpose, and whereabouts after death. These, of course, are perennial questions that still today occupy scholars and even the average man as age progresses; and no one can say with certainty what really happens to the human being after death or what was his nature before birth. Perhaps, all religions exist for the purpose of answering this question that science and speculation cannot. We have been successful in deciphering a number of Nature's secrets, and in the process we have achieved some understanding of how the physical world works. In spite of the breakthroughs in interpreting the mechanics of Nature, however, we still do not know quite a number of things. But, for today, as far as man's whereabouts after death, perhaps for those who do not accept religious dogma, the issue may be a matter of agnosticism--and thus may not present an urgent problem or bring obstacles to everyday life. These individuals probably are more concerned with pressing demands of the present, and struggling to meet the needs for survival--rather than philosophically attempting to resolve such metaphysical questions--for which there is no concrete scientific answer. But if one goes back in time, before the Christian era, it is apparent that people were vitally concerned with these issues, because for most people the impact of religion was significant. Thus, the matter of whether man is **matter (Yλη)** or **spirit**, and whether the human being has a soul, has concerned all philosophers and schools of philosophy throughout the ages. In different ways, for those who postulated that man has a soul, the establishment of a theory of its whereabouts after death becomes *a* <u>**sine qua non**</u> condition. The body obviously decomposes and returns to Earth in its basic elements, but the question of the existence of the soul and its outcome after death has been a matter of concern addressed by all thinkers and philosophers; and various speculations have been offered which were usually revised later. Before we proceed with this subject further, and explore Plato's view on the topic, it might be of interest to briefly examine the convictions and beliefs of previous thinkers on the matter of the *Soul of Man.*

1. If we study **Homer's** works (**The Iliad** and **The Odyssey**), we note that the soul is something ethereal, similar to the breath, and manifests itself through breathing; it resides inside the body, in the mind, where it derives all its strength and energy. At death it exits the body either through a wound (in case of violent death) or the mouth, and becomes an **image (Oπτασια)** of the body--resembling smoke or shadow--that cannot be seen or touched by mortals. After death the soul travels to Hades where it is judged on merit, and the souls of the **"Good" (Aγαθοι)** are rewarded; while the souls of the **"Evil" (Κακοι)** are punished.

2. The **Ionic philosophers (The Miletians)**, who were more concerned with the physical world and less with the metaphysical, considered the soul to be the power that produced life and constitutes *life itself.* They believed that the soul is the strength that moves and inspires the body, and is not something complete and self-contained--but rather another form of matter; and therefore: a *Non-Thinking Power.* If the body dies; so does the soul. These philosophers were not as interested in examining the **"Afterlife."**

3. According to the **Ephesian philosophers**, exemplified mostly by **Heraclitus**, there is no difference between soul and body--or life and death; instead, a continuous flowing condition exists from one state to another. This was an explanation of the concept of the soul on the basis of the archetypes of this school, whose tenet was that: everything is in a **flux**, and that this should be true of the soul and the body as well.

4. The **Eleatic philosophers (Xenophanes, Parmenides, and Zeno)** believed that there is a soul and that it has its own *substance*, but only in a state of energy, which is the mixing of material elements. These philosophers attempted to explain the conventional notion of the soul during their time, by incorporating metaphysical elements into the interpretation. For example: they believed that the *body consists of two parts--the light (good) and dark (evil)--and that the mind associates with the soul and depends on the two parts.* The intellectual power is affected by the existence of these two elements.

5. The **Atomic philosophers (Leucippus** and **Democritus)** believed that the principle components of the world consist of atoms and void. The atomic substances are infinite in multitude, and when they join together they create **"birth;"** but when they separate they create **"destruction."** The soul consists of small atoms that are precious, and direct the movement and life of the body. It is only through the mind that we can discover the truth of

The Panathenaic Procession, South Frieze, Parthenon

"being;" because the senses deceive. The separation of atoms from the body and the soul results in **death**; therefore, the soul has a limited life.

6. Anaxagoras believed that at the beginning there were infinite particles--divisible and non-homogeneous--which were placed in order by non-material "Mind" (the ultimate strength and power): self-contained, intellectual, and rational. The soul exists in the form of the mind; and when death comes the soul is separated from the body, and perishes with it.

7. The Pythagoreans interpreted the soul on the basis of their philosophy that everything could be explained by numbers. Thus, the soul is harmony, as part of a mathematical function of bodily elements, and after the body dies the soul returns to life in reincarnation. According to this group of thinkers, the soul is in a perfect equilibrium; the connecting link between the material part of the body and the transcendental nature of the human being. The element of reincarnation of the soul that the Pythagoreans postulated influenced Plato considerably.

Plato believed that the human being is a spirit and has a soul. The soul incarnates into the body upon birth and survives throughout life; and upon death separates from the body. After judgment it reincarnates into another human being--in a continuous cycle. The soul pre-exists and is *immortal*. The **"Theory of Ideas"** and the concept of the "soul" are interrelated in the Platonic philosophical system. Plato asserts that the soul has knowledge of the **"Ideas"** or "**Truths,**" and therefore the human being via his/her soul is a repository of knowledge through the **IDEAS**. It is through the soul that the human being can communicate with the "**IDEAS**" and thus strive toward "**Agathon**" (**Good**). This soul is of a *tri-partite* nature*: (1) The Logical (Λογιστικον); (2) The Sensual (Επιθυμιτικον); and (3) The Intellectual (Θυμοειδες).* There is strife between the Sensual and the other two parts of the soul; as the sensual part, affected by the senses, directs it toward temptations and corruption. It is the successful outcome of this conflict that leads the soul, upon death of the body, to rewards and a higher level of reincarnation: depending upon the moral and ethical state of the individual during his life. In the dialogue **Phaedrus** (#6 in this Chapter), Plato describes the *nine[1] levels of human professions and activities in which the soul reincarnates, grading them from the lowest-- a tyrant--to the highest--a philosopher.* The purpose of the soul then is to thwart the corrupt urgings of the senses in order to achieve a virtuous and harmonious life, and thus achieve higher reincarnation levels when it separates from the body and is judged by the *Super Soul*. In the same dialogue Plato describes the soul as a chariot driven by two horses--the one representing the *Sensual*--and the other the *Intellectual* component of the Soul; the Charioteer, representing the Logical part. The soul, being knowledgeable of the **IDEAS,** plays an important role in all of the Platonic works, as it provides the means for man--*by way of recollection*--to reach knowledge and "perfection": the third doctrine of the Platonic philosophy.

THE THEORY OF RECOLLECTION.

Plato emphasized the principle of self-education, because he believed that since man's soul is knowledgeable of the **IDEAS**, and the **IDEAS** are knowledge, it behooves man to ask questions of himself and inquire of what he does not know--thus "**recollecting**" knowledge. It is this concept that gives birth to the "**Theory of Recollection.**" Recollecting, then, means *obtaining knowledge from oneself*--either by asking questions or being questioned on matters that one does not know. Thus, Plato does not say "learning"--but rather "recollecting"--and proposes that through the process of intensive question and answer format, what we would call "brainstorming," knowledge can be acquired. In the dialogue "**Meno**" (Chapter 8), Plato carries out an experiment on the *Doctrine of Recollection* by having Socrates pose questions to a young servant relating to a problem of geometry. He has a youngster, with no prior education on geometry, "learn"-- through questions and answers--that if you draw a square based on the diagonal of a given square, you obtain a new square which is double in area of the original. In addition to "proving" the **Theory of Recollection** by this experiment, Plato also establishes the principle of the *pre-existence of the soul.*

In this and the next two chapters, a summary is given of those dialogues which are

---

[1] The nine levels of reincarnation are: a philosopher; a musician or an artist; a prudent king; a political leader; an economist or financier; a hard working gymnast or medical doctor; a soothsayer or priest; a poet; a worker or a farmer; a Sophist or attorney; and lastly--a tyrant.

considered genuine Platonic works. These dialogues are, in reality, Plato's effort to reach the truth and the underlying **"idea"** of the various principles that each dialogue addresses. It is not possible to cover, in such a short space, the full depth and understanding of these dialogues. Instead, a full outline is presented, and some of the points made by the individuals involved in the dialectic process are given. If one is interested in studying, in depth, the deeper meaning and salient points of these dialogues, there are several references in the bibliography that suggest pertinent reading material.[2]

---

[2] A very interesting and detailed analysis of the Platonic dialogues can be found in the book by **A.E. Taylor, Plato, the Man and His Work.** (See reference 13).

THE PLATONIC DIALOGUES

1. CRITO

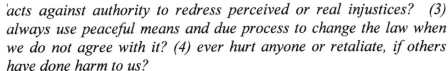

«Μητρος τε και πατρος τε και των αλλων προγονων
απαντων τιμιωτερον εστιν η πατρις και σεμνοτερον»[3]

Plato

Crito was a student and friend of Socrates. After Socrates' trial in 399 B.C., and while he was still in jail awaiting execution, several of Crito's friends decided to persuade him to escape and avoid certain death. The place that Crito chose for Socrates to go was **Thessaly**, where he had friends and would be welcome. This dialogue describes the discussion that took place at the jail, where Crito visits Socrates and attempts to persuade him to flee. The basic philosophical questions raised during this discussion are: *Should we (1) be concerned with the opinion of the majority on matters of justice, ethics, and morality? (2) ever disobey the law and commit violent acts against authority to redress perceived or real injustices? (3) always use peaceful means and due process to change the law when we do not agree with it? (4) ever hurt anyone or retaliate, if others have done harm to us?*

Herodotus

The dialogue begins when Crito, concerned and mindful of the predicament of his teacher and friend, enters the jail at daybreak and wakes Socrates, who is in deep sleep. He harbored love for him, as well as mixed feelings of enthusiasm and agony, at the prospect of this visit. **Crito** announces to **Socrates** that he has bad and good news. The bad news is that the ship that left for **Delos** the day before his trial, to offer supplications to **Apollo**, was seen at Sounion and expected to arrive at Piraeus the next day. During the absence of the ship from Piraeus no executions were to be carried out--according to Athenian custom and the law--and that was why the execution did not take place immediately after the trial. The ship is arriving tomorrow, he tells him; and therefore, according to the law, you must die the day after. Crito felt all along that it was a great injustice for such a brilliant man to die so undeservedly and so ingloriously. Socrates was not perturbed at all by the bad news. He remained calm and contented, as if nothing were wrong, and not as though the next day he would have to take the hemlock and die. The good news that Crito had was related to a plan that he and

---

[3] The Motherland is more honorable and venerable than the mother, the father, and all other ancestors.

some friends had devised to save him. He tells him that they have decided to bribe the jail warden, who would not interfere with his escape. He points out to Socrates that he and his friends are agonizing over the thought that the public will believe that they abandoned him--at the time when he needed them most--for love of money. They were fearful of facing the general public who would consider them ungrateful for abandoning him to die; rather than risking themselves and sacrificing their wealth to save him. What then, would be their position in the society? They would be ridiculed and censured; so they had decided to lead him out safely because they thought that that was their duty.

Socrates disagrees with **Crito** and reacts strongly to the proposal of escaping. He raises

Temple of Zeus, Sounion

the question: W*hy should they be concerned with public opinion when principles of justice, morality, and ethics are at stake.* **Crito** does not want to hear this and is determined to save him from an unjust death. He insists that he and the others are willing to risk their lives and spend whatever money is necessary to help him escape to **Thessaly**. Crito also has some other important points to argue. He reminds Socrates that his three young sons need his support and protection, and feels that his refusal to save himself is irrational, arrogant, self-serving, and detrimental to their welfare. *But Socrates counters that he cannot reject the principles that he advocated and preached all his life: Does that mean that he should abandon these principles now and escape death, for fear of what the public would say? There are opinions that we must respect--and there are those that we do not have to abide by.* He argues that the opinion of the experts is superior to that of the multitude-- which is not an expert. Socrates emphasizes injustices committed by the multitude in the democratic decision process. He points out that in ancient Athens three important men were exiled: **Themistocles, Miltiades, and Aristides;** and at times *incompetent and corrupt men were elected to positions of public responsibility*. He asks what the multitude knows about obeying the laws. Should we ask their opinion when we plan to break the laws? If we seek advice from the experts when it concerns matters of health, why should we not ask the experts, not the multitude, when it concerns matters pertaining to justice, morals, ethics, and the tranquility of our souls? When it comes to distinguishing **right** from **wrong**, this is not a question for the crowd, but for those who can discern the difference. Sometimes the opinion of the majority can cause harm and death; and the important point is: not *simple living* but *virtuous living*. For Socrates, then, it is not a question of whether he should be concerned with the opinion of the multitude-- but rather whether it is right to escape from prison by unlawful means.

Socrates now states an important tenet of his philosophy: *Should one commit an unjust act and hurt others (metaphorically--the Law), even if others have hurt him?* This is equivalent to Christianity's **"turn the other cheek,"** and this principle was not consistent with the conventional wisdom of the time. Compare this with the prevailing philosophy of the Sophists on this matter, as well as previous civilizations, which advocated **"An eye for an eye and a tooth for a tooth."** Socrates argues that if escaping is a just act, then he *should* escape; but if this is an unjust act--then *by no means should* he escape. He also emphatically stresses *should* versus *should not,* and adds that one must never allow himself to commit an unjust act to seek revenge, even if he has been hurt; therefore, he must not escape because escaping is an unjust act. The point that the court system hurt him does not alter the assertion, because he cannot prove that the court action is erroneous. The court is a legitimate instrument of the State and rendered a decision after it heard from the Defense and the Prosecution. To Socrates, the decision of the court was a legitimate act following a traditionally instituted due process that all Athenians had accepted--including himself. The trial was conducted properly and he was given all means to defend himself. To dramatize this Plato introduces the *Laws* metaphorically, asking Socrates to respond as to why he intends to violate them by escaping: *How am I to respond to this accusation that I abandoned all the principles that I espoused all my life concerning justice, obeying the laws, and upholding virtue and morality?* The following is a passage from **CRITO** in which Socrates responds to the "Laws."

.............*"Socrates: but let us suppose **Crito** that the Laws might ask: Is it not the agreement that we reached **Socrates**, that you should stay obedient to the decisions of the courts, whichever those might be?' And the Laws further might say: Tell us; what is your complaint against us and against your city that you plan to hurt us? Did we not give you first life, as because, thanks to us your father married your mother, and you came into this world? Do you have any complaint against those of us who provide for the marriages, that we might not be right?*

Socrates: Of course I would have said that I have nothing against the Laws.
Laws: Perhaps you have some complaint against those of us who provide for the upbringing and education of the youth--according to which you were educated. The laws appropriate in this case have directed your father to educate you properly in music and gymnastics and other subjects.
Socrates: I should have said that they have done well.
Laws: It appears, then, that through us you were born, brought up, and were educated. Would you not say, then, that you and your ancestors are ours; our children; our servants? Do you really mean to say that you have equal rights with us and that it is correct for you to hurt us in return? Of course you do know that you do not have equal rights in the case of your father, or if you have one, in the case of your employer. And that you would not do to them what they would do to you; as for example, if they scolded you, to scold them in return; and if they punished you, to punish them in return. But as far as your city is

concerned and its laws, it seems you are of the opinion that if the courts decided to punish you, because they found it to be right, that you should try as much as it is in you power to hurt the laws and your city, taking revenge?

And you will insist that you did it because it was right; you, who always fought for justice and prudence? Or are you really such a wise man that it has escaped you, the fact that your city is superior to everything else, and including your father and mother and all of your ancestors; and it is the most precious thing you have.

Socrates: *Tell me Crito, what are we going to answer to all these. Are we going to say that the Laws tell the truth, or not?*

Crito: *I think we should.*
Socrates: *Then I think the Laws would further say: Watch out Socrates, if you think that we are telling the truth, then you are committing a crime against us, if you plan on doing what you are thinking of doing.*
Laws: *We brought you into this world, we raised you and educated you, and we gave you and all others like you, the means available for growth and prosperity. We had warned you and any other Athenian who reached your age to become a citizen and learn the customs and the laws of the city, and if you did not like us, to take all your property and go elsewhere. No one of us prohibits any one of you, if you are unhappy with us or the city, from leaving and going to any of our colonies of your choice.*
If any one of you, however, decided to stay here after he has seen how we resolve our differences, and how we administer the affairs of the city, then we say that this person has practically undertaken responsibilities toward us and ought to carry out whatever he is ordered. We allow our citizens the choice: **Either persuade us with logical and peaceful means that we are unjust, so as to change, or obey our commands. You, Socrates, seem to be doing neither"**...............

The principle of civil disobedience by peaceful means is most vigorously enunciated by Plato in this passage of the dialogue.

2. APOLOGIA (ΑΠΟΛΟΓΙΑ)

«Σοφοκλης Σοφος, Ευριπιδης Σοφωτερος
Ανδρων Απαντων Σοκρατης Σοφωτατος»
Delphic Oracle[4]

In the year 399 B.C., **Socrates** drank the hemlock and died in Athens at the age of 70. The accusation that was leveled at him by **Anytus, Melitus, and Lykon**, representing respectively: *the business establishment; the poets; and the Sophist intellectual elite,* **was that he did not believe in the gods of the city, was introducing other deities, and corrupting the youth.** Besides the adverse feelings these groups had against Socrates--who was indeed antagonizing them all, making them look foolish and inept in public, there were political reasons, as well, that led to his death. In the year 404 B.C., the military collapse of Athens after a 30-year war with Sparta, the *Peloponnesian War,* brought tyranny to Athens after over 100 years of democratic rule. **Critias,** one of the protagonists of the tyranny that toppled

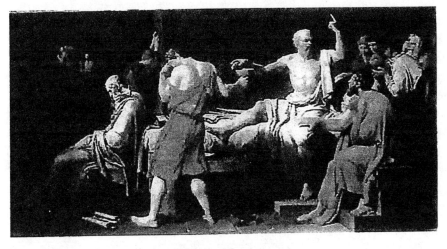

Socrates takes the hemlock

the democratic system, was a friend, relative, and student of Socrates. Thus, when the Democrats returned to power soon thereafter, they were looking for scapegoats to retaliate for the dictatorship and unfortunate turn of events that shook the city-state of Athens and caused considerable damage and death to thousands of people. Also, **Socrates** was not highly enamored with the democratic process of the Athenian democracy, and on many occasions he criticized the decision process in the Assembly, where demagogues would sway public opinion. A trial was held early in 399 B.C., and after the accusers presented their points, Socrates stood up to defend himself and, according to Plato, he spoke thus:

"…………*Some would say: Aren't you ashamed, Socrates, that by your lifestyle you are leading yourself to an early death? I would say to them that they are wrong. A man who is*

---

[4] Sophocles is wise; Euripides is wiser; but of all men living, Socrates is the wisest.

*"good" in all aspects of his life must not be afraid of death. He simply must choose between doing good or doing evil. Otherwise, those heroes who fell under the walls of Troy would not have been worth much; as for example, the son of **Thetis (Achilles)** who challenged death to preserve his honor. When he was faced with the dilemma of killing Hector or facing infamy, his goddess-mother told him that if he killed Hector the same fate would befall him. He replied: "It is better for me to die, after having revenged my friend **Patroclus**, rather than become the ridicule of the world." In whatever position one is placed in life, either by his own free will or by his superiors, he should remain steadfast at the time of danger. He must not be afraid, but he should be concerned with disgrace. It seems strange to me, Oh men of Athens, that today I run the risk of being sentenced to death, while earlier when I served in the army in **Potidea, Amphipolis, and Delium**, I obeyed the generals of the city and stood fast where they placed me in the battlefield, facing danger and death along with all others. It would be awkward if, today, I abandon my position, due to the fear of death or any other fear. I believe God placed me here to fulfill my philosophical duty to investigate you and myself. The fear of death seems logical, but it may not be so, because it presupposes that we know the unknown. No one knows whether death, which all think is the worst of evil, might be—the Greatest of Good. Don't you think it is arrogant of man to assume that he knows something, which in reality he does not? And, in this respect, I think that I differ from other people, even though it may look less wise of me. I do not know anything about the whereabouts of man after death, and I do not pretend that I do. But I do know that injustice and disobedience toward someone superior, either a god or a man, is something evil and dishonorable; and I will not be afraid of, nor will I attempt to avoid something, which could be better--as opposed to something that it is surely evil."*

Socrates now presents his basic beliefs on justice and virtue and defends himself from the accusation that he was corrupting the youth.

*"..... Men of Athens, I honor and I love you! But I prefer to obey God, rather than to obey you. And as long as I have life and strength I will not cease to teach philosophy and ask anyone that I may meet, in my own way: You, citizen of this great city of Athens, aren't you ashamed of accumulating wealth, honors, and glory, and yet be little interested in truth and wisdom and the betterment of your soul? I say that money does not produce virtue, but as it is true for any other **"good"**--be it private or public, tangible or intangible--benefits come from virtue; this is my philosophy, and if learning of this corrupts the youth, then I must be a very evil person."*

At this time a vote was taken and the jurors found him guilty by a small margin. According to the law, he was asked to propose an alternative punishment, other than the one that his accusers entered in the indictment.

"........ The law proposes death as my punishment. You ask me, as an alternative, to propose another form of punishment for myself. Oh Athenians, what can I propose as punishment for myself, since all my life I have sought to find virtue and wisdom and put these concerns above my personal interest? Certainly, such a man deserves some reward; what would such a reward be for a poor man who is your benefactor and who tries to find the time to teach you some

beneficial things? I believe that such a man should have all his living expenses taken care of by the State now and in the future. He deserves such a reward far more than the awards accorded to the winners in the Olympic Games--who have won in the chariot races. I am impoverished and these Olympic winners are well off. Such men give you a fleeting pleasure--while I give you eternal reality".

Socrates further argues that any alternative punishment (jail or exile) is not any better than death.

*"......Do you think that I say these things because I fear the capital punishment that **Meletus** proposes? Since I do not know whether death is an evil or a good thing, why should I propose a punishment which would definitely be bad? Should I propose imprisonment? Why should I spend my life in prison and become a slave of the authorities? Should I propose a fine and imprisonment until it is paid? This is the same thing because I am poor and cannot pay the fine. Suppose that I propose exile, and I suspect that this would please you. But then it would be illogical on my part; for how would it be possible for one to believe that since you, my fellow citizens, cannot tolerate my teachings and find them dangerous and offensive and want to get rid of me, that other people and strangers will tolerate me. **What kind of life would there be for me, at this age, wandering from city to city, changing venue of exile and banished everywhere?** ....And then you would say: Socrates, can you keep your mouth shut and go to another city where no one will bother you if you do not speak out? It is very difficult to explain to you that, for me, the effort to search and understand others and myself is the most rewarding pursuit; otherwise, life would be meaningless. You should know, Oh men of Athens, that had you not become so impatient to get rid of me, since I am old and approaching death now, you would have avoided embarrassment and a bad name from your political opponents for having killed Socrates--an innocent and wise man. They will refer to me as a wise man, even though I am not; but they will say so because they will want to discredit you. And I can foretell that immediately after my execution-- you, my killers--will suffer greater punishment than the one imposed on me now."*

At this time another vote was taken, and the margin against Socrates was increased. He was sentenced to die by taking the hemlock.

*"..........Let us now consider this in a different way. There is a serious reason to hope that death, after all, is not a bad thing; because only one of two things regarding death can be true: Either death is a state which can be construed as nothing, implying complete absence of the senses; or, as most people believe--a passing of the soul from this world to another. Let us assume that the first condition is true--and that there is no consciousness--and that it resembles sleep without dreams. Then death will be a beautiful state because if we compare our nights without dreams with the other days and nights, even the greatest king will admit that those were his best moments of life. If death resembles that, then it constitutes something pleasant, because eternity will be—but just a night. But if death is a journey to another world, what a wonderful thing, my friends and judges, would that be. When the traveler will reach the "other world" he will rid himself of worldly judges and meet the real judges who judge down there, such as: **Minus, Rodamanthus, Aeacus, Triptolemos,** and the other sons of God who were just in their lives.*

*Wouldn't that be a great pleasure, for someone to converse with **Orpheus, Musaius, Hesiod, Homer**? I personally will be very pleased to have an exchange with **Palamedes, Ajax,** and all those other ancient heroes whose deaths resulted from an unjust decision in this world. Perhaps, then, I will continue with my research to distinguish between real and fraudulent knowledge. What a delightful experience that would be, for one to see and converse with the leaders of the great expedition to Troy, such as: **Odysseus, Sisyphus**, and countless other men and women. What a wonderful thing it would be to ask questions; in that world they certainly do not kill people because they ask questions. Also, besides the fact that there these men are happy, as they say; they are also immortal."*

And closes his defense by stating his conviction that nothing wrong can happen to a virtuous man.

*"............I want to assure you that nothing bad can befall a just and honest man, while alive or dead...**The time to depart has come and each one of us will follow his path--you to live and I to die. Only God knows which path is better**."*[5]

---

5 Translation by the author.

3. EUTHYPHRO (ΕΥΘΥΦΡΩΝ)

Οταν μεν ημεις ωμεν, ο θανατος ου παρεστιν´
Οταν δ' ο θανατος παρη, τοθ' ημεις ουκ εσμεν.[6]
Epicurus

The system of polytheism practiced by ancient civilizations and cultures, with perhaps the only exception the Hebrews, was prevalent in ancient Greece. Beginning with Pharecydes--7th century B.C.--and followed by Xenophanes--6th century B.C.--this religious practice started

Zeus

eroding, at least in the minds of early intellectuals and philosophers. There is no question that Socrates and Plato had second thoughts about polytheism, and particularly the **"quid pro quo"** relationship that existed between gods and humans: It would be sufficient to make the right offerings, sacrifices, and supplications to the gods, and in return reap benefits and favors from them. They could not accept this relationship between gods and humans that the poets and epic writers presented in the theaters and in their literary works. It was precisely this view that caused Melitus to state in his affidavit for the indictment of Socrates: **"Socrates does not believe in the gods of the city and introduces new gods."** Note also that in the **APOLOGIA** there is no defense that Melitus' accusation was erroneous. In this dialogue Plato suggests disillusionment by criticizing the religious practices of the Athenians concerning offerings, sacrifices, prayers, and supplications in their efforts to dispose the gods in their favor. Also, in this dialogue Plato addresses the impact that the fear of God had on humans. Euthyphro was a soothsayer who claimed knowledge of coming events and peoples' future. One day Euthyphro meets Socrates at the **Courthouse (Vassilios Stoa)** and inquires about his presence there, for it seemed to him that it was a "most unusual event." Socrates responds that he is there because a fellow by the name of **Melitus** has filed a suit against him for criminal action. Euthyphro inquires as to the nature of the criminal accusation, and Socrates informs him that he has been accused of **"corrupting the youth; rejecting the gods of the city; and introducing new deities."** Euthyphro is surprised with the news and thinks that this is a foolish accusation, adding that the courts will reject such a frivolous suit. He further points out that Melitus brought the accusation against him for introducing new deities, most likely because of the **"Daemonion," the Inner Voice,** that

---

[6] When we are, death has not come; when death has come, we are not.

Socrates often mentioned and claimed to be guided by. Socrates is concerned, however, that this frivolous accusation has deeper roots and will bring him trouble. He then asks Euthyphro his reason for being there, and whether he is a plaintiff or a defendant. He replies that he is a plaintiff and has come to the "Vassilios Stoa" because he wants to find out how to file a criminal action suit. Socrates asks whom he plans to sue, and Euthyphro responds: his father. He states that his father is responsible for the death of one of their workers in Naxos, where they have their farms. One worker, he continues, got drunk and entered into a quarrel with another, and during the fight that ensued, killed him. Euthyphro's father discovered the crime and arrested the killer, tied him with ropes, placed him into a pit, and went to seek advice on what to do. But by the time he returned, the man died in the pit; now Euthyphro is suing his father for negligence and irresponsibility--resulting in the death of the worker.

This is the dramatic part of the dialogue, and the beauty of this, and all other Platonic dialogues, is that they have a certain charm--in that while dealing with such significant topics, one also enjoys their simplicity and humanity. The discussion that follows between Socrates and Euthyphro addresses the questions: *What is right and proper in the eyes of the gods and accepted religious practices?* What really caused Euthyphro to seek punishment for his father? Was it that he was afraid that the gods would not forgive him if he knew of a crime and did nothing to redress it? He was also concerned that the perpetrator of the crime was his father, and felt that he had a filial responsibility for his safety and welfare. In this dialogue Plato illustrates the suffocating impact that the polytheistic religion of the times had on people. He felt that some of the qualities attributed to gods were nonsensical, as such attributes were more appropriate for humans than gods; therefore, some human acts were justified, even if they were not sanctioned by the gods, because the gods themselves engaged in such practices. Several attempts are made to define what **"Reverence"** (Ευσεβεια=**respect for God and God's laws**) **is,** and as in most Platonic works, the various definitions given (four in total) represent diverse views and constituencies; while somewhere one may find Plato's view on the subject--if there is one. In this case, however, it is difficult to find a clear definition of what «Ευσεβεια» is--according to Plato. But even if he does not provide a clear definition of what **"Reverence" is,** we can surmise what **it is not** by following Euthyphro's dilemma of having to sue his father because he is afraid of the gods. Socrates asks him why he feels compelled to sue, and he replies that it is against the will of the gods not to report a crime--because this will displease them. Socrates then asks whether this will displease one god or all, and proceeds to show that, in the writings of the poets, the gods were often divided and had taken positions on either side of a dispute: *"How can you be sure, Euthyphro, that you are doing the right thing, and that you may not be committing an impious act by displeasing some of the gods"?*

4. GORGIAS   (ΓΟΡΓΙΑΣ)

"Man is the measure of all things; of those existing that they exist, and those non-existing that they do not exist."
Gorgias

<u>Gorgias</u> is distinguished for its literary style, but also in addressing the major problems of the society at the time. These were identified with the influence that the Sophists exerted on society by their function as **speechwriters** and **language teachers,** and as the developers of **"rhetoric."** This may be interpreted by modern readers as the art of persuading, debating, and convincing opponents through literary manipulation of grammatical and syntactical tools of the language-- similar to what is covered in a speech course at a university today: But this is not the case. The term **"rhetoric"** involved politics, a new philosophy, ethics, and way of life; and therefore had a

Ptolemy Lagus

profound influence on daily life in the free and open society of democratic Athens in the middle of the 5th century B.C.   The philosophy of the Naturalists of previous centuries, and their research efforts into the physical world was abandoned and displaced by new slogans, concepts, and inquiry. The Sophists had a significant impact on the society by their approach and recognition of the *Natural Law* as superior to Societal or Human Law. They argued that the **strongest,** by virtue of being stronger--physically or otherwise--has the right to impose his views on matters of justice, politics, or ethics.

Also, the Sophists--with their new views on relativism and skepticism--had strong reservations on the validity of **"knowledge,"** and undermined tradition. Gorgias was a renowned teacher of rhetoric who believed that **"Nothing exists, and if it exists it is difficult to comprehend; and if comprehended would be difficult to communicate to others."** Emphasis on material possessions, pompous appearances, and colorful attire, was conveying false moral and ethical values and standards for the youth.

Five individuals participate in this dialogue: (1) **Socrates; (2) Gorgias** (the main representative of the Sophists**); (3) Polos,** a well-known thinker; (4) **Kallicles,** an unknown figure; and (5) **Cherephon,** a friend of Socrates who accompanies him to the house of **Kallias** where he introduces him to **Gorgias,** visiting from Sicily, and opens the discussion. You can subdivide the dialogue into four parts, each addressing a specific question pertaining to *ethics, virtue, and justice*. A charming prologue precedes referring to the fact that Socrates and Cherephon missed the main presentation by Gorgias--exhibiting his capabilities as an orator. The dialogue continues with (1) a discussion on rhetoric between Socrates and Gorgias examining whether it is a scientific discipline or art, and if it has any significant value for the average citizen; (2) a discussion between Polos and Socrates on the subject of virtue and how prominent it should be as an ethical standard; (3) an exchange between Socrates and Kallicles on the true meaning of justice; and (4) a Socratic monologue on the subject of life after death--closing with an epilogue encompassing the basic Socratic tenet: **"What is the best way for man to lead his life."**

The main point of **GORGIAS,** which includes the first two parts of the dialogue, is to identify and emphasize the basic differences between the prevailing philosophy of rhetoricians and grammar teachers (representing the materialistic point of view) and the Socratic vein of philosophy. The Sophists stressed the superiority of "**physical**" versus "**human**" law; and this had a significant impact on the conventional wisdom. The ethical values of justice and prudence are emphasized in Socratic philosophy; while the Sophists advocate subjectivism and the will of the strongest. Plato emphatically proposes that the Socratic standard of justice and virtue is superior to all other standards because it inspires Truth. Socrates states that for these values he is willing to die, and asks: **"Is it worth winning the world and losing your soul?"** This reference also appears in the Christian Bible (**Parable of the Rich**) and constitutes a fundamental tenet of Platonic philosophy. Of significance, is the part of the dialogue that presents the exchange between Kallicles and Socrates concerning justice. The subject of justice was paramount to Plato and he dealt with it extensively, as we have seen in **THE REPUBLIC.** Kallicles enters the discussion to reverse the damage inflicted on the Sophist philosophy during the discussion between Socrates, Polos, and Gorgias. While all other figures represented are real, Kallicles is a fictitious person that Plato presents as an aggressive supporter of the Sophists. Kallicles poses a question to Socrates: whether he is really serious in suggesting that human and societal law should precede physical law. He claims that Nature sets her standards uncontestedly--that the stronger should always prevail--because this is Nature's way. The stronger are better suited to exact justice and govern; while the weak invent laws to protect themselves. The strong should disregard such laws because they are in opposition to the natural order of things. Kallicles brings hosts of examples to buttress his point and to show that the strongest, historically, always prevail. His examples relate to matters of war and relationships among nations, in what we would call today--matters of "foreign conflict." He advises Socrates to abandon his naïve philosophy, which is good only for children, and get seriously involved with important matters of political life. Socrates responds, in his usual mode of feigning ignorance, and apologizes to Kallicles--saying that he does not have complete information on the subject and does not mean to undermine his wisdom. He asks Kallicles to enlighten him as to *who is strong and who is weak.* Is it possible, he asks, that the multitude should prevail over a single individual because it is stronger? For if it is so, are their laws then "good" and beneficial to both? Considerable discussion ensues at this point concerning who is "strong" and who is "weak," and the conclusion is that the "good" (Αγαθοι), virtuous, just, and brave are the stronger--regardless of physical strength--and their laws should prevail over all others. Kallicles continues to argue that the person who lives according to the physical law (of the jungle) is a happier person because he satisfies his needs immediately. Such people, Socrates counters, cannot be happy (Ευδαιμονες) governed by their instinctive desires and lust, and do not differ from animals, stones, or the dead--

because they are *devoid of emotions*. Socrates contends that pleasures constitute a part of life, and some may be beneficial, but others harmful. Man should be in a position to distinguish among them.

The entire line of discussion, in this part of "**GORGIAS,**" examines the difference between Materialism (Sophist philosophy) and Intellectualism (Socratic philosophy), which throughout the centuries has constituted the dividing line among thinkers: the essence and substance of two diverse ways of thinking and living. It is **Matter** that counts, say the Materialists; while the **Idea (the mind)** is more important, counter the Idealists. Marx's "**Historical Materialism**" springs out of this difference that Plato so eloquently presents. The Sophists embrace rhetoric, with the physical law as the foundation of their philosophy; while Socrates and Plato represent Idealism with virtue, justice, and prudence. The Socratics argue that for man to improve and achieve happiness, he must first **understand himself (Γνωθι Σ'Αυτον)** and his environment, and secure the harmony of his body (health) and soul through justice and virtue. The true leader should direct people toward the correct path and not toward hedonistic gratification and the **rule of the jungle**. Socrates, after Kallicles exits the discussion, emphasizes that only justice and virtue can be "good," and that "pleasure" is not always associated with "good" (Αγαθον). Plato points out that perhaps the Socratic philosophy cannot always prevent injustice, but it definitely avoids doing harm--vs. being done harm. He further states that the "**rhetoric**" of politicians of his time did not lead to virtue, citing that most politicians--who were not philosophers--did not improve the lives of the people. Socrates contends that, at the risk of being harmed, he will continue to direct people toward the path of justice and prudence. He does not fear death; because only the souls full of injustice fear death. He ends the discussion by recounting a myth: The souls of virtuous people will be led to the "**Elysian fields**"; while the souls of the unjust will reside in "**Tartar**" (**Hades**) where they will be judged. The souls of tyrants and unjust kings would certainly be there; while the souls of philosophers will dwell in the **Elysian Fields.**

Today, studying these Socratic precepts, one recognizes their significance and close ties to Christian ethics that dominate Western culture. These Socratic principles, however, *preceded Christianity by over 300 years,* and how many early Christian theologians borrowed from Socratic ethics is debatable--since most of them were members of the Academy in Athens and later of the Neoplatonic School of Plotinus in Alexandria. In the area where the Christian Code has little to offer, Plato--and particularly Aristotle--expended considerable effort to emphasize *the importance of relationships among nations.* The jungle rule of the Sophists still prevails, and the powerful usually have the upper hand--disregarding justice. If there is a message to be garnered from Socratic philosophy, as presented in <u>Gorgias,</u> affecting lives in the "civilized" world today, it is this: *The implementation of unjust rules and unethical policies between nations has caused great misfortune, harm, and hatred--which has led to continuous injustice, conflict, misery, and warfare.*

5. THEAETETUS

«Αλλα γαρ ηδη ωρα απιεναι, εμοι με αποθανουμενω,
υμιν δε βιοσωμενοις; οποτεροι δε ημων ερχονται επι
αμεινον πραγμα, αδηλον παντι πλην η τω θεω.»
Socrates[7]

Temnple of Olympic Zeus, Athens

The question of knowledge and scientific inquiry had come to a test with the advent of the Sophists, who had cast some doubt about the benefit of real knowledge, and particularly **Gorgias** with his famous dictum: *"Nothing exists, and if it exists it is difficult to comprehend, and if comprehended difficult to communicate to others."* Also, the Sophist **Protagoras** had an impact with his views as exemplified by his dictum: "M*an is the measure of all things, of those that exist that they exist, and of those non-existing that they do not exist."* This statement by Protagoras had an adverse impact on the advancement of scientific pursuits and tended to emphasize the subjectivity versus the objectivity of knowledge. This view mitigated intellectual effort in searching to find answers to the problems posed by Nature and forces affecting the soul of man. According to Protagoras, man and his needs, mostly material, are what matter; and apart from an element of Humanism, this new approach had no salutary effect on uplifting the level of understanding Nature and man. In **Theaetetus** Plato discusses and attempts to define the concept of "**knowledge**," and confronts this kind of fallacious scholarship.

Theaetetus was a well-known ancient mathematician who attended a school of mathematics at **Megara,** whose director was **Euclid,** a student of Socrates and also a member of the Academy. Plato must have written this dialogue later, during the period of his high intellectual maturity and depth, probably in the early 360's B.C., but the timing and setting is prior to the period of the 30 Tyrants (404 B.C). **Theaetetus** was a very bright young man, an adolescent then, and Euclid introduced him to Socrates at the **Palaestra**--where a discussion

---

[7] "But it is already time to go, I to die and you to live; who is going to a better place is only known to God."

ensues concerning the definition of "knowledge." In spite of a lengthy and at times confusing discussion, no definitive statement of *"knowledge"* is given: but what knowledge *is not* is emphasized. The format of the dialogue is based upon the Platonic principle of **The Theory of Recollection,** and Socrates throughout the discussion attempts to lead **Theaetetus** to the point where he would discover the truth himself (**the true definition of the Idea of knowledge**) by simply asking questions. In the introduction considerable discussion ensues about the meaning and the definition of mathematical terms: square roots, cubic roots, etc. At the time Theaetetus was destined to be a mathematician, and the question of the meaning of an irrational number--the square root of 2, for example--was an appropriate diversion from the main topic of the dialogue. The second topic of discussion was the dialectic method--also known as the **"maeutic"** approach (**Μαιευτικη**). Socrates stresses the significance of the dialectic method as the only means for scientific research. On the basis of this theory, one can see why all earlier ones are undermined--even if they came from wise men such as: **Homer, Hesiod, Heraclitus and others**. The true lesson then is not seeking knowledge through external factors, but instead searching into one's soul, with the aid of sensory perceptions, in order to reach the heavenly wisdom that is projected from the eternal "**Idea of Good**" (Αγαθον). *Two conditions are necessary to achieve success and wisdom in this method, and these are: maturity in the soul of the student and dedication and conviction of purpose on the part of the teacher.* Theaetetus is the personification of maturity and readiness--*the ideal student*; while Socrates is the *ideal teacher* who is in the habit of only asking questions by the dialectic method. He is the person who dedicated his life toward the education of the youth; and his intellectual purpose was to emancipate them from bad influences and encourage them to engage in virtuous acts: *a simple life, humility, justice, and self-respect.*

After these introductory discussions between **Plato** and **Theaetetus**, attention focuses on the main topic--which is the definition and understanding of the term "**knowledge.**" In the entire dialogue three definitions are given by Theaetetus; but all are rejected by Socrates. These are: (1) *Knowledge is sense; (2) Knowledge is right judgment; (3) Knowledge is right judgment accompanied by Logos.* A discussion and critical analysis ensues after each definition; the first definition is discussed in a far more extensive and comprehensive manner. One should note that the definitions proposed by Theaetetus represented the conventional wisdom of the time and had been advanced earlier by the Sophists, particularly Protagoras, and also by other theorists (Heraclitus). The statement by Theaetetus that knowledge is "sense," which means that what is perceived by the senses **only** is knowledge, represents a summary of the Sophist philosophy that Plato strenuously disagreed with.

Protagoras' assertion that *"Man is the measure of all things" infers* that whatever man feels and understands about himself and the world around him, as well as all images generated from his senses, are true for him--and therefore constitute valid knowledge. This is a subjective way of looking at things, and Plato was alarmed that civilization and science would depend upon the perceptions and understanding of individuals, without appropriate scientific scrutiny to find: the Ultimate Truth. For example, if two people view the same object and disagree as to its apparent color--one saying it is red, while the other says it is orange—then, according to this theory: both are correct. The second disagreement challenged the statement by Heraclitus that: *"Everything is in a flux and nothing is stationary.*" The implication of this for Plato was that since everything is subject to change, ethics and morality should be variable. On the basis of this view one would be free to choose whichever moral or ethical standards one deemed convenient. But Plato had advanced **"The Theory of Ideas,"** according to which there is a *Fundamental Truth; unalterable, universally acceptable, and valid for all people at all times.* The third theory that **Theaetetus** had in mind was the conception of **relativism** and the comparison of the customs of various people—as well as the element of skepticism that this generates. In the case of less discerning individuals only sensory objects can be perceived; the more acute observer perceives movement and relationships. From this standpoint then, two opposite images emanating from the senses of two different people may be interpreted subjectively as *both being true*; while objectively--they are not.

These were, in essence, the inner workings of this dialogue, which dealt basically with the objective or subjective visualization of truth. For Plato, there is only **one** view--and that is the objective one; and it is our duty to strive for the truth that is not so easily discernible. Plato concerns himself with the possibility that if every person is the source of subjective truth, there would be no need of teachers; if either our actions or words consciously or unconsciously deceive, then what kind of learning is possible? And if we accept these views, even an animal could very well establish a rule or a truth. What would be the difference in the conception of the truth between man and God? We see in this dialogue the influence that the Eleats, with their Monist theory, had on Plato; as well as the Pluralists' views on change, relativity, and evolution. It is man's imagination and ability to think abstractly that can unravel the mysteries of Nature and explore the depths of the human soul. The intellectual objective pursuit of the truth that Plato championed throughout his life is the legacy that the West inherited from these early Greek thinkers.

6. PHAEDRUS (ΦΑΙΔΡΟΣ)

«Ο μεν ουν μη νομοτελης η διεφθαρμενος.....ωστ' ου σεβεται
προσορων καλλος αλλ' ηδονη παραδους΄, ου δεδοικεν ουδ' αισχυνεται[8]
παρα φυσιν ηδονη διωκων»

Plato

　　While Plato, in most of his dialogues, addresses one topic; in **Phaedrus** he discusses the subject of love as well as rhetoric. In the first part a short speech written by the rhetorician, **Lysias,** is analyzed. In this speech **Lysias** discusses the nature of the love *(ερως)* that the "**loved one**" (εραστης) feels, and asks whether the "**loved ones**" should or should not extend their love to the "**loving one**" (αντεραστης). It is not clear whether this relationship relates to **Platonic**

Lysias

love, hedonistic love, or both kinds; or if it relates to homosexual love--since the persons involved appear in the masculine gender. The soul, in its tripartite nature, appears in the dialogue in the form of a two-horse chariot--where the two horses represent the "**sensual**" and "**intellectual**" components of the soul--while the charioteer represents the "**logical**" part. In the latter part of this discussion Plato introduces the subject of rhetoric, and considers its usefulness as a form of education for the youth. He takes issue with Lysias' and the other Sophists' approach to the subject, compared with his dialectic method (the objective or scientific vs. the dogmatic or subjective), and praises another speechwriter, **Isocrates,** who apparently was his favorite.

　　Phaedrus, the main person besides Socrates in this dialogue, was a well-known personality in ancient Athens, and he appears also in the **Symposium, Protagoras, et al.** On his way to the country **Socrates** meets **Phaedrus** outside the city limits. Phaedrus was returning from a lecture by Lysias on the subject of **Love (Ερως).** Socrates asks if he would recite the speech, and it happens that Phaedrus has the written speech under his clothes, so they agree to go to a nice and comfortable place by the Ilissos River and

---

[8] "The person who is not law-abiding, but is corrupt; does not feel awe in facing beauty, but rather embraces hedonism, and is not afraid or shameful in pursuing unnatural hedonistic pleasures."

read **Lysias'** speech. One thing is unclear: Is the speech an attempt to show Lysias' views on love; or is it to illustrate Lysias' deficient literary style. Socrates convinces Phaedrus that Lysias is not a good speechwriter, and he recites a speech of his own on the subject to demonstrate the framework of a good speech of this kind. In the new speech on love, Socrates presents the basic concept of how the **loved one** should show devotion to the **loving one**. They analyze it along the same lines, even though on several occasions one can detect Plato's discomfort with Lysias' positions.

Isocrates

The subject of **"love"** (ερως) is discussed extensively elsewhere (**Symposium**, Chapter 8), where «love» is viewed as a very important sentiment; and Plato takes considerable time and effort to distinguish the difference between **"heavenly love"** (ουρανια Αφροδιτη)--the love that a mother feels for her child--as contrasted with **"sexual love"** (πανδημος Αφροδιτη)--the love of a lover for a loved one for sheer pleasure. The discussion in this dialogue also addresses the subjects of pederasty and homosexuality, extensively practiced in Athenian society, and some other ancient societies. Plato does not condone these practices, and on several occasions describes them with disgust and contempt. Nowhere in the dialogue will one find a reference to the love of a man for a woman--as if there were no women in ancient Athens. Perhaps Plato felt that pederasty and homosexuality are detrimental practices to the society and wanted to condemn them--thus emphasizing his comments on these practices. Was pederasty really a common practice or an aberration, as is true in most societies at all times?

According to some writers, this is a physical abnormality, and the person affected is ill and needs treatment. Plato refers to it indirectly, often in this dialogue--and as quoted above, only a corrupt and unscrupulous person would seek "unnatural pleasures." In **Phaedrus** and other dialogues, he takes considerable time to discuss it and emphasize that it is a social aberration rather than a social phenomenon tacitly accepted by society. We know that Socrates, in his encounters with the Sophists, warned of the deterioration of the moral fabric of the society; and the practice of pederasty was indeed a corrupting practice. In this dialogue one also can see how Plato, in the words of Socrates, attempts to show the detrimental effect on society due to the emphasis on material possessions; exemplified by the Sophists during the Golden Age of Athens. Socrates summarily rejects the excesses and the emphasis on materialism; and Plato, who inherited this thinking, was surely concerned that the practice of pederasty was an additional damaging factor undermining the welfare of the society. Homosexuality is a condition, however, that has existed since the formation of human societies; and while some are tolerant of the practice, others are contemptuous of it.

In the continuation of the dialogue, Plato introduces the concept of the soul into the discussion of love. As we have seen elsewhere, the soul is considered immortal and pre-existing the human body in which it re-incarnates and inhabits at birth--and where it resides until death, when it is separated from the body. The soul is further delineated into three parts: the "**Logical**" (Λογιστικον), the '**Intellectual**' (Θυμοειδες), and the "**Sensual**" (Επιθυμιτικον); and the soul is allegorically represented in this dialogue by a chariot with two horses and a charioteer. The charioteer is the **logical part** of the soul who is interested in directing it and, by extension, the human being: to the right—just--and virtuous life. The other two components of the soul, the **sensual** and the **intellectual,** are represented by the two horses. One horse signifies the **sensual part** and becomes wild when it views sensual beauty--leading the soul to temptation and toward unnatural desires and hedonism. The other horse, personifying the **intellectual part**, resists the temptation and attempts to direct the soul to the highest levels of virtue and intellectual achievement. This continuous struggle results in the human being and his soul either reaching the ideal height and the purest virtuous living, or descending into the abyss and corruption.

Lysias was a speechwriter and recognized rhetorician in ancient Athens, as was **Isocrates** --ten years younger. Plato spends more than half of the text on the subject of Rhetoric vs. Dialectic. This revisits the Socratic condemnation of the practices of the Sophists, pertaining to their methods of transmitting knowledge, relativism (traditions), intellectualism, and true scholarship. In this discussion it is Lysias who receives the scorn of Socrates, and on several occasions Plato presents Lysias as a pseudo-philosopher and thinker. Lysias was also a language teacher and court counsel who prepared speeches for the antagonists in court litigation. This was a profitable enterprise and these rhetoricians or speechwriters were paid handsomely for their services. While Plato discredits **Lysias; Isocrates** is the recipient of his praise. Considering that these individuals had acquired similar acclaim in ancient Athens as rhetoricians who had opened successful schools of rhetoric, it is unusual for Plato to praise the one but condemn the other, unless there were other reasons besides rhetoric, perhaps political, or the role that Lysias played in the conviction of Socrates.

The emphasis on early education is the most important message that one garners from most of the Platonic dialogues, and it would be surprising if it were not the underlying theme in this one as well. Which is the proper course for the education of the youth? The Socratic and Platonic position is that early and continued education leads to the discovery of the **Real Truth**-- through the dialectic process and a highly developed adherence to justice and prudence. Rhetoric is not the proper subject to educate the youth, if viewed from the perspective of rhetoricians such as Lysias and other Sophists. As we have seen elsewhere, rhetoric dealt not only with education in the correct form of written and unwritten speech, but was also a subject encompassing such topics as: politics, ethics, and morals; and according to Socrates and Plato, these values were distorted by the Sophists: hindering the full development and potential of the youth.

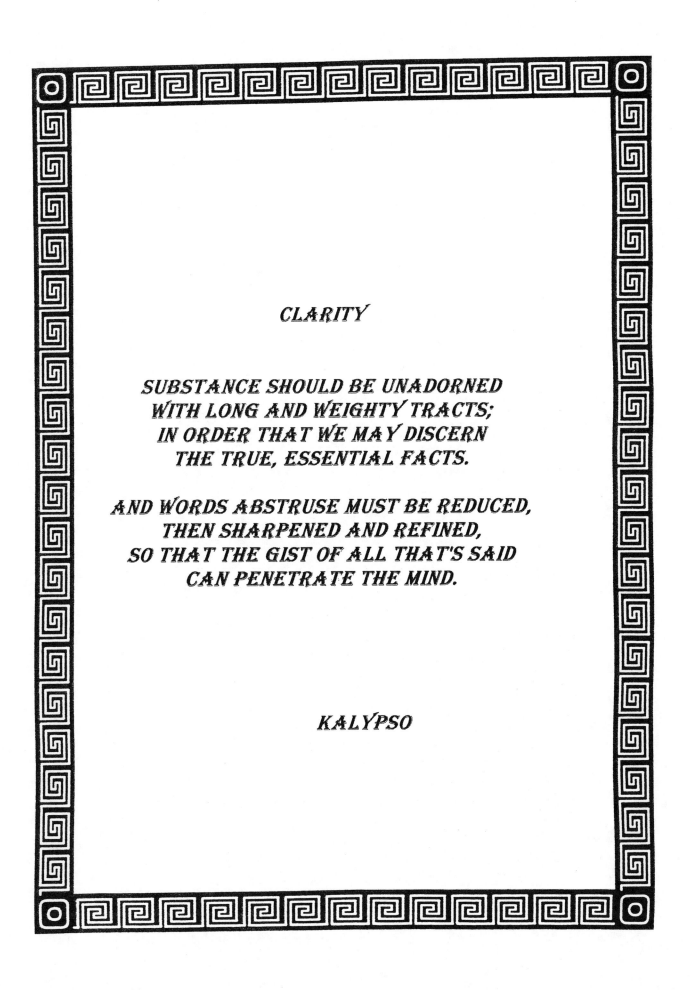

CLARITY

SUBSTANCE SHOULD BE UNADORNED
WITH LONG AND WEIGHTY TRACTS;
IN ORDER THAT WE MAY DISCERN
THE TRUE, ESSENTIAL FACTS.

AND WORDS ABSTRUSE MUST BE REDUCED,
THEN SHARPENED AND REFINED,
SO THAT THE GIST OF ALL THAT'S SAID
CAN PENETRATE THE MIND.

KALYPSO

CHAPTER 8

PLATONIC DIALOGUES

1. P R O T A G O R A S (ΠΡΩΤΑΓΟΡΑΣ)

"Περι μεν θεων ουκ' εχω ειδεναι ουδ'ως εισιν,
ουδ' ως ουκ εισιν. Πολλα γαρ τα κωλυοντα
ειδεναι, η τ' αδηλοτης και βραχυς ο βιος
του ανθρωπου"[1]

Protagoras

The difference between the philosophy of Socrates and that of the Sophists was so great that Plato addressed several of his dialogues on the subject. In **Protagoras** Plato deals with this

subject and, in his usual indirect and ironic way, attempts to emphasize the pitfalls and detrimental aspects of this Sophist vein of philosophy by targeting the *King of the Sophists*--the famous Macedonian Sophist, **Protagoras.** The Sophists claimed that they *could teach anyone the fundamental principles of managing one's political, social, and personal affairs, which would translate, in essence: that through the art of rhetoric they could foster virtue, and by extension political acumen.* At the outset then, the question was whether virtue can be taught, and we have seen that Plato dealt with this subject in another dialogue, **Meno** (p.148). At first response Socrates disagrees with Protagoras that virtue can be taught. Later on, however, he assumes a different position by introducing the principle: **If virtue is knowledge: then it is teachable.** Considerable discussion

The dramatic poet, Sophocles

in-between had ensued in an effort to show that virtue is **knowledge.** This is an interesting position that Plato advances--*that virtue is knowledge*--which was strange for his time (mid 4th century B.C.), as well as perhaps strange for our time today--21st century A.D. The main point that Plato emphasizes is that *man should always strive to perfect himself and reach maturity, and eventually virtue.* Man is by nature *"good,"* and will never consciously act in an injurious way toward himself or his fellow man, but only under the influence of ignorance and erroneous interpretation of what is *"good" and what is "evil."* It is in recognition of this nature of man that

---

[1] "As for the gods, I have no means of knowing either that they exist, or that they do not exist; for many are the obstacles that impede knowledge: both the obscurity of the question and the shortness of the life of man."

virtue is teachable; not really teaching virtue itself, but rather educating man to distinguish between **good** *and evil*. In conclusion then, the spirit of the dialogue is that **"Knowledge is Virtue"** and **"Ignorance is Evil."** Of course a very important question springs out of this statement and reasoning, which *is: "What is knowledge?"* The type of knowledge that Plato distinguishes here is not dependent on the degree of mathematical, social, behavioral, or physical science knowledge one possesses, but rather the knowledge embodied in the dictum **Know Thyself**, which is an attribute that can be acquired by the common man, not necessarily one with parchments and titles that superficially command acceptance that the possessor has knowledge and should be accorded respect. This is, in essence, the main point that one would garner by studying this dialogue.

The dramatic setting and the artistic plot, the characteristic features of all Platonic writings, are present here as well; and the dialogue begins with the young **Hippocrates**, a friend of Socrates, who stayed up all night in anticipation that in the morning he would meet the visiting **Protagoras**. At dawn he knocks at Socrates' door and asks if he would be kind enough to introduce him to Protagoras, who is staying at the home of **Callias**, a friend of Socrates. Socrates agrees to take **Hippocrates** to **Callias'** home and tells him that he will meet not only **Protagoras**, but also two other famous men: **Prodicus and Hippias,** who were also staying there. Upon introducing **Hippocrates to Protagoras, Socrates** inquires: *"If I would take Hippocrates to a musician for lessons, he would learn music; to a carpenter, he would learn carpentry; what may he now learn from you?* Protagoras responds that he will teach him to be a better person in managing his affairs, the affairs of his household, and the affairs of the State-- and *will make him just and virtuous.* Then Socrates asks whether virtue is teachable; and Protagoras enters an extensive narrative stating how he will teach him virtue, and attempts *to "prove"* that virtue is teachable. Protagoras' argument derives from the principle that there are laws in society requiring people to obey and behave in a virtuous and moral manner by not harming or causing injury to others or the State; and therefore, by extension, this can be seen as a method of educating people to be virtuous. Protagoras further argues that instruction in managing personal affairs and affairs of the State can be extended to cover the teaching of the art/science *of* **"politics."** Socrates counters that in the Assembly, if a decision required technical knowledge-- such as constructing a public building, the opinion of an expert would be sought. But in matters of politics in general, as for example policy decisions, anyone at the Assembly could stand up and offer an opinion, which would be taken into consideration. Also, how can the art of politics be taught, since famous politicians have not been able to teach their own sons to become as good as their fathers; and he brings as examples: **Themistocles, Pericles, and Miltiades.**

Plato ultimately suggests that virtue is *knowledge* and it is teachable from the standpoint that one learns of "himself" and then distinguishes what is good and what is evil. Another point that one derives from this dialogue highlights Sophist teaching versus that of Socrates. In the Socratic discussions, the essence of the *dialectic method (the scientific method)* is utilized; it is the objective truth that we are interested in pursuing--and is contrary to the Sophist dictum that

"Man is the measure of all things," or that *Subjectivity is Truth*. The Sophist method is based on myth, rhetoric, and the writings of the poets; and Protagoras embarks upon extensive narrative and employs the myth of **Prometheus** and **Epimetheus**--the two demigod brothers who were appointed by the Olympic gods to distribute attributes, strengths, and weaknesses to earthly beings--in an attempt to dramatize the natural differences in judgment and wisdom among humans. Protagoras' argument is that politics, justice, and virtue are teachable attributes, and strengthens the validity of his assertion by reasoning that if people violate these principles there is punishment forthcoming from the laws of the land--one is deprived of some valuable asset because an unjust or evil act was willfully committed--implying that a person had a choice and acted unjustly: while he could have acted justly. *The Laws then are the Teachers of justice, virtue, and morality; they do not punish someone due to an infirmity or affliction--being born feeble-minded, lame, blind, or deaf.* The crux of this position is similar to the present *"law and order"* view of a certain segment of the political right, versus *"education and reform"* from the other side of the political spectrum. The Socratic view accepts the premise that virtue

The Dionysus Theatre, Proscenium

and justice can be taught, but this education is equated with "knowledge," in that if one reaches maturity and understanding of one's self, then his choice will invariably be just and virtuous because it is to his benefit. This closely resembles the Christian dictum: *"Father forgive them for they know not what they do,"* that Christ uttered from the cross before dying. The Socratic Method respects the intelligence of the individual in that he alone will have to search for truth until he acquires real knowledge and becomes a complete virtuous individual--and ultimately a philosopher.

This is the message one gleans from this dialogue: A message of hope--based upon the ancient Greek spirit of free will and the individual dignity of man—the conviction that no one will commit an unjust or evil act knowingly, but only through ignorance, and that knowledge begets *virtue and justice.*

2. PHILEBUS (ΦΙΛΗΒΟΣ)

«Νουσος υγιειν εποιησε ηδυ και αγαθον,
λιμος κορον, καματος αναπαυσιν»[2]
Heraclitus

The eternal question: How can one achieve happiness, mental tranquility, peace, and harmony, is essentially the subject matter of **Philebus.** At the outset, this dialogue, which was probably written during the decade of the 360's B.C., addresses this question by setting the parameters of the discussion to take place between Socrates and **Philebus**, a follower of the Sophistic discipline. The position of Philebus is that to achieve the state of **"good"** (Αγαθον), *the perfect virtuous state*, one should *seek sensual pleasures and all things associated with these.* On the other hand, Socrates maintains that one should seek: *prudence, intellectual reflection, reminiscence, and all other things related* to these *in order to achieve the state of* «*Αγαθον*». Usually in his dialogues Plato selects an individual who represents an opposite opinion, in this case the *Sophist philosophical position on pleasure,* and engages this person with Socrates in an intellectual dialectic discussion. Eventually, the final conclusion, if there is one[3], amounts to a triumph of virtue, truth, right, justice, and ethical behavior. In this case, Plato selects **Protarchus** to be the main defender of the Sophist position, even though **Philebus** initially expresses the Sophist point of view on pleasure, and the dialogue is titled after him. **Protarchus** is the son of **Callias,** but it is not clear which Callias Plato is referring to, the well-known rich businessman mentioned in other dialogues (**Protagoras**), or someone else, as the name Callias was common in ancient Athens. Protarchus, however, was a student and frequent attendant at the lectures of the Sophist **Gorgias**, and adhered to the Sophist philosophy. For his dialogues Plato would select personalities of current and past times who had had an influence on the political and intellectual life of ancient Greece; but Philebus is an unknown person, and even some modern scholars believe that this is a fictitious name, as such a first name rarely appears in ancient Athenian onomastics. A short

Xenophon

---

[2] Disease, Hunger, and Weariness make Health, Satiety, and Rest pleasant.
[3] Sometimes Plato defines the opposite position, e.g. what pleasure is not.

passage of the opening statement is presented below to illustrate how emphatic Plato is on this topic of how to achieve pleasure:

"**.......SOCRATES:** *"Tell me* **Protarchus,** *which of* **Philebus'** *theory are you prepared to accept, and which of mine are you planning to oppose, if you do not agree with it? Do you wish that we summarize the two positions?*
PROTARCHUS: Very much indeed**.**
SOCRATES: *Philebus believes that for all living creatures the ultimate "good" (Αγαθον) is pleasure, entertainment, enjoyment, and all other things related to these. The opposite position, that I hold, is that these are not the fundamental principles of the "good," but rather: prudence, temperance, the right mental reflection, the process of reminiscence--and all things related to these; i.e. correct judgment, right opinion, and justice. I contend that these are far superior and have greater value than enjoyment and pleasure for all living beings capable of practicing them. Furthermore, I contend that for all people, now and in the future, these attributes are the most beneficial. Are these approximately the positions that each of us holds to be true,* **Philebus?**
PHILEBUS: *They are indeed, Socrates.*
PROTARCHUS: *I am prepared to accept this position, since our pretty Philebus is already worn out.*[4]
SOCRATES: *You do accept that we should reach a true conclusion on these matters, at any cost?*
PROTARCHUS: *We certainly must."*

From these opening statements one clearly notes the opposing positions in the attainment of "*Αγαθον*" *(ultimate good)* between the Sophists and Socrates. For Socrates, *the way people should lead their lives* is a fundamental and important tenet in order to achieve a happy, harmonious, and peaceful society. Plato proceeds, in the continuation of the dialogue, to determine how man derives pleasure, and distinguishes the *pleasure generated out of the senses (hedonism) from the pleasure generated out of intellectual thinking: the right reflection, the logical choice (prudence).* Pleasure is generated when someone satisfies his needs, those of the soul *(psychogenic or psychological needs)*, and those of the body *(physiogenic or physiological needs.)* Plato borrows from the Pythagoreans and the Ionians to distinguish the boundaries of these needs. He associates the mathematical concepts of the limit and infinity to identify the pervasiveness of these needs. The physical requirements are limited--how much one can eat or sleep--but psychogenic needs are infinite: how much wealth can one accumulate, or how much pleasure from entertainment one can derive over time. The basic question, then, is when does man feel totally contented, happy, and satisfied. Is it when he achieves satisfaction of his psychogenic needs, or when he achieves satisfaction of his physiogenic needs? The distinction between pleasures derived from material or sensual stimulation *(hedonistic pleasures),* as

---

[4] From this statement one surmises that the discussion on the subject must have taken place earlier, probably at the Academy.

126

contrasted with pleasures motivated by the intellectual nature of man, is discussed extensively. Does one achieve happiness and contentment through sensual pleasures (hedonism) alone? In other words, can pleasures derived from sensual stimulation outside the human intellect, motivated by external factors, provide real happiness or *"Ευδαιμονια,"* to borrow an Aristotelian term, as the Sophists contend? These are significant questions that philosophers, religious leaders, and social scientists-- every since recorded history--have attempted to answer, and have introduced written and unwritten laws in their efforts to supply, for the common man, the proper rule of action and behavior. Understanding the implications of these differences, and being able to apply correct judgment, determines societal tranquility, peace, equality, and *"Ευδαιμονια."* If not, the harmony in society is disturbed, and personal and societal upheavals arise that lead to unrest, crime, injustice, revolutions, and misery. Plato is concerned with how a person can distinguish the differences between the choices available to satisfy these needs in an intellectual manner from those of a sensual or materialistic manner.

Near the conclusion, Plato alters his position slightly. At the beginning, as noted, he maintained the position that to reach the state of *"good" (Αγαθον), man needs **only** prudence, intellectual reflection, reminiscence, and all other related things to these.* But later, this rigid

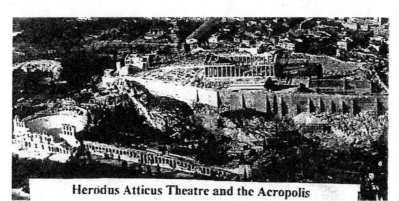
Herodus Atticus Theatre and the Acropolis

position changes. Plato eventually distinguishes the various levels of pleasure, as well as prudence, and finally concludes that what is **"good" (agathon)** for man is a mixed state of pleasure and prudence. This stance reflects the well-known Socratic position embodied in the famous Delphic epigram, *"**Nothing in Excess**" (Μηδεν Αγαν),* which requires a happy medium. He concludes that pleasure (hedonism) is necessary for ultimate fulfillment, and admits that prudence alone is insufficient and incomplete. However, Plato wants to emphasize that prudence is an **essential** factor, even though he admits that all living beings seek pleasure naturally. This is to counter the position of **Eudoxus**[5], one of the attendants of the Academy, who believed that pleasure is fundamental and dominant. This position was partially adopted by the Epicureans later on, and was influential during the Hellenistic period and throughout the Roman era. The early Christians, at the turn of the new era, adopted a radically different view: that *denial* of all forms of hedonistic needs is necessary to achieve salvation--which led to **asceticism**. Plato wishes to emphasize, however, that to achieve happiness man should not resort to intellectual pleasures alone, and accepts that human passion has its place in man's life only when it serves an intellectual purpose. Unfortunately, this emphasis was not heeded in the following centuries;

---

[5] Eudoxus had a school of philosophy and rhetoric at the beginning of the 4th century B.C. in Athens.

instead the Epicurean (emphasis on pleasure) and Stoic (apathy) viewpoints dominated societal mores, and the emphasis on sensual gratification led to extremes. Compare Roman practices which led to the various spectacles at the Coliseum involving humans vs. animals (lions devouring humans) or humans vs. humans (gladiators fighting to the death).

The influence of this dialogue on Aristotle was significant, as can be noted in his work, **Nichomachean Ethics**, as well as ***Poetics,*** concerning the theory of mixed pleasures--and the topic of "**Catharsis**" in theatrical plays.

3. PARMENIDES (ΠΑΡΜΕΝΙΔΗΣ)

" Χρεω δε σε παντα πυθεσθαι, ημεν Αληθειης ευκυκλεος ατρεμες ητορ, ηδε βροτων δοξας, ταις ουκ ενι πιστις αληθης."[6]
Parmenides

The Dramatic poet Aeschylus

Parmenides is a major Platonic dialogue and deals exclusively with the basic Platonic doctrine: *"The Theory of Ideas or Forms."* The introduction and dramatic part is most entertaining, charming, and matter-of-fact. It has fascinated readers in past, as well as present times, for its simplicity, humanism, and realism. Perhaps no one in the history of philosophy has succeeded to match this dramatic and captivating Platonic style. And in this dialogue, the introduction of personal and mundane matters-- such as an old man forgetting the name of a child that he met many years ago--is the artistic element that Plato succeeded to capture. At the beginning, **Cephalus**, a well-known philosopher from the Ionian city of Clazomenae, arrives in Athens along with several other philosophers and friends, with the intention of learning about a discussion on philosophy that took place between **Socrates, Parmenides, and Zeno**, in Athens several years ago. Upon their arrival in Piraeus they meet Plato's brothers, **Adeimantus and Glaucon**, and Cephalus inquires about Plato's other half-brother, whose name he regretfully forgets, as he met him many years ago when the child was 10

---

[6] "You need to learn all things, but above all the unshakable heart of well-rounded truth; for the opinions of the mortals are not of sure trust."

years old. He adds that he remembers the father's name, **Pyrilambis**, and when **Adeimantus** tells him that the other half-brother's name is **Antiphon**, he rejoices and expresses a desire to meet him. They walk to the house of Antiphon, who has just finished giving instructions about a harness to one of his servants. Adeimantus asks Cephalus why he wants to see Antiphon, and Cephalus reveals his real reason for wanting to meet him. Antiphon has a friend by the name of **Pythodorus**, who was present at the meeting of Parmenides, Zeno, and Socrates; and Cephalus wants Antiphon to introduce him in the hope that he will tell him about the meeting. One has the impression by reading the preliminary paragraphs, that a beautiful novel or short story is in the making, and not a discussion on the most important doctrine of the Platonic philosophy. Such departures from the subject, that Plato mastered so well, and his style of extreme civility and feigned ignorance at times--along with the famous Socratic irony-- make the reading of such dialogues most pleasurable.

A considerable part of the dialogue also addresses the philosophical position of the Eleatic School's **Monist Theory**, as it affects Plato's philosophical position on the "*Theory of Forms.*"

Homer's Apotheosis

As pointed out elsewhere (Chapter 7), the *Forms* or *Ideas* are those independent entities of all tangible and intangible, animate and inanimate things that we cannot see--but can conceive of only through our intellect; *the actual such entities, the objects of our senses that we can see, are only shadows of the prototypes.* Here Parmenides maintains that such entities cannot exist; *and particularly that insignificant, sensory things cannot have "Ideas."* One would expect Plato to defend his position and at least attempt to refute Parmenides' objections. But he does not, and instead lets Parmenides' position stand.

Parmenides brings forth four basic objections to the "*Theory of Ideas*": (1) the *existence of the doctrine of Ideas is highly improbable; for, if we have "Ideas" of Good (Αγαθον), Beauty, or Justice,* and the sensory objects are the samples or shadows of them, as asserted, then *we should also have "Ideas" of insignificant things (clay, hair, or dir)t--which could lead to the absurd;* (2) As it concerns the relationship between sensory objects and the "Ideas," there is a

129

a contradiction in Plato's assertion that sensory objects become parts (**Μεθεξις**) of the Ideas by separating and distributing them in the sensory objects. This contradiction derives from the Monist viewpoint that the *"Idea"* is considered as *one* and therefore it cannot be distributed or split. The attempt by Socrates to characterize the Ideas as *notions* that exist inside the soul of man, and as such can be separated, is opposed by Parmenides who asserts that the *notions* are Elements of the Ideas derived from them and referred to them. (3) If the Ideas are the prototypes, then between them there should exist something in common – such as the *Idea of Similarity*. The Idea of Similarity then, so defined, would necessitate similarity with other similar objects; and therefore, this would lead to plurality, which is *a priori* unacceptable according to *the Eleatic principle of Monism.* (4) If Ideas exist they should be unknown to man, because by their nature are not inside man or inside the sensory objects--as they are independent from them all. There must exist a science of Ideas and a science of sensory objects, each studying the truth of these two separate entities. We know the science of sensory objects, but we have no knowledge of the science of Ideas--as these are foreign to us. Since the science of the "Ideas" is a perfect and complete science, it can be known only by God who is perfect and omniscient, and this produces a feeling of frustration--as it would make it impossible for us to reach perfection.

One has to realize that these contradictions were written by Plato himself, and the fact that he does not refute them in **Parmenides** suggests two possible explanations: First, either the dialogue was not written by Plato, but by a student at the Academy in later years; or second, Plato revised the *Theory of Ideas,* as he did in the "**Laws,**" where he refuted some of the principles in the "**Republic,**" and indeed intended to modify some of his original convictions on the *"Theory of Forms."* There still may be another explanation: Plato attempted to present a deeper view of the concept and it was not completed, judging from the extensive discussion on "**Monism**" that follows.

The portion of the dialogue that deals with the subject of "Ideas" is only a small part of the whole. The bulk of the work addresses the Eleatic concept of *"Being" (Οντος Ον)* and its uniqueness and inalterability. This part becomes highly transcendental and dialectic, so that at times it becomes difficult to comprehend and interpret. According to the Monists the world is *"One"*--unchanging, unalterable, and unique; and what we perceive with our senses as change--*is only an illusion.* They completely disregard acquisition of knowledge through our senses--*because the senses deceive.*

Parmenides was written later in Plato's life, perhaps after considerable criticism had developed concerning his *"Theory of Ideas." M*embers of the Academy, particularly Aristotle, who was perhaps one of the most serious critics, probably forced Plato to modify his views. It was perhaps his disagreement that compelled Aristotle to leave the Academy for northern Greece and Ionia in 354 B.C., and prompted Plato to complain that Aristotle did not exhibit gratitude for the intellectual benefits he accrued while at the Academy for 20 years. Plato wanted to believe that the physical and social world, in a transcendental conception, is superior to what our senses lead us to understand. The essence of his theory, then, is that we should strive to reach this *Ideal World* because it is only through such an ambitious and honorable pursuit that society will improve and reach the *ultimate* **"Good"** (Αγαθον).

4. THE REPUBLIC (ΠΟΛΙΤΕΙΑ)

«Της δε ζημιας μεγιστη το υπο πονηροτερου αρχεσθαι»[7]
Plato

The **Republic** represents Plato's political philosophy. As pointed out elsewhere (**Laws,** p. 191), he was not enamored with the political systems of his time--including Democracy. He believed that such systems as *Aristocracy and Monarchy* were deteriorating into *Tyrannies, and Democracies into Ochlocracies:* **the mob rule**. The system that he envisions in the **Republic** is quite different from all other systems prevailing, and is based upon the creation of a separate class, the **Guardians (Φυλακες)**, who would protect the city-state from external as well as internal enemies, and also serve as *the executive, the judicial and legislative* branch of government. He outlines a detailed process of how the Guardians should be educated and prepared for their important role. The Guardian class would not possess material wealth, and the women would be equal to men in all activities--except those that require physical endurance; while the children would be raised by the State, so as to leave the women undisturbed in the pursuit of their political and social aspirations. In this respect, then, Plato can be seen as perhaps one of *the first feminists in history*. There is a stringent curriculum in the education of the Guardian class, which includes: *music, gymnastics,*

Pericles addressing the Athenian Assembly

---

[7] "The greatest punishment is for one to be ruled by a person who is his inferior."

harmonics, mathematics, geometry, and other. The objective is to develop pious and virtuous societies. The ultimate leader and head-of-state would be the *Philosopher-King: a paragon of virtue.* This Republic requires few laws because Plato believed that when people develop prudence and maturity there is no need for excessive legislation.

The dramatic part of the dialogue, for which **Plato** was a master, shows **Socrates** visiting Piraeus for a special festival honoring the goddess[8]. After the festival was over he started his return trip to Athens, when **Cephalus**, an old friend and rich entrepreneur, invites him and his companions[9] to stay at his house overnight, to watch the evening events and discuss the festival and other matters. Socrates agrees to stay, and at **Cephalus'** house he finds a number of other people waiting to meet him and enter an animated discussion on the ideal political system. Socrates begins by asking **Cephalus** to relate the most important experiences he has had in his life that he might wish to share with the group, so that the younger may learn what pitfalls to avoid on this road that they are taking, which Cephalus has already traveled. Several other matters are discussed, such as: the effect wealth and material possessions have on achieving happiness; the impact aphrodisiacs have on an individual, and the consequences of aging. After these introductory points, the discussion is geared toward the central subject which is--*the practice of justice in the society;* actually, the full title of the work is ***The Republic-- A Political Treatise Concerning Justice*** (**Πολιτεια: Περι Δικαιου Πολιτικος**).

Plato wanted to analyze and define justice in a succinct way, by the dialectic method,

The podium at the Pnyx as it stands today

because he considered "Justice," "Virtue," and "Good" (Αγαθον) to be the cornerstone of the new political and social system of government that he had really envisioned. Several propositions were made by the participants to define what justice is-- ranging from: (1) *returning what is owed;* (2) *benefiting your friends and hurting your enemies;* (3) *the right and interest of the stronger-- and others.* A rigorous

---

[8] A festival (Bendidia) for Artemis-Bendis; a Thracian goddess transplanted to Piraeus.
[9] The participants in this discussion, besides Socrates and Cephalus, were: Plato's two brothers, Adeimantus and Glaucon; Polemarchus, son of Cephalus; and Thrasymachus, a well-known Sophist from Chalcedon.

discussion ensues in Books I and II, and all agree that: *Justice is not to return what you owe, and not to hurt your enemies; in fact, one should never hurt anyone, including his enemies,* because this action will render them worse off--to the detriment of society. Also, they convincingly conclude that Justice is not *"the right of the stronger"* as **Thrasymachus,** a well-known Sophist, argued. Thrasymachus maintained that the right of the stronger is a natural principle, as the stronger were made so by Nature; therefore, they deserve to have their way because this is a natural law (the **Sophists** made a clear distinction between **Man's law and Nature's law).** **Thrasymachus** further argues that one will realize, by observation, that most of the time the unjust prosper; while the just suffer. **Glaucon,** a member of the company, proposes that it does not really matter if we are just or unjust because most people, if not all, act justly only because of necessity; and at any moment anyone could commit an unjust act if he knows that he will not be punished by a god or man. So far, Plato has masterfully avoided engaging in serious discussion on *what justice is,* but has spent considerable time on *what justice is not. Later on, justice is defined as the harmonious relationship of the three forces of the soul (Logical, Sensual, Intellectual); 440a-441c.*

After this exchange about Justice, Plato introduces the basics of the origin of the State and the development of various specializations, political organizations, and trade in an organized society.

A 5th century Athenian coin

But the crucial and seminal question for Plato is: **What kind of individuals should be directly or indirectly entrusted with the positions of leadership of the State?** He spends considerable time in identifying the leadership features of the ruling class and introduces the concept, the organization, and the qualities of the **"Guardians."** He is concerned that the "Guardians" develop feelings of love, compassion, and understanding--devoted to the needs of the citizens-- but exhibit hostility toward external enemies of the State. He compares them to the dogs, which by instinct may become aggressive toward a harmless stranger, but are friendly and playful with those whom they know--even if mistreated. He considers the proper education of the "Guardians" to be of paramount importance. He attacks the myths, which he considers to be harmful, because they are *unrealistic and convey false knowledge to the youth, and* condemns those passed on by **Homer** and **Hesiod**--as well as the plays of the dramatic poets featured after these myths. He further condemns the impact religious myths have on the youth, particularly the behavior of the gods when they are shown fighting each other and exhibiting immoral human characteristics. Another important feature of the conventional values of the society that **Plato** considers dangerous to the education of the youth is the *fear* that develops in the hearts of people: *fear of death and the* prospect of what is expected afterward. Plato disagrees with the false qualities given to the mythological heroes and the lack of temperance, compassion, and virtue exhibited by them-- which distort the perception of reality.

Concerning the education of the Guardians, Plato considers that the environment plays a significant role; and the "Guardians," if possible, should develop a character of their own, based upon virtuous qualities, and not mimicking others who have reached their state of mind by other means. *Harmony and rhythm in music is as important as physical training, gymnastics, and the development of a healthy body.* In music **Plato** selects from among the various musical modes, the **Dorian** and the **Phrygian,** which are characterized by harmony, rhythm, and melody-- and discards *the Lydian, Mixolydian, Ionic and Lydic,* as not appropriate for the education of the youth. *The Doric and the Phrygian modes inspire, sooth, calm, and provide tranquility to the soul, as well as good disposition on the part of the "Guardian."*

In general, Plato believed that the virtuous qualifications of those who aspire to political positions, particularly the Guardians, are fundamental for a successful career, and specifically refers to the following virtues that good rulers should possess: T*hey should be truthful; hate lies and lying; be prudent; hate excessive enrichment; be proud, humble, eager, and willing to learn; be mnemonic, harmonious, and pleasant.* He admits that such individuals in the current political life, who would be appropriate for political responsibilities, are usually rare--and probably unwilling to participate in the political process. If the public is to make a choice in a democratic election, it is often not the right one--either because of ignorance, or due to the influence of demagogues or special interests. When individuals who do not possess the above qualifications are elected or appointed to public office, *they cause the public great harm.*

The Karyatides on the Acropolis

After the matter of justice and the definition of the ideal, virtuous Guardian were treated, the next subject of major importance addressed in the **Republic** is the woman's role in this society and the matter of raising children. The discussion regarding the role of women is perhaps a first attempt identifying the place and perspective of women in society. Plato finds no difference between a man and a woman in carrying out all kinds of societal duties:

Women should receive the same education as men and participate in all activities with them--including physical exercise in the **Gymnasium (Παλαιστρα)** where men usually exercise nude. Even though he does not find it awkward that young women should also exercise in the nude, he cautions that the existing society might not accept such a practice; he argues that in the same way that other cultures do not accept nudity in any form (Oriental civilizations), while the Greeks accept the practice naturally, so the Greeks will eventually learn to adjust to young women exercising in the nude as part of their education. Some participants in the discussion contended that certain activities are more suited for men than women. But Plato argues that, with the exception of activities that require physical endurance, there is no difference between men and women. Thus, women could participate in war as well, but not necessarily on the front line. Women should receive the same education in *gymnastics, music, mathematics, geometry, harmonics, and other branches of knowledge.* Naturally then, the question arises about the nature of the family and the rearing of the children, since the function of the woman is no longer confined to the house. And here is another innovation by Plato: The institution of the family, only among the Guardians, is abolished. Weddings would be performed by selection of the best among the Guardians for the purpose of improving the quality of the population. The fertile age for men is set for 30 years- from 20 to 50; while the fertile age for women is set for 20 years-- from 20 to 40. But once the child is born the State undertakes its care, and the father and the mother cease to have anything to do with its upbringing.

The question of private property and accumulation of material wealth occupied the ancient scholars. We have seen that the **Pythagoreans** established the *Commune* in Croton, Southern Italy, in which all material possessions of the community were shared, *and everyone*

Herodotus

received benefits according to his needs, and contributed according to his capabilities. Plato considered the possession of material wealth among the "Guardians" a potential source of friction, disputes, jealousies, and antagonisms which would be detrimental to their welfare--and consequently to the State. *Thus, private property and accumulation of material possessions among the "Guardians" is abolished.* In this way Plato believed that harmony, peace, and devotion to the public good would be wholeheartedly carried through.

Plato, at this point, is asked what sort of administrative leader he would propose for this new government, considering the systems existing at his time-- *Aristocracy, Democracy, or Monarchy. He states that any would be acceptable if the rulers become philosophers or the philosophers kings.* For Plato the ideal ruler is a philosopher, because in that person he finds perfection *in virtue, wisdom, prudence, and knowledge.* The **Philosopher-King,** then, would have to be chosen from among the Guardians, but only after such a person had gone through a complete educational experience-- and would not rule before the age of 55. He distinguishes between **real** knowledge and the

superficial knowledge of those who aspire to political positions, and decries the unfortunate consequences that follow when a ruler has not reached the ideal state of virtue, knowledge, and wisdom. Good men and good views are often silenced by the ignorant multitude, which transforms these good men and good views into mediocrity, injustice, and ignorance.

In the **Republic** Plato revisits the doctrine of **Ideas** or **Forms,** and particularly the **"Idea"** of **"Good ("Αγαθος".)** The ultimate achievement of a virtuous man is the attainment of the state of "Good," and the struggle for this achievement is a difficult one; but if reached, he arrives at the level of the *ideal, perfect man.* He uses a very dramatic example to illustrate the struggle and the goal of reaching the **"Idea"** of **"Agathov":** Picture a man in a cave, which is enclosed on all sides, with the exception of the upper entrance; he is chained at the bottom and unable to move or turn his head. It is dark and he is sitting with the entrance to the cave behind him, and can only

The School of Athens by Raphael

see the wall ahead of him where shadows of objects outside the entrance are reflected by a fire burning behind them. He has a vague idea of what these objects are, and cannot make out their form because he sees only distorted shadows. *For Plato the shadows are only the sensory perceptions of things we do not truly see, or comprehend their real nature: the "Ideas."* For man, then, to reach perfection and learn the truth--not an image of the truth-- he has to break his bondage and climb to the entrance of the cave and see, with his own eyes, the true and real objects whose shadows were projected on the wall. In this metaphor Plato wants to dramatize the fact that we are really ignorant of the true nature of things, and that if we want to learn the "Ideas" (the **Truth),** we have to struggle and mount the steep wall (*Ignorance*) at the entrance of the cave. Education or *recollection* is the means to reach the "**Ideas.**" It is this emphasis on education to which Socrates devoted most of his strength in order to convince his fellow citizens that pursuance of *knowledge leads to happiness;* while *ignorance results in misery and evil.* Those who do not strive for real education (knowledge of the "**Ideas**") are not fit to govern; and those who have reached that state should strive to shed the light and reveal the truth to all.

The final chapters, or books, of the "**Republic**" address the feasibility of the system outlined therein. Several of the participants exhibit doubt that man can reach a perfect state and achieve the essence of **Good (Αγαθον).** Based upon the idea of a philosopher becoming the ruler of such a state, Plato's attempt to persuade Dionysius, the tyrant of Syracuse, and later his son

(Dionysius II) to become virtuous and just rulers as philosophers--landed him in jail (See **Laws**, next chapter). In the last four books he dramatizes how the political system deteriorates into either tyranny or mob rule, and ultimately an oligarchy--if the type of people he described above are not the rulers of the State. Specifically, in a benevolent, just aristocracy, the non-virtuous rulers become negligent of their duties; consequently, corruption and disharmony ensue. Instead of wisdom and stability, the rulers exhibit instability and resort to violent actions; the artisans and the farmers are treated and looked upon as slaves. Education deteriorates and instead of the principle of persuasion, compulsion is now applied. Real art is neglected and music is downgraded. The citizen lags in intellectual acumen, becomes egotistical and insensitive to the needs of others (particularly the slaves), morally corrupt, warlike, and preoccupied with the acquisition of wealth. The soul is not directed by logic, but by anger and desire for material possessions. These lead to excessive enrichment, which determines the value of the citizen. Virtue vanishes and the right of the stronger substitutes for justice. Instead of a unified society, two essential classes develop--the class of the rich and the class of the poor (the *"haves"* and the *"have-nots"*), who become antagonistic toward one another. Public services lag in quality and the number of incompetent citizens increases, as well as the number of indigent and thieves. Desire for wealth, entertainment, and power, dominate the soul of man; and the friction that the chasm between the *"haves"* and the *"have-nots"* develops: leading to the rule of the mob. The public senses that their rulers are exploiting them, and the revolutionary spirit inspires and initiates uprisings. Usually the multitude wins and commits atrocities, exiles or kills the rich and confiscates their property--which is distributed by lot. Complete freedom which borders on anarchy characterizes this kind of society--sustained on selfishness and self-gratification. In such a system it is sufficient to feign interest for the welfare of the State, deriving thus benefits and positions regardless of virtue and capability. **Equality is imposed on unequal things.** This practice eventually deteriorates into the **"rule of the jungle,"** and a tyrant ultimately seizes control and enforces a despotic rule. This occurs when selfishness supercedes all physical and intellectual values in life. Plato was correct, because after the brief experience with democracy-- from the time **of Cleisthenes (518 B.C.)** to the time of the Romans--it was not practiced again until the latter part of the 16th century A.D. (over 1900 years).

Ancient and modern critics have viewed the **Republic** as a Utopian system--highly idealized and impractical. Several of the participants in the discussions sensed this deficiency and pointed it out to Socrates. But Plato, who had conceived the **Theory of Ideas**, a concept that caused Aristotle to break with the Academy in 354 B.C., was a very idealistic individual who maintained **that the human being is made by Nature "good."** By the stringent conditions set forth in the **Republic**, and the creation of the elite class of the Guardians, he believed that a viable, peaceful, and harmonious society could evolve. Judging by what he wrote in the **Laws,** after his experiences in Sicily, perhaps he had a change of heart-- as the **Laws** could be considered a revision of the **Republic** (read on**).**

5. SYMPOSIUM (ΣΥΜΠΟΣΙΟΝ)

«Τι δητα οιομεθα, τι των γενοιτο, αυτο το καλον ιδειν
ειλικρινες, καθαρον, αμικτον αλλα μη αναπνεως σαρκων
τε ανθρωπινων και χρωματων και αλλης πολλης φλυαριας
θνητης, αλλα αυτο το Θειον καλον δυναται μονοειδες
κατιδειν.»[10]

Plato

    <u>**The Symposium**</u> represents Plato's views on the subject of **love (Ερως)**. For the ancient Greeks **"Eros"** (**Ερως**) was a god, and throughout the entire dialogue Eros is praised, glorified, and presented in many facets to emphasize its impact on man. The symposium was held at the house of Agathon, an Athenian playwright, and was given by his friends in honor of his victory in theatrical competition at the **Dionysus Theatre**. The speakers were, in order of appearance: **Apollodorus** (the narrator**), Phaedrus, Pausanias, Eryximachus, Aristophanes, Agathon, Diotima** (a female priestess from **Mantinea who speaks through Socrates**), and finally **Alcibiades**. Each one intended to speak in praise of Eros and present their view on the subject and its impact on human life. **Phaedrus** begins and praises Eros as unique and the oldest of gods; lauding love as the most beautiful, ethereal, useful, and powerful sentiment. Next, **Pausanias** separates love into two parts; **heavenly love**--which is the love for the betterment of the loved one--and pandemus **love**--the desire for sensual satisfaction. In the case of **pandemus love,** he addresses homosexuality and pederasty extensively. For **Eryximachus**, who is a physician, love is a powerful force that affects not only human sentiments, but also the human body and its related systems. **Aristophanes** follows, and being a comedian presents a comic view of the origin of Eros. But it is **Diotima,** speaking for Socrates, who summarizes Plato's view on the subject. Plato believed that the purpose of love is to unite and uplift two human beings and inspire them to recognize beauty in its magnificence; this is what is referred to as **Platonic love**. The final speaker is **Alcibiades**, a student and friend of Socrates, who praises him for his wholesome qualities and high moral standards. The subject of homosexuality, and particularly the subject of *pederasty (love for boys)*, is discussed extensively in this dialogue. **Plato** presents the subject through the speeches of **Pausanias, Aristophanes,** and others; and his intention, most

---

[10] "What indeed, if we could see beauty undefiled, pure, unmixed--not adulterated with human flesh and colors--
and much other mortal rubbish; then we could behold Divine Beauty in perfect simplicity."

138

likely, was to address and acknowledge the subject--which was a cancer in the society--treating it dialectically and demonstrating its detrimental impact on the youth. As is true in all societies at times, these aberrant practices thrive "in the closet"--while little or nothing is known by the public; and the impact on society as a whole is not properly recognized. Plato wanted to emphasize love as a powerful sentiment, and disassociate it from unnatural and sensual practices.

The Symposium at Agathon's

From the discussion it becomes clear that there were laws against these practices, with different levels of enforcement applied in the various Greek city-states. But in the case of pederasty the laws were very strict, and in some cases involved capital punishment. It is also inferred from the discussions of the speakers that this unnatural behavior was viewed with disgust and contempt by the general public. It is not clear, however, how *widespread the practice of pederasty was in Athenian society. Because of the lack of public education* in ancient Greece, there was an extensive interface between young adolescents and older men, who played the role *of tutors and guardians,* that gave rise, most probably, to these unnatural practices. An adult was chosen to serve as a guardian and teacher to advance the educational level of a young protégé, and this tradition played a significant role in the educational upbringing of the youth. The guardian assumed the same role as the **"godfather"** today in the Catholic and Orthodox churches. This individual, who could be a relative or a friend of the family, undertakes the religious stewardship of the youth at the time of baptism, and creates a bond that lasts for a lifetime. In ancient times *this trusted individual, or guardian,* was also undertaking the broader curricular education of the youngster as tutor and supervisor. By some accounts, pederasty flourished when some corrupt individuals took advantage of this close relationship with the children.

139

The **<u>Symposium</u>** is considered one of the most brilliant pieces of literature of ancient Greece; and Plato, in this dialogue, achieves a high degree of perfection in style, substance, and philosophical depth. A short analysis of the speeches at the Symposium is given below, starting with **Phaedrus**, whom we encountered in another homonymous dialogue in the previous chapter. **Phaedrus** emphasizes the importance of love and how powerful a sentiment it is, in that people in love devote themselves to each other completely and would sacrifice themselves for their loved one. What an ideal society it would be, he points out, if all people loved each other and were willing to sacrifice themselves for the welfare of their fellow human beings: A harmonious and peaceful life would result.

Phaedrus emphasizes this point by relating from mythology the example of **Alcestis** who loved her husband **Admetus** so much that she offered to sacrifice herself for him, in order to save him from Hades, even though his own parents were not willing to die for him. Phaedrus concludes his presentation by stating that: *"So I declare that Eros is the oldest, most honest, and most important (of all gods), in that he directs both the living and the dead among humans to reach and acquire virtue."*

Daidalus and Ikarus, Crete

Pausanias, who spoke second, distinguishes between the two kinds of love: **Platonic love**, the love that is beyond sensual pleasures and has as an objective a selfless interest in another human being, and **Sensual love**. He identifies two **Aphrodites** (the goddess of love): **the heavenly (Ουρανιος) Aphrodite** who inspires altruistic love, and **the common (Πανδημος) Aphrodite** who embraces sensual love. Within this context Pausanias brings the matter of pederasty and homosexuality into discussion and presents their various aspects. In describing sensual love, Pausanias associates it with the instinctive drive for immortality and the propagation of the species; this point, however, is fully explored later when Socrates speaks through Diotima and associates this love with procreation. **Pausanias** illustrates how powerful this feeling and desire is, and what a profound impact it exercises on life. The desire for survival and achievement of immortality has been the fundamental drive of every human being, as no one really wants to perish without living traces of their impact. This feeling has two views: The first is in the propagation of physical offspring; and the other is in the propagation of spiritual and intellectual offspring in the form of *fame, glory, and recognition*. **The "pandemus"** love, then, which is the desire for the satisfaction of sensual pleasures, *is the love that provides immortality through the birth of physical offspring*. The third speaker is **Eryxymachus**, who identifies Eros as a functioning entity that affects the health of the body as well as all other physical relationships in man. In the speech by **Eryxymachus** one discerns the concepts of Love (**Φιλοτης**) and Strife (**Νεικος**) proposed by **Embedocles,** as being: *the Forces that are responsible for the creation of the world.* **Aristophanes** is the next speaker, and being a comedian proposes a comic interpretation of Eros. He invents a myth-- that originally the sexes were three: male, female, and a combination of the two (**hermaphrodite)** --having four hands, four feet, four eyes, four ears and two genitals (male or female); with *Hermaphrodites* having one male and one female. Being united and having four hands and four feet, they became powerful because they could move in different directions swiftly. They developed an arrogant attitude and challenged the gods, who decided to punish them for the hubris of undermining them, and proceeded to cut them in two so as to weaken them. These single new beings, which came from the original combination after the split, tend to seek the missing part; and those who came from the male combination seek male companions; while those who came from the female combination seek female companions--the abnormal outcome of the separation (by our today's standards). Of those who came from the third kind: the male seeks its counterpart, the female; and the female seeks its counterpart, the male--and these are the normal relationships (by our today's standards). Plato, through Aristophanes' myth, probably wanted to portray that there is nothing unnatural in the tendencies for *the male-to-male and female-to-female relationships.* But apart from the myth, Aristophanes agrees with the deeper truth permeating all speeches: Love is a natural state; and a person lacking it is abnormal and incomplete.

After Aristophanes, **Agathon's** turn comes and he proposes that the god Eros is not the oldest but rather the youngest. He appears to follow the line of Phaedrus who suggested that where this god (love) is, there is *harmony, peace, and happiness.* He embraces the Platonic tenet:

Excavations at Knossos, Crete

Love is a virtue, and it is in it that human beings will find happiness. In the last part of the dialogue Plato presents his thoughts and philosophy on the subject of love in general. As mentioned above, his views on the subject pointed to two different avenues: *spiritual or "heavenly" love and sensual love.* He is emphasizing spiritual love; and the entire latter portion of the dialogue is a hymn to this kind of love. Socrates, who is the speaker of this part, recites how he learned, in the past, all about love from **Diotima,** who invented still another myth about the genealogy of Eros:

Conceived at a party given by the gods to celebrate the birthday of **Aphrodite**. Because Aphrodite was *the goddess of Beauty*; Eros' activities are always associated with beauty. His parents were **Destitute (Πενια)** and **Poros** (the son of **Metis**, the first wife of Zeus). Because he is the son of **Destitute** he is always poor, resilient to hardships, and homeless. From his father **(Poros)** he inherited cleverness and inventiveness; this is Plato's explanation of the vicissitudes of love. Socrates asks Diotima how love can be useful to humans, and Diotima undertakes a lengthy discussion and analysis of the aspect of love that relates to one's desire for propagation **(Pandemus love)**, and is used as a vehicle to immortality and fame. But either through this or through the spiritual "Heavenly" (Aphrodite) love, this sentiment is used as a means to achieve **happiness**. She further adds that every person wishes to reproduce at some point in life; she uses the expression "**give birth**" and distinguishes between the products of sensual love as well as those of the **heavenly (Ουρανια)** love. Diotima offers a paean to the values of the offspring of love which is motivated by the spiritual force. She points out the notable accomplishments of **Homer, Solon, Codrus, Lycurgus,** and others, who were motivated by the love for what is beautiful. Their works (*poems or laws*) are immortal and are glorified by generations. These are the beautiful products; and when man pursues the love of what is beautiful in the soul and spirit, he will finally sense Beauty in its true splendor. When one reaches this stage and views **Total Beauty**, he becomes perfect: avoids superficiality and meanness, and generates majestic thoughts in an inexhaustible philosophy of flawless ideas and values. When one, she continues, follows the correct path of love for what is beautiful, he elevates himself above sensual things and has the possibility of reaching Ultimate Beauty. Slowly, step by step, he will reach the **"Idea" of "Beauty" and the "Idea" of «Good» "(Αγαθον)."** It is at this level, then, that man will be happy and propagate real virtue, not images of virtue: *because he faces real beauty.* Plato concludes the speech by Diotima by stating that he who can propagate true virtue has the possibility of being loved by the gods and becoming immortal, unlike the person who follows a different path.

As a tribute to Socrates, Plato concludes the dialogue with the appearance of Alcibiades-- late, drunk, and incoherent. Through Alcibiades, Plato gives praise to Socrates for his: *honesty, outstanding traits; efforts to save the youth; steadfastness of conviction; resilience in battle; avoidance of temptation; and love of philosophy. He* ends the dialogue this way because, most likely, he wanted to show what happens to persons like Alcibiades, who caused considerable harm to Athens and to himself by following a corrupt and sensuous path, as compared with Socrates who followed the path that Diotima described above and became *a paragon of virtue.*

6. PHAEDO (ΦΑΙΔΩΝ)

«Καλλος μεν γαρ η χρονος ανηλωσε η νοσος εμαρανε,
πλουτος δε κακιας μαλλον η καλοκαγαθιας υπηρετης
εστιν, εξουσιαν μεν τη ραθυμια παρασκευαζων,
επι δε τας ηδονας τους νεους παρακαλων.» [11]

Isocrates

Phaedo explores the subject of the soul of man. The "Theory of the Soul" constituted, along with the "Theory of Recollection" and the "Theory of Ideas," the foundation of the Platonic philosophical edifice. The soul pre-exists man and is immortal. It incarnates in the human body and departs upon death. Since the soul is immortal and continues to exist after death, and is judged for its accomplishments while incarnated in the human body, the kind of life one leads determines its fate after it departs from the mortal body. In this context then, the Platonic **"Theory of the Soul"** and its **Christian** counterpart do not differ much, with the exception that the Christian soul does not pre-exist the human body. As to the immortality of the soul, the two doctrines are similar, as are the positions on judgment and the necessity of virtuous living leading to a rewarding life after death. In **Phaedo** Plato discusses these points and attempts to *prove* the pre-existence as well as the immortality of the soul. He emphasizes that a person who has led the life of a philosopher (*a virtuous life*) should not fear death, and should not agonize over the fate of his soul or of its whereabouts after death. In the dialogue some of the participants questioned and doubted the immortality of the soul, and asserted that it should be more natural for the soul to perish along with the body. At this point Plato borrows from the **"Theory of Opposites,"** advanced by Anaximander, to prove that the soul is immortal. The **"Theory of Recollection"** is used subsequently to prove the pre-existence of the soul prior to its re-incarnation in the body. These are, in essence, the main philosophical points of this discussion.

This dialogue takes place in the city **of Flis** in N.E. Peloponnesus, which was a city on the road to **Ellida**. It was in this city that Phaedo, a student and companion of Socrates, settled after he left Athens along with other students and followers of Socrates, in fear of reprisals against them by the returning Democrats. **Phaedo** is requested to relate the last days of Socrates in prison, and particularly the last moments of his life just before he took the hemlock. He recalls

---

[11] **"Because time or disease destroys physical beauty, wealth serves evil rather than benevolence, for it corrupts the leaders and leads the youth to hedonism."**

that quite a number of students and friends of Socrates were present during the final hours of his life and he identifies all by name. Phaedo describes the Socratic mood; and essentially the dramatic part of the dialogue deals specifically with the reaction of Socrates while facing death, and the reaction of his students and friends as well. Reading through one is impressed by the mood of Socrates; he is calm, tranquil, and exhibits composure of grandeur. His contented expression exudes the Socratic irony, even though subdued under the circumstances; he expresses concern over the conditions and whereabouts of each one of his fellow students and friends, and for those who had already fled Athens. It evokes a strange feeling of admiration and

The Academy of Athens

compassion for the fate of the man who is about to die, and yet maintains a gay and joyful demeanor; he converses, he laughs, he tells jokes and defends his views. His stoicism is real, not pretentious; no fear of his impending death; no boisterous speeches; just plain talk in a matter of fact way. He is simple and honest, calm and brave; he is teaching those who are depressed and crying that one should not be afraid of death. This dialogue exhibits the Platonic art in writing that was considered in ancient times and even today as *poetry in prose*. The French philosopher and poet, **Alphonse de Lamartine,** wrote: *"For Socrates this day was like any other day, with the exception that it did not have a tomorrow."* A considerable part of the discussion deals with the three aspects of the soul: (1) The soul exists and man is a spirit with a soul; disregarding completely the material aspect of life embraced by pre-Socratic philosophers, (2) The soul pre-existed the birth of the body and (3) The soul is immortal. He borrows both from the Naturalists' and the Pythagoreans' views on the subject. Plato had traveled to Croton and was acquainted with their mystic conception of the soul and its whereabouts after death

In **Phaedo** Socrates teaches his students that man should not be afraid of death because death is merely the separation of the immortal soul from the body, and upon death will travel to another world where a virtuous man, the true philosopher, will meet other virtuous souls and almighty immortal gods. He warned them that only those who reach the *"Ideas"* and live an exemplary, virtuous, and prudent life would reach this state. Phaedo describes Socrates as an exuberant person not afraid to die because he lived a virtuous life, and also taught that man should never commit suicide because he has no right to separate the soul from the body before its time.

The true philosopher, during his life, is seeking the truth: the Platonic "*Idea*" or "*Form*." There is a struggle between the soul and the senses while man lives; therefore, the ultimate goal for man is to reach perfection by leading a virtuous and prudent life. *The struggle of the soul in its tri-partite form of the "Logical", the "Sensual," and the "Intellectual"--is real, continuous, and agonizing: only the soul has knowledge of the "Forms."* The Socratic doctrine of **recollection** is extensively discussed in this dialogue and also in **Meno,** in which a geometric proof is presented through an experiment with a young servant. *Recollection is knowledge*, in that one has to search for the truth vested in the soul, and Plato suggests that if we make it a point to question and search for answers for things that we do not know, we will eventually acquire **"knowledge":** *which constitutes happiness.*

Reproduction of ancient Olympia

The proof of the immortality of the soul is important; otherwise, the suggestion that one should not fear death becomes meaningless. Unlike the Egyptians, the Greeks believed that the body disintegrates after death, and in this dialogue Plato "proves" the immortality of the soul in a logical dialectic way. He refers to the **"Theory [12] of the Physical Conception of Opposites"** advanced by **Anaximander,** and the argument is as follows: Every positive entity exists and is recognized by the understanding of its opposite, and between the two parts there are two conditions. Death is the opposite of life; and as it is with all opposites, there is an underlying state, which is life, that extends from birth to death. Also, on the basis of this thinking, there is the opposite state that extends from death to life. This concept has no meaning if the cycle is broken; therefore the soul continues to live after death until it returns in order to complete the

---

[12] Compare this with the opposites: *day and night*. There is a state from sunrise to sunset--"the day state," and a state from sunset to sunrise--"the night state."

cycle. If we do not have the second state, then we would have broken the cyclical process of the opposites and everything should perish in a linear relationship, which cannot be true, as in Nature *nothing is destroyed and nothing is created from nothing* (theory advanced originally by the Naturalists.) A passage from Phaedo (105b-107a) follows in which Plato reasons out the immortality of the soul:

"SOCRATES: Seeing then that the immortal is indestructible, must not the soul, if she is immortal, be also imperishable? CEBES: Most certainly. SOCRATES: Then when death attacks a man, the mortal portion of him may be supposed to die, but the immortal goes out of the way of death and is preserved safe and sound? CEBES: True. SOCRATES: Then, Cebes, beyond question, the soul is immortal and imperishable, and our souls will truly exist in another world?"

This Socratic dialogue addresses the most important question posed by man, and that is: **What occurs after death?** There had been considerable argumentation concerning heretical discussion among the early Christian theologians, and quite a number of early Christian thinkers were persecuted for stating their conviction that the soul pre-existed. Plato attempts to "prove" the existence and immortality of the soul through logical criteria and quasi- experimentation, but refrains from dogmatism and one-sided determinism. The important point to consider here is that, in both the Socratic and Christian tenets, the kind of life one lives in this ephemeral existence will have consequences in the other "eternal life." If one leads a non-virtuous life, according to Plato, his soul will be denigrated to a lower level, and that will be its punishment; however, if one leads a corrupted life, in the Christian ethic, he will be tortured and burned in eternal hell.

The god Hermes

The mystery of life and death has fascinated thinkers who attempted to go beyond the theocratic interpretation of the phenomenon, at all times. The process whereby a sperm from a male joins the egg of a female and eventually develops into a living being capable of feeding itself, thinking rationally, and surviving through overwhelming impediments, is an awesome phenomenon that has not been understood or explained by the simple human mind. If one considers the complicated functions that the human organs perform in the body, such as: the metabolic system, the circulatory system, the sympathetic and parasympathetic nervous system, the immunological system, the genetic code, and so many more detailed sub-functions inside each system, one cannot help but stand in awe facing such an extraordinary machine of superhuman conception and complexity. We understand quite well, through the advances in medicine, how to measure the reactions of these systems, but we are unable, even in a rudimentary level, to duplicate them.

The intellect and the reasoning process, which constitute the difference between the human and the animal worlds, present the most complicated task for the human mind to interpret, understand, duplicate, and explain. It is this intellectual, logical capability of the human being that has challenged thinkers of all ages to understand and predict. Even though the physical functions of man can be observed and analyzed, the origin and force behind these activities--the Aristotelian "*First Movement*"--cannot; the process of thinking, deciding, choosing, acting, and planning, is far beyond our capabilities to predict. Prior to Socrates most of the thinkers (Naturalists), with the exception perhaps of the Pythagoreans, attributed all phenomena to material cause. Matter was considered the basic substance of all elements on Earth, and the creation of all objects resulted from this original substance: water, air, fire etc. Socrates, or perhaps Plato, was the first to introduce the transcendental concept of the "Ideas" and the soul--which is not theocratically inspired--as were those of the pre-Greek Oriental cultures. He introduces the spirit in man as part of his being that depends on his actions, and directed by his will. Previously, such incomprehensible actions and conditions exhibited by man were set aside from the material substance that they consisted of; but now the soul plays a predominant role in the study of man and interpretation of his behavior. As pointed out earlier, previous thinkers and cultures such as the **Chaldeans, Egyptians, Babylonians, and Pythagoreans,** dealt with the matter of the soul--but none had elevated the subject to the scholarly and scientific plateau achieved by Plato. Other Greek thinkers such as **Anaxagoras (Νους) and Empedocles (Νεικος and Φιλοτης)**, did consider the spirit in man, in some form, as the force that dominates life and directs all actions and reflections.[13] Plato developed a detailed theory about the soul of man intertwined with a divinity, and presented as a function affecting behavior and life at all levels. Both Socrates and Plato preferred to believe that man is a spirit, and that *Man has a Soul.*

---

[13] Refer to the previous chapter for a narrative on early Greek views on the soul.

7. MENO (MENΩN)

«Κρειττον ενα φιλον εχειν πολλου
αξιον η πολλους μηδενος αξιους»[14]
Anacharsis

In **Meno** Socrates discusses the general subject of *"virtue"* and specifically: (1) its definition; (2) whether it is teachable; (3) if it is acquired by practice; or (4) is it innate to some, but absent in others. As is true in most of the dialogues, the theories of: *Recollection, Immortality of the Soul,* and *Ideas or Forms,* enter the discussion as well. At the beginning Socrates contends that he has no idea what virtue really is, and asks **Meno,** who is a friend and follower of Gorgias' philosophy, to provide a definition of his own. **Meno** states: "*Virtue is the act of benefiting one's friends and hurting one's enemies, and enabling one to participate in the administration of the affairs of the State."* **Meno** adds that there are quite a number of other definitions of virtue that relate specifically to women, children, old people, etc. The above definition applies to men; while for women he states that a woman's virtue would be: *"to rightly administer the affairs of her house and obey her husband."* Similarly, he gives other interpretations of virtue applicable to different people and situations. The intention of the discussion is to dramatize the fact that the current thinkers (mostly Sophists) were providing various definitions and interpretations of virtue, ethics, and other moral or political values applicable to specific conditions-- without a root of universality. With their rhetoric they were capable of convincing people of what would benefit them at the time, rather than pursuing the ultimate truth and universal values. Socrates analyzes these definitions given by Meno and refutes them all--compelling Meno to accept that virtue is the same for men, women, children--rich and poor, strong and weak. The discussants ultimately agree that virtuous is the

Euripides

person who is *prudent, temperate, just, brave, compassionate, tolerant, loving, and*

---

[14] "It is better to have one friend of great worth, than many friends worth nothing at all."

forgiving; which constitute the components of *virtue.* Also, in this part of the dialogue the role of material possessions is explored, and they agree that if accompanied by *justice, prudence, devotion, and Temperance,* they enhance *virtue;* otherwise, these possessions distract one from the road to virtuous behavior. As we have seen elsewhere (**Protagoras,** p.122), the acquisition of knowledge was of paramount importance in Platonic theory, and in this dialogue Socrates discusses the difference between his views on *knowledge* as compared with those of his contemporary thinkers. Meno introduces Gorgias' contention that ideal (transcendental) knowledge is not possible or important, and that knowledge derived only from the senses (**sensory knowledge**) is of greater significance. He further states that man cannot search either for the things that he knows, or for those that he does not know, because it would not make sense for one to pursue something that he already knows; and it is not necessary to search for things that he does not know--because he would not know where to start. The Platonic school strongly opposed this view, and to counter it, in the second part of the dialogue, Plato extensively discusses the *"Theory of "Recollection"*--which is Socrates' reply to the pessimistic view of knowledge advocated by the Sophists. Meno asks Socrates to elaborate on what he means when he says *"recollecting"* rather than *"learning,"* and to differentiate between *"learning"* and *"recollecting".* Socrates carries out an experiment in geometry with one of Meno's young servants, to prove that the servant, by responding to questions posed to him, acquired *(recollected)* real knowledge of geometry without ever having been taught the subject. This is an important point in that Plato: **First-** introduces the notion that a person, via his soul, has all knowledge stored in him--and that he only has to "search" (recollect) for it. Therefore, one has to be active and strenuously seeking knowledge, because it is there for him to acquire. This is similar to today's concept of *"brainstorming."*

The Goddess Aphrodite

Second--by proving that the young servant *"acquired knowledge"* of how to double the area of a geometric square, without previously having ever been taught the subject, Plato *"proves"* the immortality of the soul, and also that it existed prior to its incarnation in man. A narrative of this experiment is reproduced below, along with the appropriate diagrams, so that a better understanding of the principle of *"Recollection"* may be achieved and also to demonstrate the Platonic dialectic method. Socrates poses question and the servant responds, while Meno listens and at times comments. The problem posed to the young man by Socrates is: By *how much would one increase the dimensions (sides) of a square so as to double its area.*

"..........MENO: What do you mean, Socrates, when you say that we do not *"learn,"* but that we *"recollect,"* and that *"learning"* is *"recollecting."* Could you teach me on this?

SOCRATES: I commented on this earlier, Meno, that you are indeed devious, because you ask me to "**teach**" you something, while I proclaim that there is no such thing as "**teaching**"--but rather "**Recollecting**." You try to show me contradicting myself.

MENO: Not by Zeus! Socrates, I did not say it intentionally, but rather by habit. But if you can show that this is so, please proceed.

SOCRATES: It is not easy, but for your sake Meno, I will try. Could you call one of your servants near, whomever you wish, and I will prove it to you through him.

MENO: With pleasure (addressing the servants).You, young man, come near!

SOCRATES: (Addressing the servant) Are you Greek? Do you speak Greek?

MENO: Very well, as he was born and raised in my home.

SOCRATES: Watch out now Meno, and see whether he **recollects** or **learns** from me.

MENO: Of course, I will be attentive.

SOCRATES: Tell me boy, do you know that this is a square shaped (ABCD) diagram?

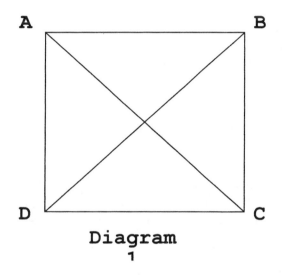

Diagram
1

SERVANT: Yes.

SOCRATES: A square diagram, then, is one that has four equal sides.

SERVANT: Certainly.

SOCRATES: Then, it should have the lines AC and BD equal.

SERVANT: Yes.

SOCRATES: Could there be a smaller or larger square diagram than this?

SERVANT: Yes.

SOCRATES: If now the side AB is two feet long and the side AD is also two feet long, how many square feet would the entire square be? Look at it this way. If AB were two feet long and AD were one foot long, would the diagram be one times two feet?

SERVANT: That should be so.

SOCRATES: But since AD is two feet long, wouldn't the square be two times two feet?
SERVANT: Yes.
SOCRATES: Then what would that be? Think carefully and tell me.
SERVANT: Four.
SOCRATES: Excellent. Could another similar such diagram be constructed and be of double size, and have all sides equal?
SERVANT: It could.
SOCRATES: How many square feet would it be?
SERVANT: Eight.

SOCRATES: Tell me now; what would be the length of each side of this diagram? The length of this one is two feet; how many feet would be the length of the new one? Would it be double?
SERVANT: It is obvious that it would be double.
SOCRATES: Do you see, Meno, that I do not teach him anything, but pose questions? He now thinks that he knows the length of the side of the new double diagram. Or am I wrong?
MENO: Yes, it is true, he thinks so.
SOCRATES: Does he really know?
MENO: Of course not.
SOCRATES: He thinks, however, that a double diagram in area will be created if we double the length of the sides.
MENO: Yes.
SOCRATES: Watch now how he will begin to recollect. Tell me boy, do you still insist that a double diagram will be created if we double the length of the sides? And I do not mean longer here and shorter there, but all sides being equal, just as the original shape--but double in area; that is, eight square feet?
SERVANT: I still think so.
SOCRATES: Is the line AE double the line AB, if we add BE to it, which is equal to AB? (See diagram 2).

SERVANT: Yes.
SOCRATES: You say then, that if we draw 4 equal lines, AE of a square diagram, we will create a diagram of eight square feet.
SERVANT: Yes.
SOCRATES: Let us now draw these 4 lines (See Diagram 2).

*(Note that Socrates by the "**question and answer**" mode of inquiry (the dialectic method) attempts to draw the servant's attention to a rigorous inductive thinking (going from the particular to the general) with the objective to make him "**recall**" the desired answer of the doubling of area of the square; reasoning out answers by simply posing questions. One obviously could argue that it is not the mind of the servant that engages in the **in-depth inquiry**, but rather Socrates' who poses the*

questions because he knows the answer. The point, however, that Plato makes, in this example, is that asking questions is tantamount to learning, because the answers or the secrets will be revealed only if one is rigorously engaged in questioning. This is a direct response to Gorgias' negative approach to knowledge: t "Nothing can be learned and communicated to others"—which, in essence, is a repudiation of abstract thinking.

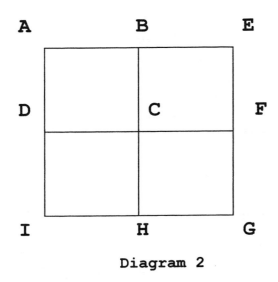

Diagram 2

SOCRATES: Aren't all four squares (ABCD, BCFE, FCHG, and DCHI) included in this new diagram AEGI-- each of equal size as the original ABCD?
SERVANT: Yes
SOCRATES: How big then should the diagram be? Isn't it four times ABCD?
SERVANT: Why not?
SOCRATES: This then, that is four times larger, can it be double?
SERVANT: Oh! By Zeus, of course not.
SOCRATES: But how many times bigger should it be?
SERVANT: Four times.
SOCRATES: Therefore, my boy, by doubling the lengths of the sides we do not double the area, but we quadruple it.
SERVANT: Truly.
SOCRATES: Four times four is sixteen, or is it not?
SERVANT: Naturally.
SOCRATES: This square, ABCD, was made of half of the line AE?
SERVANT: Yes.

SOCRATES: Very well. The diagram of eight square feet is not created if we double the line AB, but if we increase it by more than AB but less than AE, is smaller than AEGI.

SERVANT: Yes, it seems so.

SOCRATES: Very well. That is the way to respond--"that it seems so." So, now isn't AB two feet and AE four feet?

SERVANT: Yes.

SOCRATES: Thus, the length of the side of the diagram of eight feet must be larger than two feet and less than 4 feet?

SERVANT: So, it should be.

SOCRATES: Think and tell me what the length of this line should be.

SERVANT: It should be three feet.

SOCRATES: If it is three feet, we take half of AB and add to it, so it will be three feet, AB'. And if we do the same with the other side AD' we create a square that has three feet length on all sides. (Diagram 3).

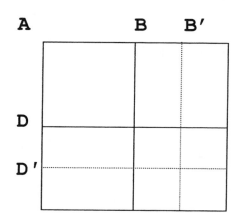

Diagram 3

SERVANT: Yes.

SOCRATES: If now it is three feet long on all sides, it should be three times three square feet.

SERVANT: It is clear.

SOCRATES: Three times three, however, is what?

SERVANT: Nine.

SOCRATES: But we said that the doubled square should be of how many square feet?

SERVANT: Eight.

SOCRATES: Thus, it is not by the length of three that the area of the square becomes eight feet.

SERVANT: It certainly is not.

SOCRATES: But of what length is this true? Try to tell us exactly. And if you do not want to express it arithmetically, just show us the line.

SERVANT: But by Zeus! Oh Socrates, I do not know.[15]

SOCRATES: Do you see now, my friend Meno, at what stage of recollection is this boy? At the beginning he did not know the dimensions of the diagram of eight square feet exactly, and still he does not know, but he thought that he knew and he responded very boldly, as if he knew, and he did not believe that he did not know. Now he is conscious of the difficulty that he is in, believing that he does not know; and therefore he does not think that he knows.

MENO: It appears so.

SOCRATES: Do you think that he would have attempted earlier to search for and learn that which he thought he knew, while in reality he did not, before he got into the present predicament? He believes now that he does not know and desires knowledge.

MENO: No, Socrates, I do not believe so.

SOCRATES: He benefited then by stumbling?

MENO: I accept it absolutely.

SOCRATES: Watch now what he will find, given his present impasse, by asking him further questions, but without instructing him on anything. Be careful and observe whether I attempt to teach him anything. (To the servant): Is this the diagram of four square feet, ABCD? (Diagram 4).

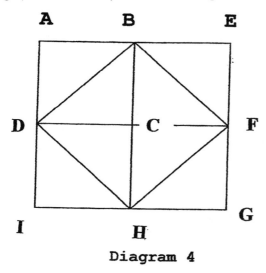

Diagram 4

SERVANT: Yes.

SOCRATES: We could add another one equal to it, BEFC.

SERVANT: Yes.

SOCRATES: And also two more, CFGH and CHID.

---

[15] This length is an irrational number, the square root of 8, and can only be understood as an approximation. The ancient Greeks never studied it extensively, with the exception of the Pythagoreans who discovered it.

SERVANT: Why not?

SOCRATES: What happens now? Did we not create these 4 equal squares?
SERVANT: Yes

SOCRATES: Therefore, the total is larger than the first (ABCD) by how much?
SERVANT: It is four times as much.
SOCRATES: We have quadrupled it, or do you not remember?
SERVANT: I remember very well.

SOCRATES: Now then, are the lines BD, BF, FH and HD, dividing these squares in two?
SERVANT: Yes.
SOCRATES: Don't these lines create the diagram BDHF?
SERVANT: Yes, they do.
SOCRATES: Tell me, what is the area of this new diagram?
SERVANT: I cannot say.
SOCRATES: The line we drew, BD, doesn't it divide ABCD in half? And one half is in DBFH, and the other half outside it?
SERVANT: Certainly so.
SOCRATES: How many diagrams like DBC are partly included in DBFH?
SERVANT: Four.
SOCRATES: And how many in ABCD?
SERVANT: Two
SOCRATES: What is four in relation to two?
SERVANT: Twice as much.
SOCRATES: Now, what is the area of the diagram DBFH?
SERVANT: Eight feet.
SOCRATES: And from what line was it formed?
SERVANT: From DB.
SOCRATES: The one that extends from one corner of the original square to the other corner.
SERVANT: Yes.
SOCRATES: The Sophists call this line **the diagonal.** If you create a new square based on the diagonal, then we double the original square; isn't that so, oh servant of Meno?
SERVANT: And certainly it is so, Socrates.
SOCRATES: How does this seem to you, Meno? Didn't he answer all these on the basis of his own opinion?
MENO: That is true; all was his.

SOCRATES: And yet we know that he did not know these things before.
MENO: Certainly.
SOCRATES: Were these opinions-- **"Ideas"**-- inside him or not?
MENO: It seems so; they existed in him.

SOCRATES: This person, who does not know, has inside him knowledge of things that he does not know.

MENO: It seems so.

SOCRATES: And now then, these **"Ideas"** *or truths* were stirred, as in a dream. If one then asks him questions many times and in different ways, concerning things that he does not know, do you not think that at the end he will acquire knowledge like anyone else?

MENO: True.

SOCRATES: He will know about these things without anyone teaching him; but by only asking questions, he will derive the knowledge from himself.

MENO: Yes.

SOCRATES: Deriving knowledge from oneself then, is it not **"recollecting?"**

MENO: Surely.

SOCRATES: Is it not, however, necessary that the knowledge that he has now was either acquired at some time or was in him all the time?

MENO: Yes.

SOCRATES: If he had it always, then he knew it always; but if he acquired it at some other time, it is not possible that he acquired it during his present life. Or has anyone ever taught him geometry or any other branch of knowledge? You are the right person to know because he was born and raised in your family.

MENO: I am sure that no one ever taught him these subjects.

SOCRATES: He has, however, these conceptions in him, or doesn't he?

MENO: It appears so, Socrates.

SOCRATES: Since he has these ideas now but did not acquire them during his present life, isn't it obvious that he had these ideas during some other period?

MENO: It appears so.

SOCRATES: This period, then, must have been one during which he was not a man.

MENO: Yes.

Aristophanes

SOCRATES: Since we are compelled to admit that at some time, when he was or was not a man, these **"ideas"** were inside him, which when prodded by questioning become knowledge; is it not appropriate then, to believe that his soul preserves these "ideas" forever? Because it is obvious that in all time he was a man or he was not a man.

MENO: Obviously.

SOCRATES: Since the truth is always inside our soul, it should be admitted that the soul is immortal. And it behooves us to seek--with determination--the truth, and to recollect that which we do not know at the moment.

MENO: It seems to me, Socrates, that by some inexplicable way you are right.

SOCRATES: *It seems to me as well, Meno. As far as other things are* *concerned, I would not dare insist on the veracity of my convictions. But I believe that it is our duty to look into and learn of things that we do not know; and I believe that we will be better men--more active and more compassionate--than if we accept that it is not possible to learn about things that we do not know.*

For this conviction I will fight with words, deeds, and all my strength for as long as I can.
MENO: I agree with you, Socrates..........."[16]

This last passage highlights the difference between Plato and the Sophists, and provides a response to the earlier negative definition of Meno--denying the validity and universality of knowledge. Socrates' view of seeking knowledge radiates a feeling of optimism and belief in humanity, as well as the need to investigate and discover the truth (*Ideas*) of things that we do not know.

In the continuation of the dialogue, the original question of teaching virtue is revisited, and Plato concludes with this important topic. The major objective that he attempts to achieve in this portion of **Meno,** is to refute the argument of the various language teachers and speechwriters throughout Greece, and particularly in Athens, that in their schools, for a handsome fee, they could teach virtue, the art of politics, morality, and other important values--in addition to language and rhetoric. There are three persons involved in this the latter part of the dialogue: **Socrates, Meno, and Anytus.** Anytus is a friend of Meno and is visiting Athens from Thessaly. He is also one of the three accusers of Socrates--representing the business establishment--who brought the court suit against him that eventually led to his death. **Meno** makes several attempts to prove that virtue can be taught; but **Socrates** consistently disregards his points. If virtue is "teachable," then there should be instructors of virtue in the city; but Anytus is not able to identify out such teachers, and eventually admits that even the Sophists cannot teach virtue.

Socrates believes that virtue is not innate; for he has never found, in spite of his search, someone born virtuous. But if that were the case, he contends, we should be in a position to recognize virtuous persons when born, keeping them secure and protected on the Acropolis, and using them to disseminate virtue when they mature. He further states that if virtue is "teachable," then the sons of famous men--virtuous and honorable men--should have taught their sons to be virtuous as well. But that is not universally true. Socrates concludes that if virtue is knowledge, then it can be taught; but he is not sure if virtue is knowledge--as sometimes it is; and sometimes it is not. At this point, Socrates introduces a new term--*Ορθη Δοξα*--translated as *"Correct Judgment,"* which is fundamental in recognizing when virtue is knowledge that can be acquired through teaching. This term refers to that knowledge which derives from a clear understanding of things directed by the intellect. He brings an example to dramatize the difference between *"Simple knowledge"* (*Sensory Knowledge*) and *"Correct Judgment"* (*Transcendental Knowledge*). If one is asked to take a passenger to Larisa (a city northwest of Athens) and he has been there before and is familiar with the road, then he has "Correct Judgment" (**Ορθη Δοξα**) of the undertaking;

---

[16] Translation by author.

but if he only knows where Larisa is and how to get there, but has never been there, he has *Simple Knowledge*. You have to have **Ορθη Δοξα** and **Simple Knowledge** in order to learn and become virtuous. The concept of *Correct Judgment* represents the essence of the **"Idea" of virtue** in Platonic philosophy: If both knowledge and *Correct Judgment* are present, then one can learn and teach virtue. Responding to Meno's protest that "*Correct Judgment*" is not always a part of the *Logical* part of the soul, Socrates states that effort and hard work are required to keep it intact. It is like the sculptures of Daidalus,[17] which if not tied down, will walk away. This infers that to have "*Correct Judgment*" present in the soul at all times, it must be anchored. In conclusion, this implies that if one is to become virtuous, honorable, and useful to himself and to

Artemis being worshipped, Relief 4th century B.C.

society, he should strive to employ his intellect to acquire true knowledge «*Ορθη Δοξα.* » For example, to be in a position to take visitors to Larisa, one should study the road and become familiar with the area-- he will then be in a position to successfully take visitors there.

The feasibility of teaching virtue and honor has concerned university curriculum committees at all times. Courses on ethics have been developed and taught at philosophy departments and schools of business in an effort to distinguish and avoid unethical and immoral practices that afflict society daily--and occupy the media continuously. But it appears that today we are faced with the same problem that concerned Socrates almost 2500 years ago. We see a number of students who have graduated from these courses on ethics, yet the practice of unethical and immoral behavior are ubiquitous. Two and a half millennia of instruction in the field of ethics indicates that virtually no progress has been made in this area since the time of Socrates. It appears that we have not heeded his conviction that ethics cannot be taught--but rather is the result of *intellectual maturity and acquisition of true knowledge (Ορθη Δοξα).*

---

[17] Daidalus was a Greek sculptor who built his statues by advancing one leg in a position of walking. Because they seemed so lifelike, a myth developed—"If you do not tie the statues down they will walk away."

8. STATESMAN (ΠΟΛΙΤΙΚΟΣ)

«Ανθρωπων, τους μεν ουτω φειδεσθαι ως αει ζησομενους,
τους δε ουτως αναλισκειν, ως αυτικα τεθνηξομενους»[18]
Aristotle

Demosthenes

The <u>**Statesman**</u> examines the subject of "politics" and the functions and responsibilities of the *statesman-politician*. In addition to **Socrates,** the participants in this dialogue are: **Socrates** (the younger); **Theaetetus** (well-known from the homonymous dialogue--Chapter 9); **Theodorus** (a renowned mathematician who had established a school of mathematics and philosophy in Cyrene--present Libya); and a representative of the Eleatic School--referred to as **Stranger** *(Ξενos)*.

As stated elsewhere (<u>**Republic, Laws**</u>), Plato was neither enamored with the politicians of the mid-5th century Athenian democracy, nor with other forms of political systems in ancient Greece. He had found that ordinary politicians did not possess what he would expect in *virtue and other moral and ethical values* required for a wise and just leadership of the city-states.

The **Philosopher-King** concept--the Ideal Ruler--as expounded in the <u>**Republic,**</u> was actually preferred by Plato in his early writings, but in his more mature years it appears that he abandoned this doctrine (**see** <u>**Laws**</u>). In the "ideal" statesman Plato *identifies all virtues, education, judgment, maturity, and experience* necessary to rule justly; and under such conditions a plethora of laws would not be necessary. In almost half of the dialogue, Plato identifies, classifies, and defines the characteristics of a "**Statesman,**" and uses parallelisms from real life-- comparing a ruler with a master weaver who uses various tools to produce a product: cloth. He spends considerable time identifying and recognizing the role of the politician-ruler as a function

---

[18] "Mankind is divided into those who are as thrifty as if they will live forever, and those who are as extravagant as if they are going to die tomorrow."

of scientific criteria and mature leadership. Decision-making is a difficult and responsible process, and the person who is in a position of authority may have to make decisions under conditions of certainty—but involving conflicting opinions decisions are made under conditions of considerable uncertainty. The application of scientific criteria in the decision process becomes necessary for valid and sound choices based on objectivity and the ultimate truth. These judgmental decisions must be made with the benefit of the public in mind. He compares a ruler,

The Epistyle block of the Dionysus Theater

in terms of decision making, with that of a shepherd, whose decisions should ultimately lead to the betterment and welfare of the flock. First, he summarizes and evaluates existing political systems in ancient Greece at his time, even though Herodotus had previously described the various systems (Greek and barbarian) extensively in his **Histories.** Plato basically recognizes systems controlled by: (1) a few--the *Aristocracies*--which deteriorate *into* oligarchies; (2) a hereditary form of government--***Monarchy***--which could deteriorate into *Tyranny*, and finally (3) the multitude--the *Democracies.* Plato had the least confidence in direct democratic rule. Most likely his thinking on this matter was influenced either by his aristocratic upbringing, or by his experiences with the system--particularly the execution of Socrates during the democratic rule of Athens in 399 B.C. Also, due to the exile of **Themistocles** and the banishment of **Aristides,** two very significant personalities of ancient Athens, and of other famous innocent Athenian politicians and thinkers (**Anaxagoras**) sent into exile following false accusations--most likely he mistrusted the system. Often the multitude was swayed by eloquent demagogues in committing these injustices, without full knowledge and cognizance of the facts and consequences. Famous is the incident, when **Aristide (***the "Just"***)** was approached by a simple citizen who asked him to write on a shell the name of the person that he wanted banished in a plebiscite. Aristide asked the citizen what name he wished written on the shell, and the citizen answered, "Aristide." When Aristide asked why he wanted Aristide banished, the citizen, without knowing that he was addressing Aristide, replied--"Just because I am tired of hearing him called "The Just."

In the description of these political systems, Plato expresses displeasure with all of them for reasons that he eloquently presents in a dialectic discussion with the participants. He makes extensive reference to the proper objectives and leadership of political systems, and concludes that the basic goal should be to secure: *freedom; peace; eradication of poverty; moderation in the acquisition of wealth; achievement of law and order; harmony; and elimination of injustice and anarchy.* He states that he does not believe that, by the very nature of these systems, any one of them would be successful in providing to the public such advantages: the reason being that they usually deteriorate into *tyrannies or the rule of the mob (Οχλοκρατιες)*. To emphasize the necessity and advantage of the scientific method in decision-making, he draws an analogy: A medical doctor will attempt to cure his afflicted patients--either with or without their cooperation--and he will or will not decide to perform an operation or prescribe therapy--with or without their consent. These doctors may be rich or poor, but still are called doctors as long as their prescriptions are issued on the basis of scientific criteria. Overall, the objective is the wellness of the body--securing it in health for a happier life; it is only in this way that one could define a doctor. Obviously, the opinion that Plato enunciates in this passage, the comparison of the public with a person needing help, and the medical doctor who is offering this help, is intended to emphasize the gravity of political decision making--which should not be left in the hands of inexperienced, immature, and unethical neophytes. In today's political systems the influence of special interests, in the form of campaign financing, is an example of serious manipulation of the political process--similar to the influences the demagogues exerted in ancient Athenian democracy.

Corinthian Style

In summary: Plato believed that the ruler, for efficient leadership, should have empathy for his people—acting *in justice, peace, and harmony--avoiding excesses in all aspects of administrative relationships.* All these would be beneficial and provide justice if decisions are based upon scientific criteria: *the Ultimate Truth--the "Ideas."* The unprepared and unscientifically minded would fail. By the thoughts expressed in this dialogue, one will conclude that Plato had in mind an ideal ruler, whom he lauded extensively in the **Republic**. He did not believe that a charismatic orator, a rich lord, a powerful military man, or any man of influence should become head of state unless he possesses the *scientific knowledge necessary for the profession, and the virtues of justice, prudence, and bravery, enabling him to guide and manage the affairs of the city-state equitably.*

9. TIMAEUS (ΤΙΜΑΙΟΣ)

«Κοσμον τονδε τον αυτον απαντων, ουτε τις θεων
Ουτε ανθρωπων εποιησεν, αλλ ην αει και εστιν
και εσται, πυρ αειζωον, απτομενον μετρα και
αποσβεννυμενον μετρα»[19]
Heraclitus

Timaeus is really a monologue, and represents Plato's conception of the Creation of the World. There are only two participants in this dialogue: **Timaeus**--a famous and renowned astronomer from **Locris,** who is carrying most of the narrative; and Socrates, who occasionally responds in the affirmative. The previous night, at **Phaleron,** a group of Socrates' companions had discussed *the ideal State*--for which Plato wrote the **Republic**--and they had decided to meet again and discuss other subjects, such as: *Atlantis, f*or which Plato wrote the dialogue **Critias;** and the *Creation of the Universe*-- which is the topic of the present dialogue.

As we have discussed elsewhere (chapters 2 and 3), the physical philosophers attempted to explain the creation of the world by the use of physical and speculative conceptions, and identified the *first principle* or *the first cause* of creation with a number of physical substances. For example, **Thales** attributed to **"water" (Υδωρ)** the magical power from which the entire living and non-living world evolved. **Anaximander** thought that **"Infinity" (Απειρον)** or the **"Boundless,"** by interaction of the forces of the opposites, was the First Cause; and

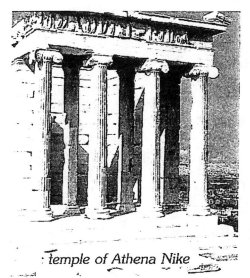

Temple of Athena Nike

Anaximenis, the last of the Miletians, had advanced the theory that **"Air" (Αηρ)**, through the forces of condensation and rarefaction, was the ultimate generating force. Others advanced different ideas; for example: the **Pythagoreans** considered *"numbers"* **(Μαθηματικοι Αριθμοι)**; **Anaxagoras**--the **"Mind"** *(Νους);* and **Embedocles**-- **"Love" (Φιλοτης)** and **"Strife"** **(Νεικος)**. But it is important to note that all of these thinkers discarded the theocratic interpretation of the creation of the world, as proposed by Hesiod and other epic poets and sages. **Aristotle** also abandoned the theocratic approach, and in **Metaphysics** directed his attention to four basic conceptual and theoretical principles, which are: *(1) the substance or essence of*

things; (2) the nature of the actual matter of things; (3) the source of the motion that caused the First Movement; and (4) the final purpose for the creation of a thing. In other words, Aristotle

---

[19] "This ordered world, the same for all, has not been made by any god or man; but it always was- is--and will be;--an ever living fire, being kindled in measures and put out in measures."

162

was directing his research in identifying the source and the reason for the existence of any thing by asking: *What is its substance, the material, the original force of motion, and the purpose of its creation.* Once one has understood or has been able to explain these four basic questions, then he has an understanding of the origin of the world around him and its purpose: *because everything has a purpose.* Plato was confronted with these questions as well, and in **Timaeus** he attempts to provide still another view of the Creation and the nature of the world around him. Unlike all previous and subsequent thinkers, he involves the notion of the Divinity. But he does not identify

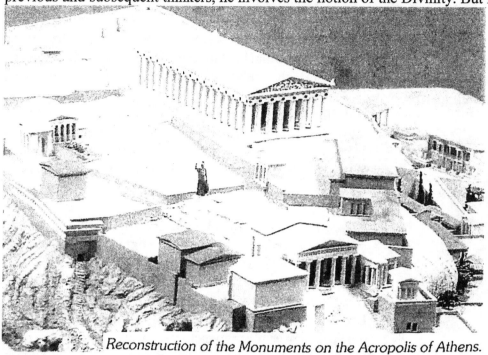

specifically the creation of the world as the work of a known god, among the well known gods, but introduces the concept of a divine **Creator**, or **Craftsman** (Δημιουργος) instead. It is as if he is saying: *I am not interested really in exactly how, and by what substance, this world has been created;*

Reconstruction of the Monuments on the Acropolis of Athens.

but I accept it as it is, and proceed with my research from there-- analyzing It, explaining It, and understanding It. On several occasions, however, he refers to God as being the ultimate **"Good"**--the Greek equivalent of (Αγαθος)--and gives some details of how God constructed the world. He recognizes that the Creator made this world in perfect harmony and order, but yet the world that we see around us--the sensory world--is not the real, perfect world, but rather a copy of the original that the **Creator** used as a prototype in the image of which he formed the universe. If one conceptualizes the *Platonic "Ideas,"* he can understand that Plato's view of the prototype-- on the basis of which this image of the world was created, is the **"Idea"** of the Cosmos. In the first part of the dialogue Plato describes how the Creator made the world in a fashion similar to the **"Genesis"** of the Christian Bible. He describes, for example, how the Creator separated the light from the dark and the wet from the dry; and in a harmonious way created the Cosmos. Plato makes use of the Theory of Averages, the Median, and the four elements--*Air, Water, Fire and Earth—in the process used by the Creator to make* the living and non-living "things" of this world and the outer universe. In this respect, then, Plato's conception of the world is not different from that of the Bible. But in the continuation of the narrative by **Timaeus** the approach differs. Now Plato attempts to introduce scientific principles, mathematics, logic, and geometry, into the process of creation. Having already identified the world of the prototype, which--in the view of the Creator--is perfect, and admitting that the world perceived by the senses--is imperfect: *he points out that this world, being created from the prototype, is a changing world*. Something that is born or created is subject to change, and this obviously is the influence of **Heraclitus on Plato**. He then departs from the creation mode and introduces the concept that everything made by the Creator had always a causative factor--*because nothing is created without a reason*. Whatever is

Evzones; Guards at the tomb of Unknown Soldier. Athens

made by the **Master-craftsman (Δημιουργος)** is made by use of the original model, which is perfect, and which can be understood only by our intellect. Plato introduces *the concept of the* He takes *soul* into this world; as he has identified a soul in every living being. The soul now is included as part of this universe and described further in its various components: **(1) the Logical (Λογιστικον), (2) the Sensual (Επιθυμιτικον), and (3) the Intellectual (Θυμοειδες)**. He takes considerable time considerable time describing the world of the planets: how the Creator arranged them in a symbiotic relationship with each other--the Earth being the center of this world with all orbiting planets, the moon, and the sun, revolving around it; the moon being the closest, followed by the sun and the other planets farther out. For the creation of the stars and their orbits, he left these to be discussed later--which most likely was never done.

The various features of the human body receive considerable attention by Plato now. He discusses all matters pertaining to the nerves, organs, and their functions. He identifies: *the circulatory system of the blood, brain, muscles, eyes, ears, mouth, and nose; the anatomy of the*

male and female body; the sexual function of all beings; and the biological and chemical functions of all living organisms. One can say that Plato, in this discussion, treats matters of physics, chemistry, medicine, biology, physiology, anatomy, and many other scientific disciplines that relate to the functions of living organisms: H*umans, Animals, and Plants.* He discusses the geometric relationship of triangles and the various kinds of triangles in relation to the functions of living beings. In other words, he employs geometry to study the motion and functions, in general, of parts of living beings, and uses the combinations of the various elements (earth, air, fire, and water) in conjunction with wet/dry and hot/cold--along with the concepts of motion and change--to describe the nature, relationships, and existence of various objects **(rocks, wood, iron, coal, etc.)** on the plane. He identifies the different states of matter; as for example, the *three forms of water: solid (ice), fluid (water), gaseous (vapors); and of air: hot and cold.* The nature of human emotions is analyzed next in conjunction with the five senses and the soul; as well as how diverse sentiments emanate from inter-relationships of the four basic emotions **(joy, sorrow, enthusiasm, and contempt)**. These are joined as a result of the sensual component of the soul and the relationships of the four elements, and follows a complete analysis of action and reaction of the five senses (*sight, hearing, taste, touch, and smell).*

An extensive discussion ensues concerning the internal anatomy of the human body and its organs **(liver, spleen, stomach, pancreas, heart, lungs, kidneys, etc.),** and the functions of these organs, along with the reason that they were created: for what purpose--and how they relate to health. Also, how the three parts of the soul identified above are related to the various organs and senses and combine to define: the functional living being. In this part of the discussion, Plato identifies the Creator as being the One causing all of these changes; but he makes it a point to include geometry, mathematics, and logic to justify the functions and purposes of the various components of living things. *Matters of nutrition, the digestive and nervous system, and the functions of the heart and the brain are discussed in this section as well.* Reasons for illnesses and epidemics are examined and a full course on dietetics, nutrition, and exercise is presented for the prevention of these diseases and maintenance of good health.

The discussion continues with **Timaeus** treating the creation of the myriad kinds of animals—their forms and functions--and suggests that all come from some combination of an original human subject. He distinguishes **animals under the water (fishes); animals in the air (birds); and animals on the surface of the Earth (humans and other)**. In this part, the dialogue also covers the question of how women—who were a part of man—were created, and how the male's sperm joins with the female's egg to procreate life. **Timaeus** concludes the discussion by addressing problems of a psychological nature. *All psychological disturbances or illnesses relate to the body's malfunction: mania, ignorance, depression, excesses in pleasures and sorrows, insanity, timidity, arrogance, forgetfulness, incomprehension, dementia and others.* No one is willingly sick. The only therapy is a combination of: *caring for the body and the soul; acting in moderation and in symmetry; studying philosophy; adhering to physical and aerobic exercise, and listening to music.* Drugs should not be used at all--unless necessary--and only in moderation. The search for truth and refinement of the soul achieves happiness: and possible immortality for man.

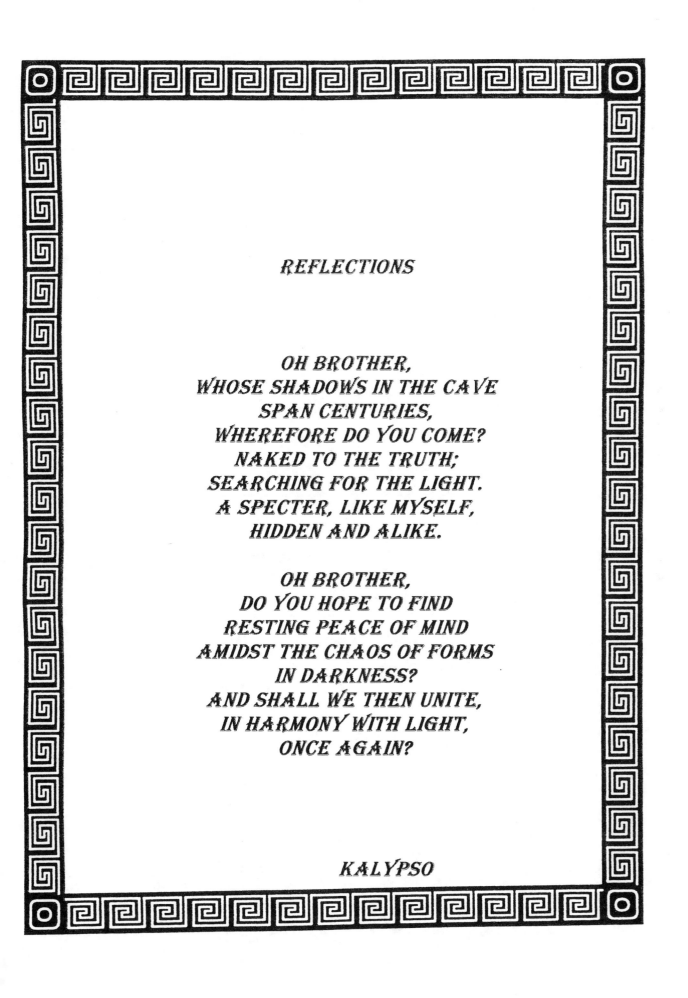

REFLECTIONS

OH BROTHER,
WHOSE SHADOWS IN THE CAVE
SPAN CENTURIES,
WHEREFORE DO YOU COME?
NAKED TO THE TRUTH;
SEARCHING FOR THE LIGHT.
A SPECTER, LIKE MYSELF,
HIDDEN AND ALIKE.

OH BROTHER,
DO YOU HOPE TO FIND
RESTING PEACE OF MIND
AMIDST THE CHAOS OF FORMS
IN DARKNESS?
AND SHALL WE THEN UNITE,
IN HARMONY WITH LIGHT,
ONCE AGAIN?

KALYPSO

CHAPTER 9

THE PLATONIC DIALOGUES

1. ALCIBIADES I, II (ΑΛΚΙΒΙΑΔΗΣ I, II)

"I am fortunate that I was born a human and not an animal;
A man and not a woman; a Greek and not a barbarian."
Thales

The main theme of this dialogue refers to the qualifications, virtue, and intelligence of those who aspire to political positions. This is a tenet that Plato was mostly concerned with, and referred to often throughout most of his writings. He believed that only the *best should direct the affairs of the State,* and that most of the miseries encountered in the life of the city-states were

Alcibiades

due to the inferior quality of their leaders. As emphasized in **The Republic** and the **Laws**, the matter of leadership was so important that the institution of the *"Guardians"* and *Philosopher-King"* was intended to address this problem. It was also mentioned elsewhere in this work, that during the session of the Assembly in ancient Athens, anyone could step up to the podium and address the public and offer either advice, commentary, or make a proposal on the topic being discussed.[1] Therefore, this system was replete with potential abuse, and the intention of this dialogue is to increase awareness of the qualifications of people who undertake political positions, and to emphasize the impact that demagogues and special interests have on the voting public. The protagonists are **Socrates** and **Alcibiades**, a prominent young Athenian destined to play a significant role in the politics of Athens during the Peloponnesian War. He descended from an aristocratic family related to Pericles, who had the responsibility of his upbringing after the death of Alcibiades' father in 446 B.C. The time when this discussion occurred coincides with the beginning of the Peloponnesian War (431 B.C.), when Alcibiades was a young man—20-23 years old.

---

[1] In a prominent spot inside the Athenian Assembly, the statement "Τις αγορευιν Βουλεται" (Who is interested in speaking?) was conspicuously displayed, encouraging the audience to address the Assembly.

The stage of the exchange is the marketplace where Socrates meets young Alcibiades and tells him: *"I have been in love with you--for a long time;"* but Alcibiades pays no attention. The expression «Ερaστης Σου Γενομενος» (I am in love with you) can be misunderstood today, because the translation would connote a different meaning from that in ancient times[2]. But for Socrates the expression "Ερaστης Σου Γενομενος" indicates Platonic love, in that he had a great interest in the character formation of young Alcibiades and wanted him to become a virtuous and useful man. Socrates realized how ambitious young Alcibiades was, and could predict that because of his aristocratic background and innate intelligence, he was destined to be involved in politics. He intends to advise and teach him what he should know and be aware of, if he intends to pursue such a career. As has been noted throughout Plato's writings, **Virtue** is the most important attribute that **Socrates** wanted to instill in this young student, so as to be useful to himself and to his country. Socrates asks him if he knows what the ultimate good is in a particular case concerning a public issue that may come up for discussion in the Assembly. Alcibiades admits that he does not know, and Socrates adds that if he does not know, he cannot distinguish what right and justice are; therefore, he commits a dishonorable act by involving himself in politics to counsel the Athenians on matters that he is ignorant of. But Alcibiades rejoins that even though he does not know what **Justice** and **Right** may be, he knows what would be profitable and beneficial for the State on a particular issue--particularly in case of war or peace. Socrates proceeds to prove to him, dialectically, that useful and just are not the same thing; therefore, if Alcibiades does not know what justice is, he neither knows what useful is. This is dangerous ignorance if one does not know of something, but thinks that he does; it is this brashness that urges him to enter politics very early--which is a dangerous thing to do. Alcibiades admits this; but he argues that he has other important attributes and characteristics-- such as bodily beauty, intelligence, and rhetoric--that will enable him to prevail over his opponents in the Assembly. Socrates advises that it is not his opponents in the Assembly that he should be concerned with, but instead should be prepared to face his true opponents, in case the State enters hostilities with other States; referring to the kings of Sparta and Persia.

Socrates concludes by urging Alcibiades to be conscious of his abilities and particularly cognizant of the dictum **"Know Thyself"** (Γνωθι Σ' Αυτον) for whatever task he undertakes. This is a difficult challenge because it does not really mean what the words imply-- *knowing of material self*--but rather knowledge of what kind of person one is in terms of talents and inclinations--and the state of his soul; as the soul controls the body. When he understands his character, by learning of his real self--his soul, then Alcibiades will know when and whether he should enter politics. Without full knowledge he will never become truly successful. The best asset a politician must have is virtue, and he should strive to impart such virtue to his fellow citizens: because it is only then that peace, progress, justice and harmony will prevail.

---

[2] Ερaστης(Lover)= Admirer, enthusiast, follower, close friend. The person that is Ερaστης is called Εταιρος or Παιδικα or Φιλεραστης. The feeling of Ερaστης is friendship. There is a difference between the common meaning of the term (lover) given today and that which Plato used (See also **Symposium**).

167

There is another dialogue titled **ALCIBIADES II,** attributed to Plato. There has been substantial evidence, however, that this is not a genuine Platonic work, as there are quite a number of points of language, grammar, events, and style that that it was written during the time of Alexander the Great (latter part of 4th century B.C.) by some unknown author. We give a summary of it here because it touches on some aspects of polytheism practiced at the time-- significant to the evolution of religion. Socrates discusses with Alcibiades the question of the value, significance, and kind of prayers usually recited. The dialogue begins when Socrates encounters Alcibiades on his way to the temple to pray, and tells him that people often do not know what to pray for, or to whom. This dialogue raises the important question of the "**quid pro quo**" relationship between humans and gods; devoid of moral and ethical standards. The message is that making offerings, rich sacrifices, and long prayers to a god, does not yield forgiveness and redemption of one's sins and infractions of the moral and ethical code. Transgressions will be forgiven only if one sincerely repents and becomes a virtuous person from then on, and refrains from committing unjust acts. Perhaps the author was concerned with the immoral practice of offering rich sacrifices to please the gods, and in return expecting forgiveness for the perpetration of unjust acts.

Plato wrote **ALCIBIADES I** during the 370's B.C., and by then Alcibiades was dead. He had enemies among the Athenians, Spartans, and Persians who conspired against him; and ultimately killed him. He was an arrogant, opinionated and ambitious person, but intelligent--and a very capable politician and military leader. He had an adventurous nature and in spite of Socrates' admonition **"Know Thyself,"** and **"Learn to be Ruled so as to Rule"** (Αρχεσθαι Μαθων Αρχειν Επιστησει), he committed a number of mistakes in his life. Athens lost a competent leader who might have led her to victory against the Spartans during the Peloponnesian War. Plato attempted to dramatize the mistakes made at the Assembly, where the demagogues, because of their envy and jealousy of Alcibiades, succeeded twice in swaying public opinion against him--and while in Sicily condemned him to death--forcing him into exile. Among other things, they accused him of cutting off the heads of "Hermes"--the statues of the street signs in Athens in 416 B.C. The events that occurred during Alcibiades' political life must have been significant in developing Plato's political philosophy--which was distrustful of the democratic system as practiced then. The story of Alcibiades is an intriguing sequence of events influenced by both the politics of the time, as well as by the personality of the man. He was a smart, ambitious, corrupt, capable, and ruthless politician. His youth was replete with ignoble, as well as noble encounters that engendered mistrust as well as admiration. He created enemies, as well as friends among the population. Declared a general in command of the Athenian fleet, when he was almost 30 years old, he undertook a military expedition to attack Syracuse in Sicily- -416 B.C., which led to an Athenian disaster; but his enemies conspired, persuading the Assembly to recall and try him for offenses that he had never committed. Alcibiades, fearful for his life, instead of returning to Athens and facing his accusers, decided to flee to Sparta--where for several years he acted as advisor in successfully administering the war against the Athenians. He developed enemies in Sparta as well, and facing prosecution fled to Persia and then back to

Athens. The Athenians accepted him because they admired his military genius, and under his command they were successful in several battles and appeared to be winning the War. Because of an insignificant event during a sea-battle, when the Athenians did not prevail, his enemies in Athens persuaded the Assembly to again recall him. This time he fled to Thrace, leading a private life, when the Spartans defeated Athens and the city-state was occupied. Alciabiades took the defeat gravely and undertook new efforts to save his city--befriending Tissafernes, a Persian satrap in Asia Minor, in the hope that with his assistance the Athenians could remove the Spartans. The Spartans learned of his efforts and demanded that the Persians arrest and execute him. In a conspiratorial fashion they encircled and set fire to the house where he was resting (on his way to Sousa), and when he attempted to flee, killed him. He was only 47 years old.

Two things are significant in the development of these events: (1) **The character of Alcibiades**--who acted in a self-serving, ambitious way--ignoring the interest of his city and engaging in immoral, unethical and superficial behavior; (2) **The influence of the demagogues**--enemies of Alcibiades in the Athenian Assembly--swaying public opinion and accusing him of acts for which he was not guilty. Plato was a young man (actually a teen-ager) when these events took place, but they influenced him immensely--coupled with the interest that Socrates exhibited toward Alcibiades and the vicissitudes of his character. This dialogue, then, *is an effort by the writer to pinpoint potential problems brought about when an individual is not mature and* **"good"** *enough to undertake the leadership of a nation.*

2. MENEXENUS (ΜΕΝΕΞΕΝΟΣ)

«Καλον μεν η αληθεια, ω ξενε, και μονιμον,
εοικε μεν ου ραδιον (ειναι) πειθειν.»[3]
Plato

MENEXENUS addresses the subject of a special kind of oratory, the *funeral oration*, which would be equivalent to what we would call today, *a eulogy*. In ancient Athens the custom prevailed that each year a ceremonial burial would be carried out for those soldiers who died in battle. This custom was initiated by Solon, a lawmaker of Athens, and was practiced until the fall of Athens to the Romans in 146 B.C. After the burial of the remains of the dead, an individual elected by the Assembly would approach the podium and deliver an address to the gathered public--which would include the immediate families and friends of the dead soldiers. A famous such funeral oration is reported by Thucidides, the Athenian historian, which was delivered by Pericles, the Archon of Athens, during the burial of the dead soldiers at the end of the first year of the Peloponnesian War (431 B.C.). [4] Plato's concern in writing this dialogue is to emphasize the importance of this kind of oratory, which, in the hands of a demagogue, could turn into a lecture of platitudes and false impressions; misleading, exciting and fanaticizing the public while emphasizing false values. Such an address, if delivered by a mature thinker-philosopher-statesman, could create a positive environment for great ideas, as well as compassion and enthusiasm contributing to the future development of the city. In dramatizing the adverse impact this speech could have on people, Socrates confesses, in an ironic way, that:

The Zappeion Megaron, Athens

"…… The speakers enchant my soul when they describe all those virtues that we all have and all those that we do not. They praise the city in many different ways, and all those who fell in battle and all our ancestors and us who are still alive. Their words cause in me a feeling and disposition of magnanimity; and each time when I hear them speaking I stand still, in awe, enchanted by the magic of their words and their artistic linguistic capabilities. I feel at that time that I have become taller, kinder and prettier. And sometimes when visitors come with me, which is frequent, I feel proud and strong--and their esteem for me and for the city increases; they find the city more wonderful than they thought it was before, because they believe the orators when

---

[3] "Truth, oh stranger, is a fair and durable thing. But it is a thing of which it is hard to persuade men."
[4] See Chapter 5, where a part of Pericles' funeral oration is presented.

170

they praise her grandeur. The excitement lasts more than three days; the influence of these speakers is so intense over me that it is only the fourth or fifth day that I start to recognize myself and understand in what part of the planet I reside.....[5]

In a democratic system, as that of ancient Athens, where the public participated in the decision process, either at the Assembly **(Εκκλησια του Δημου)**, the Parliament **(Βουλη),** or the courts, public speaking was an important component of the decision-making process. It was the orator who presented arguments favoring or opposing legislation, or presented the points in the disputes adjudicated in the courts: and he played a decisive role. The majority of the people were semi-literate; as most of them, particularly the older ones, were farmers who had little opportunity or time to educate themselves to the point where they could understand and distinguish the linguistic tricks of the orators and differentiate between spoken truth and truth-- becoming a victim of special interests and ambitious and capable speakers. There is no question that there were intelligent and educated people who could distinguish very early in the oratory the true intentions of the speakers, and would most likely walk out in protest, or attempt to reveal the truth--if they would sense demagogy--but their voices would be ignored by an excited audience in a semi-frenzied state. Thus, what Plato emphasizes in the above passage is the level of abuse possible that could take place at any moment when sincerity, truth and candor is important for the survival of democracy and the city-state. Instead, special interests sabotage the fundamental requisites of the system: *Honesty and Truth.*

The characters in this dialogue are: **Menexenus**, a respected Athenian politician, and **Socrates.** Plato presents Menexenus as a young man who meets Socrates in the marketplace by chance, and Socrates asks him where he is coming from. Menexenus responds that he is coming from the Assembly where he has been all day long, waiting to find out who was to be elected to speak in the forthcoming funeral of the dead soldiers, planned two days hence. He seems surprised that the Assembly had not made a decision, but would reconvene the next day, leaving the prospective speaker only one day to prepare his speech. Socrates assures him that this is not a problem because these speeches have already been written, and usually compiled from older ones, so that no serious thinking goes into writing them. Menexenus asks Socrates his opinion of these speeches, and Socrates responds that they make him feel very tall and proud! And in the continuation of this dialogue, Socrates delivers a funeral oration that he claims **Aspasia,** *Pericles' mistress from Miletus,* had prepared for him. In this speech Socrates presents what a funeral orator would have said during the burial of the dead soldiers. The first part of the delivery refers to the past and praises the achievements of their ancestors. This is full of exaggerations and misrepresentations of historical facts concerning wars and conflicts that the city-state had experienced during its long life. In the second part, he encourages the children of the dead to be proud of the achievements of their fathers; and the third part addresses the parents and relatives of the dead, and lauds the achievements of their sons.

---

[5] See Reference 11, Book 4, p.21 (Translation by the author)

171

In Plato's judgment, the teachers of the schools of rhetoric, which flourished widely in ancient Athens, were taking advantage of the need to develop skills in addressing the Assembly, courts, or other public places that a democratic system requires, and were undermining the city by developing demagogues rather than mature and serious speakers. Plato's intended exaggerations and platitudes in this delivery emphasize the detrimental impact that the speechwriters and teachers of rhetoric had on the uneducated populace.

3. AXIOCHUS, (ΑΞΙΟΧΟΣ)

«Ως γαρ επεκλωσαντο θεοι δειλοισι βροτοισιν ζωειν αχνυμενοις»[6]
Homer, Iliad

__AXIOCHUS__ addresses the matter of death and what happens to man when the end comes. We have seen, both in "__APOLOGIA__" and "__CRITO,__" that Socrates maintained the position that death has two possible outcomes: Either we enter an eternal sleep without consciousness and dreams; or the soul of man is transported to another world--the world of **"Ideas"** and judgment--where virtuous people will experience eternal happiness and contentment. Plato suggests that the second state is the most probable one, and that achievement of virtue (Αγαθον) should be the objective of any rational man if he wants to live a less tumultuous life--and one of eternal happiness after death. As we have seen in the chapter on *"The Epicurean Philosophers"*--(chapter 12), **Epicurus**, the founder, maintained that we should never fear death because *when death occurs we do not exist; and therefore, there is nothing that we should fear since then we will be devoid of sensory feelings.* Also, when we exist *death does not;*

Temple of Olympic Zeus and Acropolis

and we should not be afraid of something that does not exist. Strangely, this position regarding the fear of death advanced by the Epicureans, surfaced during Hellenistic times--over 50 years after the death of Plato. Given some anomalies in the language, grammar and vocabulary, along with a displaced time frame of this Epicurean viewpoint on death, scholars in ancient times (**Thrasyllus**), as well as the modern era (**A. E. Taylor**), believed that this dialogue was not a genuine Platonic work. Most likely, it was written by a student of the Academy who listed Plato's name as the author. The points that it makes about the fear of death, however, are very important because, most likely, they represented the views of the Academy that were flourishing during the Hellenistic Era.

The dramatic part of this dialogue involves **Socrates** and **Axiochus** (an influential Athenian politician), who is depicted as ill and near death. **Socrates** accidentally meets **Kleinias, Axiochus' son,** in the marketplace, and **Kleinias** asks **Socrates** to talk to his father and alleviate his fear of dying. Axiochus tells Socrates that during his lifetime he has never harbored fears of what was to become of him after death, but now that the end is near, he is tormented by anxiety. Socrates assures him, first, that there is nothing to fear of death because it is nothing for a mortal who, after death, does not experience sensory sensations anymore. This, of course, is the Epicurean philosophical belief on death. But Axiochus does not seem less anxious with this

---

[6] "So the gods destined unfortunate mortals to live in sorrow"

prospect, because he will miss the enjoyment of life. Socrates then introduces his philosophy on death: One should not be afraid of death, for if one has lived a virtuous life and achieved the state of "Αγαθος," his soul will experience a state of complete happiness. At the end of the discussion between Axiochus and Socrates, Axiochus admits that he feels relieved after hearing Socrates advance his thoughts on death and the "**Immortality of the Soul**." He concludes, therefore, that he no longer fears death, but rather *welcomes it!*

4. CRITIAS (ΚΡΙΤΙΑΣ)

Ουδεν εστιν, και ει εστιν, ακαταληπτον εστιν,
και ει καταληπτον ανερμηνευτον τοις αλλοις[7]
Gorgias

<u>**CRITIAS**</u> addresses the legendary lost continent of Atlantis. It is difficult to decide what Plato's intention was in writing this dialogue. It is, perhaps, the missing part that would have supplied the answer. Either Plato never completed the missing section, even though he indicates there is one, or it was written--but lost. The first part describes the Great War between Athens and Atlantis that occurred 9,000 years before Plato's time. The second describes the system of government and the society of the city-state of Athens during that period. The first ends so abruptly that the theory that Plato never completed the work appears more plausible.

Discuss Thrower

Atlantis was a great island beyond the Herculean Gates (today's Gibraltar). It was a prosperous and strong state, administratively divided into ten kingdoms; governed by the ten king-sons of god Poseidon and the mortal Cleto. The ten kings governed very successfully and brought prosperity to the island, **which was larger than Africa and Asia combined** (as the two continents were known to the Greeks then), but these kings became ambitious and greedy, and carried out a military campaign outside their island, conquering all of Europe and Africa—with the exception of the city-state of Athens and Egypt. The city of Athens had a magnificent system of government, which was very efficient, and resisted the armies of Atlantis. In the battles that ensued, the Athenians drove the invaders out and humiliated them totally**. Zeus** was upset by the behavior, greed, ambition and arrogance of the Atlantis' rulers, and called a meeting of the gods at Mount Olympus to determine the island's fate. It is at this point that the dialogue ends, but it is identified elsewhere (<u>**Timaeus**</u>) that soon thereafter earthquakes and cataclysmic volcanic eruptions sank Atlantis into the Atlantic Ocean.[8] The present Athenians are unaware of their ancestors' successes because references and evidence were lost when the island sank. History, then, from

---

[7] Nothing exists; and if it exists, it is not understandable; and even if it is understandable, it cannot be conveyed to others.

[8] Modern geologists (Jacques Collina-Rigard, French; in Washington Post, 12/27/01) believe that indeed Atlantis was an island in the Atlantic Ocean off the coast of Spain and Morocco. It was supposedly swamped by rising seas, along with another six islands, at the end of the last Ice Age--probably 11,000 years ago. Collina-Rigard says that today the islands are shoals concealed anywhere from 175 to 410 feet below the ocean's surface.

both sides of the conflict, is unavailable to document the Athenian achievement; but Critias relates that all this information was recorded in the Holy Books of the Egyptian priests. The priests relayed this information to Solon when he visited Egypt many years ago, and he, in turn, *recounted all this information to Critias' great-grandfather, from whom Critias obtained all the facts that Plato presented in this dialogue.*

Athens was a prosperous and successful city-state at the time, because of its unique and outstanding system of government, and as a city-state was the envy of her neighbors and of all Greece. **Critias**, the narrator, never describes this system of government in detail, which would constitute the second part of the discussion. Noting two important elements that Critias mentions at the beginning, in his general comments, one can draw an inference as to Plato's possible intent. These elements are: **First**—in the ancient Athenian system women had equality with men in the administration of the State and were participating in wars alongside them. **Second**--the system had **"Guardians"** who were charged with the defense and administration of the State, as well as a **"Philosopher-King"** as the ultimate authority. These two features of the old Athenian system--the equality of women and the establishment of the **Guardians** and **Philosopher-King**-- are the fundamental precepts in the **"The Republic"** that Plato thought would be the **"sine qua non"** condition for an *Ideal State*. Perhaps he intended to identify the old system, which was so successful in resisting the invading armies of Atlantis, as the preferred one for the modern city-state of Athens, and therefore proposed a similar one in the **"Republic."** This dialogue was intended to be one of three: **Timaeus, Critias**, and **Ermocrates;** but Plato never wrote **Ermocrates**, and **Critias** is incomplete.

5. EUTHEDEMUS (ΕΥΘΥΔΗΜΟΣ)

«Αριστοτελης ημας απελακτισε, καθαπερ
τα πωλαρια γεννηθεντα την μητερα»[9]
Plato

Plato wrote this dialogue during the decade of 380's B.C. It is, perhaps, one of his best in exhibiting Socratic irony and feigned ignorance--used so skillfully by Socrates to trap his adversaries in discussions held at the marketplace. The basic theme is Plato's ridicule of the light philosophical nature and superficial approach that the Sophists assumed in the area of **wisdom and virtue.** As mentioned elsewhere, Platonic philosophy advocated real wisdom and pragmatic understanding of virtue and knowledge as cornerstones of a healthy society. There were a number of schools of rhetoric and philosophy flourishing in Athens, promoting diverse philosophies on this subject, and, according to Plato, were distorting the real meaning of these concepts--in contrast to Socrates who had conceived, taught, and died for them. The acquisition of wealth was the main motivation that drove these individuals to open their schools of rhetoric, and the distortion of truth through pretentious speech, with promises of delivering real wisdom and virtue, had brought discomfort to Plato then and Socrates earlier.

Temple of Olympic Zeus

Plato brings forth two relatively unknown Sophists, **Euthedemus and Dionysodorus** (brothers), who had come to town with the expressed purpose of teaching wisdom and virtue to all those who wanted to listen, and had promised that they would do this more effectively than anyone else. The venue is the marketplace where these "**wise**" men enchanted their audiences with their boastful, rhetorical schemes and impressive argumentation. Opposing these arrogant and pretentious Sophists, a new figure appears--a humble and unimposing man; a real philosopher, fighter, and brave personality: **Socrates.** Using his well-known method of irony and feigning ignorance, he manages to bring these two lightweight Sophists down to Earth. He proves to the audience that their so-called wisdom is nothing more than emptiness, Para logy, and distortions of reality. In a demonstration at the Agora, Socrates challenges the two Sophists to abandon their rhetorical manipulations of the language and prove their wisdom by teaching two of his friends, **Kleinias** and **Critias,** how to

---

[9] "Aristotle spurns us as colts kick out at the mother who bore them."

acquire true virtue and wisdom. Plato illustrates the folly of these Sophists by having them direct questions to Kleinias. Their questions confuse the young man--due to their irrelevance and inappropriateness--which creates laughter in the audience. In spite of derision they continue asking immaterial questions, which is Plato's method of ridicule, and finally are exposed as superficial fools uttering paradoxical syllogisms. Examples of the brothers' absurd arguments that Plato provokes, in his efforts to dramatize the shallowness of their wisdom, would include: Responding to how they would make **Kleinias** wise and virtuous, *they argue that they have the skill to make him turn "bad" into "good" and "good" into "bad"; and can eliminate that which exists and bring forth that which does **not exist**.* Their knowledge enables them to calculate how many stars are in the firmament and how many grains of sand are in the sea. They assert that they can prove that Socrates did not have a father, and that their father is the father of all humans and animals.

In **EUTHEDEMUS** Plato takes issue with other thinkers and scholars of his time, such as **Antisthenes,** the father of the Cynic philosophy, who was a student of Socrates and the only one who stayed in Athens during the years of persecution from 399 B.C. on--when Plato abandoned Athens for thirteen years--following the death of Socrates. He differed with **Antithesis** on several aspects of Cynicism and the use of the dialectic method; and also had misgivings about the Eleatic tenets of "monism" promoted by some of the Sophists. In this dialogue Plato assumes an adversarial position toward the "**speech-writers" and "language teachers"** flourishing in Athens at the time. The rhetorician 'Lysias' indirectly becomes the recipient of Socratic scorn as well, as is the case in other dialogues (**Phaedrus**). This exchange ends with an admonition extolling the benefits of true philosophy: and the basic principles of virtue and wisdom as being the pillars and foundation of a healthy and sound society. The period referred to must have been prior to the disastrous expedition to Sicily (416 B.C.) that led to the destruction of Athenian military might. It was written, as pointed out earlier, immediately after the establishment of the Academy (387 B.C.), when criticism that he was not presenting Socratic views properly was circulated against Plato by other Socratic schools. Thus Plato, using **Dionysodorus and Euthedemus** as the main protagonists, responded to his critics and established that he was a true presenter of the **complete, orthodox and uncorrupted** philosophical teachings of his mentor.

6. E R Y X I A S (ΕΡΥΞΙΑΣ)

«Πολλακις δ' αφορων εις τα πληθη των πιπρασκομενων
ελεγε, προς αυτον 'ποσων εγω χρειαν ουκ εχω'»[10]

Socrates

ERYXIAS explores the subject of **wealth**: What constitutes wealth; its usefulness; how it relates to happiness and well being; its impact on people, and whether it leads to: **virtue or evil.** Some scholars think that **ERYXIAS** was not written by Plato himself, but rather by a student at the Academy during the beginning of the third century B.C. (280-290 B.C.). There are quite a number of characteristics in this dialogue--such as style, depth of argument, and historical anachronisms--that indicate that it is not a genuine Platonic work. Perhaps it was written with the intention of countering the Stoic philosophers who, at that time, were very popular *and had*

Attalus I

proposed that apathy, tranquility of the soul and elimination of emotion are the fundamental ingredients for achieving happiness and a "good" (αγαθον) state. Because, however, there are some significant points regarding wealth and necessities that the discussants make, it was thought worthy of presenting here; after all, it represents the position of the Academy at that time. The dramatic part of the dialogue involves a conversation concerning wealth among a group of four participants. The timing was around 420 B.C., and coincided with the arrival of a visitor in Athens--the richest man in Syracuse. It was the presence of this visitor on his way to the Assembly, pointed out by one of the group (**Erasistratus**), that prompted the discussion of wealth. The names of those involved in the dialogue are: **Socrates**, representing the Socratic-Platonic philosophy, advocating **virtue and prudence; Eryxias,** an unknown figure, representing the conventional man of the time **(c. 280-290 B.C.),** and not of the historical setting of the dialogue (c. 420's B.C.); **Critias**, the well-known oligarch and leader of the 30 Tyrants (an early student and relative of Socrates); **Erasistratus**, a known historical person who had just returned from a trip to Sicily, and only entered the discussions at the beginning to point out the visiting Sicilian and share his views on conditions there.

In an attempt to define wealth, *Eryxias* proposes that a person is wealthier than another *if he possesses more of the material means of existence.* Critias is not satisfied with this definition and raises the question of what is meant by **material means of existence.** Could it be that

---

[10] "Often when he looked at the multitude of wares exposed for sale, he would say to himself: How many things I can do without!"

someone could have more of some other non-material possession--such as health or happiness--and be considered wealthy as well? In combining the two definitions, then, they all agree: One is happier and better off if he is in good health, even if poor in resources; as compared with one who is in poor health, but wealthy. If one can find some other resource better than health, and has more of it, which contributes to **well being**, this resource is also wealthy--and superior to that derived from material possessions. So far, health is regarded as a better definition of wealth than the possession of monetary assets or material resources. Critias, who has misgivings about these definitions, asks what is the most precious thing for man to possess in order to procure happiness: for *one could be healthy but unhappy.* He proposes that the capacity to make correct decisions is a better definition of wealth, because happy are those who commit fewer mistakes in their life. Socrates introduces the subject of wisdom and suggests that wisdom is the most precious possession--because wise is the person who makes the best decisions. This statement represents the view of the Academy and infers the well-known Socratic principle*: A virtuous person will always do the right thing.* Eryxias, representing conventional wisdom, disagrees. He challenges the importance of wisdom in the life of man, who can acquire wisdom, but cannot acquire happiness if he does not have the material means of existence. Socrates counters that those who have professional skills, and by extension wisdom, can use their skills to procure the material means of existence.

Up to this point, wealth is analyzed in terms of material or other possessions, and how it relates or leads to happiness; but now **Critias** asks whether wealth is "good" or "evil." **Eryxias** thinks that wealth is good, but **Critias** contends that for some people wealth is evil; and after some discussion regarding "**just**" and "**unjust**" actions, **Eryxias** concludes that for some wealth is evil because they have the means to escape punishment if they use it to commit unjust or criminal acts: while the poor cannot. Therefore, in terms of justice and injustice and the development of a virtuous and useful man, *it is better to be poor and honest than wealthy and corrupt, as concerns the welfare of society.* Agreeing now that wealth does not necessarily make a man just and virtuous, **Critias** asks: W*hat is the nature of possessions that make one wealthy?* The utility or usefulness of possessions is the determinant factor for wealth, and the things that are not useful cannot be construed to constitute wealth. Furthermore, if we do not have needs, the value of money is zero; and the opposite is true if we have means to preserve our body--at which time money is useful. *Is it possible to say that things are sometimes good (useful) and sometimes not?* Critias does not agree that money is not always a useful commodity. It is argued that something is useful only if one knows how to use it; for example, a horse could be useful if one knows how to put it to work for him. Socrates reiterates his original argument: that *the wise man is one who knows how to use things properly*--including money, gold, or silver,

Critias, representing materialism, consistently maintains that wealth and happiness represent the possession of material goods--including money. He does not feel comfortable when Socrates attempts to assign wisdom, virtue, and health--in that order--as the most useful resources or wealth that one could have. He rejects the concept of **"utility"** and the idea of wisdom constituting wealth for the satisfaction of one's needs, and now introduces the ethical nature of wealth and its usefulness. Critias indirectly introduces the principle: **The End Sanctifies the Means,** and questions whether an unethical action is ever acceptable for the achievement of a certain goal. Ethical acts are those derived from man's virtuous behavior. While examining the ultimate purpose of wealth and ethics, Socrates disregards the contention of Critias, **by** stating: "For the acquisition of knowledge, hearing is necessary; therefore, hearing is a useful thing--because through it we gain knowledge." All money spent at the doctor's for the care of the ear is a useful expenditure, since it becomes a means of attaining knowledge and eventually virtue. But if this money was acquired by unethical means, it implies that an unethical resource becomes useful for securing "good"--which is the "hearing." **Socrates** finds this unacceptable and introduces the role needs play in the discussion of wealth. He asks: *Is man happier and better off when he has greater--or fewer needs?* When one is sick he requires more needs than when he is healthy; at which time he has fewer needs. What is then preferable? He proposes that it is preferable to be healthy with fewer needs, and consequently, limited resources. Ultimately then: Whom of two people should we consider happier and better off?--the one who has the most means to care for his needs--or the one with less resources and fewer and less important needs. This leads to the general conclusion that man is better off when he has fewer needs. This is also true of two people when one is moderate and the other prodigal. Things cannot be useful for a certain goal or purpose except when we have need for them, which would enable us to achieve the satisfaction of this need. The Socratic position prevails and all agree that the more needs we require and the more means we have to satisfy these needs--the worse off we will be. This leads to a constant struggle--which cannot produce happiness. *Wealth, then, seems to create an unhappy state: as it fosters the need for so many "useful" things.*

7. CHARMIDES (ΧΑΡΜΙΔΗΣ)

« Παντα χρηματα ην ομου´
ειτα Νους ελθων αυτα διεκοσμησε.»[11]

Anaxagoras

<u>Charmides</u> addresses the subject of Prudence (**Σωφροσυνη**). In this dialogue, Plato most probably attempted to portray the real Socrates; the person who was very much concerned with the welfare of the youth; interested in instilling in them *virtue,* increasing their true knowledge, and improving their ethical and moral life. These assets would not be acquired from the Sophists if they attended their schools. His accusers portrayed Socrates as a person who was corrupting the youth, and Plato attempts to dispel these accusations. Prudence, along with *wisdom, justice, and bravery* constitutes one of Plato's four basic components of *virtue*. Prudence is understood to include: *continence, humility, purity, discipline, balance (the mean), morality, temperance, and honesty.*

Antisthenis

The major participants in this dialogue are: **Charmides**, a young upcoming Athenian; Critias**,** a well-known politician related to Charmides, who was the leader of the 30 Tyrants--and **Socrates.** Charmides was a smart and handsome (**καλος**) young man, respected by his friends and admired by his elders. Socrates meets Charmides at the Palaistra upon returning from a war in northern Greece, where he was engaged in battle at Potideia, and from what we know (<u>**Symposium**</u>**)** had risked his life and saved his companion, Alcibiades. When he arrived in Athens he decided to visit the places he frequented before he was drafted, to discover the developments in the field of philosophy and the activities of the youth during his absence. At the Palaistra he meets young Charmides, along with his young friends, and Socrates engages him in conversation. Charmides asks him if he knows of any medicine to cure his continuous headaches, and Socrates responds that there is a certain herb that will help him--but along with the herb he should receive special incantations that he is willing to provide. He adds, however, that in order to rid himself of headaches, all aspects and conditions of his body--particularly his

---

[11] "All things were together; then came Mind and set them in order. "

soul--should be attended. Socrates then asks him if he possesses a good soul and if he is *prudent and temperate*. Charmides responds that he is not sure whether he I*s* or *Is Not* prudent, and Socrates asks him to give a definition of *prudence*. Charmides submits three definitions. The first definition is: *Prudence is a good (αγαθον) thing*-- as it relates to **self-awareness**. Socrates introduces arguments against this definition and Harmides advances another: *Prudence is exhibiting proper behavior on all occasions*. This definition is also opposed by Socrates as not being universally applicable; citing that in some instances prudent behavior may be loud and unconventional. Charmides now proposes a third definition: *Prudence is the action and behavior of someone who minds his own business*. Socrates again disagrees, for it does not stand the test of dialectic analysis. Since Charmides failed three times to give a definition of Prudence that could withstand Socratic dialectic reasoning, it is to be concluded that Harmides does not know what Prudence really **Is.**

Several definitions and points made were positions on the subject taken by the Sophists, and it is known how strongly Socrates opposed these (See **<u>Gorgias.</u>**) Critias enters the discussion by adding that prudence is the act of a **"good"** (Αγαθος) person--a slight modification of the last definition of Charmides. Socrates then adds that for this to hold universally, it is necessary for people to know what is "Good" and what is "Evil." Often individuals are not aware of what is good for them, even if they are "Good." Critias modifies this meaning by saying that: *Prudence is the act of a "good" person who knows what is good for him and **knows himself** as well, and also gauges the limits of his actions and their consequences. T*he conversation--among Critias, Socrates and Charmides--now examines the concepts of moderation and knowledge of the external world, as well as the world within. The famous dictum, *"Know Thyself" (Γνωθι Σ' Αυτον)*, is discussed at length, and another, *"Nothing in Excess" (Μηδεν Αγαν),* is introduced. These two dictums constitute the foundation of Socratic philosophy. According to Diogenes Laertius, the latter is attributed to the Lacedaemonian sage, Chilon, who was considered one of the Seven Wise Men of antiquity, and was placed at the entrance to the Temple of Apollo at Delphi as a greeting to those entering--in contrast to the usual Greek greeting, *"Χαιρε" (Rejoice.)* Socrates exhibits a certain degree of uneasiness about these definitions and concludes that one should exercise prudence for things known; as well as for those unknown. The conclusion drawn from this discussion is that Plato wants the reader to understand that *prudence cannot be defined by what* **it is or is not** but rather pertains to a way of life and proper attitude people exhibit under certain conditions:, *at any time*. It is a behavior that demonstrates respect for institutions and understands the needs and considerations of others, as well as being cognizant of one's limitations. It exhibits understanding for what one really knows, and respect and humility for what one does not know or understand.

For Plato, the conditions in the Athenian democracy at the time of this dialogue, circa 432 B.C., were not favorable to his philosophy. There was a moral crisis eroding the standards and ethics of the citizenry--and particularly the youth. It is perhaps this point that Socrates was most interested in making when prompting Charmides to give him an acceptable definition of **prudence.** In conclusion, the message that is applicable to a modern society is that peace and tranquility prevail, not necessarily within the soul of the individual, but in the entire society--when one recognizes the importance and validity of *"Nothing in Excess."* In the area of seeking continuous pleasure--there is no limit. It is significant that in societies of plenty--artificial, external means (in the form of drugs and other substances) are endemic--particularly among the youth. This search for satisfaction in the form of drugs, even today in the 21st century, reflects complete ignorance and lack of understanding of the dictum: *"Μηδεν Αγαν» (Nothing in Excess).* Current conditions strongly resemble those prevailing in Athenian society during the period of this dialogue. Socrates had perceived the slippery road that the youth of his time were entering, and ultimately sacrificed himself to communicate his views on what he thought society needed to achieve *harmony, tranquility, justice and peace*. These very principles that Socrates and Plato advocated so strongly--drastically different from those of the Sophist schools--were not advanced again to the same degree until the advent of Christianity--300 years later. It is perhaps because of this similarity that all of Plato's writings survived, while those of other authors perished.

8. KRATYLUS

«Ποταμοις τοις αυτοις εμβαινομεν τε και
εκβαινομεν, ειμεν τε και ουκ ειμεν.»[12]
Heraclitus

Plato's intention in writing this dialogue is not very clear, because his position on the subject is not explicit. **KRATYLUS** examines why ideas, objects, persons or situations have a specific name, and whether such a name represents the nature of the subject and is independently determined; or subjectively given by someone, and by convention accepted by the people.[13] This point may not be clearly understood by an English speaking person, because the English language does not have the same etymological structure as Greek, particularly at the time of Plato. What is, in essence, the question that I think would not occur to an English-speaking person: Why this

**The Goddess
"Peace"**

object, on which we place things, is called a **"table?"** Was the name given because of its function, nature, substance, purpose and usefulness; or was it arbitrarily given by someone who decided that it should be named so. Indeed, in the Greek language there are quite a number of words representing verbs, nouns, adjectives or other parts of speech, which are etymologically structured so that the nature of the object and the name itself are correlated. Thus, the main part of this dialogue addresses this matter; and the names of gods, heavenly bodies, ethical and moral terms--being either simple or compound—are critically analyzed to establish the correlation. In some way, this could be seen as a discussion of the *theory and origin of language,* were--it not for the fact that Plato did not clearly define a path toward that direction. The divergent views on the origin of name identification are represented by two well-known individuals at Plato's time. The first was **Ermogenes,** a relatively unknown philosopher, representing the arbitrary view; the second, representing the correlation between the name and the nature of the subject, was **Kratylus,** a well-known philosopher of the Ephesus School who was a follower of **Heraclitus. Ermogenes** believed that the names of objects, concepts and persons are arbitrarily given by someone without any special reason, theory or plan. **Kratylus** maintains that there is a causal factor and reason why things are named the way they are, and that the name represents the *nature* or *purpose* of the object. Considerable discussion ensues between Socrates and Ermogenes, and it appears in this part of the discussion that Socrates is of the

---

[12] "We enter and exit the same river at once; we are (in it) and we are not."

[13] An example of a concept represented by a word that physically associates the word with its meaning, is the verb «Γραφειν» (to write) in Greek. The first two letters of the word (Γρ), if pronounced together, sound as if one is scratching a sharp metal on a rock. This was how the action of carving letters on a plaque presumably sounded: the first attempt at writing.

opposite opinion--that there was a name-maker or a legislator who established the names of things--and this is the point that he stresses during the discussion with Ermogenes. Close to the end, however, **Socrates and Ermogenes** decide to ask the opinion of Kratylus on the matter. Kratylus maintains his position--that the names of things are not arbitrarily set--and one might think that Socrates will concur; but this is not the case. He seems to alter his point, disagreeing with Kratylus, and all three participants agree to discontinue the discussion and pursue additional research on the subject later on.

Scholars and analysts differ as to what Plato really intended by this discussion, which was written late in his life, and by that time he had received considerable criticism from other schools of philosophy (**Aristotle, Antisthenes**) undermining his "**Theory of Ideas**" and "**Theory of Recollection.**" Given that the nature of the exchange is sometimes bordering on the comical, one will have to decide which school of philosophy or to what individual he was addressing this dialogue. We do know, from other works, that he was opposed to the dictum of the Sophists: "**Man is the measure of all things.**" This principle, advanced by **Protagoras** (Chapter 8), stated that subjectivity is superior to objectivity, and that knowledge derived from the senses is superior to intellectual and transcendental knowledge. It is also the basis of *Materialism versus Idealism*. The Platonic School of philosophy objected strenuously to this principle, and in **Theaetetus** Plato wrote extensively on the *"Theory of Knowledge"* and the significance of objective knowledge. In this dialogue, the idea of impartially determining the names of things fits within the position of the Platonic School; while the idea that they should be determined subjectively would be unacceptable--and one might think that Plato would support Kratylus' position. He did not; and therefore, this dialogue cannot be seen as an attack against the Sophists' "Theory of Knowledge." The second principle that Plato addresses is Heraclitus' dictum: "**Everything Is in a Flux and Nothing Is Stationary,**" and it is brought into the discussion later, near the end of the dialogue. This principle would corroborate Ermogenes' position that the names of things are subject to change, and that language is in a continuous flux. The position that Socrates assumes at the beginning, by opposing Ermogenes, seems to challenge this point. The uncertainty of this argument, advanced by some, is that while Plato opposed Ermogenes in the first part of the dialogue and agreed with Kratylus (a proponent of this principle), he reversed his position at the end. The "**Theory of Ideas**" represents Plato's conviction that certain values in this world are **Unchanging;** and therefore, **the Ultimate Truth** has a *constant* value. In this way, Plato would have defended the validity of his theory had he advanced the concept that the "Idea of Language" is unalterable and permanent. Therefore, names are given on the basis of some rational principle--but he is inconsistent throughout this discussion.

9. LACHES (ΛΑΧΗΣ)

" Der Herr Gott rafiniert ist, aber boschaft ist Er nicht"[14]

Einstein

LACHES is one of the minor Platonic dialogues whose originality has been challenged by some scholars in ancient, as well as modern times. The style does not fit perfectly with the Platonic narratives of other dialogues; and the language, depth of analysis and some inconsistencies on the subject of *"Αρετη"* (Virtue), as compared with other dialogues, e.g. (**Protagoras**), cast uncertainty as to whether it was Plato or a student at the Academy who wrote it in later years. Yet, since the timing of the writing is not exactly certain, some believe that Plato probably wrote the dialogue during his early youth, before his style and depth matured into such

Epidaurus Theatre

dialogues as **Protagoras, Phaedo, Theaetetus** and others, which were written later in his scholarly career. This argument lends credence to those who claim that this is indeed a Platonic work. There are scholars today, as well as in ancient times (**Thrasyllus**), who believe that **Laches** is indeed a Platonic product, and note that it was classified as such and placed in the fourth tetralogy by ancient sages.

Lahes addresses two different subjects. In the first part, the matter of raising children is discussed, and the responsibilities of parents for their children's education is emphasized. In the second part **bravery (courage)** is addressed, and, as usual, efforts are made by the participants to arrive at an acceptable definition. The dramatic setting is the marketplace, where a famous athlete, **Stesilaus**, is exhibiting his art in the use of arms. Two elderly Athenians, **Lysimachus** and **Melisias**, had brought their two sons to the exhibit to benefit from the demonstration, because they believed that the handling of arms is a useful tool to acquire and use--either at war or at other times for protection. They were not sure, however, that this was a good idea, and consulted with two retired Athenian generals, **Laches** and **Nikias,** who happened to be present at the demonstration.

---

[14] The Lord God is subtle, but He is not malicious."

In the first part, the responsibility of parents to see to it that their young children receive the best education available, both the curricular and encyclopedic kind, is discussed extensively. Also, the cost for such an education is considered insignificant if one weighs the lasting benefits the student will receive in the future. Plato and Socrates, as we have seen in other dialogues, believed that only through education and knowledge will a person achieve a virtuous state and intellectual maturity. This will enable the human mind to ascend to the soul: where knowledge is stored in the form of *"Ideas"*.

The second and major part of the dialogue, centers on the definition and understanding of "B*ravery.*" The discussion includes Socrates, on the one side, and **Laches** and **Nikias** on the other; and the latter define bravery *as the strength and ability to remain steady in battle and constant in the defense of yourself and your country.* Plato identifies *"bravery"* as a component of virtue, and as the resiliency and composure that one exhibits at all times; at times of high joy and pleasure, as well as at times of sorrow and misfortune. Brave is the one who faces the vicissitudes of life with continence, determination and perseverance in the pursuit of Truth and Justice. Socrates advises **Lysimachus** and **Melisias** to carefully monitor the education and upbringing of the youth, because the education they receive in the fields of physical education, music, mathematics and other encyclopedic subjects will determine their eventual character and personality. At the conclusion of the dialogue, Socrates is invited to the house of the gentlemen to have a tutoring session with the youngsters. Most likely this was written by Plato to emphasize to the Athenians how unjust the accusation of Meletus was: that Socrates was fostering injustice and corrupting the youth.

10. LYSIS (ΛΥΣΙΣ)

«Τα εναντια ερωσι των εναντιων»[15]
Heraclitus

This dialogue examines the basis of friendship. **Lysis** was a young Athenian whom Socrates met at the Palaistra, along with several of his friends. The other youngster who engages Socrates in the dialogue is **Menexenus**. The youth had finished their exercises at the Gymnasium and were awaiting their servants to take them home. The style of this exchange does not follow the question and answer format, but rather is a narrative in which Socrates relates his encounters with the youth. At first a discussion ensues between Socrates and **Lysis,** and **Menexenus** enters near the middle of the narrative. The ages of the youth are uncertain, but judging from the questions answered, they must have been in their early teens--as Lysis responded that his father and mother would not permit certain

The Port of Piraeus

things--such as driving a chariot and going out without their permission. The concept of friendship and that of *Platonic love* do not differ in Platonic philosophy, and in **Phaedrus** and **The Symposium** Plato expounds on their significance. The subject of pederasty is present, as at the beginning, **Ippothales,** a member of the group that met Socrates before he entered the Palaistra, was pressured to reveal that he was in love with one of the youth; but apart from some questions concerning how a lover should approach his loved one, there is no sequence to the incident. Reading through this narrative, one will discover what friendship *is not* rather than what friendship *is*. Plato explores and evaluates these concepts, but leaves the audience to think and judge for itself. Altogether, four definitions of friendship are given, along with extensive commentary in the dialectic mode, but in a narrative format. Socrates appears to reject all of them--including the fourth one that he proposed. This is the typical approach that Plato follows, in that he wants the reader to examine and search for the truth through his "*Method of Recollection*": because it is only then that true wisdom is achieved.

The first definition states: By detailed dialectic analysis this definition is shown not to hold true in general; because if the devotion is not of mutual intensity, it is feasible that one could befriend his *enemy*. The second definition is borrowed from earlier sages--**Embedocles and Homer**--according to which: **"Like is attracted by Like"** (Ομοιος Ομοιω αει Πελαζει). By the dialectic method this definition is also rejected, in that two bad people cannot be friends because, due to their nature, they are bound to hurt each other. The definition stands when a friendship develops between two good people who are similar, but does not hold between two bad people who are also similar;

---

[15] "Opposites attract."

189

therefore: we have a partial truth but false definition. A third definition of friendship is taken from Heraclitus, according to which: **"Two dissimilar subjects attract each other (opposites attract)."** Initially this definition appears correct, in that sometimes opposites attract; as for example: the weak are attracted to the strong to gain support; the uneducated are attracted to the educated and wise--also to derive benefit and support. By the dialectic method this definition is also rejected by Socrates, illustrating that it may be partially true, but not universally--in that injustice cannot be attracted to justice; or the good to the bad; or the corrupt to the virtuous. The fourth definition is proposed by Socrates himself: **"Friendship is the love and devotion that attracts one who is neither good nor bad to the good."** He uses as an example, metaphorically, the human body--which is neither bad nor good--but neutral. When it is healthy it does not exhibit attachment toward a doctor; but when ill responds with devotion toward a doctor, due to the presence of illness. This definition appears to have as a base in it the element of utility, in that there is a benefit that one hopes to derive from the relationship. This element in the definition also appeared in earlier ones and is apparently defective. The discussion enters a vicious circle and Plato ends it abruptly, admitting that, in spite of the extensive discussion one may not know what friendship is. Suddenly, the servants of the youth appear and take them home. Ultimately, no definition or final conclusion is reached; but then, as we mentioned earlier, one would expect such an outcome because this is the way Plato often presents his views. He encourages mature audiences to consider and arrive at the conclusions themselves--not through lectures--by using their intellect to achieve knowledge: which is unique and natural. This subject is examined further by Plato in other dialogues, in which he introduces the concept of Platonic love *(the epitome of friendship)*, where friendship and love between two people is intended to reach the *ultimate good* (Αγαθον) and achieve *the happiness of those involved* **(Symposium).**

11. LAWS (NOMOI)

« Ο γαρ ακοινωνητος ων εξουσιας του συνδικαζειν
ηγειται το παραπαν της πολεως ου μετοχος ειναι»[16]
Plato

During ancient times, and particularly at the beginning of the 4th century B.C., the main political systems in practice were: T*he Monarchical, the Aristocratic, and the Democratic,* which--according to Aristotle **(Politics Πολιτικα)**--could deteriorate into *Tyranny, Oligarchy, and Demagoguery.* Plato was familiar with the practice of democracy, because it was the political

Modern Athens and the Acropolis

system in Athens during the years that he lived there. He must have been disillusioned, however, with the democratic system, as was probably true of quite a number of other Athenians who witnessed, under this regime, the decline and eventual fall of Athens as the dominant power in Greece. The indication that democracy would deteriorate into *"mob rule" (Οχλοκρατια)* was probably evident, as there were some bad decisions made by the Assembly; for example, in 416 B.C. it authorized the ill-fated expedition to Sicily, which resulted in the destruction of the Athenian navy and the deaths of thousands of Athenian soldiers. Political figures, such as **Cleon**, and military leaders, such as **Alcibiades,** contributed significantly to the development of demagogy, which dominated the Assembly and the decision process for some time. It was a democratic system, in that decisions were made at the **Assembly (Εκκλησια του Δημου)** by all of the people, but it was a participative democracy--without checks and balances--where a demagogue could step to the podium and sway public opinion, toward his point of view, before a vote was taken on some controversial issue.

Plato seemed to have no confidence in the other political systems as well, and in the **Republic** he attempted to create a new system based upon justice and virtue, with the expectation that citizens, particularly the *Guardian Class*, would set a high moral and ethical standard--to the degree that they would be self-governed under the direction of a virtuous and moral leader: the **"Philosopher King"** that the public would look up to. The Philosopher-King would be a paragon of virtue, and Plato provided considerable guidelines devoted to the education and

---

[16] "He, who is not a participant in the political process, should feel that he has completely lost his political rights."

upbringing of such a leader. There were few written laws in the **Republic** because Plato believed that when virtuous people rule: there is no need for excessive legislation. He also maintained that if an arrogant and uneducated individual takes control, who usually would not accept other opinions--even when conditions require change--he could inflict considerable damage to the

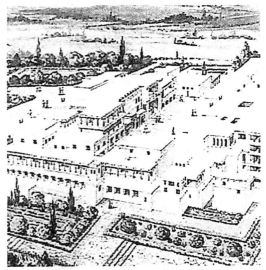

Knossos, Reconstructed Model

Republic by manipulating existing laws. He also pointed out in the **Statesman (Πολιτικος)** that it is impossible for written laws to cover all possible circumstances. It is to Plato's credit that he attempted to establish the validity and viability of the **Republic,** instead of arbitrarily and arrogantly proposing it as a system that could meet all peoples' needs. He believed that a benevolent king or tyrant, if properly prepared, could become a virtuous ruler. For this reason, in 386 B.C., he went to Sicily, at Syracuse, to the court of Dionysius I, hoping to convert him into a philosopher-king who would rule justly, morally, and ethically. Some say that on that trip[17] he visited Sicily and Southern Italy to acquaint himself with the landscape and political environment. **Dion**, who was the King's

brother-in-law, was sympathetic to Plato's ideas; but **Dionysius** was not, and when Plato advised him that in order to be a good king he should be virtuous, Dionysius became angry, had him arrested and delivered to a Spartan by the name of **Pollin**--with instructions to either kill or sell him as a slave: *Fortunately, for Plato, he chose to sell him as a slave; and at the Aegina slave market a friend paid his ransom and freed him.*

In 366 B.C., Dionysius I died in Olympia from excessive drinking and celebrating after he won at the Games, and Dion, who became the Regent, invited Plato to Syracuse. He attempted, one more time, to educate and reform the new king, Dionysius II, young son of Dionysius I; but his program did not achieve much success because Dion, his protector and supporter, had fallen in disfavor with the new king and was exiled. Plato stayed awhile at the court of Dionysius II, but eventually returned to Athens in 365 B.C. without any success. He felt that this expedition to Syracuse was not an outright loss, however, because he had the chance to meet **Archytas**, a *Pythagorean mathematician*, and through him he was introduced to some of the successes the Pythagoreans had achieved in the field of mathematics. Later, Dionysius II felt that Plato could provide help in improving the image of his rule by bestowing intellectual stature to his tyrannical regime. Plato attempted to persuade Dionysius to become virtuous and modify his lifestyle--particularly his desire for wine. It appears that at the beginning the plan was working, because in the fourth book of the **Laws** it is stated that *the reformation of the State can be achieved if a strong dictator or tyrant selects an advisor with wisdom and eloquence.*

---

[17] Since it was the first year after he returned from Egypt and before establishing the Academy.

Ultimately, however, the third experiment failed when Dionysius engaged in hostilities with Dion, Plato's friend, and Plato decided to return to Athens because he had had enough of his adventures at Syracuse. Dionysius did not permit him to leave at the beginning, but finally, with the help of Archytas, acceded and allowed him to return-- never to set foot in Syracuse again. He must have been disappointed that he was unable to persuade these rulers that virtuous and ethical behavior would bring harmony, peace, benevolence, and ultimate stability to the affairs of the city-states. Most likely this affected his thinking about the tenets of **The Republic,** and some claim that the "**Laws**" is a repudiation of some of the views expressed earlier in **The Republic--** particularly the **Philosopher-King** principle.

What is missing in Plato's political writings, and particularly in **The Republic,** is *the Separation of Authority (Executive, Legislative, and Judicial)* in the various levels of government; this principle is not mentioned anywhere prior to the **Laws.** In the Spartan system there was some semblance of separation of powers: the **Ephors (**selected directly by the people); the two **Kings** (hereditary succession); and the **Assembly** (also elected by the people) could be viewed as three independent levels of authority.   For example-- *the Ephors were independent from the Kings and played the role of the Judicial; the Kings played the role of the Executive, and the Assembly the Legislative.* This is not exactly the same type of system that eventually evolved in modern times;

The Temple of Hephaestus, Athens

but nevertheless, the idea of separation of authority with the concept of checks and balances is present. This system was discussed by Aristotle in "Πολιτικα" (**Politics**), and one might say that he officially introduces, for the first time, the separation of powers in the administration of the affairs of the city-state. **Polybius,** a later historian who discussed the Federal System practiced by the Achaean League, also dealt extensively with the separation of powers concept. But the full identification of the system in modern times was not achieved until 1748 when **Montesquieu,** the famous French philosopher, published **L'Esprit des Lois** and established the principles and philosophical doctrines of the separation of powers--*Legislative, Executive, and Judicial.* Plato believed that a division of power was necessary in order to create checks and balances to make the system work efficiently.   He considered *a blend of the Monarchical, Aristocratic, and Democratic practices as a possible structure to separate and balance authority.*

NOMOI is the only dialogue in which Socrates is not a participant; instead, three old men: **Kleinias** from Crete, **Meggelus** from Sparta, and a **Stranger** from Athens meet at Knossos,

Crete, and decide to travel to the top of **Mount Heda** to offer sacrifice at the Temple of Zeus. The purpose of the trip, besides the sacrificial ceremony, is to discuss the formulation of a constitution for a new city-state that was to be created in Crete, for which the government at Knossos would provide the land and the people. *It is of interest that Plato selects these three elderly people representing Crete, Sparta, and Athens.* Plato, as mentioned above, was concerned with devising a new system which would encompass those practiced in the three cities that these elderly men came from: *Aristocracy in Crete; a Quasi-Monarchy in Sparta; and Democracy in*

The Library at Pergamum

Athens. Kleinias, the Cretan, announces that he has authority from Knossos to build a new city in western Crete which would consist of 5096 inhabitants--most coming from Crete--but if necessary, immigrants from Peloponnesus would be added. The number 5096 is chosen as being a number perfectly divisible by most integers. Here one views Plato's final political convictions, as he was almost 80 years old when he was writing the **"Laws."** The existing property of the new city would be divided equally among these 5096 inhabitants, and everyone would be allowed, by becoming progressive and productive, to increase

his lot four-fold--but no more. The people, then, as political and economic entities, would be divided into four classes: The First Class would comprise *those who did not improve*; the Second--*those who doubled their possessions;* the Third--*those who tripled their possessions;* and the Fourth would include *those who quadrupled their property.* Note the limitation on material possessions as compared with the similar concept in **The Republic,** where, in the case of the Guardians: material possessions were completely eliminated.

What were the motivating factors for such an extensive and complicated plan? After his expeditions to Sicily, and considering the experiences that he encountered there, Plato apparently abandoned the idea of a **Philosopher-King** as the ultimate alternative to the existing political systems. Yet, it is clear that he did not abandon the underlying concepts in the **Republic** concerning *Virtue, Education, and Justice as the fundamental philosophical doctrines.* If, in his old age, Plato believed that people would not find their way to a virtuous life just by being properly educated and shown the way, then surely the **Republic** was due for a revision. We do know, however, from his writings in the **Laws,** that the principle of the **"Philosopher- King"** was definitely up for revision; for he says that only when people *become sons of "God"* is there hope of ultimately achieving a virtuous status, so that the Philosopher-King" will become effective. In the third book of the **Laws,** Kleinias asks the Athenian guest what kind of system he contemplates for the new city-state: *"Would it be Monarchy, Aristocracy, or Democracy?"* He excluded Tyranny outright: *"I do not believe that you would ever consider tyranny."* After several passages one surmises that he envisions a combination of the three. Here is the first subtle appearance of the Separation of Powers in government. He despised Tyranny and

Monarchy, and doubted the effectiveness of Democracy without checks and balances. The implication, then, that he considered a mixture of the three systems suggests that he wanted to set limits that would prevent **"mob rule" (Οχλοκρατια)** *and the tyranny of the majority of the parliamentary rule.*

Plato envisioned the following division of authority in the new city-state. (1) **The Assembly *(Εκκλησια του Δημου or Συλλογος)*:** The ultimate authority and power regulating the governance of the people; (2) **The Legislative Body or Parliament (Βουλη):** consisting of 360 deputies elected from the four classes of the society--90 from each; (3) **The Guardians of the Laws (Νομοφυλακες)** (37 in number): elected by members of the Parliament; (4) **The Body of the Ministers (Ευθυνοντες):** originally set to be 12, with provisions to replace 3 annually-elected directly by the people. These ministers would function as the Executive Branch of the government and have ministerial duties, i.e. Ministers of Education, Gymnastics, etc. The Minister of Education would be the most important authority, acknowledged by both the elected officials and the electors as the highest office of the State, and would not allow the education of children to become a secondary or incidental matter. (5) **The Nocturnal Council (Νυκτερινος Συλλογος):** so named because it is to meet early in the morning before the business of the day begins--composed of ten senior "Guardians of the Law," the Minister and Ex-Minister of Education, and ten men between the ages of 30 to 40 who are trained to recognize the *One in the Many,* and know the value of virtue and prudence. Thus, this Council composed of men who have knowledge of God and of the ideal pattern of goodness, will be sanctioned to watch over the Constitution and be *the Guardians of the government and the laws.* The role of women in the **Laws** reflects the one described in the **Republic:** Women would receive equal education and military training, and participate in the defense of the city-state; however, the commonality of women and children is abandoned. They could enter politics and assume public duties as *Ministers* after they reach the age of forty. They would supervise and license marriages and be in charge of legislation affecting the upbringing of children. As far as slaves are concerned, Plato adheres to the established practices applied in the entire ancient world.

In the following, a short summary of the contents of the 12 books of the **Laws** is presented. As we have seen, there are few laws in the **Republic,** but now Plato provides a system of laws that cover every aspect of the civil, social, religious, and political life of the citizens of the new state. There are provisions for practically all aspects of human activity, from tariffs and demography to litigation for civil and criminal offenses and the election of governing officials. In this system there is no Philosopher-King; no Monarchical King; and no Benevolent Dictator.

Book 1. The systems of Crete and Sparta are discussed, as well as the "symposia"[18] in Athens and the practice of open drunkenness--which gives an indication of the true character of the individual. Plato concentrates on the harmful effects that drunkenness and immorality have had on Athenian society and the resulting collapse of democracy.

---

[18] **Drinking parties which could evolve into intellectual exchanges.**

Book 2. The significance of education is stressed, and suggests that man should pursue knowledge and try to improve the quality of his life. Excessive drinking is condemned and prohibited for adolescents younger than 18 years old.

Book 3. The discussion covers the matter of how states either advance toward progress and harmony, or follow the road to self-destruction. The question is: What are the institutions in a society that lead to moral excellence? The organization of a society should have as an objective the virtuous development of its citizens, through the education of its people, which leads man to rational thinking and prudence.

Book 4. Discussion is centered on the actual legislation that should be enacted in this newly created city in Crete, of over 5000 people, and for which three old wise men are about to provide laws that would govern it. This book serves as a preamble to the principles of the legislation, which are to be presented in the remainder of the books.

Book 5. Questions on morality, faith, and values are discussed. A comparison of the virtuous life versus the immoral life is made, in order to prove dialectically that the virtuous life provides more pleasure to the individual. Provisions are made for the distribution of land, and controls are set which would regulate the acquisition of wealth; the population is then divided according to its four economic classes.

Book 6. There is a discussion concerning the method of electing those who would govern and the kind of laws that should be introduced for the leaders to follow. Specific legislation is provided for the police (rural and urban); deputies of the Legislature; the clergy; the judicial system; the Supreme Court; military service (men and women); building codes; rules pertaining to servants (slaves) and marriages. The maximum age of 40 is set for a woman to bear children, and 50 for men to marry. Balloting and regulations for free elections are described and set forth.

Book 7. In this, the longest book, the matter of education is covered extensively. The question is: What kind of education should be provided, because a person will be either temperate and akin to virtue--or a **wild animal**, depending on the quality and extent of his exposure to education. Education should be compulsory for both male and female and consist of: physical education, reading and writing, music, drama, arithmetic, geometry, astronomy, logic, and harmonics.

Book 8. Holidays and State celebrations are discussed, as well as the population's participation in these events. It also addresses preparation for the eventuality of war; and rules and regulations are established for the protection of morals, ethics, and traditions. Finally, agricultural, professional, and business laws are added.

Book 9. The criminal code of the State is drafted. Crimes against religion and murder are covered first, and the gravity of these crimes is analyzed-- followed by procedure and punishment. The crime of theft is next discussed; while distinction is made between voluntary and involuntary crimes, and specific articles of the Law are given concerning punishment and rehabilitation.

Book 10. In this book the matter of "atheism" is discussed, and it is, in some sense, a preamble to Book 9, in which the matter of the criminal code is covered--even though it is presented later. According to Plato: *All evils in the society derive from the fact that most people do not believe in God.*

Book 11. Matters pertaining to the criminal code that were interrupted by the discussion of atheism in Book 10 are now discussed. The issues for which legislation is provided are: differences between citizens; relations between freed slaves and their masters; business transactions; family law (wills, custodies, parental rights), and other matters (including begging, court procedures, libel et.al).

Book 12. This last book covers legislation governing various areas such as: embezzlement of public money, military crimes and military honors. Further, the chapter presents views on: the Supreme Court; oaths in courts, foreign policy matters; protection of visitors and tourists, and safeguarding the rights of the individual in his home.

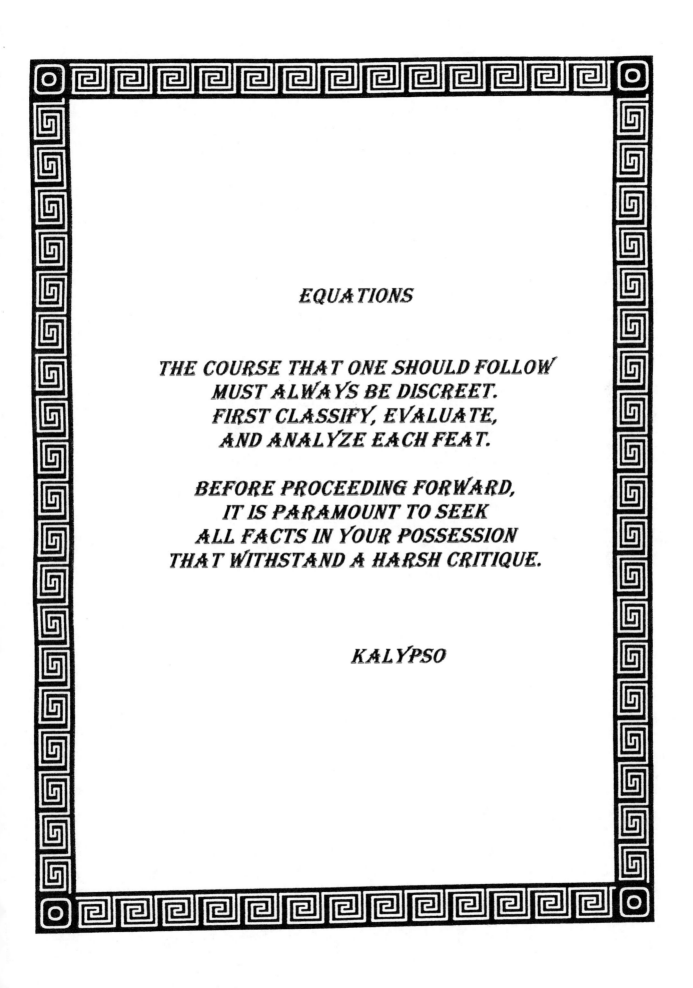

EQUATIONS

THE COURSE THAT ONE SHOULD FOLLOW
MUST ALWAYS BE DISCREET.
FIRST CLASSIFY, EVALUATE,
AND ANALYZE EACH FEAT.

BEFORE PROCEEDING FORWARD,
IT IS PARAMOUNT TO SEEK
ALL FACTS IN YOUR POSSESSION
THAT WITHSTAND A HARSH CRITIQUE.

KALYPSO

CHAPTER 10

ARISTOTLE--THE MAN AND HIS WORK

«Ει μεν φιλοσοφητεον, φιλοσοφητεον, και ει μη
φιλοσοφητεον, φιλοσοφητεον παντως αρα
φιλοσοφητεον»[1]
Aristotle

THE MAN

Aristotle dominated the intellectual world of his time and has been the most respected thinker of all ages. As was true with all ancient thinkers, Aristotle's influence diminished during the Medieval Age, but re-emerged during the **Renaissance** and had a considerable impact thereafter.

Aristotle

At that time (c.1400's A.D.), the advancement, both intellectually and commercially, of the Italian city-states took place, and new scholars emerged who studied Aristotle's doctrines and principles, and developed original ideas and breakthroughs in the world of science and philosophy-- creating the impetus for what we call today the **Western civilization** and **culture**. Aristotle followed Plato as the leader of the Greek thinkers during the middle of the 4th century B.C, and directed the **Lyceum** until his death. To paraphrase Goethe: *Aristotle was a builder, a creator who looked around and collected the appropriate data, analyzed them and then started building an edifice. Plato was a floating spirit that looked down into the human soul and tried to analyze it, and searched for its origin and whereabouts.* Aristotle was born in the city of Stagira, in Macedonia, in the year 384 B.C., and died in Chalkis, Euboea, in 322 B.C. His father descended from an old family of physicians and was a prominent physician himself; employed in the court of King Amyntas II, of Macedonia, grandfather of Alexander the Great. Aristotle lost his mother when he was quite young, and was an early teenager when he lost his father. **Proxenus,** a close friend of his father, undertook to raise Aristotle and his younger brother, and

---

[1] "If we do not have to philosophize, still we shall philosophize to prove that we must not philosophize."

198

took them, along with his family, and moved to Atarneus, a city in Asia Minor across from the island of Lesbos. In reality, it was Proxenus' wife that raised the youngsters, and eventually Proxenus adopted the brothers. In 368 or 367 B.C., at the age of 17, Aristotle moved to Athens and attended various schools of rhetoric; and since he descended from a family of medical doctors, he had some knowledge of medicine and used it in practice. Finally, he settled and attended classes at a school of **Eudoxus',** a philosopher and mathematician, where he learned the first ethical lessons on prudence and moderation. He inherited a sizable property from his father, and while in Athens,

Apollo with his Mother (Leto) and Sister (Artemis)

according to Diogenes Laertius, he was living an ostentatious life. Laertius further reports that he spoke with a lisp, had slender calves, small eyes, and was conspicuous with his attire, rings, and hairstyle; and was most concerned with his appearance. Some other biographers, however, claim that this is not entirely true, but rather because he was short, skinny, and not particularly good looking, was concerned with his appearance and spent money for his grooming and dress. He did not last long at Eudoxus' school, as he did not find it sufficiently challenging, and soon joined

Plato's Academy where he distinguished himself as an intelligent and promising young student. Plato, at the time, was in Sicily. Early at the Academy Aristotle exhibited his interest in serious research, not only on the subjects that the Academy was pursuing, but also on matters pertaining to what we would call today the physical sciences and biology. He left the Academy shortly before Plato died in 347 B.C., and returned to Atarneus--the city where he grew up--at the invitation of Hermeias, the ruler of Atarneus. Diogenes Laertius claims that he left the Academy because he took issue with some of the Platonic tenets, particularly the" **Theory of Ideas**"; but still others claim that he left because the wave of anti-Macedonianism was growing stronger--due to the conflict between King Philip of Macedonia and Athens--and he felt that the environment was not very comfortable for him. Upon learning of Aristotle's departure, Plato purportedly said: *"Aristotle spurns me, as colts kick out at their mother who bore them."* (Αριστοτελης ημας απελακτισε καθαπερ τα πωλαρια γεννηθεντα την μητερα). Hermeias, a very intelligent man whom Aristotle met at the Academy when he was a student there, left prior to Aristotle's break and became the ruler of Atarneus--where he distinguished himself as a benevolent ruler--and was recognized as the protector of the interests of the city-states of Asia Minor from the Persian Satraps. But within a few years of Aristotle's arrival in Atarneus, the city was captured by the Persians and Hermeias was arrested and executed. This was a serious blow to Aristotle, who hastened his departure from Atarneus before he could be arrested by the Persians. He had a companion and friend with him by the name of **Xenocrates,** who later became the Director of the Academy, and they were encouraging **Hermeias** in his efforts to save the Greek city-states of Ionia from the Persians. He moved to **Mytilene,** along with his family, where he met Theophrastus, a native of Mytilene and a close friend; he had married one of Hermeias nieces (Pytheias) and had a daughter also named

Pytheias. He stayed in Mytilene several years, and during that time wrote some of his early works. By then, Aristotle had developed a great reputation as a scholar and teacher, and King Philip of Macedonia invited him to Pella by sending him the following letter:

"I have a son and I am so grateful to the gods, not only for the birth of the child, but of the fact that he was born at a time when you are a distinguished teacher. I hope that you will agree to undertake his education and upbringing so that he may become a worthy successor."

Aristotle, in 340 B.C., went to Pella to serve as the tutor of young Alexander, and stayed there until Alexander began his campaign to Asia in 334 B.C. While in Pella, he had a son by the name of Nichomachus. Aristotle continued his research and writing at the Macedonian palace, and edited and published the **Iliad** by Homer, at the request of Alexander; it was this issue of the **Iliad**

Relief Sculpture of Hegesus

that **Plutarch** refers to in his biography of Alexander that he carried with him in his campaign to Asia. Aristotle, while in Pella, wrote a series of books, particularly dialogues, concerning subjects of philosophy and rhetoric, and two: **On Monarchy** and **Politics,** which were meant for Alexander: these books are not extant. After Alexander departed, Aristotle returned to Athens where **Speucippus** was the Director of the Academy, but instead of joining him and becoming a research associate, he decided to establish his own school of philosophy and rhetoric in a northeast suburb of Athens--near where today is the hill of Lycabettus--and dedicated it to Luceus Apollo. The school became known as the **Lyceum,** also as the **Peripatetic School**[2]—because Aristotle used to promenade through the porticos of the school while lecturing-- and flourished for several centuries. Scholars from all over the known world assembled there pursuing research and studies in the various aspects of philosophy, as well as the physical and social sciences. The classes and lectures were divided into two groups: one in the morning hours, in which the attendees were usually mature students with advanced knowledge and experience on the subjects; these lectures came to be known as the **"Acroamatica."** There are some writers who claim that there was some degree of secrecy associated with these lectures, because most of the notes and writing concerning the discussions perished. In the afternoon there was a series of other lectures, devoted mostly to younger students and beginners, and these lectures came to be known as the **"Encyclical Lessons"**--which dealt mostly with general subjects on Nature. At the beginning, Alexander paid considerable amounts of money (thousands of talents) in support of the Lyceum, before he came in conflict with Aristotle[3], and it is reported by biographers that he invited scientists

[2] From the Greek word «Περιπατος», meaning "promenade."
[3] Before Alexander left, Aristotle introduced his nephew Kalisthenes to him--who served as observer and advisor-- and followed Alexander on his expedition. This nephew was accused of conspiring to kill Alexander, and Alexander had him tried and executed. This event considerably cooled the relations between Alexander and Aristotle.

from the School to accompany him on his campaign--to collect data on fauna, flora, geography and geology--on the basis of which most of the work on these subjects by Aristotle was done. The variety of subjects that he wrote about, and the way he systematically classified these data, comprised an encyclopedic knowledge for his time. It was so well prepared, meticulous with attention to detail and the application of the scientific method, that the accuracy, even today, fascinates students of his work. A German philosopher once said: *"Another Aristotle was not born,*

will not be born; and there is no need for another." In the year 323 B.C., Alexander died in Babylon, and the Athenians, who had never harbored warm feelings for the Macedonians, revolted against their rule. Aristotle felt that his sojourn in Athens must come to an end, and is quoted as having said: **"Let me leave Athens before the Athenians commit another blunder."**[4] Also, at the time when he was in Athens, the Delphic Oracle reportedly bestowed on him honors, crowned him, and recognized him as a significant scholar. But at the news of the death of Alexander, the Oracle stripped him of the honor, and Aristotle commented: *"As of the honor conferred on me at Delphi, and of which I have been stripped, I am neither greatly concerned nor greatly unconcerned."* According to one biographer, Aristotle was accused of impiety by a person named **Euremedon**, and by some others, for an epigram that he wrote and inscribed on a statue of Hermeias that he had built at Delphi. He left Athens and moved to **Chalkis,** on the island of Euboea, where his mother had an estate, and died there a year later (322 B.C.) from a

Zeus and his Wife Hera

short illness--at the age of 62. Aristotle was a very pious man, protective of his friends and family; and from his will we know that he cared for his wife and children and distributed his wealth in an equitable and honorable way. He had many enemies, however, particularly among the members of the Academy, because he espoused different views on a number of issues and disagreed with the Platonic **Theory of Ideas;** and of course, most importantly: because he was a Macedonian. Aristotle was more of a pragmatist; while the Academicians were idealists.

The following anecdotes characterize his personality, his maturity, and compassion for his fellow human beings. When he was once asked what people gain by telling lies, his answer was: **"Just this, that when they speak the truth they are not believed."** Once he was accused of giving money to a bad man; he responded: **"It was the man and not his character that I pitied."** He was fond of mathematics and used to say: **"Mathematics shines and illuminates the environment as the sun."** Aristotle is credited with the famous motto: **"The roots of education are bitter, but the fruit is sweet."** Once he was asked what is it that soon grows old; he responded: **"Gratitude."** And when he was asked to define "hope," he replied: **"It is a waking dream."** He used to say that three things are indispensable for education: **natural endowment,**

---

[4] **Aristotle** was referring to the unjust execution of **Socrates** by the Athenians 77 years earlier.

study, and constant practice. When someone abused him, he responded: **"It is all right as long as it is in my absence."** Beauty, he declared to be: **"a greater recommendation than any letter of introduction."** Some say that Diogenes, the famous Cynic philosopher, devised the following definitions referring to Aristotle's and others' views on beauty: Socrates defined beauty as: "A short lived reign"; Plato as: "Natural superiority"; Theophrastus as: "A mute deception"; Theocritus as: "An evil in an ivory setting"; Carneades as: "A monarchy that needs no bodyguard"; and Aristotle as; "The gift of God." Once, when Aristotle was asked to describe the difference between the educated and the uneducated, he replied: **"As much as the living from the dead."** He used to refer to education as: **"An ornament in prosperity and a refuge in adversity."** Regarding teachers, he said that: **they should be given more honor for educating children than the parents who bring them into this world, because the parents provide the bare life; while teachers ensure the good life."** To one who boasted that he belonged to a great city, his reply was: **"That is not the point to consider, but who it is that is worthy of a great city."** When asked what friendship is, he replied: **"A single soul dwelling in two bodies."**

"Mankind," he used to say, **"is divided into those who are as thrifty as if they would live forever, and those who are as extravagant as if they were going to die tomorrow."** When one once inquired why we spend so much time with the beautiful, he said: **"That is a blind man's question."** When asked what advantage he had ever gained from philosophy, he replied: **"This-- that I do without being ordered what some are constrained to do by their fear of the Law."** Responding to the question of how we should behave to friends, he answered: **"As we should wish them to behave to us."** Justice, he defined as: **"A virtue of soul which is distributed according to merit."**

ARISTOTLE'S WILL.

Because there are certain elements in Aristotle's will relating to his humanity, his devotion to those who worked for him, his children, and his wives, and also because it gives a rare picture of practices of ancient Greeks concerning matters of heredity, disposition of property, and handling of servants, it is considered worthwhile to present it here--as published by Diogenes Laertius:[5]

*"All will be well; but if at any time something should happen to me, here are Aristotle's dispositions: I appoint **Antipater** as the executor of my will for all my possessions and in general. Until **Nicanor (The son of Proxenus)** returns, I appoint **Aristomenes, Timarchus, Ipparchus, Dioteles, and Theophrastus**—if he can and wishes so--as caretakers of my children, wife **Herpyllis**, and all my possessions. And when the time comes, my daughter should be married to **Nicanor**. If anything should happen to my daughter--and heaven forbid nothing happens to her--before or after the marriage, and if there are children, **Nicanor** will be in charge of the children and all my possessions; managing them worthy for his sake and my honor. Nicanor should take care of both*

---

[5] Translation by author.

*my boy, **Nichomachus,** and my daughter, as it is proper, and be to them as father and brother. If something should happen to Nicanor--heaven forbid that it does not before he marries my daughter or afterward, and if there are children, if he had made provisions already for their care, let it be so, as he ordered. But if not, then let **Theophrastus** live with the girl in the same way as **Nicanor** would. If this is not possible, then the Caretakers should consult with **Antipater** about the future of the boy and the girl, and they decide, in their judgment, the best means for their care. The executor*

Perdicas coin

*and Nikanor, in my memory, should take care of all **Herpyllis'** needs, because she has been good to me all my life. If she wishes to marry, they should see to it that she gets a worthy husband. In addition to those things that have been given to her already, she should also receive one silver talent from my estate and three servants--to choose whomever she wants--as well as the maiden that she already has, and the child **Pyrrhaeus.** If she wishes to live in Chalkis, she should have the house by the garden; but if she wishes to live in Stagira, she should have the family house there. Whichever of the two she chooses, the executors should see to it that they provide for the furnishings of the house, according to her wishes and their judgment. **Nicanor** also should take care of the boy, **Myrmex,** as is proper and worthy, in my memory, and see to it that he receives the property that belongs to him, and returns to his people. **Amvrakis** should be given her*

*freedom, and when she marries, 500 drachmas from my estate, as well as the little maiden that she now has. To **Thale** should be given 1000 drachmas--the girl that he has now, whom he bought--and a maiden. **Simon** should receive, besides the money already given to him to secure a servant, an additional servant or money. When my daughter is married, **Tycho** should be set free; as well as **Philo, Olympius,** and his child. None of the children of my servants should be sold, but should be retained in employment, and when they come of age should be freed upon confirmation of their worth. The statues made by **Gryllion** should be taken care of, and when completed should be dedicated; these are the busts of **Nicanor, Proxenus** (which I was planning to dedicate), as well as the one of **Nicanor's** mother. The bust of **Arimistus** (his brother), which has been completed, should be dedicated as a monument to him because he died childless. My mother's bust should be dedicated to **Demeter in Nemea** or in any other place the executors see fit. Wherever they choose my burial, they should bring the remains of **Pytheias** (his first wife) there, as she has so wished. The executor should install in Stagira, stone animal statues, life size, in honor of Savior **Zeus and Athena**: in celebration of Nicanor's safe return, as I have wished."*

From this testament we note that many of the themes that he was discussing with his students at the Academy and the Lyceum, are reflected in the way that he distributed his wealth, honored his friends, and took care of his family. He provided amply for the care of his teenage children and saw to it that they would be safe and successful. He cared for those people who worked for him, compensated them, and granted their freedom--releasing them from slavery and making them free citizens. He honored the dead among his friends and family by paying to erect statues of them, and provided amply for his common-law wife, Herpyllis, and honored his dead wife, Pytheias-- the mother of his children. These are characteristics of a virtuous and honorable man.

Aristotle ushered in a new era, which was not only a natural evolutionary period that developed as a result of the teachings and theories of the philosophers prior to his time, but also the result of the extended boundaries of the Greek world—then reaching from Macedonia to India, and from Egypt to Persia. New ways of life were introduced, and new philosophies and cultures clashed with the world of the Hellenes. This is the period known as the **Hellenistic Period,** and Aristotle's writings exercised a strong influence, not only on the world of the Greeks, but also on the **new** world of Alexander.

HIS WORK

As we have seen earlier, Aristotle was as much concerned with the physical world-- the plants and animals on the planet--as well as the physical characteristics of the environment; more so than anyone before him, including the Naturalists. The endowment of the Lyceum by Alexander, and the assistance provided scientists following him in the campaign to Asia to study the physical world there, was definitely a major factor contributing to the success that he achieved. To reveal a picture of Aristotle's views on philosophy, which is the main purpose of this work, it is worthwhile to examine some of his writings at the beginning of his career. Just before he left the Academy, in his mid-thirties, he wrote a book by the title of **Προτρεπτικος** loosely translated as **Exhortations to Philosophy,** in which one can find Aristotle's perceptions of the purpose of philosophy and how people should lead moral lives guided by ethics. It is worthwhile to stop and examine this, because the values and ethics exhibited in his will are reflected in **Exhortations to Philosophy. Aristotle** viewed the human soul from a different angle, as compared with Plato; yet he did consider the soul as being connected with the way of life one leads--similar to the tripartite nature of the soul that Plato presented in **Phaedrus.** The soul, then, is connected with the moral and ethical values that one espouses, and a good soul is superior to wealth and health. It is a question of behavior, disposition, and prudence that count more than wealth-- and even health. Aristotle recognizes a soul in plants and animals, but accepts that *rationality is more important than irrationality*--which is not a characteristic of plants or animals. It is essential that people develop their rationality for a life of happiness (**Ευδαιμονια**). Plato strongly emphasized the importance of *knowledge* in achieving happiness and well-being; and Aristotle, as well, points out this important principle as a component of a rational and happy life. It is the privilege of man to exercise rational thinking and prudence that makes him unique; otherwise, he would not differ from plants or animals. The mind of man is a divine component of the human being, and can be utilized by virtuous reasoning to achieve happiness. Aristotle emphasizes the significance of rational thinking: Man can be divine if his mind is devoid of irrationality; but he can become a brutal entity if he is void of rationality; and a plant--if he is deprived of perception and mind.

He urges people to study the subject of philosophy for its own sake, and not for the purpose of direct and instant return, because the good from the study of philosophy will accrue gradually--not as an instant gratification. It is quite a different thing to endeavor toward something with the view of the benefits derived, rather than pursuing an endeavor for its own sake: *if it is worthwhile.* Plato, in creating his ethical edifice, emphasized the importance of knowledge in achieving the **"Idea of Good";** Aristotle emphatically underlines the importance of education, as well, and in addition stresses the distinction between *a life of hedonistic pleasures vs. a life of understanding and moral behavior.* Aristotle must have written **Exhortations to Philosophy** early during his sojourn in Athens, but in his major works-**Nichomachean Ethics** and **Eudemean Ethics**--he vividly outlined these points and amplified on the tenets of virtuous and rational living. In a vein similar to Aristotle's view of pursuing research for its own sake, and not for some immediate benefits, the Ionian philosopher **Anaxagoras,** when once was asked, while in Athens, if he missed his home town, **Clazomenae,** looked up to the sky, pointed to the stars, and said: *This is my home.*

Aristotle was a prolific writer, and Diogenes Laertius reports that he wrote in total 354 books, or 445,270 lines; but from these books only about 20 per cent have survived. Most probably, some of these books were written by his associates at the Lyceum, or by some of his most advanced students--under his direction. Also, the size of these books must not have been the size of today's, because if we divide the number of lines by the number of books, we obtain 1258 lines per book. We do not know the line length of an ancient papyrus roll, but if a page of a papyrus roll were about the same as an average book today, say 30 lines, then each of Aristotle's books would have, on the average--30 pages. If we look across Diogenes Laertius' list, we find titles such as: **On Justice; Poets; Soul; Prayer; Wealth; Education; Extracts from Plato's Laws; Motion; Controversial Propositions; Art of Rhetoric; Reply to the Writings of Gorgias; Concerning Physiognomy; etc.** Obviously, some of these must have been simple monographs or short articles and not full length books.

While Plato and other ancient writers wrote on a specific topic only, Aristotle's writings covered an extensive array of subjects and areas. Judging from the titles provided by Diogenes Läertius, both the physical, as well as the social and behavioral sciences are addressed. From the existing books, we note the following areas that Aristotle covered: Logic; Physics; Biology; Metaphysics; The Soul; Ethics; Poetry, and Politics. We present below the titles of the extant Aristotelian works and a summary that follows.

A)   **Concerning Logic and Methods of Research**: **The Organon** (not the original title):

1) **Categories** (Κατηγοριες)--1 book
2) **Interpretations** (Περι Ερμηεινας)--1 book
3) **Topics** (Τοπικα)--2 books
4) **Prior Analysis** (Ανα λυτικα Προτερα)--8 books
5) **Posterior Analysis** (Αναλυτκα Υστερα)--2 books
6) **Sophists** (Περι Σοφιστικων Ελεγχων) -- 1 book

B) **Concerning the Physical World (ΦΥΣΙΚΑ)**: In this category Aristotle included 18 titles dealing with the following subjects:

On the Heavens (On Creation and Destruction)
Meteorology
On the Soul
On Generation and Corruption
On Sense and Sensibilia
On Memory and Recollection
On Sleep and Walking
On Dreams
On Prophesying by Dreams
On Youth and Old Age
On Length and Shortness of Life
On Breath
On Respiration
History of Animals
On the Parts of Animals
On the Progression of Animals
On the Generation of Animals
On the Motion of Animals

C) **Concerning Metaphysics: (Μετα τα Φυσικα or Πρωτη Φιλοσοφια).** In this category Aristotle analyzes questions referring to the realm of the transcendental world and the mind (beyond the physical world)--14 books. The title that Aristotle gave to this series of treatises is ***First Philosophy* (ΠΡΩΤΗ ΦΙΛΟΣΟΦΙΑ).**

D) **Concerning Ethics and Politics (Ηθικα and Πολιτικα).** In these books Aristotle presents his philosophy on ethics and politics, including his views on political systems and government.

Ethics (1 book)
Nicomachean Ethics (1 book)

<u>**Eudemian Ethics (1 book)**</u>
<u>**Politics (8 books)**</u>

E)   <u>**Partially Saved Books**</u>. In addition to the above, the following books are available--but not in complete form. These are:

<u>**Philosophy**</u>
<u>**The Soul**</u>
<u>**Justice**</u>
<u>**The Politician**</u>
<u>**Poetry**</u>
<u>**Eugenics**</u>
<u>**Dialogues (5)**</u>
<u>**Rhetoric**</u>
<u>**Ideas**</u>
<u>**Agathon**</u>
<u>**The Athenian Republic**</u>
<u>**Homer**</u>
<u>**Pythagoras (7)**</u>
<u>**Archetian Philosophy**</u>
<u>**Democritus**</u>

Most of these books are available today, and one can step into any major university library and study them. There are quite a number of other books that perished, and the only thing known about them is their title--as provided by ancient biographers. For example, it is reported that Aristotle wrote and described the constitutions and the political systems of 158 city-states of his time, but only the one referring to the Republic of Athens has survived (partially); the beginning of this treatise is missing, but has been reconstructed from fragments.

We present below a summary of Aristotle's views, listing the general categories of research that are identified with the books above. One should realize that this is a brief-format description and certainly does not do justice to the Aristotelian work. It is recommended that the interested reader check out these books or study the bibliography references, commentary, and analyses that are available, in order to achieve a deeper grasp of the Aristotelian scholarly work. Also, one should familiarize oneself with the conditions, life patterns and history of the Greek world during the time of Aristotle, so as to have a clearer understanding of the views expressed in his writings. (See a short Greek history at the end of Chapter 1).

TREATISES DEALING WITH LOGIC AND RESEARCH

It was Aristotle who, for the first time, formally introduced the tenets of logic and the scientific approach to research. To be sure, scientists before him: such as the Eleats, the Pythagoreans, and the Atomists dealt extensively with these subjects; but it was Aristotle who formally presented logic in a scientific manner. He was the first to formally collect and analyze data by using logic and developing hypotheses to prove or disprove a proposition. This is the only way that science can advance, and this is the way that scientists throughout the world apply the scientific method today-- and have at all times since the Greeks. All the work by Aristotle in this area is included in a collection of writings known as **The Organon** (not Aristotle's title), and consists of the books shown in list (A). In these books Aristotle addressed questions pertaining to structural matters of the language, and meanings of expressions in terms of: substance, quantity, quality, relationships, place, time, position, state, and action. These matters were covered in the treatise **"Categories"** (ΚΑΤΗΓΟΡΙΑΙ). In the treatises **"Prior Analysis"** and **"Interpretations,"** Aristotle dealt with various forms of logical statements and theories and their relationships, such as: methods of inductive and deductive reasoning, syllogisms, hypotheses, and propositions. The significance of direct statements of fact is contrasted with

Gathering of Gods, Parthenon (East)

those statements which contain expressions of condition or contingency. In the treatise on **"Posterior Analysis,"** Aristotle examines with the methodology of scientific research--rather than logic. In the treatise on "**Topics**," he discusses how one should approach matters involving argumentation. This treatise addresses issues concerning debate, and particularly how one should develop an argument that would support or refute a given thesis: the general area of laws or **"rules of logic."** In the treatise on **"Sophistical Refutations,"** Aristotle examines forms of reasoning that appear valid on the surface but actually conceal a delusion or deceit. These would include (1) **"Circular Reasoning"**--*The soul continues to exist after death because it is immorta*l." (2) "**The Fallacy of the Consequent"**--*If a man is a drunkard, he becomes destitute; therefore, if a man is destitute, he then is a drunkard;* or (3) "**The Fallacy of the Irrelevant Conclusion"**--*Instead of proving the point in a dispute, the contestant seeks to gain his point by directing attention to some extraneous fact.* The **Organon** was the handbook and textbook of students of research and scientists for centuries, and in some respect, in reference to logic and the scientific method, still is.

TREATISES CONCERNING NATURE (ΦΥΣΙΚΑ)

In these treatises Aristotle dealt with the natural "body"--living or not-- and all that is corporal. He covered such ideas as: the intrinsic elements of a natural body--"matter" and "form"; the phenomenon of change and its "causative" factors; as well as the topics of space, position, and

208

time. Their magnitudes, continuity, and the cause of movement in natural bodies were studied, as well as the notions of immovability and eternity. Under the title **"On the Heavens"** (**Περι Ουρανου**), Aristotle treated other subjects, such as: a mechanical, geocentric model of the cosmic universe with the Earth at rest--broadly suggesting the notion of gravitational theory for the first time--and the heavenly bodies (planets and stars) viewed in a three dimensional space orbiting the Earth. Also, in the treatise titled **"On Generation and Corruption"** (**Περι Γενεσεως και Φθορας**), Aristotle examines the mutability of earthly material bodies. This investigates changes in size, quantity, and even substance. The notion of **causes of change** was applied to the problem of the interrelationship between the constitution of things in various degrees of structural complexity, and their qualities and functions.

Under the title **"Meteorology"** (**Μετεορολογικα, η Περι Μετεορων**), Aristotle examines such physical phenomena as: **weather, wind, the various forms of precipitation (rain, hail, snow); cloud formations,** and general topics concerning meteorology. Finally, in a series of treatises dealing with the animal world, Aristotle covers such biological problems concerning the general field of what we call today **zoology, botany,** etc. The problems which Aristotle observed and analyzed in detail are related to the functions of life itself. These cover: **generation; sex; environmental adaptation; the struggle for existence; locomotion; growth, and nutrition.** The orderly interrelationships of the kinds and functions of animals are set forth, together with rules and exemplifications of the method adapted to their study.

TREATISE ON THE SOUL (Περι Ψυχης)

Aristotle approaches the matter of the soul differently from the way Plato treated the subject. The relationship between the body and the soul in human life, and to all of life's biological and psychological phenomena, was explored by Aristotle; while rejecting the Platonic transcendentalist and the pre-Socratic materialistic theories on the nature of the soul. The complexities and universal conditions constituting: *birth, nutrition, growth, the senses, experience, movement, and thought were* viewed from the perspective of life's material and formal causes. The *vital principle* was identified with the soul (the formal, efficient, and final cause of living), and the various processes involved in sensation and thought were elaborated on in relation to the proper objects: sight, for example, is identified as the process of seeing visible objects. Aristotle insisted on the distinctions between thought, perception, and imagination; and he establishes the purpose of psychology to be the exploration of the nature, essence, and pertinent associations of the soul of man. To Aristotle, unlike so many other philosophers, the soul is not a spiritual entity--but rather in an integral relationship with the body, and it derives its growth and function from the body's organs of sensation. Since the senses nourish the mind and the intellect of the body, the soul is the means through which **intermediation** and growth are realized. Aristotle then, being a pragmatist--unlike Plato-- attributes significance to the senses and assigns to the soul: the function of **communication** between the intellect and the senses. Through the function of the soul, the moral and intellectual aspects of man are developed; and in this sense the soul provides the link for the bodily organism and the virtues--which are generated in man through his conduct and behavior. Aristotle does not want to explain the theocratic nature of the soul, but associates it with the functions of the organic life of man: **growth, sensation, motion, and thought**. By associating the soul of man with his physical being (unlike Plato, who considered the soul to be a spirit), Aristotle contributes to the development of: (1) an attitude that rejected much of the mysticism previously associated with the soul and its function, and; (2) provided a method for dignified scientific investigation, thus setting the stage for the development of modern psychosomatic medicine in the field of **psychoanalysis.**

TREATISES ON METAPHYSICS (Μετα τα Φυσικα)

The term **"metaphysics"** was not the original Aristotelian title. Aristotle's original title on the subject was **"First Philosophy,"** and he intended to address matters other than the physical objects that were covered in previous treatises. In 14 books, Aristotle investigates issues pertaining to the subjects of: *being, unity, continuity, identity, theology, the problem of causal explanations, principles of science, metaphysical puzzles, conditions of existence, the nature of substance, and mathematical problems*. The reason these treatises came under the title of "Metaphysics" was only that they were meant to be read after the treatises on **"Nature" (Physics).** They contain information concerning the writings of pre-Socratic philosophers on the subjects, and it is through these treatises that we learn of the Eleatic, Pythagorean, and Ionian philosophers' writings in these areas. As was the case with all previous philosophers that we have studied so far, the question of the origin of the "world" has always been a difficult and intriguing concept to tackle. Most Greek philosophers considered God as "existing"--and this was true of Aristotle, as well. But for Aristotle, God is **"Pure Intelligence";** and as such, God is completely **indifferent** to the affairs of the world. Aristotle did not believe that the world was created by God; but rather that the world had existed for all eternity and will continue to exist forever. He begins with the saying: **"All human beings naturally seek knowledge"** (Παντες ανθρωποι του ειδενα ορεγονται φυσει), and states that the knowledge of "why" is superior to the knowledge of "how"; therefore, in these treatises the basic purpose is to seek the knowledge of "why": the knowledge of the principles and causes of all things. This knowledge Aristotle calls **"wisdom,"** which is knowledge for the sake of knowledge itself-- and not to serve some other purpose. He stated: **"This science investigates the being as being and its parts . . . no other science deals with the being as being, but only of some part of it."** (Εστιν επιστημη τις η θεωρει το Ον και τα τουτο υπαρχοντα καθ' αυτο.....ουδεμιαν γαρ των αλλων επιστημων επισκοπει καθ'ολου περι του οντος ει ον, αλλα μερος αυτου τι). Aristotle further states that it is only when we investigate the principles and causes of "being" that we have real knowledge, because then we know the **First Cause**: the beginning of "Being." This area is very complicated to follow and difficult to explain.[6] But in summary, and in a simplified format,

---

[6] A famous Arab philosopher, who had studied and translated Aristotle's "Metaphysics," stated that he had read the subject 40 times, and still he could not say that he understood it.

one can conceive the extent and depth of the problems involved by observing the basic areas that Aristotle devoted most of his scientific research to, which have challenged philosophers and scientists from the beginning of recorded history until today, and these are: *What makes things be what they are? What makes things transform into the various forms that they take? What is the substance that things are made of? What are the fundamental components of matter; do they exist independently, and can they be known and defined?* Research in these fields continues today and will continue in the future. During the period from **Thales** to **Democritus**, phenomena and things were identified by their constituent elements, which Aristotle called **"Material Principles and Causes"** He further enumerated four causative factors to explain change in any thing or situation; although on any occasion only two or three might be amenable to investigation: **(1) the Material Cause; (2) the Form or Definition; (3) the Efficient Cause, and (4) the Final Cause.** In other words, if we assume that we are standing still, the "universe exists." What is this force that precipitates change--because Aristotle accepted Heraclitus' proposition of "**change.**" An example of these four causes would be the following: *Consider the making of a vase or cup: The "**Material Cause**" would be the substance the vase would be made of; the Form or Definition Cause would be the design or shape; while the Efficient Cause would be the method employed to construct the vase; and finally, the Final Cause would be the purpose of the vase (for what reason was it made).*

TREATISES CONCERNING ETHICS (ΗΘΙΚΑ)

There are three basic works by Aristotle addressing the subject of ethics. By time sequence, these are: **Ethics, Eudemian Ethics,** and **Nicomachean Ethics**. Some of the conclusions reached in the last treatise can be found on a less refined level in the other two works, which leads to the conclusion that Aristotle completed it near the end of his life. It bears the name **"Nicomachean"** because some claim the work was actually edited by Aristotle's son, **Nicomachus**. The title of **Eudemean Ethics** also has two possible sources of parentage: (1) either Aristotle dedicated it to his friend and scholar, Eudemus of Euboea, or it was written for a young Cypriot friend by the same name. The work on *ethics,* in all his treatises, summarizes his conclusions on the behavior of man in society after he had extensively studied all the work completed by previous Greek philosophers, including: Plato, Socrates, the "Eleats," "Pythagoreans," Ionians," and others. An ethical life, according to Aristotle, is one that is based on: *"logical, virtuous behavior accompanied by free will."*

Aristotle begins his study on ethics by stating: *"Every art and every method, as well as every action, choice, purpose, and intention seems to have an end that leads to something "good"* (Αγαθον); *and for this reason the "good" has rightly been declared to be that at which all things aim."* (**Πασα τεχνη και πασα μεθοδος, ομοιως τε πραξις και προαιρεσις, αγαθου τινος εφιεσθαι δοκει. Διο καλως απεφαιναντο τ'αγαθου, ου παντ' εφιεται**). By this statement, one immediately grasps the idea that Aristotle, as was true of most Greek thinkers, believed in the innate good nature of the human being. As one notes, examining Aristotle's writings, it is the manner in which the individual will be educated and nurtured by societal institutions that will allow attainment of *"the good"* that all strive for; and which should dominate for the benefit and advancement of society as a whole. In spite of the fact that several aspects of the Aristotelian Ethics reflect Platonic and Socratic concepts and tenets, Aristotle is considered the dominant personality in this area among all ancient Greek and medieval writers until **Immanuel Kant (1724-1804 A.D.),** employed modified versions of some Aristotelian tenets to reflect value changes through time.

The Tholos, Delphi

The notion of *"Prudence"* **(Σωφροσυνη),** an important component of the "Platonic Ethics," also appears in Aristotle's view that it is the *ultimate virtue* that leads to the acquisition of good habits in behavior that the mind requires for a superior and virtuous life. Aristotle accepts the other three virtues advocated by Plato: **"Temperance," "Justice;"** and **"Bravery"** as necessary for a virtuous life; but Aristotle goes beyond the pure acquisition of these virtues and analyzes and corroborates the effect other extraneous factors have, by constructing a theoretical framework that determines the practical application of virtuous principles. For Aristotle, the ultimate objective is *"Happiness"* **(Ευδαιμονια),** and he spends considerable time in his writings defining "happiness" and how it should be pursued. Prior to him and afterward--**Stoics, Epicureans,** and **Skeptics** have defined "happiness" in different ways. Aristotle defines what happiness **"is not":** one will not find happiness in the pursuit of hedonistic pleasure, power, glory, wealth; or even as Plato maintained--in an ideal, virtuous life: happiness is to be found somewhere in-between. The theoretical foundation that Aristotle builds toward a definition and understanding of happiness is evident in the statement: *Every theoretical or practical action of man has a purpose; an end; a goal* **(Τελος)**—a teleological purpose. However, for man to pursue this purpose there must be some *"good"* **(Αγαθον)** value for him in it. The notion of this value is then understood in conjunction with the "good." But the good should strive toward some superior value; to some higher objective: and that is *"happiness"* **(Ευδαιμονια).** Aristotle finds happiness to be something unique and special for man as a human being. The artisan, the artist, the shoemaker, the carpenter; each one carries out a particular activity-- in the same way as the eye, hand, and foot of the human body can execute a specific task. So man carries out, in this world, a distinctive purpose as well: which differs from all other creatures on this Earth.

With this syllogism, Aristotle connects ethics with metaphysics; because, according to Aristotelian metaphysics: everything exists for a purpose. He applied this basic teleological (ultimate purpose) principle faithfully in all the writings and subjects that he studied. Man differs from all other creatures on Earth due to his ability to think rationally. The **mind,** then, is the differentiating factor; therefore, according to Aristotle, man has as a final purpose: to perfect his mind--the nucleus of his personality. Man, then, by perfecting his mind and achieving his objective in life, will eventually attain "happiness." But this alone does not fulfill happiness; because man, in order to secure *complete* happiness, needs other material, external things. These include: friends, wealth, political influence, beauty, noble background, good children, and many others. (This addition to the definition is the factor differentiating Aristotle's philosophy on ethics from Plato's). Aristotle is a pragmatist; a realist who believes that material means are necessary for complete happiness. He hastens, however, to add that even if all of these external, material means are missing, happiness that relies on the proper use of the mind and the conscience that accompanies it, is not disturbed: but it remains incomplete. The notion that the mind or logical reflection, and the struggle for its perfection, is the source of man's happiness, is an essentially Socratic and Platonic concept. The difference, however, is that Aristotle introduces additional external factors needed for the achievement of total happiness; and it must be noted that this Aristotelian principle represents a typical ancient Greek view. The Greeks admired beauty and artistic expression--exhibited in their writings, art, and theater--from the early Ionian philosophers to modern times.

It is on this particular point that Aristotle deviated from the Platonic and Socratic philosophy--which was entirely ideological and very demanding. As Goethe pointed out, Aristotle was: **"a pragmatist, a builder, a realist, and a thinker,"** who viewed man as a spiritual entity with a mind. He maintains that man can only achieve happiness in direct relation to the degree of prudence and other virtues he possesses. Since the definition of happiness involves two factors, it is necessary to establish a representative amount of these factors. Aristotle follows a new course and divides virtue into two categories: (1) **Intellectual Virtue**--virtue dominated by the logical mind, and (2) **Virtue dominated by Ethics.** The first is dependent on the mind or intellectualism (the ideal goals in life); while the second is dependent on the sensory component of the human soul (Επιθυμιτον). For ancient Greek philosophers, the idea of virtue had a wider and more encompassing meaning than what we consider virtue today. To the ancients, it meant not only a state and a condition, but also a struggle for the perfection of a: *"thing," "being," "action" or an "activity."* It is through this type of understanding that we can comprehend the division of virtue by Aristotle into theoretical and practical aspects, in the same way that he divided theoretical and practical reason. And the action of both (the theoretical and practical mind) is directed toward the knowledge of *Truth.* The difference, however, is that theoretical reasoning strives toward knowledge and truth; while the practical mind strives toward the truth that conforms with **rational desires (Επιθυμια).** Thus: science and wisdom are associated with theoretical reason; whereas: art, prudence, and professionalism are synonymous with practical reason. We can say then, that Aristotle distinguishes "theoretical reason" from "practical reason," in that the first involves something that is changeable--and can be created or perfected. Practical reason, however, is neutral, and only seeks a **means to achieve an end.**

But now let us discuss the "medium"; the "moderation"; the "mean": as it relates to the degree of pragmatism and idealism that is necessary for the achievement of complete happiness.

213

We have repeatedly seen, in the works of other Greek philosophers, the precept of moderation that dominated the minds of these thinkers. One can return to the writings of the pre-Socratic philosophers who had advanced the idea of moderation with such slogans as: **"Nothing in Excess"** (Μηδεν Αγαν); or **"Everything in Moderation"** (Παν Μετρον Αριστον). Plato repeatedly referred to these concepts and counseled strongly against excess. Aristotle now gives virtue a slightly different definition as it concerns moderation, by stating that, **". . . *hence, in respect to what it is, i.e., the definition that states its essence, virtue is a mean; with regard to what is best and right, it is an extreme."* (. . . Κατα μεν την ουσιαν και τον λογον του τι ειναι λεγοντα μεσοτης εστιν η Αρετη, ´κατα το Αριστον και το Ευ, ακροτης)** In other words, as it concerns the "goodness" of virtue, there can be **no mean or average.** The following is a passage from **Nicomachean Ethics B-6**[7], in which Aristotle discusses the extreme and the mean of virtue.

" Not every action nor every passion admits of a mean; because some have names that already imply badness; e.g.: spite, shamelessness, envy, and in the case of actions: adultery, theft, murder; for all of these and similar things imply by their names that they are in themselves bad, as well as the excesses or deficiencies of them. It is not possible then, to be right with regard to them; one must always be wrong. Nor does goodness or badness depend on committing adultery with the right woman at the right place, in the right way; but simply to "engage" in "bad activity" is to go wrong."[8]

In summary then, Aristotle accepts the notion of moderation advanced by earlier philosophers, but provides the interpretation that in ethics: there is no moderation; because in certain situations by the very committal of the action there is **no degree of being better or worse.** Aristotle, in his total work on ethics, also addresses the subject of **"free will"** and the concept of choice (**Προαιρεσις**). He recognizes in man free will and free choice and holds him responsible for his actions. In the 5th book of **Nicomachean Ethics,** Aristotle deals extensively with this subject and also the topic of **"justice."** Aristotle's views on free will and choice, and the fact that he would hold an individual responsible for his actions, is a fundamental departure from Oriental fatalism (fate, "kismet") and of man's bondage to the will of the gods.

Aristotle could not accept the Platonic transcendent concept of **"Ideas,"** and the hypothesis that whatever we see and perceive with our senses is nothing but an imperfect copy of the true original (**"Idea"**). During his 20 years attendance at the Academy under Plato's tutelage, he

---

[7] See Reference #2, under the title of **Nichomachean Ethics.**

[8] What Aristotle tries to affirm in this passage, is that there are certain actions where the notion of the mean and extreme are meaningless. This contradicts earlier assertions by previous philosophers who preached **"Nothing in Excess"** (Παν Μετρον Αριστον). **There is no mean in "cruelty" and no extreme in "love".** It would be equally absurd to expect an unjust, cowardly, and unfair action to have a mean, an excess, or a deficiency. Conversely, there is no excess or deficiency in temperance and courage; because what is intermediate is, in a sense, an extreme.

developed a Skeptic view of this highly theoretical and transcendental Platonic concept. But it was after he left the Academy and went to **Atarneus (Assos)**, in Ionia, and later to the Island of Lesbos that he formulated his own ideas about this concept and the most pressing question that Socrates originally posed: **"How man should live his life."** Aristotle, even though highly motivated in pursuing theoretical (philosophical and metaphysical) questions, was basically a natural scientist; a pragmatist; an empiricist; and was more interested in discovering how things work by observing man and society in action, rather than attempting to locate the "First Cause" or the "First Principle" of the underlying power or force that affects the existence and function of things. Thus, it is not surprising that he approached this investigation from an empirical and biological perspective-- regarding man as a living entity--and formulated his theories on these matters in **Ethics** and **Politics** on the basis of this approach and analysis.

Plato suggested that if man becomes virtuous (temperate, just, prudent, and brave) and understands himself (**Γνώθι Σ'Αυτόν**) through *knowledge*, then the society, composed of virtuous people, will also be virtuous--and the **"Ideal System"** will be implemented. Later, Plato seems to have changed his mind, because while in **The Republic** he postulated that education and the proper division of functions in the State (**Philosopher-King, Guardians**) and clear delineation of the roles of its members, was deemed to be the means to achieve this goal, in the **Laws**--after his repeated trips to Sicily and Southern Italy--he introduced additional conditions: strict adherence to the laws of the State; and discipline to regulate behavior, and education and knowledge as tools for achieving a peaceful and harmonious people. Aristotle takes a different view of how man can reach **"perfection"** and the **"Ideal Society."** Through observation, he notes that every living thing starts from an imperfect state, proceeds through a cycle to maturity (perfection within the species), then declines, and eventually dies after it has reproduced itself. This is true for plants, animals, and humans. A calf or a small plant is as vulnerable and imperfect as a small baby, if left alone to cope with the vicissitudes of Nature. Through time they all grow and each one naturally achieves a state of perfection according to its *intended purpose*. All calves are alike and can perform whatever functions a calf, dog, or cat can when they reach *maturity (perfection)*. They develop their senses and instincts equally within the species; these elements (*sense and instinct*) lead them to self-preservation through defense, feeding, and propagation.

There are basically three factors that impede the development of all living entities in achieving their *talents and inclinations*: (1) Natural factors; (2) Societal; and (3) Personal factors (for humans). Natural factors mitigate the development of their attributes into "perfection": often animals are unable to cope with the environment and are handicapped, maimed, or perish before reaching maturity. For example, a beehive left out in freezing temperatures will be destroyed; and disease and predators adversely affect the cycle of all animals. An animal, if physical factors do not affect it negatively, will reach perfection and perform its pre-destined functions: feeding, surviving, and propagation. All dogs, cats, or horses are more or less equal, and may reach perfection within their species.

According to Aristotle, all humans, as far as their intellect is concerned, are not equal--but are endowed by Nature with different talents, inclinations, and capabilities. Therefore, we cannot say that all humans, once they have reached maturity within their kind, are capable of equal levels of perfection (achievement). Each can reach a level of potential achievement--depending upon innate inclinations and talents--which are natural. Also, human beings, unlike other animals--due to their intellect--are in a position to cope with natural factors and thus modify the environment to their benefit. Yet, in our efforts to reach perfection we are affected by the conditions (laws, traditions, lifestyles) that the society artificially creates--which sometimes thwart this goal. Thus, if these adverse societal factors are not present, it can be concluded, considering Aristotle's "teleological" hypothesis, that every action and every choice or intention leads to something "good"--that *if man is left alone*, he will be successful in perfecting his natural drive to achieve his talent or inclination. Ultimately then, he will have the same effect as the Platonic "*ideal or virtuous man*": and eventually a perfect society will be achieved.

The Archaeological Museum of Athens

Of great importance, is the issue of how a society should establish perfect conditions or factors that will motivate or allow man to achieve his potential. Peace, justice, prosperity, and proper legislation are the fundamental conditions necessary to ensure attainment of this goal. These conditions may be achieved with relative ease in a proper political system of government. But Aristotle now brings another important factor that mitigates achievement of this perfection--and this is: **"man himself."** While in the animal world we noted that the physical conditions are the mitigating factors, as the animal lacking intellect cannot cope with them; man can. Man, as a consequence of his free will, freedom of choice, senses, sentiment, and intellect, may impede his natural potential--which is not true of other animals. While animals are adversely affected by external factors, man, in addition to societal restrictions, may be **adversely affected by himself**: in that he is often unable to exercise self-control. All human activities are directed toward a good and satisfactory life; but there are many subordinate aims--controlled by emotion--that are sensible ends only as far as they serve an ultimate purpose: that of the society at large. According to Aristotle, there are three basic "*factors*" or "*conditions*" emanating from **man himself**, that adversely affect him in his efforts to reach his teleological goal--which is the *good*--and these are: **"Enrichment,"** **"Power,"** and **"Pleasure."** It is acceptable for man to enrich himself, as long as in the process the general societal "*good*" is served as well. If the general "good" is not served while the individual's subordinate aim is reached, then the society as a whole suffers. **"Money"** is a store of value and a medium of exchange and, according to Aristotle, when the illusion is formed that it is acceptable to accumulate unlimited wealth, man harms both the community and himself; because, while concentrating on such a narrow purpose, his soul and spirit are deprived of larger and more rewarding experiences. Accumulation of wealth cannot bring happiness; therefore, the pursuit of money is a factor that mitigates against achieving perfection.

The second element of adversity by which man harms himself, according to Aristotle, is **"Power"**—which is only useful and beneficial if used for achieving a goal within a talent or inclination. **Power** exercised by a talented individual, a teacher or an architect, in directing subordinates (students or workers) toward a goal (such as achieving education or constructing an edifice) is **"good"**--and benefits both the individual and the community. But there is another type of power, exercised for its own sake, the power for achieving a subordinate aim that does not benefit the society-at-large. This kind of power is harmful, because it becomes oppressive to those subdued by it and harmful to the oppressor who incurs the enmity of the oppressed. The third element that mitigates achieving the Aristotelian teleological goal is: **"Pleasure."** Man, according to Aristotle, also needs entertainment and amusement as respite, in order to engage in serious and fruitful activity. This is one of the psychogenic needs that must be satisfied. Because man tends to work beyond his limit, either to acquire the necessities of life or for personal or idiosyncratic reasons, entertainment and joyful experiences are necessary to strengthen the intellect. However, man often develops the illusion that a life of constant amusement would be the most pleasant and joyful, and this emanates out of fixed habits and addictions. Aristotle claims that such a life, in reality, is very **difficult and disquieting to the soul** and the normal function of the being.

Aristotle's observations on the influence that **"power,"** **"enrichment,"** and **"pleasure"** exert on the individual and the society as a whole, are pertinent today at the beginning of the third millennium, 2328 years after his death. Under the political and economic systems practiced in the "Western World," primarily the democratic and capitalistic systems, we note an obsession with the accumulation of wealth, and the disquieting effect this obsession has on the opportunities for fair distribution of wealth and its concomitant results: abject poverty; deteriorating middle class; enlargement of the lower class; crime; drugs; destruction of the family, and deterioration of ethics and morals. Also, the incessant pursuit of entertainment, which is dominated by mediocre Hollywood productions through cinema and television, creates an environment which curtails intellectual maturity and pursuit of knowledge toward understanding ourselves and our environment--because there is no time left for such pursuits. This leads to the deterioration of quality education and limited curriculum offerings. The desire for **"power,"** which provides gratification only to the power holder, leads to the election of mediocre individuals with myopic vision and low intellectual maturity--unable to direct communities and nations of the world toward higher standards and achievements. Similar conditions led to the deterioration of the moral and ethical strength of the Greek states, their demise, and the collapse of the democratic city-state of Athens at the close of the 4th century B.C.

TREATISE CONCERNING POLITICS (ΠΟΛΙΤΙΚΑ)

The treatise that deals with the subject of **Politics** (Πολιτικα) consists of eight books divided into three parts. In Part A, which consists of three books, Aristotle examines such concepts as: What defines a State and how it develops—as well as the issue of wealth and its impact and evolution. In this part we could say that Aristotle presents a basic course in **"Economics,"** which, with the exception of Xenophon's **"ΟΙΚΟΝΟΜΙΚΟΣ"** ("Economics"), is the only treatise that serves as an introduction to the science of political economy written by the ancient Greeks. The various political systems practiced by the ancients, until the time of Aristotle, are also covered in this first part. Aristotle categorizes these systems in three parts: (1) One in which authority is in the hands of one person (**Monarchy**); (2) One in which authority is in the hands of a few (**Aristocracy**); (3) One in which authority resides with the people (**Democracy**).

Macedonian Coin

In Part B, which consists of three books, Aristotle discusses various combinations of **political systems** and lists three possible outcomes: **Monarchy** leads to tyranny; **Aristocracy** leads to oligarchy; **Democracy** leads to demagogy. He also distinguishes the various branches of government: The Legislative, Judicial, and the Executive. The topic of revolution is also treated, and Aristotle questions when and why revolutions occur, and criticizes the Platonic system enunciated in the **"Republic"**--considered the **"Ideal State"** by Plato. The subject of "tyranny" (dictatorship) is also discussed. In Part C, which consists of two books, Aristotle deals at length with what he would consider the **"Ideal Society,"** as well as with the relations between the sexes, and the topic of education (concerning children as well as the general public).

Aristotle treats the matter of politics extensively, and begins by dealing with man and the conditions that led to organized societies, stating: **"Man is a political animal by nature"** (Ανθρωπου φυσει πολιτικου). Furthermore, he points out that, by nature, man needs to socialize and interact with others--stating: *"He who does not socialize, or participate in the political process, is either a beast or a god"* (**Ο δε μη δυναμενος κοινωνειν η μηδεν δομενος δι' αυταρκειαν, ουδεν μερος πολεως, ωστε η θηριον η Θεος**). Aristotle notes that the whole is more important than the part (**Το ολον προτερον του μερους**), and asserts that the "genesis" of society starts with the family. The individual desires association and begins with marriage. Thus, the first community in life is between a man and woman--which leads to the reproduction of the human family. What about the *"Ideal Society"*? We have seen in the writings of Plato, the need for a system, based on justice, which would provide equal opportunities--leading toward a virtuous and happy life

(EYΔAIMONIA). Aristotle embraces this same principle, but rejects several premises of the Platonic "Ideal Society"--the common ownership of the material means of existence and of women (in the case of the "Guardians") -- because common ownership of women and children leads to moral decay; while common ownership of goods cannot be equitably distributed in the community, which leads to disputes and friction.

Aristotle accepts the ownership of private property, but considers the overall societal problem of the distribution of wealth: if it is not distributed in an ethical and moral manner, it leads to poverty. He states that: **"Poverty leads to riots and crimes"** (Η πενια στασιν εμποιει και κακουργιαν). Aristotle's "Ideal Society" is one in which all citizens participate in its well-being and happiness in a virtuous manner. The **best life** is nurtured in a society that is well-educated and well-governed **(EYNOMIA).** He did not favor large populations, and as a result condoned abortion--as long as the embryo had not developed: *"Prior to the feeling of life and sense"* (Πριν αισθησιν εγγενεσθαι και Ζωην). The objective of an ideal society, according to Aristotle, is achieved not only by internal order and education, but also by a foreign policy based on the same principles that guide domestic policies. He opposes violence and accepts only **defensive wars.** Plato was concerned with the education of the population, and in The Laws (as we have seen earlier) extensively outlined the type of education an individual should receive. The purpose of a state, according to Aristotle, cannot be found in wealth or military might alone, but rather in the practice of virtue which would lead to: justice, tranquility, and peace. The image of the State is reflected in its constitution. The use of political authority, in all of the three systems identified above, can deteriorate into three possible alternatives--good or bad. Aristotle does not specifically describe what constitutes a "good" or "bad" system of government. He rather prefers to state that the constitution or political configuration depends upon the **"level of virtue and moral strength"** that citizens have achieved.[9]

A good system is one where the rulers are superior in virtue, prudence, and education: and where the citizens obey and follow. The system that Solon developed in Athens was a good one, according to Aristotle, because the citizens of the middle class and average economic strength governed the State. This median group is usually logical; whereas, the rich tend to be "arrogant," and the poor "canny and perfidious." The rich do not obey the laws, and when they govern they become autocratic; while the poor become subservient and generally cannot rule. In such instances, you have a society that is despotic and consists of members who are not free--but slaves--and in such a society jealousy and contempt dominate; while friendship, camaraderie, and cooperation are void. The democratic system that ancient city-states, particularly Athens, experienced from mid 6th century B.C., to the time of the fall to the Romans (146 B.C.), was the only democratic system that the world had experienced prior to the American and French Revolution, 1776 and 1789 respectively. Aristotle was not so enamored with the democratic system, and neither was Plato,

---

[9]Even though Aristotle admits that if such a condition has not been reached, constitutional democracy is the best choice--given the alternatives.

because they were concerned that such a system would lead to chaos and demagogy if the population is not equipped with: virtue, justice, and equality. It appears from the writings of these two great men of antiquity, that primary prerequisites necessary for the smooth governing of the State are: **"knowledge"** and **"virtue."** It is only when these two conditions are met that one would expect a contented society with equal opportunity for all--and diminished strife and revolution.

While Plato, both in **The Republic** and the **Laws,** identifies no inherent differences between men and women in intellectual and other characteristics, save only those of physical endurance, and makes no mention of the institution of slavery, Aristotle, in this treatise, distinguishes between those born to rule and those to be ruled-- including both genders. On the basis of this principle, he accepts the institution of slavery as a practice based upon *natural differences.* In ancient Greek societies menial and manual professions were considered degrading and unbecoming to a free people, because they believed such activities would detract from man's dignity, honor, and freedom; and was the domain of slaves. This view, among some people, also applied to the merchant profession, industrialist, and rich entrepreneur. It appears that Aristotle intellectually accepted this view; and it is this position that makes him an apologist for slavery. He does not summarily accept it, however, as in Book 1 of **Politics** (5-8) he cites some reservations. For example: (1) *He considers unacceptable the practice of slavery acquired by force--including prisoners-of-war; (2) He recognizes that there are free men who should be slaves and slaves who should be free; (3) He considers enslaving one who is your equal a crime against humanity and God; and (4)* He does not accept the continuation of slavery in the children of slaves. Yet he believed that some men were born to be free and others slaves; and, in the case of prisoners-of-war, he modifies his position and accepts that it befits the victors to make slaves of the vanquished--because by their victory they have exhibited qualities of superiority. It is indeed strange that Aristotle, a spirit of exceptional values and moral and scientific conscience, would side with the institution of slavery. But we should not forget that this institution was so embedded in the conscience of ancient societies, Greek and barbarian, that it would be awkward to rail against it. One should be careful, however, when judging this practice as embraced by ancient societies--and by some in modern times—because the definition of *"free man"* may be blurred if one considers that, even today, wages paid to many workers are insufficient to provide for a family, home, and an honorable lifestyle.

CHAPTER 11

THE HELLENISTIC PHILOSOPHY: THE ACADEMY AND LYCEUM

**"The roots of education are bitter: but the fruit
is sweet."**

Aristotle

INTRODUCTION

With the end of the discussion on the life and work of Plato and Aristotle, we concluded the second period of Greek philosophy, which extended from the end of the Persian wars in 479 B.C.,

Cleopatra

until the death of Aristotle in 322 B.C. After the death of both **Plato** and **Aristotle,** the **Academy,** established by Plato, and the **Lyceum,** established by Aristotle, progressed rapidly and continued the tradition set forth by these two scholars--until the beginning of the Christian Era and beyond. During this third period, which extended from 322 B.C. to about 313 A.D., when Constantine the Great, the Roman emperor, sanctioned freedom of religion and accepted Christianity as the official religion of the Roman Empire, the philosophical tradition was dominated by six schools that flourished primarily in Athens. Athens was the center of the intellectual world of the time, which was formed by Alexander's conquests, and extended from Egypt to the Caspian Sea, and from Macedonia to India. This was known as the **"Hellenistic World."** Around the middle of the second century B.C. (146 B.C.), the Romans completed the conquest of the Hellenic World, replacing part of Alexander's empire with a new political regime, and a number of Roman thinkers and philosophers appeared, such as: **Cicero, Ovid, Horace, Seneca, Tacitus, Virgil, Lucretius,** and others.

Six philosophical schools that dominated the intellectual world at the time were:

1.   **The Academy (Plato's legacy).**

221

2.   **The Lyceum (Aristotle's legacy).**
3.   **The Stoic Philosophy (established by Zeno).**
4.   **The Epicurean Philosophy (established by Epicurus).**
5.   **The Skeptics (established by Pyrrho).**
6.   **The Cynics and the Neo-Cynics (established by Antisthenes).**

In this chapter we shall discuss the Academy and the Lyceum, based on information provided by ancient biographers, and introduce the individuals who were responsible for their success and fame--as well as summarize the kind of philosophy that they espoused. In the following three chapters we conclude the **Hellenistic** philosophy with the **Stoics,** the **Epicureans, the Cynics** and the **Skeptics** (Chapters 12, 13, 14).

THE ACADEMY

When Plato died in 347 B.C., he left behind a flourishing school with over 2000 individuals directly connected with the **Academy.** The leaders who dominated the Academy changed some of Plato's teachings, and the work they engaged in involved teaching and research on numerous subjects.   This was perhaps the first established **University** where rich and accomplished individuals were able to educate themselves and their children. Those who became the directors were scholars recognized by their peers, and considered qualified to be leaders.   The Academy flourished for over 900 years--well into the Christian Era. We can divide its life into three periods:

The Old Academy	**(347 - 250 B.C)**
The New Academy	**(250 - 318 A.D)**
The Neoplatonic Period	**(--527 A.D. closure)**

Some of the scholars associated with the old Academy were:

> **Speusippus**
> **Xenocrates**
> **Heraclides**
> **Eudoxus**
> **Polemo**
> **Crates**
> **Philippus**
> **Crantor**
> **Ermodorus**

These individuals continued the old traditional philosophy on: **ethics, morals, metaphysics,** and **politics** as conceived by both Socrates and Plato, and enunciated by Plato, with minor deviations and revisions. The New Academy, from 250 B.C. to the beginning of the

Christian Era, was heavily influenced by new schools and the new theories that developed as a result of the influence of the Stoic, Epicurean, and Skeptic philosophies. Quite a number of tenets that were espoused by both Socrates and Plato, as well as those of the Old Academy, were now being modified by these external influences; and quite a number of revisions occurred.

Some of the scholars who led the Academy during its second period were:

Arcesilaus
Carneades
Clitomachus
Philo
Antiochus and others

Unfortunately, there is not enough material available to judge some of the changes that took place in the Academy during this period, because most of the writings of these thinkers are lost. As

a result of the expansion of the Hellenic World all the way to India--and the association of the educated people of Greece with other Oriental philosophies--new doctrines, philosophies, ethics, and traditions were introduced into Greek life; and therefore, changes were inescapable. We present below some information about the leaders of the Old and the New Academy--as people, scholars and researchers--as well as information about their philosophies and academic achievements.[1] It is truly unfortunate that thousands of books written by these eminent scholars perished; and we depend entirely on the writings of subsequent individuals who provided a subjective glimpse of what they said.

Oenochoe, Sphynxes with
Hermes

XENOCRATES (396-314 B.C.) was from the city of Chaldedon, and was in his twenties when he began his association with the Academy and developed a close relationship with Plato, accompanying him on his trips to Sicily. He assumed the directorship of the Academy from 339 B.C., until his death. He was dignified and grave in demeanor, which made Plato chide him continuously: **"Xenocrates, sacrifice to the Graces!"** He was entirely trustworthy; so much so, that although it was illegal for witnesses to give unsworn evidence, the Athenians allowed Xenocrates alone to do so. He wrote over 100 books.

SPEUSIPPUS (407-339 B.C.) was an Athenian who distinguished himself as the Director of the Academy after Plato died in 347 B.C. He was very intelligent and authored over 300 books;

---

[1]Some of the material presented below has been summarized from the writings of Diogenes Laertius in his Biographies of Ancient Philosophers. See reference #8. Book II

but almost nothing has survived. He was, unlike Plato, prone to anger and easily overcome by pleasures.

POLEMO (Head of the Academy, 314-276 B.C.) was an Athenian. When he was young he was a delinquent, and the following story is related about him. One day, in agreement with his drunken young friends, he burst into the Academy where Xenocrates was lecturing--with the intention of creating a disturbance. Xenocrates, however, without being at all flustered, continued with his discourse as before: on the subject of **"temperance."** Polemo was so impressed that he repented and regretted his silly act. He later became a student and eventually leader of the Academy, where he wrote a considerable number of treatises.

CRATES (326 --? B.C.) was from Thebes and a protégé and good friend of Polemo. He shared the same beliefs and convictions as his mentor, and wrote extensively. Upon his death, he left to the Academy library a number of treatises--some on philosophy and some on comedy--as well as speeches delivered at the Assembly and those from his service as an envoy. He left behind him a distinguished group of pupils.

CRANTO (340 to 290 B.C.) was from the city of Soli, and even though he was much esteemed in his native land, he left it for Athens and attended the lectures of Xenocrates at the same

time as Polemo. He wrote memoirs which extended to 30,000 lines, but none survived--some of which were attributed to **Arcesilaus** by some critics. He was once asked what he admired most in Polemo; he replied: **"The fact that I have never heard him raise or lower his voice in speaking."**

Funeral Monument

ARCESILAUS (318-242 B.C.) was from Aeolis, and with him begins the New Academy. He was the first to suspend judgment-- owing to the contradictions of opposing arguments. He was also the first to argue on both sides of a question; and the first to meddle with the system handed down by Plato: the **"Dialectic Method"**--and followed a system approaching the **"Eristic"** system of argumentation. One has to remember that by this time new philosophies, mores, and influences of the **Stoics** and the **Epicureans**, as well as foreign philosophical thinking, had had a significant impact on the Academy. The old Platonic ideal and highly sophisticated dialectic system was attacked from all sides. Arcesilaus was one of the most influential leaders of the Academy and died at the age of 75.

BION (3rd century B.C.) was a citizen of Borysthenes. He was in some respect a shifty character; a subtle Sophist, and one who had given ammunition to those contemptuous of philosophy. Bion also became pompous and arrogant. He left numerous memoirs and pithy sayings, such as: **"Old age is the harbor of all ills; at least they all take refuge there."** Referring to a wealthy miser, he said: **"He has not acquired a fortune; the fortune acquired him"**; and

"Misers take care of property as if it belonged to them, but derive no more pleasures or benefits from it than if it belonged to others."

LACYDES (Director of the Academy c. 242-216 B.C.), the successor of Arcesilaus, was from Cyrene and the main force responsible for the founding of the New Academy. He was a man of very serious character; industrious from his youth, and though poor, of pleasant manners and admired by many.[2] Lacydes assumed the leadership of the Academy around 240 B.C., and he led the school for 26 years.

CARNEADES (c. 213-129 B.C.) was from Cyrene. He carefully studied the writings of the Stoics, particularly those of Chrysippus, and by challenging them successfully he became so famous that he once said: **"Without Chrysippus where should I have been?"** His industry was unparalleled; although in physics he was not as strong as in ethics. He would let his hair and nails grow long from intense devotion to study. Such was his expertise in philosophy, that even the rhetoricians would dismiss their classes to attend his lectures. His voice was extremely powerful, and the keeper of the Gymnasium requested that he lower it; to which **Carneades** replied, **"Then give me something by which to regulate my voice."** He died at the age of 85 in 129 B.C., after directing the Academy for several years. He left nothing behind of his own writing, but his students published his extensive correspondence with the King of Cappadocia.

Carneades

CLITOMACHUS (Director of the Academy from 129 B.C.) was a Carthaginian whose real name was **HASRUBAL.** He taught philosophy in his native tongue at Carthage, and was 40 when he moved to Athens and became a pupil of **Carneades,** who recognized his potential. He assisted in his education and mentored him; and to such an extent did **Clitomachus'** diligence grow, that he composed over 400 treatises. He succeeded Carneades in the leadership of the Academy, and through his writings did much to clarify his opinions. Clitomachus was well acquainted with the prevailing three schools of philosophy: the Academy, the Lyceum, and the Stoics.

There were quite a number of other eminent scholars who either directed the Academy or

---

[2]A most amusing story is told of his housekeeping. Whenever he brought anything out of the storeroom, he would seal the door back again and throw his signet ring inside, through the opening, to ensure that nothing stored there could be stolen or carried off. When his servants became aware of this, they broke the seal and carried off what they pleased, afterwards throwing the ring through the opening into the storeroom--always undetected.

were scholars-in-residence who published an extensive roster of treatises--which, unfortunately, did not survive. The Academy was a center of research and teaching, and some of the treatises that came out of this institution covered subjects that had been previously discussed, but were amplified upon, and included the latest developments in the field.

NEOPLATONISM

Quite a number of scholars attended or taught at the Academy until its demise and closure by **JUSTINIAN** in 527 A.D. Of course, by then, new approaches and doctrines had affected the field of philosophy extensively, as well as the Academy and the original Platonic concepts. The advent of Christianity and the conversion of the Roman Empire into a Christian Empire introduced drastic changes. Now everything taught at the Academy was considered "pagan," and if it did not conform to the existing religion, was banished. Before we conclude the discussion on the Academy and the influence that the Platonic work had on ancient philosophical thinking, it is appropriate to make some additional comments about an offshoot of Platonic thinking that flourished in Alexandria, Egypt, around the third century A.D. This philosophy is known as the "Neoplatonic" philosophy, and its originator is believed to have been an individual by the name of **PLOTINUS**.

PLOTINUS was born in **Lykopolis, Egypt, c.204 A.D.**, and was of an aristocratic background. He studied philosophy and other subjects in Alexandria at the school of **Ammonius Saccas,** and it was Saccas' lectures on philosophy that motivated him to pursue further studies in this field. At the age of 28, he was a recognized scholar and seriously embarked upon the study of Platonic philosophy. It is not clear whether he attended the Academy in Athens, but his interest in the subject of philosophy propelled him to establish a new brand of the Platonic doctrine: "Neoplatonism."[3] He was also interested in studying other philosophies and religions--particularly the philosophy **of Zoroaster and Hinduism.** He joined an expedition to Persia and India with **Emperor Gordian,** but the expedition had an unfortunate end when the Emperor was assassinated in Mesopotamia, and Plotinus returned to Egypt without having accomplished his objective of visiting the birthplace of these two religions. At the age of 40 he opened a school of philosophy in Rome and gained wide respect and fame. He requested permission and money from **Emperor Gallienus** to establish a city in Campagnia, Italy--modeled after Plato's **Republic** and **The Laws**--to be named **Platonopolis**. The Emperor, however, withdrew his original authorization because of bureaucratic opposition, and the project did not go forward. Plotinus himself left no writings in the form of books published and distributed for mass consumption. However, a student from his school in Rome, by the name of
Porphyry (Πορφυριος), edited his voluminous notes and lectures and published them in six books (extant), each containing nine chapters, known as the **Enneads (Εννεαδες)**—from the

---

[3] There are some who believe that it was Ammonius Saccas who should be credited with the establishment of the philosophy of Neoplatonism.

Greek word for nine. Plotinus was a gentle, ascetic, and pleasant man who had a great number of friends--and no enemies. He had great compassion for his fellowman, as well as for the oppressed and handicapped. While the parents of his teacher, Ammonius Saccas, were Christians, Saccas himself was not--even though he received a Christian upbringing from his parents. Plotinus, however, neither joined the new religion nor worshipped or practiced Christianity. **Porphyry**, from whom we have most of our information, writes that Plotinus opened an orphanage and acted as the guardian and financial supporter of the orphans. He was deeply spiritual and, according to Porphyry, had four actual encounters with god--not the Christian God--but one that he envisioned. Plotinus died in the year 269/270 A.D., at the age of 66.

There is no reference in the writings of Plotinus concerning Christianity, which was underground during his time, but because of his advocacy of a branch of Platonic philosophy--akin to Christianity--his views and doctrines were viewed favorably by the Church. As we have seen elsewhere (Chapter 6), the fundamental tenet of Platonic philosophy is the emphasis on the metaphysical world, as contrasted with that of the sensory world: the difference of what we can visualize with our mind, from that which we see with our eyes. **Plotinus** reasserts this important difference and establishes his philosophical beliefs on this fundamental doctrine. The departure of the mind from the sensory world, and its association with the transcendental, establishes an immediate communication with God. There was no attempt by Plotinus to prove the existence of the Divinity. The transcendental world is revealed to man by some action of the mind, not found in the world of the senses; therefore, Plotinus' philosophy is highly theoretical and spiritual. He revisits the principle of the **Master-craftsman (Creator=Δημιουργος)** of Plato's **Timaeus,** and incorporates the "Creator" as the architect of the physical world. Plotinus' god is the **"One"** and the **"Good"**--transcendental--and has no multiplicity: a concept of monotheism--unlike the existing polytheistic ancient religions of his time. This monistic concept is not related to Parmenidian **"monism,"** because Plotinus' monism is idealistic--while Parmenides' is materialistic. This god is beyond being; indivisible, unchanging, eternal--without past and future—a constant self-identity; an ultimate "Principle." Plotinus distinguishes two souls; unlike Plato, who distinguishes only one: A Higher or World Soul, and a Lower soul that he named **"Nature" (Φυσις).** The concept of the Platonic "Ideas" is revisited and identified with the second component in Plotinus' hierarchical classification of entities: the **Mind (Νους)**--not Anaxagoras' Mind. Plotinus subdivides the soul into two parts, unlike the Platonic three; the first relates to the Mind, and the second to the body. *The soul pre-exists, unlike Christian doctrine, transmigrates upon separation from the body, and continues to exist after death.* Below the sphere of the soul is the material world and Matter, which then forms the lowest stage of the universe--the opposite of the "One." At the level of Matter--what Aristotle called **Υλη**--*Plotinus* recognizes "evil" and the existence of "demons" which are invisible to man. The part of the soul that enters the body may become contaminated, and resembles the Platonic component of the soul controlled by sensual desires (Επιθυμιτικον); while the other part transcends into God--the "One."

227

Neoplatonism was a refined view of the universe and a fresh answer to the question that early physical philosophers posed: *"What is the original Substance that all things are made of?"* There is a dogmatic answer--a transcendental answer--not a pragmatic, scientific response. It is beyond the dialectic Platonic view, as it presupposes faith. After disposing of the question regarding the **"substance"** of the universe, by identifying the One as the source of all change and all form in the physical world, the human being is left to struggle for his/her salvation and attainment of the Socratic **"good"** and his/her betterment. Plotinus reintroduces the notion of theocratism that tethers man to the will of God--who holds him accountable for his misdeeds. Neoplatonism becomes a highly mystic and transcendental philosophy that does not differ much from early religions. It contributed significantly to the formation of Christian philosophy, as most of the early theologians (**Origen**[4], **Clement, Eusebius, Athanasius, Basil, Gregory, John Chrysostom, and others**) who edited the Christian scriptures were first Neoplatonists. **Neoplatonism** represents the final form of the pre-Christian Greek philosophy, and was not necessarily a combination of philosophies, as was the case in later years with new schools, but rather a genuine, if one-sided, extension of ideas originated by Plato. Plotinus did incorporate important Aristotelian and Stoic elements in his new philosophy, but only to the degree necessary to complete his doctrine. There may have been some Oriental influence, but it is not so apparent because there are not enough writings to provide a sound basis for judgment. As we have seen so far, all philosophies tend to provide answers to the pressing questions of life and death, and the correct way of living which will lead to happiness and well-being. Neoplatonism, as a philosophical doctrine, was attractive because it provided a genuine philosophy to guide the conduct of man toward attainment of happiness and fulfillment: by leading an ethical way of life. It contained a strong element of mysticism and asceticism, and placed little emphasis on the material means of existence. As a result, it exercised a strong influence on Christian philosophers who already were sympathetic to the Platonic philosophy: the true origin of this doctrine. Individuals such as: **St. Augustine (354-430 A.D.); Dionysius Aeropagite (5th century A.D.); Johannus Scotus Erigena (810-878 A.D.),** and the Renaissance scholars: **Georgios Gemistus Pletho (1355-1450 A.D); Ficino (1433-1499 A.D.); Jacob Boehme (1575-1624 A.D.); Spinoza (1632-1677 A.D.), and Leibniz (1646-1716 A.D.)** were influenced strongly by the Neoplatonists. Neoplatonism declined considerably after the death of one of its strongest supporters, **Proclus (401-485 A.D.),** and **Christianity** became the only religion and philosophy tolerated by the Roman Empire.

THE LYCEUM--(THE PERIPATETIC PHILOSOPHERS)

After the death of Aristotle, the Lyceum was taken over by **THEOPHRASTUS** (from

---

[4] He was a pre-eminent Christian martyr, but he became a heretic in his later life because he believed in the pre-existence of the soul and disagreed with the Christian authorities at the time about the interpretation of the **Old Testament.** He was a student of **Plotinus',** even though he was his elder.

Eressos) who directed the school from **322 to 286 B.C.**--in total, 36 years. The Lyceum did not last as long as the Academy, and by the beginning of the Christian Era it closed its doors permanently. During the years that this school flourished, it became the home of some brilliant minds who left impressive work behind--reflecting the standards of its founder, **Aristotle.** The individuals who directed the Lyceum most successfully were:

THEOPHRASTUS	**(322-286 B.C.)**
STRATON	**(286-270 B.C.)**
LYCON	**(270-225 B.C.)**
ARISTON	**(225-180 B.C.)**
KRITOLAUS	**(180-170 B.C,)**
DIODORUS	**(170 B.C.--)**
ERRIPUS	**(1st Half of 2nd century B.C.)**
SOTION	**(later part of 2nd century B.C.)**
DEMETRIUS FALIREFS	**(350-280 B.C.)**

Most of these scholars succeeded in keeping the school as an institution of research and teaching, and maintained a high quality of scientific inquiry and scholarship. However, with the

Theophrastus

exception of **Theophrastus**, very little improvement was made beyond the level that Aristotle achieved.   But these scholars were successful in preserving the existing advances, as they defended the Aristotelian philosophy amidst the continuous changes that were developing during the Hellenistic Era. The nature of the Lyceum was different from that of the Academy and of the other schools which developed during this era, because of the nature of **Aristotle's** teachings. Aristotle developed, in essence, the foundation of many scientific disciplines found in universities today; while others were merely concentrating on one discipline or school. It was difficult for the scholars of the Lyceum to take positions on all individual areas of the Aristotelian system, because the concept of "specialization" did not exist. A philosopher was a **"pansophist"** (a person embracing universal wisdom).   Thus, the Lyceum started deteriorating after the first generation of scholars and directors, and with the beginning of the Christian Era, closed its doors. We provide some information below about some of the most known and influential directors of the school:

THEOPHRASTUS (370-286 B.C.), a native of Eressos, was a man of extraordinary intelligence and industry, and remarkably kind and fond of discussion. He was so esteemed in Athens, that when someone ventured to prosecute him for impiety--the prosecutor himself narrowly escaped punishment. In Athens, if you could not prove your accusation in court, you could be penalized with the same punishment that you demanded for your opponent. At one time **Theophrastus** had 2000 students in the Lyceum; and although his reputation was exemplary, he had to leave the country when an Athenian ruler (**Sophocles)** decreed that any philosopher presiding over a school, without the permission of the Assembly and of the people, risked the penalty of death. There must have been a local political dispute, involving the teachings of some philosopher, that led to the passage of this decree by the Athenian Assembly. The following year this decree was rescinded, and the instigator of this legislation was punished, allowing all philosophers--including Theophrastus--to return to Athens.

Theophrastus repeatedly stated: **"In our expenditures, the item that costs the most is time."** He wrote quite a number of treatises and over 350 books, but the only ones remaining are: 30 partial references in **Metaphysics;** three of 18 from **Physica (Περι των Φυσικων);** partial references **On the Senses** (Περι Αισθησεων); 20 partial references on **Reverence (Περι Ευσεβειας) (Reverence towards God),** and three complete books on **Botany.** Theophrastus is particularly known for his analysis of human character. In his book **Characters (Χαρακτηρες),** he gives a detailed description of 30 different traits of people: fortunately this book has survived intact. He died at the age of 85.

STRATON (Head of the school from 286-268 B.C.) was the successor to the directorship of the Lyceum after the death of Theophrastus. Straton was from the city of Lampsacus, and was a distinguished man. Generally, he was known as a physicist because, more than anyone else, he devoted himself to the most detailed study of Nature. He was a Director of the Lyceum for 18 years and authored 55 books.

Demetrius Phalirefs

LYCON (299-225 B.C.), from the city of Troy, was the successor of Strato as Director of the Lyceum. He was a master of expression and excelled in the education of young people. He used to say: **"Modesty and love of honor are as necessary equipment for boys, as spear and bridle for horses."** His voice was exceedingly sweet; so much so, that some altered his name to **Γλυκων** (sweet) from Λυκων, by prefixing the letter **"Γ."** Lycon presided over the school for 44 years and died at the age of 74.

DEMETRIUS PHALIREFS (350-280 B.C.) was a native of Phaleron, a suburb of Athens, and a pupil of **Theophrastus;** and, due to his oratory in the Athenian Assembly, held the chief power of state for 10 years. He was so admired, because of the many benefits that he secured for the Athenians, that they erected 360 bronze statues of him--most of them representing him either on horseback or driving a chariot on a pair of horses. He entered politics and rendered his city splendid services; but in spite of all these accomplishments, his popularity with the Athenians declined--due to the machinations of jealous rivals. He left the city and went to Egypt, where he died of complications from "snakebite". While in Egypt, he became an advisor to Ptolemy Soter, and in c.290 B.C.--following his recommendation--the famous **Library of Alexandria** was built. He worked at the library until his death and was instrumental in developing a scientific complex-- including a university and a museum that was unparalleled at the time. In terms of volume of work and number of books published, he surpassed most of his contemporary Peripatetics; and in learning and versatility: he had no equal. Some of his works are historical and others political, and also include public speeches and embassy reports, as well as collections of Aesop's fables and much more.

Neoclassical Building in Athens

HERACLIDES (c. 360 B.C.) was from Pontus and an extremely wealthy man. In Athens, he first attached himself to Speusippus, attended lectures by the Pythagoreans, and admired the writings of Plato. He became a pupil of Aristotle and was mild and dignified. Heraclides wrote, in total, 60 books--comedies as well as tragedies (none survived)--and had the capacity to charm the reader's mind. He was an adroit conversationalist and moderator, and was able to converse with philosophers, generals, and statesmen equally well. Furthermore, he wrote books pertaining to geometry and involved himself extensively in writing in the dialectic style; but **Heraclides** never ascended to the directorship of the Lyceum. He earned the unique distinction, however, of being a member both of the Academy and the Lyceum at the same time.

With this we conclude the discussion on the philosophy of Socrates, Plato, and Aristotle-- and of their students who espoused the same or similar doctrines. In the next three chapters we shall discuss other special brands of philosophy that were developed during the Hellenistic Era. These philosophies were significantly influenced by the prevailing conditions in Greece at the time- -as well as the Oriental views on philosophy: the concept of "fatalism," for example, had spread via Alexander's extensive conquests and expansion into Asia.

REVELERS

LET US FROLIC TOGETHER
AND GAZE AT THE MOON,
LIFT OUR GLASSES IN TOASTING
AND SING OUT OF TUNE.

LIFE SHOULD BE A BANQUET,
DEVOID OF ALL FEAR,
WHILE TRUSTING OUR INSTINCTS
AND LIVING WELL HERE.

THE PROPHETS WHO FORECAST
ETERNAL DAMNATION,
ARE MISSING THE CHANCE
TO INDULGE IN CREATION.

WE HAVE NO FRUSTRATIONS,
MAY SLEEP WELL PAST NOON,
AND ALL THE DIRE WARNINGS
JUST LEAVE US IMMUNE.

KALYPSO

CHAPTER 12

THE EPICUREAN PHILOSOPHY

"Pleasure is our first and kindred good."
Epicurus

INTRODUCTION

A new era begins with the death of Alexander (323 B.C.), and of Aristotle a year later (322 B.C.). The Hellenic World was no longer as it used to be. The city-state (Πολις) had been the dominant political unit until then, and Athens was still the center of the political and intellectual world, but with time this changed and other cities claimed prominence as centers of intellectual activity, research, and scholarship. **Alexandria, Pergamum, and Rome** also became established cultural centers that attracted serious scholars. New libraries and schools were established, and local rule was replaced by huge political entities with a distant **king or emperor** directing the affairs of the people. The distinction between **Greeks** and **"barbarians"** ceased to have any meaning with the expansion of the Empire to unprecedented boundaries. Provincial and tribal loyalties were destroyed by Alexander, first, and by the Roman legions later. The concept of **"democracy,"** as it was experienced by the Greek city-states, particularly Athens, was replaced by **empires, kingdoms, and tyrannies.** Traditional mores gave way to uncertain and transient values. Civic and social harmony was replaced by societal and political unrest. Alexander's soldiers traveled to India and other places, and discovered new philosophies, customs, and attitudes that some adopted and carried back to Greece when the war ended. These diverse ideas, practices, and religious beliefs began affecting people's perceptions of social order, religious values and the family: as well as their

Epicurus

232

allegiance to the **"polis"** or the **"demos."** These changes and other factors, such as military conquests, trade expansion, and cultural exchanges resulted in altered attitudes toward the old philosophies. Even though the **Academy** and the **Lyceum** continued to flourish and teach the **Socratic/Platonic and Aristotelian** doctrines, until the time of the Christian Era, several new philosophies appeared and established a foothold. These primarily were: the philosophies of the **Epicureans, Stoics, Skeptics, and Neo-Cynics.** We discuss the Epicurean philosophy in this chapter, and the Stoic and other philosophies follow in Chapters 13 and 14.

In some ways, the background of the **Epicurean and Stoic** schools of thought does not

A Macedonian Coin

differ significantly. In many respects these two philosophies represent a departure from the Socratic and Aristotelian tenets and, according to some, the Epicureans were influenced significantly by the pre-Socratic thinkers; while the Stoics were influenced more by Oriental viewpoints. The pre-Socratic philosophers, the **Naturalists**--particularly the **Atomists**--exercised a strong impact on the Epicureans in forming their basic philosophical principles. The Melitians, as we mentioned in Chapter two, had called attention to **"cosmic order"** and the **"beauty of Nature,"** and this teaching had a strong impact on **Epicurus,** the founder of Epicureanism. **Parmenides** had stressed the power of reason and reflection; but the strongest influence on Epicurus comes from Democritus, the Atomist, and the Pythagoreans--as Epicurus adopted the communal style of living and advocated abstention from politics and other social associations. The communal way of life of Epicurus most likely influenced subsequent communal and monastic living patterns practiced by early Christians in monasteries and church enclaves. We first present a few thoughts and facts about Epicurus as a man and as a philosopher, and then summarize the core of his philosophy. We conclude the chapter with: (1) a letter that Epicurus sent to one of his students, **Menoeceus,** in which he expounds on his beliefs and convictions regarding the way an individual should lead his life; and (2) a list of 40 moral maxims, known as "moral principles," which were published by his associates. Both the letters and the maxims were preserved and published by Diogenes Laertius[1].

---

[1]See Reference #8, Volume II. p. 663.

EPICURUS AS A PHILOSOPHER AND AS A MAN [2] (341-269 B.C.)

Epicurus was born in Samos, in the year 341 B.C., from Athenian parents who had emigrated there when it was a colony of Athens. When **Alexander** died, the Macedonian king, **Perdiccas,** expelled all Athenian settlers from Samos; and Epicurus--along with the other members of his family--emigrated to Colofon, in Ionia. When he was 18, he went to Athens and studied philosophy at the Academy--where Xenocrates was the Director and Lecturer. After completing his studies he joined his father, a school-master in Colofon, where he stayed for several years. In Colofon, he opened a school of philosophy and taught there for awhile. He returned to Athens soon afterwards and pursued further studies along with other philosophers at the Academy; but he was not contented with what he was learning and soon developed independent thoughts and views about philosophy. He separated from the Academy and opened a new school of his own, and named it **"The Garden" (Κηπος**), where he taught his philosophy for 36 years. It is related that the citizens of Colofon, who were very proud of him, collected the necessary money and bought the property where he founded the **"Garden,"** and presented it to him as a gift. Epicurus originated a new brand of philosophy: a departure from existing doctrines of his time. His philosophy differed significantly from the Platonic and Aristotelian principles taught at the Academy and the Lyceum, and blended his own thinking with tenets borrowed from the Physiocrats and pre-Socratic philosophers. It was, however, a philosophy of pure Greek origin and lasted for many years, even during the Christian Era. Epicurus was a controversial figure because his philosophy challenged the existing "**Establishment."** According to Diogenes Laertius, there was a book published by **Timocrates** about Epicurus, in which he made some derogatory allegations. Timocrates was one of Epicurus' students; but he rejected the "Garden" and joined the Academy.

Timocrates stated that Epicurus' acquaintance with philosophy was negligible--and his acquaintance with life insufficient as well; that his bodily health was pitiful (Timocrates alleged that Epicurus was unable to rise from his chair for many years); that he spent a whole **mina** (monetary unit) daily for food--an extraordinary figure and that, in his treatise "**On Nature"** (37 books, perished), he was repetitious and primarily wrote in sheer opposition to others. It also appears that Epicurus had used some harsh epithets characterizing other philosophers. He called Aristotle a "profligate," because he supposedly squandered his father's estate and then peddled drugs ("medicines"...Aristotle's father was an eminent physician). He called **Heraclitus "a meddler"; the Cynics, "foes of Greece"; the Dialecticians,"despoilers";** and **Pyrrho,** the Skeptic philosopher, **"an ignorant boor."** Even today, the term **"Epicurean"** implies an individual who enjoys good food, and is a connoisseur of eclectic cuisine. Concerning this, Timocrates further states that Epicurus was eating so much that,

---

[2]Almost all of the information about **Epicurus** comes from Diogenes Laertius, who devoted a full chapter (Chapter X, of Volume II) to him in his work --unlike other **philosophers,** who often received scant coverage. See Reference #8.

on several occasions, he would throw up twice a day from over-indulgence. There are additional accusations, but Diogenes Laertius, who preserved some information about his life and held him in high esteem, has some laudatory remarks. He writes;

> *"But these people (his accusers) are mad. For our philosopher has numerous witnesses to attest to his unsurpassed goodwill towards all men; his native land, which honored him with statues of bronze; his friends, so many in number that they could hardly be counted by whole cities; and indeed all who knew him held fast, captivated by the charm of his doctrine."*[3]

It appears from the above and further evidence, that Epicurus was well liked by the masses and disliked by the intellectuals of his time. He exhibited great gratitude towards his parents, generosity to his brothers, gentleness to his servants--as shown by his will--and by the fact that his servants were also members of his commune--including a slave named "Mys." He was respected for his benevolence to all mankind, his piety towards the gods, and his affection for his country. He never entered public life. He spent his entire life in Greece, in spite of the calamities that Greece suffered during that time, but he did travel once or twice to Ionia to visit acquaintances there. Many friends came from surrounding areas and stayed with him-- living a simple and frugal life. In his **"Garden"** they were content with half a pint of watered wine: and most drank water. The **"Κηπος"** (**Garden**) was a communal lifestyle, but Epicurus did not allow common ownership of property--as the Pythagoreans had required--because he believed that such a practice implied mistrust; and without confidence--there is no friendship. In his correspondence Epicurus states that he is content with: **plain bread and water.**

The Goddess Tyche (Fortune)

Epicurus' teachers were the Platonic philosopher **Pamphilus** and the **Atomist-Skeptic Nausiphanes.** He never married, taught for 36 years, and died at the age of 71 or 72. The "Garden" developed eventually into a peaceful community devoid of politics, and maintained its Hellenic traditions and humanity. There was no distinction between free men and slaves. All the members were bonded in friendship. Epicurus was slim, tall, peaceful, and very polite to everyone. Education at the "Garden" was achieved through daily social interaction and impromptu lectures.

---

[3] See Reference #8. Volume II: Book X (p.528).

THE EPICUREAN PHILOSOPHY

Epicurus believed that philosophy should lead man **towards his happiness.** Knowledge that deviates from this purpose is **meaningless.** Because of this tenet, Epicurus criticized: **Homer, Hesiod, Aeschylus, Pindar, the Sophists, Socrates, Plato, Aristotle, the Stoics and the Skeptics.**

Another Bust of Epicurus

He complained that all these men--with their **myths**--brought **"darkness" to the mind of man and placed fear in his heart.** It has been stated that Epicurus embraced philosophy when disillusioned with his schoolmasters, while he was young, because they could not tell him the meaning of **"Chaos" (Χαος)** in **Hesiod**. He was critical of astrology and rhetoric. In criticizing rhetoric, he used to say that it is necessary to follow the language that comes directly from **"real"** things. **"Substance,"** he said, **"is to be found only through our senses."** Everything depends on the senses: and we will never be cheated by them. If we view certain things altered in shape, color, or size, it is because of the position that we take facing them. For the mistakes that we make; we should blame our reasoning. **The senses are always right: the intellect is sometimes right and sometimes wrong.** Sense and understanding go together. Epicurus accepted the world of sensory perceptions as a means to accumulate knowledge, but on the other hand, affirmed the superiority of reason and reflection. He admitted that there are certain phenomena which cannot be perceived by the senses; yet we know that they exist--as for example: we cannot see the wind, but can infer that it exists. Material things radiate small particles, and our senses act as receivers that react to this radiant energy.[4] In the same way that the sense "sight" is affected by the radiation of "beings," so too are the senses of "hearing" and "taste." Epicurus believed that the universe is, and will be forever--as we know it. It is formed from atoms and void and has no end. The atoms present a variety of shapes, weights, and sizes; and move incessantly. There is an infinite number of "worlds" (similar or different from ours), and life exists there. The soul is part of the body, and is composed of small particles dispersed throughout. When the bond of soul and body breaks, the soul loses all its strength and is no longer viable. The soul is not bodiless; for Epicurus, **"bodiless"** would imply the void: and there is no meaning if the soul is void. The soul is viewed as matter by Epicurus, and relates to the body as a soul-matter--body-matter relationship: when one dies--so does the other.

---

[4]This is the influence that the **Atomists,** particularly **Democritus and Leucippus,** had on **Epicurus.** He wrote extensively on the physical sciences and added a number of refinements to the Atomic Theory of Democritus'; but unfortunately, out of his over 300 books, nothing is available except the titles and three letters addressed by Epicurus to three of his students. For example, Diogenes Laertius lists the following treatises by Epicurus: **On Nature** (37 books) and **Of Atoms and Void** (one book). We know much about Epicurus, however, from Roman writers.

Physical phenomena are not caused by the acts or the supervision of "gods," because such activities should be unfit for "gods." *There are "gods"*--but they are not interested in the world and

Schliemann's Residence in Athens

its inhabitants. Man's needs make the creation of arts, science, and social laws necessary. Humans should live together in harmony, and the State's sole purpose is to safeguard its citizens from harm. Epicurus was interested in **astronomy** because he believed that the explanations provided by this science disprove quite a number of myths and redeem man from the agony and anxiety of fear. In a letter to Herodotus[5], one of his students, Epicurus examines the composition of the world and gives explanations and interpretations of: the sun, moon, stars, sunrise, sunset, phases of the moon; eclipses of the sun and moon; the length of day and night; clouds, thunder, lightning, earthquakes, winds, hail, snow, dew, ice, comets, planets, and other meteorological phenomena. Epicurus notes the relative size of the sun and stars as compared with their apparent size, and acknowledges the fact that the moon may have its own light--but most likely receives it from the sun. He attributes phenomena in this world to many and diverse causes, and does not preclude other causes unknown to him and to his contemporaries. There is **one practice that he detested:** the invention of **"myth" to explain physical or human phenomena (Μον' ο Μυθος Απεστω).** His purpose was clearly enlightenment. From the very beginning, Epicurus was interested in the tranquility of the soul and of the mind; and he advised that **man** can achieve happiness by himself, with the help of science, in the struggle against all those disturbances which emanate from: Fear, Ignorance, and excessive Ambition. **"The highest virtue is the tranquility of the soul; for if we have peace we do not need pleasures or joys, because these sentiments also generate disturbances."** Epicurus finds a relationship between the tranquility of the soul and **material pleasure;** because, as he states it: **"Satisfaction is an indicator of a normal function of every organism. Since, by nature, all beings avoid pain and search for pleasure, this means then that pleasure is related to our nature; while pain is foreign."** Epicurus restores pleasure as a **purposeful function** of life, which differs significantly from the Platonic conception that pleasure is not necessarily a means to happiness. The way he understands and explains pleasure, however, is not the pleasure of the profligate: but the *pleasure that precludes pain in the body and disturbances in the soul.*

---

[5]If one is interested in the views of **Epicurus** and the **ancient Atomists** on matters of physics and other areas of the physical sciences (such as astronomy and meteorology), this letter and one to another student, **"Pythocles,"** preserved by **Diogenes Laertius**, are very informative and provide considerable details. These letters are a summary of Epicurus' views, and refer to topics discussed in his 37 books: <u>On Nature.</u>

One will not achieve a happy life through drunkenness and excess, nor by indulgence in erotic joys and rich foods; but rather will find joy through prudent, logical behavior which searches for the causes of every preference and choice and dispels the fantasies which bring anxiety and disturbance to the human soul. **Prudence** plays an important role in Epicurus' philosophy, because he recognizes that, through it, all virtues are generated; and we learn that life without beauty and justice is unbearable. But even life itself--with prudence, beauty, and justice--is impossible without pleasure, because: **virtue** and a **pleasant life** go together (Maxim 5).

Epicurus proposes that if one wishes to achieve a happy, prudent, and tranquil life: politics should be avoided: **"Live in obscurity"** (Λαθε Βιοσας). As far as love **(Eros)** is concerned, one must recognize that this is one of those strong, natural, and pure desires which must be satisfied--but always within the limits of prudence and logical behavior--because it can become a passion which will destroy man's tranquility. **Regarding friendship**: Epicurus attaches great significance to it. "We pursue friendship because it helps us in securing our peace; but we must seek friendship for its own sake. We

An Aegean Island

do not need the help of our friends as much as we need the assurance of their help. The person who seeks to benefit from your friendship, or the person who avoids obligation, is not a real friend: because the first uses you, and the second cuts off any hope of a bond."(Maxims 27, 28) As far as death is concerned, Epicurus believed that the true philosopher has an obligation to **"redeem man from fear."** *"It makes no sense to fear Death."* Strive to understand, he states, that death has no meaning because everything good and everything bad emanates from the senses. But, of course: **senses cease to exist after death.** When we exist, death does not exist; and when death exists, we cease to exist. Thus, death bears no significance for the dead or for the living (Maxim 2). When one dies, he shall become what he was before: **"nothing."** Generally, Epicurus' contribution towards decreasing the fear of death was significant during his time. As we pointed out earlier, Epicurus was a rare phenomenon: a man as much criticized as praised. Many of the ancient thinkers, such as: **Possidonius, Epictetus, Dionysius from Halicarnassus; Plutarch, Clement, Eusevius, Laktanius, Hieronymus, Saint Augustine** of the Christian Era, and many more, were very critical of him. They accused him of being illiterate because he showed contempt for some branches of philosophy that were not concerned with problems relating to man, and of being an advocate of corruption--due to his acceptance of material pleasure as a fundamental "tenet" of happiness.

But on the other hand, as indicated earlier, the public adored him and he had an **extensive**

following. His school, according to Diogenes Laertius, lasted as long or even longer than any other, and the great Roman poet, **Lucretius**, praised him lavishly (*see Chapter 1*). He said that Epicurus was the first Greek "**who looked straight up to the Heavens without fear,"** and taught man the true meaning of existence--saving him from the agony that the myths had planted in his heart. What we know about Epicurus and of the hundreds of books that he wrote is condensed in three letters published by Diogenes Laertius hundreds of years after his death, and from what **Cicero, Seneca, and Lucretius** wrote about him and of his work. These letters were sent by Epicurus to three of his students, and in some sense they summarize his philosophy and understanding of the physical world (astronomy and physics), ethics and morality. The first letter was addressed to **Herodotus** and relates to physics; while the second is addressed to **Pythocles** and discusses astronomy; the third was addressed to **Menoeceus** and concerns the proper way for one to lead his life and achieve happiness. This letter follows:

EPICURUS' LETTER TO MENOECEUS

"Let no one be slow to seek wisdom when he is either young, or weary in the search of wisdom when he has grown old. For no age is too early or too late for the health of the soul. And to say that the season for studying philosophy has not yet come, or that it is past and gone, is like saying that the season for happiness is not here yet, or that it is now no more. Therefore, both old and young ought to seek wisdom; the former in order that, as age comes over him, he may be young in good things because of the grace of what has been; and the latter in order that, while he is young, he may at the same time be old; because he has no fear of the things which are to come. So we must exercise ourselves in the things which bring happiness, since if that be present, all our actions are directed towards attaining it. Those things which continuously I have been sending you and have advised you to study and carry out, constitute the elements, I think, of the right life. First, believe that God is a living being, immortal and blessed, according to the notion of a god indicated by the common sense of mankind; and so believing, you shall not affirm or deny his immortality or his blessedness, but shall believe about him whatever may be upheld both about his blessedness and his immortality.

For truly there are gods, and the knowledge of them is manifest; but they are not such as the multitude believes, seeing that men do not steadfastly maintain the notions they form about them. It is not the man who denies the beliefs of the multitude about the gods that is impious, but rather he who affirms what the multitude believes about them. For the utterances of the multitude about the gods are not based on superstition, but rather on false assumptions; hence it is that the greatest evils happen to the wicked and the greatest blessings happen to the good from the hand of the gods, seeing that they are always favorable to their own good qualities and take pleasure in men like themselves--but reject as alien whatever is not of their kind. Accustom yourself to believe that death is nothing to us, for good and evil imply sentiments, and death is the deprivation of all sentiment; therefore, a right understanding that death is nothing to us makes the mortality of life enjoyable, not by adding to life unlimited time, but by taking away the yearning after immortality.

239

*For life has no terrors for him who has thoroughly apprehended that there are no terrors for him in ceasing to live. **Foolish, therefore, is the man who says that he fears death, not because it will pain when it comes, but because it pains in the prospect.** Whatsoever causes no annoyance when it is present causes only a groundless pain in the expectation. Death, therefore, the most awful of evils, is nothing to us, seeing that: when we are, death is not come; and when death is come; we are not. It is nothing, then, either to the living or to the dead; for with the living it is not, and with the dead exists no longer.*

But in the world, at one time men shun death as the greatest of all evils, and at another choose it as a respite from the evils in life. The wise man does not deprecate life nor does he fear

Attalus I

*the cessation of life. The thought of life is no offense to him; nor is the cessation of life regarded as an evil. And even as men choose of food not merely and simply the larger portion, but the more pleasant, so the **wise seek to enjoy the time which is most pleasant and not merely that which is longest.** And he who admonishes the young to live well and the old to make a good end speaks foolishly, not merely because of the desires of life, but because the same exercise at once teaches us to live well and to die well. Much worse is he who says that it were good not to be born, but when once one is born to pass with all speed through the Gates of Hades. For if he truly believes this, why does he not depart from life? It would be easy for him to do so, if once he were firmly convinced. If he speaks only in mockery, his words are foolishness; for those who hear believe him not. We must remember that **the future is neither wholly ours nor wholly not ours;** so that neither must we count upon it as quite certain to neither come nor despair of it as quite certain not to come. We must also reflect that of desires, some are natural, others are groundless; and that of the natural some are necessary as well as natural, and some natural only. And of the necessary desires some are necessary if we are to be happy; some, if the body is to be rid of uneasiness; some if we are even to live. He who has a clear and certain understanding of these things will direct every preference and aversion toward securing health of body and tranquility of mind, seeing that this is the sum and end of a blessed life. For the end of all our actions is to be free from pain and fear, and, when once we have attained all this, the tempest of the soul is laid; seeing that **the living creature has no need to go in search of something that is lacking,** nor to look for anything else by which the good of the soul and of the body will be fulfilled. When we suffer pain because of the absence of pleasure, then, and then only, do we feel the need of pleasure. Wherefore we call pleasure the alpha and omega of a blessed life. **Pleasure is our first and kindred good.** It is the starting point of every choice and of every aversion, and to it we come back, inasmuch as we make feeling the rule by which to judge of every good thing. And since pleasure is our first and native good, for that reason we do not choose every pleasure whatsoever, but oftentimes pass over many pleasures when a greater annoyance ensues from them. And often we consider pains superior to pleasures when submission to the pains for a long time brings us as a*

240

consequence a greater pleasure.

*While therefore all pleasure, because it is naturally akin to us, is good, **not all pleasure is choice worthy;** just as all pain is an evil and yet not all pain is to be shunned. It is, however, by measuring one against another, and by looking at the conveniences and inconveniences, that all these matters must be judged. Sometimes we treat the good as an evil, and the evil, on the contrary, as a good. Again, we regard our independence of external factors as a great good, not because we may use little of them, but so as to be contented with little if we have not much of them. Because then we are honestly persuaded that we have the sweetest enjoyment of luxury if we have little of it. **Whatever is natural is easily procured and only the vain and worthless hard to win.***

***Plain fare gives as much pleasure as a costly diet,** when once the pain of want has been removed, while bread and water confer the highest possible pleasure when they are brought to hungry lips. One then should habituate one's self, therefore, to a simple and inexpensive diet that supplies all that is needful for health, and enables man to meet the necessary requirements of life without shrinking, and it places us in a better condition when we approach at intervals a costly fare, and **renders us fearless of fortune.** When we say, then, that pleasure is the end and aim, we do not mean the pleasures of the prodigal or the pleasures of sensuality, as we are understood to do by some through ignorance, prejudice, or willful misrepresentation. **By pleasure we mean the absence of pain in the body and of trouble in the soul.** It is not an unbroken succession of drinking bouts and of revelry; not sexual love, not the enjoyment of the fish and other delicacies of a luxurious table, which produce a pleasant life; **it is sober reasoning,** searching out the grounds of every choice and avoidance, and banishing those beliefs through which the greatest tumults take possession of the soul. Of all this, the **beginning and the greatest good is prudence.** Wherefore prudence is **a more precious thing even than philosophy;** from it springs all the other virtues; for it teaches that we cannot lead a life of pleasure which is not also a life of prudence, honor, and justice; nor lead a life of prudence, honor, and justice, which is not also a life of pleasure. For the virtues have grown into one with a pleasant life, and a pleasant life is inseparable from them.*

*Who then is superior in your judgment to such a man? He holds a holy belief concerning the gods, and is altogether free from the fear of death. He has diligently considered the end fixed by Nature, and understands how easily the limit of good things can be reached and attained, and how either the duration or the intensity of evils is but slight. Destiny, which some introduce as sovereign over all things, he laughs to scorn, affirming rather that some things happen by **necessity,** others by **chance,** others through our **own doing.** For he sees that **necessity destroys responsibility** and that chance or **fortune is not constant;** whereas **our own actions are free,** and it is to them that praise and blame naturally attach. It was better, indeed, to accept the legends of the gods than to bow beneath that yoke of destiny which the Naturalists have imposed. The one holds*

241

*out some faint hope that we may escape if we honor the gods, while the necessity of the Naturalists[6] is deaf to all entreaties. Nor does he hold chance to be a god, as the world in general does, for **in the acts of a god there is no disorder;** nor to be a cause, though an uncertain one, for he believes that no good or evil is dispensed by chance to men so as to make life blessed; though it supplies the starting-point of great good and great evil. He believes that the **misfortune of the wise is better than the prosperity of the fool.** It is better, in short, that what is well judged in action should not owe its successful issue to the aid of chance. Exercise yourself in these and similar precepts day and night, both by yourself and with him who is like you; then never, either in waking or in dream will you be disturbed, but will live as a god among men. For man loses all semblance of mortality by living in the midst of immortal blessings."[7]*

These are Epicurus' views on life and conduct, and he has addressed these matters at great length elsewhere, in more than 300 books that he wrote, in which he rejects the whole notion of destiny and predictions, by writing: *"No means of predicting the future really exists, and if it did, we must regard what happens according to it as nothing to us."* He meant that regardless of our knowledge, we cannot change the outcome. As we pointed out earlier, the students of the **"Garden"** published 40 "Maxims" (even though later more were discovered--over 80) after Epicurus' death, representing his beliefs on moral standards. These maxims follow:

EPICURUS' MAXIMS

1. *"A blessed and eternal being has no trouble himself and brings no trouble upon any other being; hence, such a person is exempt from outbursts of anger and partiality, for every such outburst or partiality implies weakness.*

2. *Death is nothing to us; for the body, when it has been resolved into its elements, has no feeling, and that which has no feeling is nothing to us.*

3. *The magnitude of pleasure reaches its limit when it removes all pain. When pleasure is present, so long as it is uninterrupted, there is no pain either of body or mind, or of both together.*

4. *Continuous pain does not last long in the flesh; on the contrary, pain, if extreme, lasts a very short time, and even that degree of pain, which barely outweighs pleasure in the body, does not last for many days continuously. Even illnesses of long duration allow for more pleasure over pain in the body.*

---

[6]He refers to the philosophers and scholars prior to him: "With their myths, they brought darkness into the soul of man."

[7] See Reference 8, Volume II, pp. 648-661.

5. *It is impossible to live a pleasant life without living wisely, well, and justly; and it is impossible to live wisely, well, and justly without living pleasantly. Whenever any one of these is lacking--when, for instance, a man is not able to live wisely, though he lives well and justly--it is impossible for him to live a pleasant life.*

6. *Obtaining security from other men is a natural good; therefore, any means of obtaining this security is also a natural good.*

7. *Some men sought to become famous and renowned, thinking that thus they would make themselves secure from their fellowmen. If, then, the life of such persons really was secure, they attained this natural good; if, however, it was insecure, they did not attain the end, which by Nature's own prompting, they originally sought.*

8. *No pleasure is in itself evil, but the things that produce certain pleasures entail annoyances many times greater than the pleasures themselves.*

9. *If pleasure could be accumulated, regardless of time, in total, and in all principal parts of human nature, then there would never be any difference between one pleasure from another; even though there is.*

10. *If it would be possible to free the profligate from fears of the mind--fears inspired by celestial and atmospheric phenomena, fear of death, and fear of pain-- and also teach them to limit their desires, then we would have no reason to criticize them because they would have overflowing pleasures coming to them from everywhere, which would exempt them from all pain--whether of body or mind: that is, from all evil.*

11. *If we had never been tortured by suspicions or alarms of celestial and atmospheric phenomena, nor by the misgivings that death somehow affects us, nor by neglecting to comprehend the proper limits of pains and desires, then we would not have the need of natural sciences.*

12. *It is impossible to banish fear on matters of highest importance, if man does not know the nature of the whole universe--but lives in suspicion of what legends tell us. Thus, without the study of Nature there can be no enjoyment of pure pleasure.*

13. *There would be no advantage in providing security from our fellow men, so long as we are alarmed by occurrences over our heads or beneath the earth, or in general by whatever happens in the boundless universe.*

14. *When tolerable security is attained, on the basis of power sufficient to afford support and material prosperity, the guarantee of a quiet private life--withdrawn from the*

243

multitude--arises in its most genuine form.

15. *Nature's wealth is given and easy to procure; but the desire of the vain is unlimited.*

16. *Fortune seldom interferes with the wise man; his greatest and highest interests have been—are--and will be--directed by reason throughout the course of his life.*

17. *The just man enjoys the greatest peace of mind; while the unjust is full of the utmost disquietude.*

18. *Pleasure in the flesh admits no increase once desire has been satisfied; after that it only admits variation. The limit of pleasure in the mind, however, is increased when we reflect on those things and their consequences which cause the mind the greatest anxiety.*

19. *Unlimited time and limited time pleasure are equal, if we measure the limits of those pleasures by reason.*

20. *The flesh considers as unlimited the limits of pleasure and time to satisfy them. But the mind, grasping what the end and limit of the flesh is, and banishing the terrors of the future, provides a complete and perfect life, and has no longer any need of unlimited time. Nevertheless, it does not shun pleasure, and, even in the hour of death, the mind so arranges circumstances so that it will not be deprived of the enjoyment of the best life.*

21. *He who understands the limits of life knows how easy it is to procure enough to remove the pain of need and make the whole of life complete and perfect. Hence, he has no longer any need of things which are to be obtained by labor and conflict.*

22. *We must take into account all that really exists and becomes clear evidence to our senses, and on which we base our opinions; for otherwise, everything will be full of uncertainty and confusion.*

23. *If you fight against all your senses, you will have no standard reference, and thus no means of judging even those events which you pronounce false.*

24. *If you reject, absolutely, any single sense without stopping to judge with respect to that which awaits confirmation between matter of opinion and that which is already present, whether in sense, feelings, or in any perception of the mind--you will throw into confusion, even the rest of your sensory perceptions, by your groundless belief; and so you will be rejecting the standard of truth altogether. If, in your ideas based upon opinion, you hastily affirm as true all that awaits confirmation--as well as that which*

244

does not--you will not escape error; as you will be maintaining complete ambiguity whenever it is a case of judging between right and wrong opinion.

25. *If you do not refer, on any separate occasion, each of your actions to the end prescribed by Nature, but instead, in the act of choice or avoidance, swerve aside to some other end, your acts will not be consistent with your words.*

26. *All such desires which lead to no pain when they remain ungratified--are unnecessary, and the longing is easily dispelled when the things desired are difficult to procure--or when the desires seem likely to produce harm.*

27. *Of all the means which are procured by wisdom to ensure happiness throughout the whole of life, by far, the most important, is the acquisition of friends.*

28. *The same conviction that inspires confidence that nothing we have to fear is eternal, or even of long duration, also enables us to see that, even in our limited conditions of life, nothing enhances our security so much as friendship.*

29. *Of our desires, some are natural and necessary; others are natural, but not necessary; others are neither natural nor necessary, but are due to illusory opinion. (Epicurus regards as natural and necessary desires those which bring relief from pain: drink when we are thirsty; while by natural and not necessary he means those which merely diversify the pleasure (without removing the pain): costly foods; neither natural nor necessary: desires for crowns and erection of statues in one's honor).*

30. *Those natural desires which entail no pain when not gratified, though their objects are vehemently pursued, are also due to illusory opinion; and when they are not dispelled, it is not because of their own nature, but because of man's illusory opinion.*

31. *Natural justice is a symbol or expression of expediency--to prevent one man from harming or being harmed by another.*

32. *Those animals incapable of making covenants with one another, to the end that they neither inflict nor suffer harm, are without either justice or injustice. And those tribes which either could not or would not form natural covenants to the same end are of like kind.*

33. *There never has been an absolute justice, but only agreements made in reciprocal relation, in localities from time to time, safeguarding against the infliction or suffering of harm.*

34. *Injustice is not in itself an evil, but only in its consequence, viz. the terror which is excited by apprehension that those appointed to punish such offences will discover the injustice.*

35. *It is impossible for the man who secretly violates any article of the social contract to feel confident that he will remain undiscovered, even if he has already escaped ten thousand times; for right on, until the end of life, he will always fear detection.*

36. *Taken generally, justice is the same for all--something found expedient in mutual relations; but in its application to particular cases of locality or conditions of whatever kind, it varies under different circumstances.*

37. *By conventional law, whatever serves the needs of the people and found to be expedient, is considered just. Any law that does not serve the interests of the society cannot be considered just. And should the expediency expressed by the law vary, it may no longer be just, even though it was just at one time, so long as we do not distract ourselves with empty words-- but look simply at the facts.*

38. *Where, without any change of circumstances, conventional laws--when judged by their consequences--are seen as incompatible with the notion of justice, such laws are not really just; but wherever the laws have ceased to be expedient in consequence of a change in circumstances, in that case the laws were just when they were expedient for the mutual relations of the citizens, and unjust when they ceased to be expedient.*

39. *He who best knows how to meet fear of external foes, makes into one family all the people he can; and those he cannot, he, at any rate, does not treat as aliens; and when even that is not possible, he avoids all relations with them, and, so far as it is expedient, he keeps them at a distance.*

40. *Those who were best able to provide themselves with the means of mutual security, and passed the most agreeable life in each other's society, feel mutual support for one another; and their enjoyment of the fullest intimacy is just that, if one of them dies before his time, the survivors do not lament his death as something terrible.*[8]

This concludes the discussion and commentary on Epicurus and his philosophy, which exerted great influence on Hellenistic and Roman societies for several centuries. Epicurus was venerated as a philosopher who advocated a new style of life, directed primarily towards **ridding man of fear.** It was a pragmatic philosophy based upon the premise: to achieve happiness and tranquility of the soul, one has to dispel fear. Epicurus'

---

[8] Reference #8, **Diogenes Laertius**, Volume II, pp.662-667.

research and writings on the subject of atomic theory is of considerable significance to us today, for due to these writings, though unavailable, we are in a position to learn the nature of the philosophy of the Atomists--since all of their original writings perished. Lucretius, the Roman philosopher and follower of Epicurus, wrote extensively on the works of Epicurus and the Epicurean school: these writings have survived.

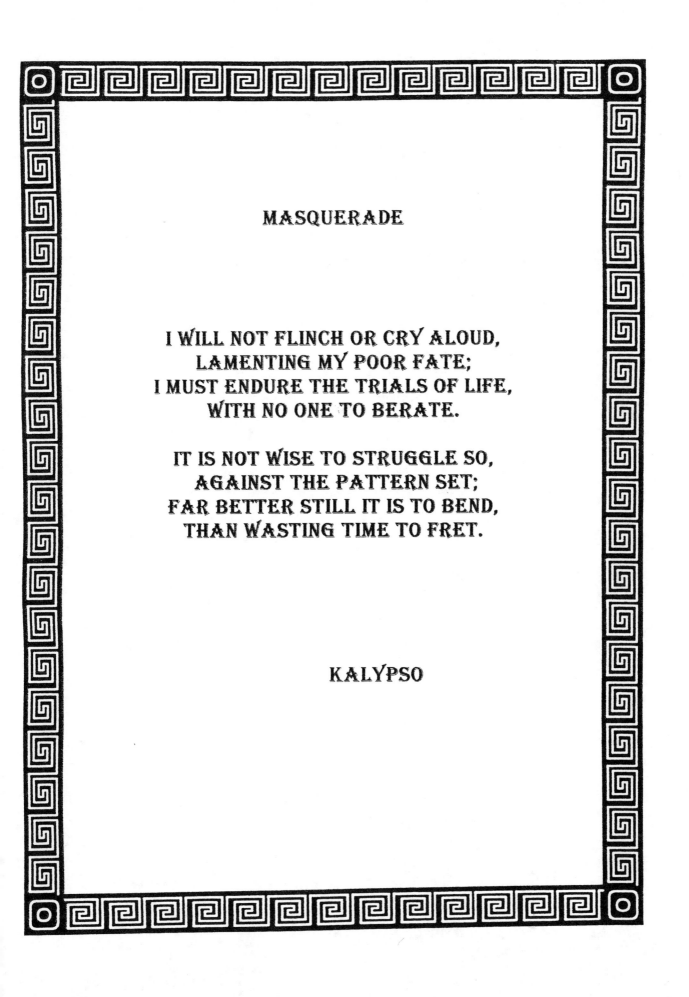

MASQUERADE

I WILL NOT FLINCH OR CRY ALOUD,
LAMENTING MY POOR FATE;
I MUST ENDURE THE TRIALS OF LIFE,
WITH NO ONE TO BERATE.

IT IS NOT WISE TO STRUGGLE SO,
AGAINST THE PATTERN SET;
FAR BETTER STILL IT IS TO BEND,
THAN WASTING TIME TO FRET.

KALYPSO

CHAPTER 13

THE STOIC PHILOSOPHERS

"The reason that we have two ears and only one
mouth is that we may listen more and talk less."
Zeno

INTRODUCTION

Zeno from Citium

At about the same time the **Epicureans** founded the **"Garden"** in Athens, the **Stoic philosophers** established the **"Stoa,"** also in Athens, where they taught their philosophy--which came to be known as **Stoicism.** Zeno, from Cyprus, was the founder of the **"Stoa,"** which lasted well into the middle of the third century A.D. The same introductory remarks from the previous chapter, with regard to the **Epicureans--** as far as the political and social conditions prevailing at the time-- could also apply to the **Stoics.** The **Stoa** was established in **301 B.C.,** and the **Garden** in **306 B.C.** The environment, following Alexander's conquests, fostered new conditions in the Greek world affecting social life, customs, and prevailing standards, which influenced and led to the establishment of these two **new schools of philosophy.** We noted that the **Epicureans** were highly motivated by their desire to emancipate man from the **fear of death; the anxiety of uncertainty;** and the **agony of survival.** They also introduced the idea that **pleasure** is not a sentiment that should be banished, but rather pursued, and if experienced in moderation and within certain prescribed limits, would prove beneficial in alleviating the **anxiety** besetting man. Also, as noted earlier, the **Epicurean philosophy was entirely Greek** and borrowed heavily from the **pre-Socratic philosophers:** the Eleats, the Atomists, Ephesians, *et al.* The **Stoic philosophers** were also concerned with the quality of life in the new environment, and sought to provide advice on how to **improve social conditions.** Alexander introduced the idea of intermarriages between Greeks and other races, and he himself married **a Persian princess.** Thousands of his soldiers married Persian women in a mass wedding ceremony--which resulted in altered attitudes towards mixed unions, intercultural relations, and the prevailing distinction between **Greeks and barbarians.** The Stoics introduced a

248

new concept as part of their philosophical doctrines: **apathy.** If you reduce your activity and let Nature take its course, all problems in life will fade away. Today, we view **apathy** as a state of mind indifferent to triumph or disaster; while for the Stoics, **apathy** implied that one is impervious to emotion. The meaning of the word *stoic* differs also from the meaning attached to it by the Stoics. Today, a stoic is an individual who does not show an interest and seeks no involvement; while for the ancients, quite the opposite; a stoic would show interest and seek involvement but would eradicate emotion in doing so.

How much the **Stoics** were affected by Oriental philosophical principles is not clear, but we know that they believed that all is pre-ordained by Fate. **Zeno** was of **Phoenician** descent; his parents had emigrated from **Sidon** to **Citium in Cyprus,** many years earlier. But he lived in a Greek city, was influenced by **Greek culture,** and all of his education was in Athens at the Academy and Lyceum. He spoke Greek and is not known to have traveled to the East; so that any Oriental influence must have resulted from conditions following Alexander's conquests. Socrates and Plato, a hundred years earlier, were looking for an **Ideal Society** and an **Ideal Man,** and prescribed some guidelines to achieve these goals. But **Plato's and Socrates' impact** on their contemporaries was minimal. Similarly, **Aristotle** had advocated logical, pragmatic, ethical standards; and above all, the pursuance of **education**--in order to improve society and refine the mores of the people. **Zeno** had noted a deterioration of standards and the quality of life--resulting in continuous strife, wars, and hostilities. The **city-state** had practically vanished, and the **democratic system** was semi-abandoned; **oligarchic** and **monarchical** systems of government appeared to dominate the political landscape. The diminished influence that the ancient **Greek myths** of **Homer, Hesiod, and the dramatic poets** had on the people, also significantly affected **Zeno's** perceptions of the world during his time. More than two hundred years before, **Xenophanes** and other pre-Socratic thinkers punctured holes in the religion of the **Olympic gods,** and many scholars lost their lives: **Socrates** and others (**Anaxagoras, Empedocles**) were banished from their cities for advocating new deities, or merely criticizing the existing polytheistic system. Zeno discovered that the period in which he lived was exhibiting rapid changes that necessitated a re-examination and a new approach to the eternal **questions of existence, and the way that people should lead their lives.**

We present first, the life and activities of the representatives of the Stoic philosophy: **Zeno, Cleanthes, and Chrysippus**--as scholars and as men--and then a summary of **Stoicism.** It is unfortunate that none of the hundreds of books written by these three men survived, and we only know about them and their philosophy from what others have written--particularly Roman writers who embraced but modified Stoicism considerably.

ZENO FROM CITIUM

Zeno was born in **Citium, Cyprus,** in the year **333 B.C.;** a year after Alexander started his campaign to Asia. He died--**261 B.C.--in Athens.** He completed his early studies in Cyprus and, according to ancient biographers, was involved in the textile trade--most likely the trade of his father. It is not clear when he became a citizen of Athens or how he spent the remainder of his 72 years there; but one explanation is provided by **Diogenes Laertius,** who describes a business trip to Piraeus from Cyprus that was shipwrecked and left him penniless. He arrived in **Athens** and decided to remain after he attended some lectures at the **Academy--where Xenocrates** was the Director. Another version is that he came to Athens to study philosophy, and liked his classes so much that he decided to stay there permanently. It is also related that when he was young, he consulted the Oracle at Delphi, asking what he should do with his life. The Oracle responded: "Ει Συγχρωτιζοιτο τοις Νεκροις"--"**That you should associate with the dead.**" He took that to mean that he should study the ancient authors, and immediately embarked upon the study of the Socratic and other philosophers. It was perhaps this undertaking that drew him to **Athens** to attend lessons at the **Academy** and the **Lyceum.** He studied under **Crates** (the Cynic), **Stilpo** (the Megarian), and **Xenocrates** (the Academician)--which indicates that he had a well-rounded education from all prevailing schools at the time. He must have learned rapidly, because he soon developed his own ideas about philosophy, which most likely did not coincide with those of the **Academy** and **Lyceum.** As a result, he started delivering lectures at the Painted Colonnade (Ποικιλη Στοα, **Portico),** a famous and sacred place painted with scenes from the battles at Marathon and Salamis, where, during the reign of the "Thirty Tyrants," a number of Athenian opponents were slain. Usually idlers would concentrate there. Due to the fact that he was delivering his lectures at the "Stoa," his followers came to be known as the **"Stoics."**

Zeno became so popular, with his new ideas and doctrines, that the Athenians honored him with a large bronze statue; and the people of Citium claimed him proudly as one of their own. At that time, Athens was under the political jurisdiction of **Macedonia.** King Antigonos sent him a letter inviting him to **Pella,** to instruct him in philosophy--which the King indicated would be not only for his own good, but also for the good of the entire population. Zeno replied with the following letter:

"I welcome your love for learning so far as you stay to that true education which tends to advantage and not to the phony one which serves only to corrupt morals. But if anyone has yearned for philosophy, turning away from much wanted pleasures which effeminate the souls of some of our young, it is evident that not by Nature only, but by strong will also, he will achieve nobility of character. But if a noble nature be aided by moderate exercise and further receives instruction ungrudgingly, it easily comes to acquire virtue in perfection. But I am constrained

by bodily weakness, due to old age, for I am eighty years old[1]; and for this reason I am unable to join you. But I am sending you certain companions of my studies, whose mental powers are not inferior to mine--while their bodily strength is far greater--and if you associate with these you will in no way fall short of the conditions necessary for perfect happiness."[2]

Once, a young man from **Rhodes** who was rich and good-looking, but not of good character, asked to attend **Zeno's lectures;** Zeno did not want him but, unwilling to hurt his feelings, allowed him to attend. Instead, he made him sit in the dusty benches, with the intention of having his clean and brand new cloths dirtied, which caused the young man to flee and never return. *Nothing, he declared, was more unbecoming than **arrogance**; especially in the young.* He also used to say that *it is not words and expressions that we ought to remember, but rather we should exercise our mind to **evaluate** what we hear.* The young, he stated, should behave with perfect propriety in **walk, manners, and dress.** When he died, he was younger than his colleague, **Cleanthes,** who eventually took over the Stoa and died at the age of 99. **Zeno** did not die a natural death, but rather took his own life in the following manner: One day, while exiting the school, he fell and broke his toe; he then struck the ground with his fist, shouting a passage from a poet, and held his breath until he died from asphyxiation. The **Athenians,** who held him in high esteem, buried him at the **Ceramicus** (the public burial grounds) and honored him with a decree passed by the **Assembly**--as testimony to his good character.

CLEANTHES

Cleanthes was born in **Assos,** a city in Asia Minor, 331 **B.C.** (two years later than **Zeno),** and died there in 232 B.C. When he went to **Athens** to study philosophy, he had only four drachmas—a very small amount. He took a job as a **gardener** and **laborer,** pumping water from a well for irrigation purposes. He met Zeno and adhered to the principles of the Stoic philosophy until the very end. He was renowned for his industriousness, as he had to work hard to make a living--being extremely poor. At night he used to work pumping water in the garden; by day he attended lectures and was a lecturer himself as well. He was summoned to court to explain how he was making a living, since he was seen at the **Stoa** all day long. He brought witnesses to testify that he was working at night as a **gardener.** The court appreciated and admired his desire for education, awarding him ten **mina;** but **Zeno** persuaded him not to accept. However, **King Antigonos of Macedonia,** who held him in high esteem, sent him a gift of 3000 drachmas--which he accepted. When it became known that he was pumping water from the well, they nicknamed him "Φρεαντλης" (Well-Pumper)--from the words "Φρεαρ"=**well** and "Αντλειν"=**pump-up,**

---

[1]This reference makes Zeno older than other sources indicate.

[2]Notice the importance of **true education** that is emphasized in the letter, and how he implies that **excessive pleasures effeminate the souls** of the young men of his time.

which rhymes with **"Κλεανθης"= CLEANTHES**. Once, when conversing with a youth, he asked if he could see. The youth replied: *"Indeed I see."* Then **Cleanthes** said: *"Then why don't I see what you see?"* And while at the theater, a poet uttered a derogatory phrase about Cleanthes; Cleanthes ignored him, and the audience was astonished that he reacted so calmly. He replied: *"Since Dionyssus and Heracles were ridiculed by the poets without getting angry, it would be absurd for me to get annoyed for such a casual abuse."* To the solitary man who was talking to himself, he remarked: *"You are not talking to a bad man."* When someone teased him about his old age, he replied: *"I too am ready to depart, but when again I consider that I am in all points in good health, and that I can still read and write, I am content to wait."* He wrote in total, 56 books, but unfortunately none exist. He died in a manner similar to his mentor and teacher, Zeno. He had a gum inflammation and his doctor advised him not to eat for two whole days; the treatment succeeded, and the doctors allowed him to continue his normal diet. He did not accept the doctor's advice and declared: *"I have already gone too far on the road."* He continued his fast until he died.

CHRYSIPPUS

Chrysippus was born in the year **282 B.C., in Tarsus**, a city in Asia Minor, but moved to Athens when he was young--and became a pupil of **Cleanthes.** He died in 210 B.C. Before settling in Athens, he had been a long-distance runner. While **Cleanthes** was still living, **Chrysippus** withdrew from the School and achieved great eminence as a philosopher. He was very intelligent and versatile, understanding all aspects of philosophy. He differed in quite a number of points from both Zeno and Cleanthes--to whom he often said that all he wanted was to be told what the doctrines were: **he would discover the proofs for himself.** He was so renowned for his capability in **dialectics** that they used to say: *"If the gods would ever want to practice dialectics, they would certainly use Chrysippus' style."* He was solid in substance but lacking in presentation. Diogenes Laertius reports that he was a prolific writer who wrote over **700 treatises** and surpassed all of the ancient authors. He was famous for his quotations and references, and was sometimes unduly criticized. It was noted that what Epicurus wrote with force and originality, unaided by quotations, was far greater in volume than the books of Chrysippus. Even though he came from a prosperous family, most of his property was confiscated by the **King of Pergamum.** Diogenes Laertius states that **Chrysippus** was not very impressive in stature, as was evident by his statue at **Ceramicus.** When once he was asked why he was not going with the multitude to hear the speaker, **Ariston**, he replied: *"If I had followed the multitude, I should not have studied philosophy."* When a dialectician rose and attacked Cleanthes, presenting sophisticated fallacies, **Chrysippus** reprimanded him: *"Cease to distract your elder from matters of importance; bring your quibbles to us juniors."* He had a high opinion of himself, and when once one asked: *"To whom shall I entrust my son?"* he replied: *To me, for if I had dreamed of there being anyone better than myself, I should myself be studying with him."* He enrolled at the **Academy** for several years, studying under **Arcesilaus** and **Lacydes,** and at times he would be seen arguing both sides of an issue. He studied **mathematics** under the **Academicians**--which was not the case with most of the Stoics. Diogenes Laertius notes that **Chrysippus** was an arrogant man, and it appears that from all of his many writings, none were dedicated to any of the kings. When **Ptolemy,** the **King of Egypt,** asked **Chrysippus** to send someone of renown to his court, **Chrysippus** refused to send someone or go himself. He, however, was very kind to his family and educated his sister's sons at his own expense. He liked to lecture in open space and was the first to have done so in his time--besides Aristotle.

Chryssippus

Chrysippus enjoyed playing with words and complicated concepts. He is quoted as saying: "*What is not in the city is not in the house either. Now then, there is no well in the city; therefore there is none in the house either.*" Or yet another: "*There is a certain head, and that head you have not; now this being so, there is a head which you have not, therefore, you are without a head.*" Again: "*If anyone is in Megara, he is not in Athens. Now there is a man in Megara; therefore there is not a man in Athens.*" Also: "*If you say something, it passes through your lips, now you say "wagon"; consequently a wagon passes through your lips.*" And further: "*If you never lost something, you still have it; but you never lost horns, therefore you have horns.*" [3]

Diogenes Laertius tells us that **Chrysippus** was criticized for using vulgar language in his writings, but none of his books exist and we do not have firsthand knowledge of what he wrote. To be sure, this was a time when morals and ethics were deteriorating, and Greek society was continuously influenced by other cultures and practices. Note, for example, that both **Zeno and Cleanthes** died a voluntary death--unheard of previously. Note also, that the Buddha and the leader of Jainism, **Mahavira,** as well as his father and mother, all died from self-inflicted starvation[4]--which possibly indicates an oriental influence on the Stoic philosophy.

THE PHILOSOPHY OF THE STOICS (THE MAJOR POINTS)

The original **philosophy of the Stoics** was formulated by **Zeno.** Essentially, it addressed the idea that we should live our lives with **as little disturbance as possible:** avoiding passion and learning to dispel all emotions that disturb the tranquility of the soul. People should strive to reach

---

[3]The idea of a man having horns (allegorically) is considered a loss of honor in modern Greece, and apparently in ancient Greece as well. If a wife commits adultery, it is accepted that she "put" horns on her husband, and therefore dishonored him.

[4] See Chapter 16, where a short discussion on Jainism and Buddhism is presented.

a state of **apathy** and let Nature take its course. In addition, the **Stoics** promoted the idea that pleasures and other comforts of life do not assist in achieving happiness. Their total philosophical system consists of three parts: **Logic; Physics,** and **Ethics.** We present some points concerning their conceptions on logic and physics, and concentrate subsequently on ethics. The Stoics rejected the Atomists' theory of the world consisting of atoms and void, and instead believed that God, the Creator, is an active force in the physical world--consisting of the finest and most active form of **matter, fire, and air**--mixed to produce a Divine Spirit; and that God goes about his work as a skilled craftsman. Their vision of the world was materialistic: viewing everything as corporeal,

unlike the Socratic spirit--and this applies to the human soul and God as well. They believed that a human being is born without any preconceived notions on knowledge, similar to John Locke's **Tabular Rasa;** unlike the Socratic "Ideas" and Aristotle's conception that one is born endowed with certain talents and inclinations--differing from person to person. They were interested in the development of a theory of knowledge using logic to provide a basis for assured understanding, similar to the Platonic model, as a foundation for rational conduct.

THE ETHICS DOCTRINES

Wisdom, according to Zeno, is the final goal in life, and consists of theoretical and practical virtue. The former (correct ideas on the nature of things) is subordinate to and exists only to aid virtuous living and rational behavior. The study of **practical virtue,** then, typifies or characterizes the philosophy of the

Attic Amphora

Stoics: which places emphasis on the ethical behavior of man and identifies practical ways to achieve it. As we pointed out earlier, the writings of the three major proponents of this philosophy, **Zeno, Cleanthes, and Chrysippus,** have vanished--and therefore, our knowledge about them comes to us secondhand. Unlike the **Socratic and Aristotelian philosophies,** of which we have Plato's original writings and some of Aristotle's, the major Stoic doctrines come from indirect sources. **Diogenes Laertius** also presents some additional information in his narrative on the life of Zeno. Stoicism considerably influenced Roman thinkers such as **Marcus Aurelius** and others, but they significantly modified the original doctrines, which were indeed austere, and developed a system of benevolence and empathy. We have considerable information from these Roman writers, and without their recorded treatises we would know little about this philosophy that played an extraordinary role in the life of the ancient world during the Hellenistic and Roman Eras, until the advent of Christianity.

The basic concepts of the Stoics' "Ethics" doctrines were originally formulated by **Zeno;** but **Chrysippus, the theoretician** of the School, eventually modified and perfected them. Thus, the Stoics' main points of research addressed: **impulse, good and evil, the passions of man, virtue, the end, values, duty, and inducements to act or refrain from acting. Self-preservation** is man's first impulse; as it is with all other animals. It would have been unlikely for Nature to have estranged the living thing from itself. Contrary to Epicurean belief (pleasure is a natural impulse), Stoics asserted that this is false. If pleasure is really felt, they said, it is to be a by-product-- comparable to the condition of animals thriving and plants blooming: as part of the process of life, not an end in itself.

Nature regulates plant life without impulse or sensation; but, in the case of animals, Nature added **impulse** and directed its command. But with reason bestowed on beings we call **"rational,"** then life, according to reason, rightly becomes still Nature's life. And that is what the Stoics call **life in agreement with Nature** (living in harmony with Nature)--which is the same as a virtuous life; virtue being the **"good"** towards which Nature guides us. The principle, *"living according to Nature,"* does not mean, however, returning to Nature and living an ascetic life--in denial. But, since Nature is ideally ordered by Divine Reason, it follows that "living according to Nature" means living up to one's true nature as a rational being, in conformity with Nature's law. The important point in this discussion on "impulse," is that the Stoics deviated drastically from previous philosophers regarding the behavior of man--emphasizing the notion of **"Nature"** (the **"Force"** that regulates all beings on this planet) and insisting that it should not be any different in the case of man. Plato wanted man to become a **son of God**; the Stoics--a **"son of Nature."** This concept approaches the notion of fatalism; but in the Stoic view, fatalism is not destructive to morality: either theoretically or practically. For the Stoics the ultimate goal was morality: not based on irrational free will, but on voluntary action. **A man is responsible for his actions;** whether or not he could have acted differently, is a moot question. The Stoics exemplified morality in their conduct, and as time progressed they emphasized it more and more in their lectures and writings. Their ultimate objective is **rational action--**a life according to Nature: not the bestial nature; one of virtue. To desire the impossible is irrational; and we should concern ourselves *only* with what is in our power--not wealth, pleasure, or reputation--but our inward reaction to the circumstances of life.

Because reason, which provides choice, has been bestowed on human beings, the Stoics spent considerable discussion on "virtue"--which leads to **"Nature's way."** All Stoic philosophers believed that living virtuously (temperate, prudent, just, and brave) is equivalent to living in harmony with Nature, for its own sake, and not due to hope, fear--or any external motive. Moreover, it is in virtue that happiness will be found: for virtue is the state of mind that leads to a balanced life. When a rational being is **"perverted,"** this is due to the deceptiveness of external pursuits or influences of associates: which deviate from the course of **Nature: because Nature is never perverse.** According to the Stoics, man is required to do what is morally and objectively good. Right action constitutes virtue--which leads to happiness. Vice means choosing the wrong action. **Virtue is absolute good**; while **vice is absolute evil.** There are various objects of desire or aversion in-between that are morally neutral, because they all can be used to promote or impede a person's true interest, such as: *life-death; health-disease; pleasure-pain; beauty-ugliness; wealth-poverty.* The wisdom of the sage resides in his ability to distinguish between *apparent* and *real* good.

255

The Stoics classified **virtues** as **Primary and Subordinate**. **The Primary would be:** **Wisdom (Σοφια), Courage (Ανδρεια), Justice (Δικαιοσυνη), and Temperance (Σωφροσυνη).** **Subordinate virtues would be: Magnanimity (Μεγαλοψυχια), Continence (Εγγρατια), Endurance (Καρτερια), Presence of Mind (Αγχινοια), and Good Counsel (Ευβουλια).** The above classification of virtues does not differ substantially from those of the Socratics and Aristotelians, but only in the approach suggested to acquire them. The Socratics believed that virtue can be achieved through knowledge; the Peripatetics maintained that rationality and education lead to the same end. The Stoics, however, advocated following the course of Nature to achieve a virtuous life.

In a similar manner, Stoics classified vices as **Primary and Subordinate**. The Primary would be: **Folly (Αφροσυνη), Cowardice (Δειλια), Injustice (Αδικια), and Profligacy (Ακολασια). The Subordinate would be: Incontinence (Ακρασια), Stupidity (Βραδυνοια), and Ill-Advisedness (Κακοβουλια).** They believed that vices are forms of *ignorance* of those things whose corresponding virtues are *knowledge*. An advantage is derived from **Good (ΑΓΑΘΟΝ)** that is either identical to or not distinct from *benefit*. They further define **"goods"** of the mind (virtues) and "goods" of an external nature (a good friend or a good country). The Stoics also defined goods as ends in themselves (**confidence, liberty, delight)** or means to an end (**a friend)**. Chrysippus, who was the articulator of the Stoic philosophy, had extensive monographs on these definitions and identifications of various virtues and the concept of **"Good" (ΑΓΑΘΟΝ)**; unfortunately, what has survived is only a summary that Diogenes Laertius preserved--from over 700 treatises that have vanished. Furthermore, the **Stoics** introduced the concept of **"Indifference" (Αδιαφορια),** to which they gave two meanings: The first denotes those things which neither contribute to happiness nor misery; such as: **wealth, fame, and strength.** It is possible to be happy without these; although, if they are used in certain ways--happiness or misery may result. The other meaning of **"Indifference"** conferred by the Stoics refers to the things that do not have the power to stir inclination or aversion. Another concept they discussed extensively within the ethical branch of their philosophy, is the concept of **"Duty" (Καθηκον).** Zeno was the first to use the term and it was presented as an action taken voluntarily--not dictated by a written or an unwritten law--but *rather as something that should be embraced as a virtue in the pursuit of "Good."* And it is the action of the duty itself that must be adapted to Nature's arrangements. For of the acts committed at the prompting of impulse, some are fit towards good, and others the reverse; while there is a third class which is neither the one nor the other. "Befitting acts" are those that reason prevails on us to perform; such as: **honoring one's parents, kin, and country.** While "unbefitting" or contrary-to-duty acts would be all acts that relate to *neglect;* for example: *one's parents, kinsmen, and country.* The Stoics believed, as the **Epicureans**, that **man has a soul** that is part of the body; but when the body dies, the soul perishes with it.

The Stoics defined eight parts of the soul: **the Five Senses; the Faculty of Speech; the**

Intellectual Faculty (the Mind), and the Reproduction (Regenerative) Faculty. It is in this area that the Stoics differed substantially from other Greek philosophers. They introduced as the root of all ills in man, his **"Passions"**--which disturb the soul and bring instability. Perversion results from falsehood, and extends to the mind and generates many passions or emotions that cause instability. Passion or emotion is defined as: an **"irrational and unnatural movement in the soul"** or **"impulse in excess."** Therefore, a good Stoic should suppress his irrational impulses which agitate the soul. Pleasure was discouraged, because it is not the first impulse of Nature; but preservation is. Emotion is a defect of the soul. This concept, along with that of apathy, is the negative side of Stoicism. They exhorted people to embrace fortitude to rid themselves of anxiety, and self-control to suppress desire. They identified four classes of passions, and these are: **Grief (Λυπη), Fear (Φοβος), Desire (Επιθυμια),** and **Pleasure (Ηδονη).** Grief or pain is caused by irrational mental contraction and derives from: **Pity, Envy, Jealousy, Rivalry, Annoyance, Distress, Anguish, and Distraction.** **Fear** is **expectation of evil**, and the following emotions are classified under fear: **Terror, Shame, Nervous Shrinking, Consternation,** and **Panic.** Desire or craving is an irrational appetite and can be subdivided into the following states: **Want, Hatred, Contentiousness, Anger, and Love.** Pleasure is an irrational elation upon the acquisition of what appears to be preferable. They provided the following sub-classifications: **Ravishment, Malevolent Joy, Delight, and Transport.** While other **philosophers** stated that **man** should apply moderation in controlling his emotions, the Stoics advocated suppressing them completely to avoid disturbances to the soul. If this is achieved, they believed, the result would be a wise, contented, and happy man. They asserted that the wise man is passionless, because he is not prone to fall into such infirmity. But they did add that such a person, in another sense, is not callous or pitiless. The **Stoics** were accused of contributing to behavior leading to **apathy** and stagnation for the individual. They retorted that this would be true only in the case of the **"Bad"** man: not the **"Good"** man.

Furthermore, they believed that **wise men are genuinely earnest and dedicated to their own improvement; following a manner of life which banishes evil and makes what good there is in things apparent.** They stressed honoring one's parents and siblings: after paying homage to **"God"** first. They advised wise men to participate in politics; unlike the **Epicureans,** who counseled against involvement. They were in favor of marriage and children, and admonished that one should: never give allegiance to anything that is false. Also, they would not allow for self-pity and would not make exceptions for anyone. The Stoics would never relax the penalties fixed by law *because they considered that indulgence and pity are marks of a weak mind, which promotes kindness at the expense of "order." Regarding punishment, they did not consider it unwarranted or severe.*[5]

The wise man does all things well and holds that virtues are interrelated; so that the possessor of one is the possessor of all, in as much as they have common principles. It is a tenet of

---

[5]Today's principle of **"Law and Order."**

the Stoics that *between virtue and vice, there is nothing intermediate*; for *just as a stick must be either straight or crooked: so a man must be just or unjust.* Another Stoic tenet is the perpetual exercise of virtue; for virtue can never be lost, and the good man is always utilizing his mind: which is perfect. They also maintained that justice, law, and right reason *exist by Nature and not by convention.* Their definition of love is: "An effort towards friendliness, due to visible beauty--not necessarily that of the body." *Its sole end should be friendship--not bodily enjoyment--*and depends entirely upon an appreciation of what is "beautiful." Of the three kinds of human dispositions: **the Contemplative (Θεωριτικον), the Practical (Πρακτικον), and the Rational (Λογικον),** they declare that we should develop the latter--because **a rational man is expressly produced by Nature for contemplation and action.** The wise man, for reasonable cause, makes his own exit from life: on his country's behalf (in war); for the sake of his friends; or if he suffers from intolerable pain, mutilation, or an incurable disease **(euthanasia).** It is also their doctrine that among the wise there should be a community of wives--with free choice of partners. Under such circumstances we would feel parental affection for all children equally, and the jealousy arising from adultery would be eliminated. Plato advocated the same practice among the **"Guardians"** of his **Republic,** but he discarded the idea in the **Laws. Aristotle** disagreed with the concept from the very beginning. One has to realize that the ancient **Greeks** never afforded women equal rights as achieved in modern times in the Western World. The **Stoics'** expressed views on the political system were similar to those of **Aristotle:** the best form of government was thought to be a mixture of **Democracy, Monarchy, and Aristocracy--**depending upon the society's level of development in terms of virtue, education, and the particular conditions prevailing in the State.

These are, in summary, the views of the **Stoics** in the area of **"Ethics."**[6] They, as well as the **Epicureans,** had a significant impact on their and subsequent generations, until the **Christian Era,** and exercised a considerable influence on the development of Roman law and society. They also affected **Christianity,** in spite of striking contrasts; as there are elements in **Stoicism** that parallel those of **Christianity.** The Stoic felt safe under the protection of **"Nature"--**similar to the Christian concept that **God** is the protector of **man.** Stoicism played a major role throughout the ages in the theological formulation of Christian doctrine--as well as in the actual realization of Christian ideals. Contemporary philosophy has borrowed from **Stoicism,** at least in part, its conviction that **man is closely connected with the entire universe,** and the solidarity of all people is based upon their common nature and the primacy of reason.

THE STOICS DURING ROMAN TIMES

There were quite a number of Roman thinkers who adhered to the principles and ethical values of Stoicism, even though they introduced significant modifications to the original philosophy of Zeno, Chrysippus, and Cleanthes to accommodate the Roman mentality--which was more inclined to look for practical applications. Two Greek individuals, **Panaetius from Rhodes, (c.**

---

[6] Most of the information about the Stoics is extracted from Diogenes Laertius, Reference #8, Book II, pp.111-262

185-110 B.C.) and Poseidonius from Apamaea (c.135-51 B.C.), were the personalities who directed Roman thinkers towards the Stoic philosophy and established what came to be known as the Middle Stoa. They modified the original doctrines and adopted a number of Platonic and Aristotelian concepts that earlier Stoics had rejected. They also were responsible for rejecting preceding Stoic notions of "apathy" and the eradication of pleasure, and instead attached value to external goods. **Panaetius** had influence on the Roman historian **O. Macius Scaevola**, who developed a new theological division: (1) the theology of the poets; (2) the theology of the philosophers; and (3) the theology of the politicians. **Poseidonius**, who was a student at Panaetius' school in Athens, traveled extensively in Egypt, Spain, and elsewhere--finally returning to Greece where he opened his own school of philosophy at Rhodes--in 97 B.C. Poseidonius is perhaps the first of the Greek thinkers of that period who made considerable modifications to the original Stoic tenets, and added empirical evidence to some of the speculative doctrines of earlier philosophers. He was considered a brilliant man and was a prolific writer. Unfortunately, all of his writings perished. He advanced the Platonic concept of the immortality of the soul that the earlier Stoics had rejected, and became known for his outstanding ability to consolidate all this wealth of empirical knowledge and incorporate it into a philosophical system determined to find connections, interrelationships, and harmonies in the physical world. He tried to penetrate and illustrate the rational structure of the universe and the rational development of history. Following the impact of **Panaetius** and **Poseidonius** on the Stoic doctrines, three individuals (two Romans and one Greek) influenced this philosophy further and modified it considerably--well into the new era. These were: **Seneca of Cordoba** (4 B.C to 65 A.D. - a Roman); **Epictetus of Hierapolis**, (a Greek, c. 50 - 138) A.D.); and **Marcus Aurelius** (Roman emperor, 121- 180 A.D.).

Seneca, in his early life, was a tutor and minister in the government of Emperor Nero. He emphasized the practical aspects of philosophy and was more concerned with the practice of virtue within the sphere of ethics than with theoretical investigations into its nature. He did not seek intellectual knowledge for its own sake, but pursued philosophy as a means to the achievement of virtue. Philosophy is necessary, he contended, but it is to be pursued with a practical end in view. He developed a series of ethical doctrines relating to virtue, which encompassed the old Stoic ethic and made a significant contribution to ethical and moral philosophy. Of course, his voice and the voice of other philosophers who strongly advocated moral and ethical standards, was not heeded by the Roman world--which deteriorated into an immoral, cruel, and materialistic environment leading to its demise, and eventually ushering the world into the medieval Dark Ages (See Chapter 1 for a wider discussion on Seneca).

Epictetus of Hierapolis was a Greek slave who bought his freedom and left Rome to establish a school of philosophy in Nicopolis, Epirus (outside the city limits of the modern city of Preveza). He taught the Stoic doctrines--which he drastically modified. In the area of ethics he taught that God has given to all men the capacity and means to develop virtue, happiness, steadfast character, and self-control. He stated that man's nature is not to bite, kick, punish, and behead, but rather to do good, to cooperate with others and wish them well. He believed that all men have sufficient innate

259

moral intuitions on which they can build a virtuous life. He advised people, in order to understand themselves, to observe those they praise without partiality: Are they just or unjust; moderate or immoderate; temperate or intemperate. Epictetus is distinguished as the author of the **Egheiridion (Handbook- Εγχειρίδιον)**, an extant primer for moral and ethical behavior available in any library.

Marcus Aurelius--a Roman Emperor from 161 A.D. to 180 A.D. He was a Stoic philosopher who recorded his thoughts and convictions in 12 books in Greek titled **Meditations**. Marcus Aurelius admired Epictetus and was considerably influenced by him in the area of philosophy and ethics. He taught that "*It is man's duty to feel compassion for human infirmity*"; and "*It is man's special gift to love even those who transgress.*" This should happen the very moment we realize that: men are brothers; sin results from ignorance and is unintentional; and in a short time--we shall all be dead. That above all, no injury should befall us; so that our inner self is not made worse that it was before. He posed the following question: "*Does the eye demand compensation for seeing or the feet for walking? Just as this is the end for which they exist, and just as they find their reward in realizing the law of their being, so too, man is made for kindness; and whenever he performs an act of kindness or otherwise helps forward the common good, he thereby fulfills the law of his being and comes into his own.*" [7]

The entire work of **Meditations** survived and can be found at any library today. Notice the resemblance between the basic tenets of Epictetus and Marcus Aurelius on ethics, as compared with those advocated by Christians. Nevertheless, Marcus Aurelius--acknowledged as one of the five **good** Roman emperors--allowed the persecution of Christians because he could not reconcile their Christian doctrines, which paid allegiance to God—over and above the Roman Empire.

---

[7](Meditations 9.42)

SOPHISTRY

YOU SAY THE WORDS I WANT TO HEAR,
AND YET THE SOUND RINGS HOLLOW,
AND TOO THE SMILE THAT GLIDES ABOUT,
BUT STILL I WANT TO FOLLOW.

WHY DOES MY MIND NOT HEED THE CALL
OF PRUDENCE, AND RETREAT?
INSTEAD, I AM ACKNOWLEDGING
THE VOICE OF PURE DECEIT.

KALYPSO

VAGABOND

I DO NOT NEED THE COMFORTS
OF A HOME AND HEARTH TO WARM,
A BED WITH DOWNY COVERS,
OR A PRETTY GIRL TO CHARM.

JUST LEAVE A FALLEN MORSEL
ON THE ROAD, IF I MAY ASK,
AND ANY EMPTY BARREL,
ONE THAT I MAY USE TO BASK.

THE MERCHANTS DO NOT LOVE ME,
FOR I CAST THEM NOT A GLANCE,
BUT ALL THE DOGS BEFRIEND ME;
ONLY PEOPLE LOOK ASKANCE.

KALYPSO

SUBTERFUGE

YOU SAY THE FACTS
ARE VERY CLEAR,
NO REASON TO DISPUTE,
BUT WHAT IS IT
YOU HAVE TO GAIN
IF ONE DOES NOT REFUTE?

YOU SAY THE FACTS
ARE VERY CLEAR,
AND DO PROMOTE YOUR CAUSE,
BUT WHAT IS IT BEHIND THE PAGE
THAT OUGHT TO MAKE ME PAUSE?

KALYPSO

CHAPTER 14

THE PHILOSOPHY OF THE SKEPTICS AND THE CYNICS

"The love of money is the mother-city of all evils."
Diogenes

INTRODUCTION

The concepts of **Skepticism** and **Cynicism,** which relate to man's natural doubt that apparent evidence reflects **truth** and **reality,** and to some men's contempt for excessive and unnecessary means, have existed in organized societies since their beginnings. They reflect man's experiences in life: that often outcomes do not meet expectations; and the realization that his needs could be satisfied with fewer resources and effort. Characteristic of this is Socrates' comment, while going through the market and seeing so many things for sale: **"How many things I have no need of!"** Skepticism and Cynicism also developed out of man's inability to remove the impediments which hinder the discovery of Nature's secrets and man's "being."

As we indicated earlier, the objective of the first Greek philosophers, from the time of Thales, was to unlock the secrets of Nature and answer such questions as: Why does it rain; why the sun rises in the east and sets in the west without fail; why the moon shines at night; why the planets follow different paths in the firmament from that of the stars, and--what are things made of? Understandably, the process of providing answers to these questions is a very difficult one indeed, and passes through stages. Different explanations are given at one time, and later repudiated, amended, adjusted, or eliminated; to be substituted with new ones. As we have seen in preceding pages, Greek scholars--who were concerned with problems in the social and behavioral environment--were also seeking answers to such questions as: What is the best way that one should lead his life; the best political and educational system, and the ideal role of various members in the society. Again, answers to these questions varied, and individuals gave responses which were adjusted, revised, repudiated--and altogether abandoned later. **So then: What is the truth? And what explanations should one believe?** Can we ever really **"know"** the correct answer to these questions?

261

In spite of considerable advances and understanding of some of the secrets of Nature and of the social environment in the 21st century, we are still far away from fully answering, with certainty, all questions in the physical, social, and behavioral world. We essentially have solved all of the important questions pertaining to our solar system, in that we understand and can predict the movements of planets, satellites, and the sun; but we still do not understand what magnetism or electricity **is,** even though we can measure their reactions. Also, we may have advanced considerably in the area of medicine, preventing death from bacterial and infectious diseases, but we have not been able to combat cancer or viruses effectively: even though we have traveled to the moon and returned to Earth. We remain mystified in fully understanding how the universe works; what it is; how it was created, and what its future is. We are still searching-- trying to understand our environment and our souls. We have developed systems which we hoped would provide peace, stability, prosperity, and tranquility among people and nations; yet we find that the scourge of war, crime, poverty, exploitation, starvation, anarchy, injustice, unethical and immoral behavior, and serious instability persist today—intranationally and internationally.

Mykonos

Apart, then, from established truths (knowledge) substantiated by evidence supported by our senses--e.g., the use of electricity and magnetism in creating machines, and some advances in communication, transportation and use of atomic physics--uncertainty still persists: maybe to no less an extent than during the time of the ancient Skeptics. Skepticism continues today, perhaps even stronger than the doctrines embraced during the time of **Antisthenes**, the father of **Cynicism**; or **Pyrrho**, the father of **Skepticism**.

The original Skeptics claimed that knowledge is only an untested **hypothesis** with concomitant **Type I** and **Type II errors:** if we respectively reject them--and they are true (**Type I**), or we accept them--and they are false **(Type II).** When, for example, at the beginning of the last century, Marxian doctrine stated that societal strife would cease with the elimination of private property, the Skeptic would have claimed, at the collapse of the experiment (the demise of the Soviet Union), that it was a **Type II error.** There have been a number of Type II errors throughout the years, particularly in ancient times, that we are in a position to recognize today, which were committed as a result of man's effort to understand himself and his environment.

Skepticism, in ancient times, raised questions about the validity of knowledge and religious beliefs espoused during this period--which contributed to debunking the myth of the Olympic Gods. There were a number of skeptics such as: **Xenophanes, Socrates, Anaxagoras, Empedocles,**

Democritus, *et al.,* who had serious doubts that blind acceptance of religious dogma was valid. The division of Christianity from its original form of Orthodoxy—into Catholicism and Protestantism—resulted from the assaults of skeptic heresies on the original doctrines.

With this as a background for the establishment and **"raison d'etre"** of Skepticism and Cynicism, we proceed to discuss these **Schools of Thought** as they were developed and practiced by their main proponents (from the time of the Sophists throughout the Hellenistic period). These two Schools had a strong influence on the thinking of scholars and intellectuals of ancient times, as well as on thinkers of future generations. One can say that they continued to affect "dogmatic" philosophies, religion, and established practices during medieval times, the Renaissance, and subsequently.

The God Dionysus

The Skeptics doubted **knowledge, truth--and man's capacity for learning.** Differences and contradictions in perceptions of social and physical phenomena convinced them to suspend judgment on knowledge. As a matter of fact, one of the Skeptics, **Aenisidemus** (1st century B.C.), developed a list of "contradictions" (**Τροποι**) concerning man, Nature, and the social system, to substantiate their doctrines.

The Cynics developed a theory of life based upon the principle: **Man can live with minimum goods and services.** An organized society places too heavy a burden on him by making life unreasonably difficult and complicated. The Cynics were using as an example--the dog--which requires the least to survive; and advocated that man should pursue such a life. It was from the name "dog" in Greek **(Κυων=Dog)** that they came to be known as **"Cynics" (Κυνικοι).** Neither the Cynics nor the Skeptics acquired or built an edifice or school in which to deliver lessons for pay--as was the case with all other philosophical groups. In fact, their main representative, **Diogenes,** lived in a tub (See picture on p.272). Their doctrines were mostly exemplified by their life-styles--which were indeed **frugal and undemanding.**

THE SKEPTIC PHILOSOPHERS[1]

We address the philosophy of the Skeptics first, and present some information about the proponents of this philosophical School, to be followed by a summary of the Cynics' philosophy--using the same order and format. **Skepticism** (*lack of confidence in apparent truth*) originated with

---

[1]Most of the information about the personal experiences of the Skeptics and Cynics is provided by Diogenes Laertius. See Reference #8, Volume II.

the Eleats, who challenged the doctrines of the Ionians, and progressed further with the Sophists, the Socratics, and others subsequently. The Academy, in its later years, was completely dominated by Skeptics, and a significant number of them, advocating that brand of philosophy, flourished. Beginning with the 3rd century A.D., a new Skeptic current appears with **Aenisidemus** and **Sextrus Empiricus**, who lived in the latter part of the 2nd century A.D. and wrote the broad outlines of Skepticism (Πυρρωνειων λογων). We present two of the main Skeptic philosophers: **Pyrrho**, the founder; and **Timon**, his student.

The Satyr in good Humor

PYRRHO.   Pyrrho was born in the city of Elis, in Peloponnesus, in the year 360 B.C., and died there 90 years later. Initially he was a painter, but very poor, and soon he abandoned painting and pursued other activities. According to some writers, he accompanied Alexander on his campaign to Asia where he came in contact with Indian philosophers, as well as the **Chaldean Magi,** and became acquainted with Oriental beliefs and practices. It is perhaps from this experience that he developed his philosophy of **"agnosticism."** He led a life consistent with this doctrine, maintaining the same composure at all times; so that even if left alone in the middle of a speech, he would finish--without an audience. He was so respected by his native city of Elis, that they bestowed on him great honors and voted that all philosophers should be tax-exempt. There is the following story related about him: Once, when aboard a ship, a fierce storm erupted and the ship tilted so dangerously that everyone was panicked. Pyrrho remained calm and confident, and pointing to a pig that was eating and oblivious to the commotion, said: **"This is the undisturbed life that a wise man should secure for himself."** He had a great number of students who distinguished themselves--particularly Timon.

Pyrrho followed a life resembling that of a recluse, living in solitude and **avoiding even his own relatives.** Occasionally, he left home without telling anyone his destination, and kept company with whomever he would find on his way. He followed an approach to life similar to that of the Indian philosophers (**Gymnosophists, Fakirs**), and related that once he heard an Indian philosopher state that it would be impossible to teach his way of life, and yet be patronized by kings in their courts.

Pyrrho had a number of students; the most famous of these being: **Hecataeus of Abdera, Timon from Flios, and Nausiphanes from Teos.** They came to be known as the **"Pyrrhoneans,"** after the name of their master. But they were also known by other names, derived from the principles of their philosophy, and these were: **"Aporetics,"** from the Greek word **"AΠOPEIN" (wonder); "Skeptics" (inquirers),** from the Greek verb ΣΚΕΠΤΕΣΘΑΙ, because they were always seeking a solution to a problem, but not finding one; **"Ephectics"** (**Doubters**), because of the state of mind which followed their inquiry, and **"Zetetics,"** from the Greek verb (Ζητειν=inquire) **"seeking,"** because they were always pursuing the truth.

TIMON

Timon was born in the city of Flios, in the year 320 B.C., and died in Athens 90 years later. He was the one who established the Skeptic School in Athens, after the death of Pyrrho. When he was young he lost his parents and became a stage dancer and actor in the theater, but soon developed a dislike of this profession and left for Megara. Eventually he went to Illida with his wife, where he met and became a student of Pyrrho.

The Island of Poros

He composed iambic poetry and theatrical plays, and when economic conditions were bleak he practiced rhetoric. This indicates that he was offering lessons or writing defenses or position papers for court cases for pay. It was only after he earned money in this area that he established himself in Athens--where he lived until his death. Timon was an accomplished gardener and preferred to mind his own affairs. *They used to say that among philosophers there were those who recruited students by "pursuing them," and those who attracted students by "fleeing from them." Timon was one of the latter.* He was perceptive and scornful--fond of writing and good at sketching plots for poets and dramatic writers.

THE SKEPTIC PHILOSOPHY

The Skeptic philosophy derives its name from the Greek word **"ΣΚΕΠΤΕΣΘΑΙ,"** which means: **"to reflect"; "to theorize"; "to submit to scrutiny."** This verb implies that one should question a proposition and reject its veracity unless a full investigation verifying its validity is carried out. The idea of doubting the true nature of things was not really developed by Pyrrho; as previous philosophers had expressed doubt about the validity of knowledge. Heraclitus had proclaimed that **"Everything is in a state of flux"**; therefore, it would be difficult to have solid opinions about things that will not be tomorrow what they are today. Also, the Sophists had been influential relating to the notion of skepticism; as one of their representatives, Gorgias stated: *"Nothing is true and nothing exists."* Socrates too, when once asked to respond to the Delphic Oracle's pronouncement that he was the wisest of men, replied: **"One thing I know--that I know nothing."** Thus, the notion of doubting the validity of doctrines, opinions, or ideas had been introduced by pre-Socratic thinkers--and by Socrates himself. Throughout the centuries Skeptics had developed arguments to undermine the contentions of dogmatic philosophers, scientists, and theologians. Their arguments against various forms of dogmatism have played an important role in shaping both questions and solutions offered in the course and development of Western philosophy.

As ancient philosophers, thinkers, and scientists were enunciating their theories and principles, doubts started developing about conventional views of the world, particularly when contradictory views were introduced. The Skeptics challenged the claims of all ancient philosophical schools, including: **Platonism, Aristotelianism, Stoicism, and Epicureanism.** Skepticism developed in tandem with various disciplines in which men claimed to have knowledge. It was questioned, for example, whether one could gain knowledge from metaphysics or the sciences--due to the uncertainty of observation and the *inherent lack of experimentation.*

They strongly opposed the possibility of serious progress in the area of medicine, and questioned whether one could establish with certainty the causes of, or cures for, diseases. In the area of "Ethics," the Skeptics rejected various mores and customs--claiming that it would be impossible to make objective value distinctions. They also attacked religion by challenging the doctrines of theology, claiming that no knowledge can be gained beyond the world of experience; and that one cannot discover the causes of most physical and social phenomena. Their main tenet was: *all things are equally uncertain and in substance unknown to us;* and therefore, we should be **"indifferent"** to them. Our understanding and conception of "things" is **neither right nor wrong.** The Skeptic would prefer to leave physical and other phenomena alone, and neither support nor refute them; but rather accept them as they appear and draw conclusions about them only so far as their obvious characteristics imply. For example: *Fire burns; it is admitted that it does so, but this is the only conclusion that the Skeptic would reach. He does not care to go beyond this admission-- analyzing what else fire can be or do.*

Skeptics differ from the Stoics, in that the Stoics accepted rationality as the preferred method of explaining our external world. An ethical approach to life--devoid of passion and sentiment--is their basic tenet. The Skeptics, however, maintained that some emotions and passions are so deeply based that it is impossible to uproot them by a simple command from the brain; therefore: *moderation--rather than complete eradication of emotions and passions--is required.* The Epicureans employed the concept of "indifference" in viewing material things, in order to achieve ethical behavior, but demanded "emancipation" from fear; while, in the case of the Skeptics, **indifference** to fear is sought, due to the fact that *it is impossible to eradicate fear.* Both the Stoics and the Epicureans pursued knowledge, but the Skeptics resigned from the search. They believed that all misery in man results from disturbances that occur: either because of an **intense pursuit** of some objective or from an **intensive effort to escape from one.** They claimed that other dogmatic philosophers desperately seek what they consider **good,** and avoid what they consider **evil;** but in truth, they claim, **we really do not know what constitutes good and what constitutes evil.** They proposed that we should abolish that which is considered "true" or "virtuous" because **truth means nothing certain** and can become harmful. Their basic position is that we will never comprehend the inner relationships of Nature and the soul of man; therefore, it is absurd to accept any theoretical definitions with complete certainty. There are quite a number of things which appear to be of a certain kind, but in reality are not; or things do not appear to be--but are. Based upon this principle, suggested by the Stoic philosopher **Epictetus,** the Skeptics developed their **Ten Modes of Contradiction (Τροποι,)** in which they demonstrate how things appear to be-- but are not.

THE TEN MODES OF CONTRADICTION

One must realize, by now, that the Skeptics were unwilling to accept the subjective claims of various theories, misleading concepts, and doctrines advocated by various schools--or abide by dogmatic positions. Their work was further curtailed by the lack of tools needed for laboratory research to prove hypotheses and establish truths--particularly in the physical world. It was a time when the results of laboratory research were first surfacing, and scientists in Syracuse, with **Archimedes** as the leader, began mechanical experiments and developed machines that were used effectively in practical applications. The scientists in **Alexandria, headed by Eratosthenes, Euclid, Hero,** and others, were developing automated systems by using steam or compressed air.[2] The ten "Modes of Contradiction" (Differences), as developed by **Aenisidemus,** are:

1. Differences between types of living beings imply different and so relative "ideas" of same object.
2. Differences between individual men imply the same.
3. The different structure and presentation of our various senses.
4. The differences between our various states, for example: walking or sleeping; youth or age.
5. Differences of perspectives.
6. The objects of perception are never presented in their purity; a medium is always involved,
7. Differences in perception due to differences in quality.
8. Relativity, in general.
9. Differences in impression due to frequency or infrequency of occurrence.
10. Different ways of life, moral codes, laws, myths, philosophic systems, etc.

The first four **"Modes of Contradiction"** address the limits of knowledge due to differences within the same species; for example--variations in animals and man--and how one can be deceived by circumstances that are not always as they seem: Some creatures procreate with intercourse; while others do not. Some are distinguished in one way; some in another--and for this reason they differ in their senses also. Hawks, for instance, are keen-sighted, and dogs have an acute sense of smell. It is natural, then, that if the senses (seeing or other) in animals differ, so also will their response to their surroundings. For the goat, vine-shoots are good to eat; to man, they are bitter.

---

[2] See the Introduction for information related to the mechanical achievements of Hellenistic engineers and of the pioneers in applied science in **Alexandria** and **Syracuse.**

The next six Modes address differences resulting from combining elements: differences in quality; variations in Nature; coincidences and circumstances; and, in conclusion, ethics. Some situations that would confound Skeptics, forcing them to suspend judgment, would include: The same action is regarded by some as just, and by others as unjust; or as good by some and bad by others. Persians did not consider it unnatural for a man to marry his daughter; Greeks did. Some cultures had wives in common; the Greeks did not. Different people adhered to different traditions and practices. For example, in disposing of their dead, the Egyptians embalmed them; the Persians burned them; the Phoenicians threw them over a sacred lake, and the Greeks buried them. When mixing elements, nothing is distinguished by itself, but only in combination with: air, light, moisture, solidity, heat, cold, movement, exhalations, and other forces. The color purple exudes different tints in sunlight, moonlight, and lamplight; and our own complexion does not appear the same at noon and at sundown. With reference to distance, position, and place, large things may appear small; square things round; flat things projected; straight things bent, and colorless colored. The sun, relative to its distance, appears small; mountains, when far away, appear misty and smooth--but when near at hand, rugged. Furthermore, at sunrise the sun has a certain appearance-- at midday another--and the same body, viewed from a wood or open country, differs still. The image again varies according to the position of the object: a dove's neck--according to the way it is turned. With reference to things being light or heavy; strong or weak; more or less; up or down: that which is on the right is not so by Nature, but rather by virtue of its position relative to something else; and if that position changes, the object is no longer on the right: Day is relative to the sun--and all things are relative to our mind. Thus: *relative things are intrinsically **unknowable**.*

Questions raised by the Skeptics in ancient times--concerning the social, behavioral, and physical world--are, in some ways, still concerning us today: but we have learned to accept uncertainties without suspending judgment. However, the important point is that the Skeptics were establishing the foundation for modern science, because--in the Greek tradition--they were questioning **"why"** events occur in a certain manner, which naturally promoted an environment of doubt. They were not willing to accept conventional wisdom; instead, choosing to challenge foolish explanations and theocratic interpretations.

THE CYNIC AND NEO-CYNIC PHILOSOPHY

The **Cynic** philosophy had its beginning during, or shortly before, the time of Socrates-- about 450 B.C. It was established by a student of Socrates, **Antisthenes** from Athens, who set the foundation, which is based on complete self-denial and an orientation towards simplicity, self sufficiency-- and total dependence on Nature. The **Cynics,** unlike other established schools of philosophy, did not have a physical edifice or research facility similar to a university today. Instead, their philosophy was formulated by the writings of one of their greatest proponents, **Diogenes,** and exemplified by their lifestyle. During Hellenistic times it was known also as the Neo-Cynic School, which modified the original examples of Antisthenes and Diogenes and molded their teachings towards conformity to various life situations. The Cynics of the Hellenistic period compared life to a theatrical play, where each one performs his role under the direction of God and Fate. They remained individualistic and cosmopolitan, but ridiculed religion, science, civilization--and even life itself--because they proclaimed that: **Life is short, and therefore should not be taken seriously.** They showed a special interest in satire, and the most known Cynics of this period were **Menedemus** and **Menippus.**

The Cynics disdained the pleasures of life, and declared war against organized society and the affluent classes. They proclaimed their own ethical "standards" and were influential in this respect, proclaiming religion and philosophy: "morally bankrupt." We review the lives of the two major representatives of this philosophy or way of life, and in doing so provide additional information about their doctrines. The following were the most well-known Cynics of ancient times:

Antisthenes

Antisthenes	**446-366 B.C.**
Diogenes	**404-323 B.C.**
Monimus	**4th century B.C.**
Onesicritus	**Approx. 330 B.C.**
Crates	**Approx. 326 B.C.**
Hipparchia	**(Crates' wife) c. 300 B.C.**
Menippus	**?**
Menedemus	**?[3]**

ANTISTHENES

Antisthenes was a student of the Sophist Gorgias, and during his early life followed Sophist doctrines. Later, however, he abandoned the Sophists and became a student of Socrates: they never forgave him for that. He lived in Piraeus, but was commuting to Athens daily to attend Socrates' lectures, and was the only Socratic student who remained in Athens after his death. For a time he practiced the art of rhetoric, defending or prosecuting cases in the courts. He was a talented writer and composed a number of tragedies and poems--but nothing exists today. He wrote extensive essays and treatises on philosophy, criticizing Plato because he opposed his idealistic views. Antisthenes' teachings essentially were concerned with how man should behave and order his life. He followed the Socratic (Delphic) concept, **"Know thyself,"** which he considered a virtue in which **one would find "happiness, self sufficiency, and self-respect."** However, he did not equate virtue with

---

[3] **Diogenes Laertius** mentions the names of these two Cynic philosophers, but he does not give the time of their birth or death. Usually he provides information about the lives of ancient scholars by mentioning the Olympiad held during the period of their lives, but not in this case.

knowledge--the Platonic tenet--because he suspected irrational forces in the soul of man. Instead, he lectured that the road that leads to happiness is through **work, hardship,** and **self discipline.** Ethical prudence is the prerequisite of virtue; but for Antisthenes the Socratic quest for **"knowledge"** takes second place, because he believed that: **hard work is essential for self-discipline.** He acknowledged intelligence, however, because he considered *pure virtue the by-product of true intelligence.*

The idea of **"being,"** independent of external factors, was fundamental for Antisthenes' claim that **"self sufficiency"** is the **"sine qua non"** for happiness. As for hedonism: *he would prefer to die than be driven by passion.* He sought the **measured satisfaction of needs,** and claimed that, for man to be "free," he must contain his needs and desires as much as possible. The wise man in society behaves according to the **"Law of Virtue"**--not written laws--and emancipates himself from all legal and religious requirements: depending entirely on the **Law of the Mind.** He used to say: *"He who has virtue does not need knowledge."* Antisthenes rejected science and the arts; and his indifference to geometry and other scientific achievements made him an adversary of science and technology. *"We should return to physical simplicity and self-sufficiency,"* he argued. He opposed the polytheistic system of religion, and claimed only **one God.** Many opponents, particularly the Sophists, persecuted him for having abandoned their movement. Plato also opposed his "simple and naive" philosophy, because Antisthenes had rejected his "Theory of Ideas." He died in 366 B.C., in Athens, at the age of 80.

Some personal musings about Antisthenes, saved by Diogenes Laertius, include the following: Antisthenes was critical of the daily affairs, disputes, and idiosyncrasies of his contemporaries, and developed the reputation (mid-5th century B.C.) of being a caustic critic of the political, social, and behavioral life of Athenians--similar to that of Diogenes, a century later. When Antisthenes opened a school of philosophy in Athens around the latter part of the 5th century B.C., a young man from Pontus was about to attend his lectures and asked what was required; the answer was: *"Come with a new book, a new pen, and new tablet--if you have a mind also."* When someone inquired what sort of wife he ought to marry, Antisthenes replied: *"If she is beautiful, you will not have her to yourself; if she is ugly, you will be penalized"* "άν μέν καλην, εξεις κοινην, αν δε αισχραν, εξεις ποινην" (which plays with the words κοινην= common and ποινην= punishment). Being told that Plato was abusing him, he remarked: *"It is a royal privilege to do good and be ill spoken of."* When he was being initiated into the Orphic mysteries, the priest said that those admitted into these rites would be partakers of many good things in Hades. "Why then," said he, "don't you die"? Being reproached because his parents were not both free-born: "Nor were they both wrestlers," he responded, "but yet I am a wrestler." One day, upon seeing an adulterer running for his life, he exclaimed: *"Poor wretch, what peril you might have escaped at the price of an obol."* (a meager monetary denomination). He used to say: **"It is better to fall in with crows than with flatterers, for in the one case you are devoured when you are dead; in the other case, while alive."** *As iron is eaten away by rust, so,* said he, *the envious are consumed by their own passion.* When he was asked what advantage had accrued to him from philosophy, his answer was: **"The ability to converse with myself."** He advised that men should endure slander more courageously than if they were pelted with stones. He used to recommend to the Athenians that they vote the donkeys as horses. When they deemed it absurd, his reply was: *"But yet generals are found among you who have no training but were merely elected."* The following sayings are attributed to Antisthenes: *"To the wise man nothing is foreign or impractical. A good man deserves to be loved. Men of worth are friends. Make allies of men who are at once brave and just. Virtue is a weapon that cannot be taken away. It is better to be with a handful of good men fighting against all the bad, than with hosts of bad men against a handful of good. Pay attention to your enemies, for they are the first to discover your mistakes. Virtue is the same for women as for men. Good actions are fair; and evil actions foul. Count all wickedness foreign and alien."*[4]

DIOGENES OF SINOPE

He was born of Greek parentage in the city of **Sinope, in Asia Minor,** and moved to Athens at an early age. Some say that either he or his father defrauded a local bank, and as a result was banished from Sinope. He was a student of Antisthenes; and while Antisthenes was a measured

Diogenes the Cynic

philosopher, Diogenes became an extremist in Cynic philosophy. He was, in essence, the bold ideologue of the Cynic School, and introduced a **completely free style of living.** He had contempt for theoretical philosophy and science in general, and wanted philosophy to serve practical needs--not lofty concepts and ideals. He also considered the core of his philosophy to be "virtue," which would coincide with a **simple, natural life.** *He exemplified, by his behavior and style of living, the epitome of self-sufficiency and self-contentment; so much so, that for a time he lived in a tub.* He exhibited contempt for the mores of society, and had no respect for societal practices in general—to the extent that he was satisfying his physical needs in public. His message was that **everything in society should be turned upside down** and the system of values re-evaluated: pitting Nature against law; and passion against intelligence. He argued often with the rich and held them in contempt. He branded Plato's "ideal" philosophy as "utopian;" and rejected all other philosophical structures and schools at his time, snubbed social and political life, noble backgrounds, glory, and wealth. He advocated a primitive society where all men, women, and children would live together. Diogenes wrote quite a number of treatises on various subjects, and had many students; among those known were: **Crates, Onisikritus, and Monimus.** Later in his life he was bought as a slave by a rich Corinthian, and served as a tutor for his children. He lived in Corinth and died there in 323 B.C.--the same year that Alexander died.

---

[4]See Ref.8, Diogenes Laertius, Vol.2, pp. 12-14.

When Diogenes arrived in Athens, in exile, he went to Antisthenes and asked him to accept him as his student; Antisthenes refused but Diogenes persisted. One day Antisthenes raised his staff, ready to strike him, when Diogenes said: *"Go ahead and strike me; but you will find that there is no wood strong enough to keep me away from you as long as you have something to offer."* From that day on, he became his pupil. He was known for expressing contempt and scorn for his contemporaries. The school of Euclides, he called **"bilious"**; Plato's lectures, **"A waste of time"**; the performances at the Dionyssus Theater, **"Great peep-shows for fools"**; and demagogues, **"the mob's lackeys."** He also said that when he viewed *physicians, philosophers, and pilots at their work, he deemed man the most intelligent of all animals; but when he saw interpreters of dreams, diviners and their attendants, and those who were puffed up with conceit of wealth: he thought no animal was sillier."* Once, when he was speaking seriously in public and no one paid attention, he began whistling, and as people clustered around him, he reproached them for coming in all haste to hear "nonsense" (whistling), but paying no attention when the subject was serious.

Alexander and Diogenes

One day he shouted, **"Men!"** and when people turned he lashed out at them with his stick, saying: **"It was men I called for; not scoundrels."** Upon observing a child drinking out of his hands, he threw away his cup and proclaimed: *"A child has beaten me in plainness of life."* Seeing a woman kneeling before the gods in an ungraceful posture, and wishing to free her from superstition, he came forward and said: *"Are you not afraid, my good woman, that a god may be standing behind you? For all things are full of his presence, and you may be put to shame."* While sunning himself at the Craneum, Alexander approached and stood over him and said: **"Ask of me anything you like,"** to which Diogenes replied: **"Move away from my light!"** When Lysias, the druggist, asked him if he believed in the gods; he replied: *"How can I help believing in them, when I see a god-forsaken wretch like you?"* One day, in broad daylight, he took a lantern and roamed the streets. When asked what he was doing, he replied that he was looking for: **"one real man."** Still, he was loved by the Athenians. Once, when a youngster destroyed the tub in which he was living, they gave the boy a flogging and presented him with a new one. It was said that, after the battle at Chaeronea, he was seized and dragged off to Philip II (father of Alexander the Great) and asked to identify himself; he replied: **"A spy upon your insatiable greed."** For this, he was admired and set free. He once saw temple officials leading away someone who had stolen a bowl belonging to the Treasury, and said: **"The great thieves are leading away the petty thief."** Being asked why athletes are so stupid, his answer was: **"Because they are built of pork and beef."** When asked what creature's bite is the worst, he said: **"Of those that are tame, a flatterer's; of those**

272

that are wild, a sycophant's." Being asked whether death was an evil thing, he replied: "How can it be evil, when in its presence we are not aware of it?" When Alexander stood opposite him and chided: *"Are you not afraid of me?"....* "Why, what are you," said he, "a good thing or a bad?" Upon Alexander replying: *"A good thing."* **"Who then,"** said Diogenes, **"is afraid of a good thing?"** Being asked what is the most beautiful thing in the world, he replied: **"Freedom of speech."** One day he saw the son of a courtesan throwing rocks at passers-by: **"Watch out, lad,"** Diogenes said, **"you may hit your father!"**

Both Skeptic and Cynic philosophers had a strong influence on Roman philosophers, as well as those of the Renaissance and current times. These were the thinkers who cast doubt on man's dogmatic beliefs and one-sided determinism. They encouraged people to distinguish what is really true from what appears to be. They meant to instruct people on how to emancipate themselves from materialistic needs and survive with less. Of course there are Cynics and Skeptics today, and there will always be as long as man has not been able to eradicate injustice, poverty, racism, chauvinism, conflict, and despair—to achieve a complete understanding of the physical world around him and of the inner relationships of his **psyche**.

With this we conclude a bird's-eye view of Greek philosophy--from the time of Thales to the advent of the Skeptics and Cynics. Admittedly, this is a condensed coverage of the subject and of each one of the topics discussed in this work; there are hundreds of books available that can provide an in-depth study. The purpose of this work, however, is intended for lay people who have limited knowledge of the subject, and have heard so much about these individuals--but have not had an opportunity to familiarize themselves with their accomplishments. In the next two chapters a brief discussion of the pre-Hellenic civilizations is presented. The purpose of this discussion is to acquaint the reader with developments prior to the Greeks, and gain an understanding of the level of science and philosophy in Egypt, Babylon, Sumeria, and other civilizations. These early societies had an influence on pre-Socratic philosophers, as well as on Hellenistic thinkers. Admittedly, the discussion is short and does not do justice to the subject; but ample references are provided in the bibliography for those readers who wish to delve deeper into this topic.

SENTRY

THIS ROCK HAS LAIN FOR CENTURIES,
AND HUGS ITS MOTHER, EARTH,
LISTENING FOR THE FOOTSTEPS
OF THOSE WHO TREAD ITS TURF.

IT HAS WITNESSED COUNTLESS BATTLES,
MANY WON AND MANY LOST;
I WONDER IF IT MEASURES
THE GRIEVING AND THE COST.

THE BONES THAT LIE BENEATH IT
ARE A TESTAMENT TO MAN,
AND HIS RECURRENT STRUGGLE
THAT LONG AGO BEGAN.

THIS ROCK HAS NEVER VENTURED,
IT MUST BE MOVED BY FORCE;
PERHAPS THIS TOO IS WISDOM
FROM YET ANOTHER SOURCE.

KALYPSO

CHIASMA

THREE RIVERS OFFERED WATER,
AND SHORES WITH FERTILE SOIL;
THE TIGRIS AND EUPHRATES
WERE FIRST TO HOST MAN'S TOIL.

SUMERIANS SET LUNAR MONTHS,
AND CODIFIED THEIR LAWS;
EGYPTIANS NEAR THE RIVER NILE
MADE PYRAMIDS THEIR CAUSE.

THREE RIVERS AIDED HARVEST;
THREE RIVERS PROFFERED PEACE;
AND EACH ONE WITTNESSED PROGRESS
AS KNOWLEDGE DID INCREASE.

KALYPSO

CHAPTER 15

THE EARLY CIVILIZATIONS

**"The misfortune of the wise is
better than the prosperity of the fool."
Epicurus**

INTRODUCTION

Ever since man abandoned a primitive, nomadic life and decided to settle in a place permanently, the most important element needed for such a life was water. Without water nothing can grow; plant or animal or man himself; and consequently, the first civilizations that appeared on this planet must have started and developed near rivers. The most famous of these that we know of today, which left traces of their appearance and existence, are those that flourished near three rivers of the Middle East and Northeast Africa: **the Nile, the Tigris,** and **the Euphrates.** The civilizations that progressed near these rivers, based on scientific evidence, appeared almost simultaneously around the period that started with the 5th millennium B.C.; even though the people who lived in these areas most likely had resided there for a much longer time period. These were: the **Egyptians,** near the river Nile; the **Sumerians, Akkadians, Babylonians, Chaldeans, Assyrians**, and later the **Persians** et al.--situated near the Tigris and Euphrates rivers. In this chapter we discuss the Egyptians first, and then continue with the Sumerians--followed by the Babylonians, Assyrians, Phoenicians, and Persians in chapter 16. Due to Alexander's invasion into India, it is believed that the Indian philosophies of **Jainism** and **Buddhism** may have influenced the Hellenistic philosophers; and for this reason a short review of these philosophies is presented in the next chapter.

THE EGYPTIANS[1]

The Egyptians flourished as a civilization from approximately 4500 B.C. until around the 7th century B.C., when they were conquered by the Persians, subsequently by the Greeks and Romans--and finally by the Arabs. They lived on either side of the river Nile, but predominantly around the area of the Delta, which is approximately 20,000 square kilometers. As they advanced and grew in population, they moved south and eventually extended beyond the Aswan area and the first cataract to the area of Abu Simbel, where they were halted--probably by local

---

[1] Most of the information regarding the Egyptians comes from **Herodotus**, Books I, II (see reference #6), and also reference #5.

tribes or extreme desert conditions. (See Map 6). The Egyptian system of government was dominated by the **Pharaohs** and the **Priests.** The Pharaoh was an inherited king; and this monarchical system continued throughout the ages in an absolute oligarchic manner, unaltered until the very end. It did not exhibit any serious evolutionary flexibility over centuries, as one might expect, because the system was highly theocratic and completely dominated by the priests. The priests lived in Thebes, the capital, secluded in the temples of Karnak and Luxor, from

The Royal Symbol of the Falcon

where they exercised absolute control of State affairs century after century. The concepts of political liberties, freedom, choice, and democracy were foreign elements in their civilization. The Egyptians, however, made important advances in architecture, medicine, mathematics, astronomy, engineering, building, agriculture--and many other areas. The construction of the **Pyramids of Gizah** (one of the **Seven Wonders** of the ancient world) is considered, even today, as an unparalleled engineering marvel that is admired and praised. Their achievements in medicine and anatomy are extraordinary; and they are credited with quite a number of breakthroughs in this area. Even now, we are astonished by their method of preserving the human body through **mummification** of the dead.

The world knew very little about the Egyptians until recently, with the exception of what Herodotus left in his **Histories.** Herodotus gathered information about their life and State, and described a number of their accomplishments--but stated[2] that most of his information came from the priests at Thebes--and it may not be accurate, considering the theocratic system at the time. It was not until the turn of the 19th century that we learned much more about the Egyptians (1802 A.D.), when Napoleon's soldiers discovered the **Rosetta Stone** with an inscription of a decree passed by the government of Ptolemy V, 196 B.C., written in three languages: Egyptian hieroglyphics, Greek, and Demotic (a common Egyptian language during Hellenistic times). This discovery made it possible to decipher quite a number of tablets and inscriptions in tombs and other monuments found through subsequent excavations. This achievement and the work done by **Champollion**, the French scholar who accompanied Napoleon to Egypt and engaged in considerable research on the subject, advanced our knowledge of Egyptian civilization considerably. Historians have classified this civilization, which lasted over 5000 years (4500 B.C. to c. 500 B.C.), into the following four time spans:

1. **The Old Kingdom--Dynasties** I-VI (4500 - 2631 B.C.)
   This period was followed by an interval of chaos.

2. **The Middle Kingdom--Dynasties** XI - XIV (2375- 1800 B.C.)

---

[2] See reference #6 in appendix. Book I.

This period was also followed by another chaotic interlude.

3.   **The Empire--Dynasties** XVIII- XX (1580 - 1100 B.C.)
        This period was followed by a period of divided rule from rival capitals.

4.   **The Saite Age--Dynasty** XXVI (663 - 525 B.C.)

As stated earlier, the system was theocratic, and full power resided with the god-kings and priests. Every acre of land belonged to the Pharaohs; common people could use the land for cultivation only by the King's indulgence, and were forced to pay a sizeable annual tax. Also, large ground tracts belonged to feudal barons or other wealthy men. In spite of this suppressive and highly centralized system that lasted for so many years, there is no record of significant political revolts or labor unrest. However, one incident, referred to by **Herodotus[3],** states that the soldiers of the Pharaoh at Upper Egypt revolted, because they felt neglected, and joined the Ethiopians. The behavior of the State towards the population, particularly the labor class, is not known to have been benevolent. Condemned prisoners who had violated the civil or criminal code, and prisoners of war, were treated ruthlessly and forced to work for the State with no hope of gaining their freedom.

The Seated Scribe, 4ᵗʰ Dynasty

The Egyptians were the "pragmatists" of the ancient world: the arch-conservatives of history. Plato, in **"Timaeus,"** refers to the Athenians as *craving knowledge*; while the Egyptians pursued *wealth*. They built **extraordinary monuments (Pyramids, Karnak, Luxor, obelisks)** and elaborate irrigation systems **(canals)** to direct the water of the Nile. It is interesting, however, that over centuries they copied their earlier artists religiously, and little progress or originality was exhibited in the fine arts. Because of the fact that Egypt is surrounded by desert in the south, east, and west, and only by the Mediterranean in the north, it experienced long periods--sometimes centuries--of peace; and this was the factor that made the continuous maintenance of military power unnecessary They did not consider anything without a theological base worthwhile. The long periods of peace made it possible to discontinue all military preparedness; and as a result of this practice, a few Persian soldiers were able to conquer all of Egypt.

The Egyptians first introduced **hieroglyphics,** which were symbols and pictographs representing animals, objects, and concepts: very similar to Chinese symbols. By practice, slowly throughout the centuries, these symbols eventually evolved into syllabic forms resembling

---

[3] See Reference #6, Book II, 30-32, and Book III, 1-66

the Sumerian model--and in time the letter was developed. Gradually the Phoenicians, probably because of trade requirements, *developed the alphabet* which most ancient people adopted; including the Greeks--who modified and perfected it to become the Greek alphabet of 24 letters, which is still used today. The Etruscans eventually transformed the Greek alphabet into the Latin alphabet practiced today by the Romance languages. **We owe then our system of writing and the alphabet to the Phoenicians and the Egyptians.** The Egyptian priests refined the Sumerian calendar and developed mathematics and geometry, chiefly for the need to calculate land areas before and after inundations of the Nile. Judging only from the Pyramids, we could consider their **architecture** as one of their finest achievements as well. We know little of their accomplishments in the area of the physical sciences, but we do know that the **zenith of Egyptian science was medicine.** They were the first to introduce **dietetics:** stating that the main part of food consumed daily is superfluous--and due to this excessive consumption, diseases originate. Herodotus relates that the Egyptians were the first to introduce **specialization** in medical practice. For example: doctors specialized in internal medicine, [4]and concentrated on various parts of the body: **nose, eyes, ears, etc.**

Regarding art, all progress occurred during the Old Dynasties. The chief characteristics of art and architecture changed little throughout the millennia. Quite a number of buildings at Karnak and Luxor in Upper Egypt, and other locations, display these characteristics today. The Pyramids, the Sphinx, the temples at Saqqarah and the Valley of the Kings also display this art. None of the sculptures of subsequent centuries in any way surpass the achievements of the art and architecture of the early dynasties. Because most of the statues made for temples and tombs were constructed for religious purposes, the priests determined, to a great extent, what forms the artist should follow; and the natural conservatism of religion affected art, not allowing for **avant-garde** experimentation. It should also be noted that the individual in ancient Egypt had little involvement with art; the homes made of mud and straw exhibited no statues or artistic ornaments. The main reason for this was that the people were, for the most part, impoverished--because everything belonged to the Pharaoh and the priests. The only remnants unearthed by archaeologists in Egypt are statuary and temples of the gods and Pharaohs. One also has to admire the Egyptian bas-relief, which effectively presented their lifestyle and depicted their legends and rulers on temple walls and statues. In the area of philosophy and philology, ancient Egyptians are not known to have progressed significantly. Philosophy is generated out of the concern of humans to achieve an ideal society by establishing justice, freedom, and equality in the enjoyment and distribution of goods, as well as understanding themselves and the world around them. But in the case of the Egyptians, the Pharaoh and the priests provided all the answers. Due to the nature of the system and the grip that religion had on the people in ancient Egypt, pursuits such as the ones above were allowed no place in the minds of the Pharaoh's subjects. Speculation on difficulties of life appeared in the writings of one thinker, **Prah-Hotep,** during the period of the Old Kingdom, but he was primarily concerned with the fatalistic aspects

---

[4] See Reference #6, Book 2.

of life and preparation for the afterlife.[5]

Initially, Egyptian religion considered all objects as "gods." Celestial bodies, animals, plants: all were gods. Human gods, such as the Pharaohs, were not worshiped until later. Of importance was the concept of "Immaculate Conception" and how gods were born divine. The predominant gods were: **Ra (Amon), Osiris, Isis, Horus,** and others. There were countless lesser divinities, such as: **Anubis** (the **Jackal), Su, Tefunt, Nephthys,** and **Ket Nut.** Later on, the Pharaoh was accepted as a god--always the son of **Amon Ra;** ruling not merely by divine birth, but as a deity transiently tolerating Earth as his home and anticipating movement to the hereafter. What characterizes and distinguishes this religion, above all, is the emphasis on "immortality." The rationale was that since OSIRIS and the Nile, reappeared every spring: so would man. They also believed that the body, properly prepared (mummification), could live forever. These beliefs dominated the Egyptian faith for thousands of years, and the notion of immortality and the concept of an "afterlife" influenced a number of other religions subsequently.[6]

Thutmose III

The notion of Paradise, Hell, and the Last Judgment of Christian faith is comparable to the Egyptian belief that the soul transcends death. For ancient Egyptians, both soul and body could escape mortality by preserving flesh from decay. This explains the special effort to preserve the body. If the deceased would come to **Osiris,** cleansed of all sins, they would be permitted to live forever in the **Happy Fields of Food** (heavenly gardens with an abundance of means and security). **Herodotus,** in his **Histories,** describes in detail the various methods of preserving the body by mummification, which had achieved a high degree of scientific refinement.[7] By the 14th century B.C., change was imminent--and established patterns of life, religion, and monarchical rule were coming to an end. As we noted earlier, all kings were gods and their name connected with **Amon Ra.** But by the year 1380 B.C., a new king abolished all other deities and introduced a new god, "**Aton,**" and named himself **IKHNATON (or AKHENATON).** As stated earlier, the theocratic system of Egypt did

---

[5] See Reference #5, Chapter XII

[6] See, Reference #5, ibid.

[7] See Reference #6, ibid.

not allow for revolutions and violent change. King IKHNATON'S revolution was the first, and one might expect it to alter the social fabric-- as well as diminish the power of the priests and the Pharaohs (similar to Xenophanes' revolution that affected early Greek theocratic polytheistic system in the 6th century B.C). But this did not happen. Had IKHNATON succeeded in his uprising, the evolutionary path of Egyptian civilization would have been altered.

Ikhnaton introduced **monotheism** and rejected and persecuted all other gods. But he encountered the wrath of the priests and feudal lords, and the resistance that followed weakened Egypt dramatically--not only domestically, but externally as well. The **Libyans, Nubians, Assyrians** and other groups were on the warpath ready to attack **Egypt.** The reason that **IKHNATON** revolted was not only that he was against the multitude of gods, but because he was wary of the strong power of the priests. The system, up to that point in time, had developed a successful society; but this society rested solely on the exploitation of the masses under the direction of the priests who controlled the resources and wealth of the land. The system was corrupt and the practices abhorrent. When **IKHNATON** died in **1362 B.C.,** the State

Guardian Statues, Abu Simbel

was bankrupt; the exterior enemies were encroaching and the Empire was penniless and close to collapse. After his fall, the priests recovered their power; the old gods were reinstated and the new kings followed in the footsteps of the Old Dynasties. The system returned to former practices, and some prosperity followed during the Ramses Dynasty; but eventually the whole system collapsed by the 6th century B.C., when Cambyses, the Persian king, conquered Egypt. Ancient Egyptian morality and practices were unique, in that the kings had several wives and were allowed to marry their daughters or sisters. This practice (incest) prevailed due to the belief that this would preserve the royal lineage. Ramses II is known to have had 50 daughters and 100 sons--and married several of his own daughters.

THE SUMERIANS

It is not clear when the first stages of organized societies started. It seems that the appearance of both the Egyptian and Sumerian civilizations coincided. From some tablets found by archaeologists at the turn of the 19th century, and after successfully deciphering the old Semitic writing, known as *cuneiform writing* (wedge-shaped impressions on clay that originated around the 4th millennium B.C.)), we can be relatively confident in assuming that the Sumerians were the first civilization to surface. They also may have been the first to move from a nomadic, unorganized lifestyle into an administrative organization headed by a god-king. **Sumerians** can be placed at about 4,600 years B.C. (prior to the Egyptians), and lived in the area of Mesopotamia (today's Iraq) between the Euphrates and Tigris rivers. It was in many ways a primitive culture that made use of copper and tin, occasionally mixing them to make bronze. Now and then, they went so far as to make implements of iron; but metal was still a luxury and a rarity. Most Sumerian tools were made of flint, and some, like the sickles for cutting barley, were made of clay; while certain finer articles, such as needles and combs, were made of ivory and bone.[8]

Medicine flourished and there was a specific cure for every disease, but it was still bound to theology. Practitioners professed that sickness, being due to possession of evil spirits, could never be cured without exorcising these demons. A calendar of uncertain age and origin divided the year into lunar months, adding a month every three or four years to reconcile the calendar with the seasons and the sun. Each city gave its own name to the months. [9] The government was run by god-kings and had full control of the population via the priests. The god-king lived in a palace which had only two narrow entrances--fitting one man at a time for security reasons.[10] Smaller kingdoms were formed, but because of trade requirements did not survive--in spite of the fact that the competition and individualism of these separate kingdoms

The Pyramid at Saqqarah

stimulated life and art. They engaged in conflict, which weakened them and eventually led to their demise--and ultimately to the whole of Sumeria. Sumerians did develop a body of laws-- already rich with precedents--when their kings, **UR** and **DUNGI,** codified the statutes. This was the foundation stone of the famous **Babylonian Code of Hamurabi.** According to Herodotus, this earlier code was a bit more lenient than Hamurabi's Code; for example: under the Sumerian Code, a wife caught in adultery would be reduced to a lower status and the husband allowed to remarry; under the **Code of Hamurabi**: the wife would be executed. Even at this early age, the great myths of religion were taking form; and certainly the **Sumerians** developed their own mythology as well. Since food and tools were placed in the graves with their dead, we may assume that they believed in the afterlife. But as the Greeks, they pictured the other world as a dark abode of shadows to which all the dead descended indiscriminately. They had not yet conceived the idea of Heaven and Hell: eternal reward and eternal punishment.

---

[8] See Reference #5, ibid.

[9] Herodotus, in Book II, discusses aspects of this civilization.

[10] See Reference #6, Books II and III.

Like the Greeks, the Sumerians offered prayers and sacrifices--not for eternal life, but for tangible advantages here on Earth. Later, legend told how they should prepare for the afterlife. Another myth narrated how God had made man happy; but man, by his free will, had sinned and been punished with a flood from which one man--**TAGTUG**--survived. **Tagtug** forfeited longevity and health by eating the fruit from a forbidden tree.[11] **Sumerian** writing reads from right to left. The **Babylonians** were, as far as we know, the first to write from left to right. Sumerian script was a symbolic convention of writing derived from signs and pictures of animals, things, or objects painted or impressed upon primitive pottery: similar to hieroglyphics. Presumably, by repetition and innovation over centuries of time, the original pictures were gradually contracted into signs, so unlike the objects they had once represented, that they became symbols of sound syllables rather than things. We could have an analogous process in English: a picture of a dog that, in time, is shortened and simplified *to signify,* not a dog--but the sound *"do,"* and then serve to indicate that syllable in any combination: as in "do-good." The Sumerians and Babylonians never advanced beyond such representations of syllables to the formation of letters and an eventual alphabet. The Sumerians, as a nation, did not last for an extended time--even though it was long by subsequent standards. By the late centuries (approximately 2200 B.C.) of the 3rd millennium B.C., new ethnic groups were developing strength and soon replaced or absorbed the **Sumerians** as the dominant power in the region of ancient Mesopotamia. These were the **Babylonians** and other groups that we shall discuss in the next chapter.

Both the Egyptians and Sumerians contributed to the development of what we call basic sciences today. They were the ones who initiated the study of mathematics; the first steps toward development of the alphabet; and the science of medicine, astronomy, and architecture. Subsequent civilizations built on the fundamentals of these early pioneers. However, the Egyptians and Sumerians contributed little in such areas as: **freedom of choice; democracy; political systems; scientific research,** and the **dignity of man**. Their political structure was highly theocratic and left scant room for experimentation in the social and behavioral sciences. It remained for the **Hellenes** to investigate and advance these areas of research.

---

[11] Compare these concepts with equivalent Christian ones.

MAP 5

THE STATES OF THE MIDDLE EAST ESTABLISHED NEAR THE EUPHRATES
AND TIGRIS RIVERS
BABYLONIA, ASSYRIA AND OTHERS
AND THE EXPANSION OF THE PERSIAN EMPIRE.
(4300 B.C - 334 B.C.)

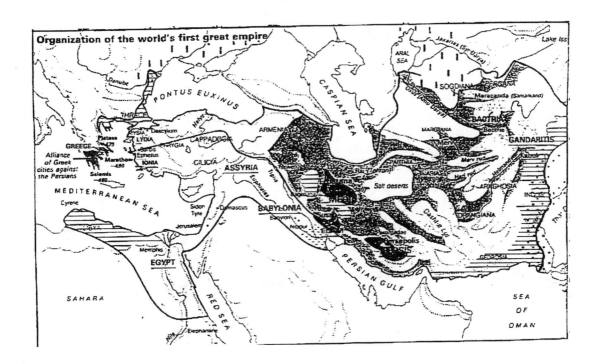

This map shows the **Mesopotamia** region where human civilization began and flourished in **Sumeria, Babylonia, Assyria, Persia, Phoenicia, and others**--from the beginning of recorded history until the time of Alexander the Great. It also details the expansion of the first known world empire (Persian), which prospered from approximately 700 B.C. until it was dissolved by Alexander in 331 B.C.

MAP 6
EGYPT AND THE NILE RIVER

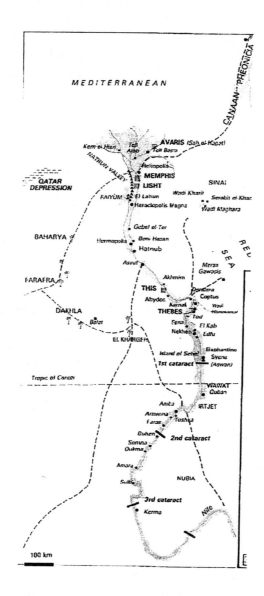

*This map shows the **Nile River** and the **Egyptian State** that flourished from approximately 4300 B.C. to 500 B.C. At that time, the **Persian King, Cambyses,** conquered Egypt. The cities of **Memphis** and **Thebes** were the centers of Egyptian civilization.*

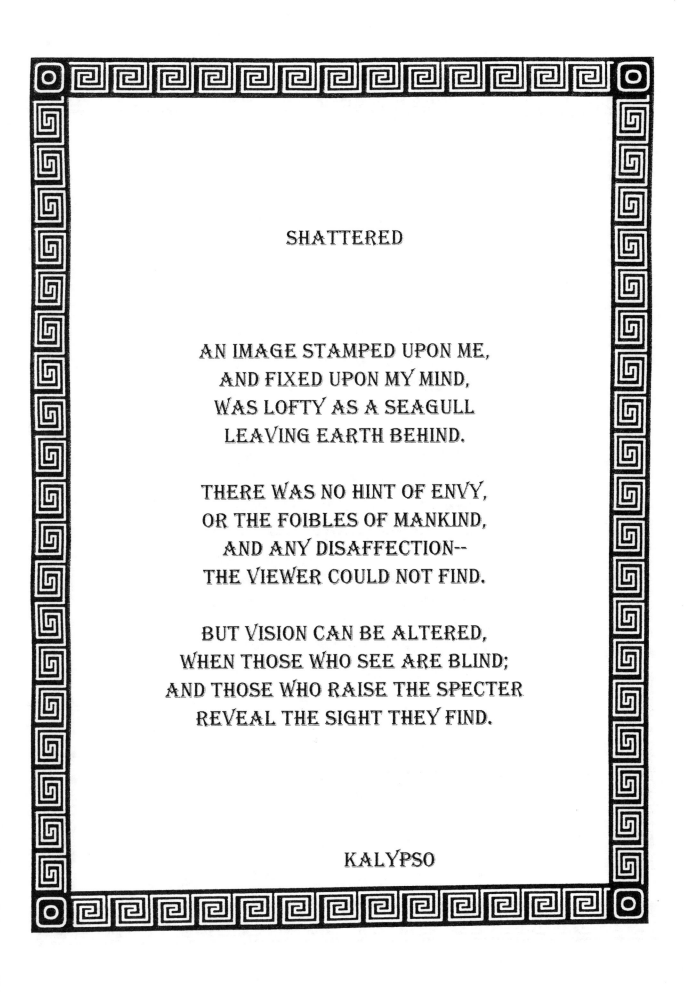

SHATTERED

AN IMAGE STAMPED UPON ME,
AND FIXED UPON MY MIND,
WAS LOFTY AS A SEAGULL
LEAVING EARTH BEHIND.

THERE WAS NO HINT OF ENVY,
OR THE FOIBLES OF MANKIND,
AND ANY DISAFFECTION--
THE VIEWER COULD NOT FIND.

BUT VISION CAN BE ALTERED,
WHEN THOSE WHO SEE ARE BLIND;
AND THOSE WHO RAISE THE SPECTER
REVEAL THE SIGHT THEY FIND.

KALYPSO

MERGING

I VIEWED A GREAT COLOSSUS,
ONCE CRAFTED HAND BY HAND,
AND PALED BENEATH ITS SPLENDOR,
WHICH ENCOMPASSED ALL THE LAND.

I WONDERED IF I MATTERED,
SURROUNDED BY SUCH MIGHT,
AND QUESTIONED YET MY PURPOSE,
WHICH WAS NOWHERE IN MY SIGHT.

BUT THEN I SAW A VISION
OF A BRIDGE WITH ENDLESS SPAN,
CONNECTING PAST AND PRESENT
WITH SMALL FOOTSTEPS MADE BY MAN.

KALYPSO

CHAPTER 16

THE BABYLONIANS AND OTHER EARLY CIVILIZATIONS

> "It is not necessary to assume a Creator or a First Cause, because any child can refute this argument by showing that an Uncreated Creator or a Causeless Cause is just as nonsensical as an uncaused or uncreated world."
>
> **Mahavira**

THE BABYLONIANS

The **Babylonian** civilization developed several centuries after the Sumerians. They lived in the same region of ancient Mesopotamia, along both sides of the rivers **Euphrates and Tigris,** but settled in the lower part of the country near the sea. There they built the city of **Babylon** and progressed rapidly, both culturally and commercially, from approximately 2200 B.C. until 1000 B.C., when the **Assyrians** first, and the **Persians** subsequently, conquered them. Historically and ethnically, the Babylonians were the product of the union of early **nomadic tribes** and the **Sumerians.** But unlike Egypt, where foreign invasions and subjugation were limited, in the region of ancient Mesopotamia (due mainly to its geographic location) the ethnic boundaries were often changing. A group would advance and prosper for a while, but external forces would eventually disrupt and alter their cultural base. During the same period when the Egyptians prospered (4500 B.C. until the Persian conquest), other groups such as: the **Sumerians, Babylonians, Assyrians, Chaldeans, Phoenicians, Hebrews, Hittites, Medes, Persians**, and other less known ethnicities, made their presence felt at one time or another.

Herodotus describes a number of features of the Babylonian culture, and gives some detailed information portraying the morals and ethics of the time. He must have visited Babylon during his extensive travels to the Middle East, collecting information for his **Histories.** [1]The various nomadic groups that intermingled with the Babylonians were of Semitic origin, which leads

---

[1] *See Reference #6, Book A (201 ff). Herodotus describes Babylonian custom--according to which a woman would not be considered suitable for marriage unless she would first dedicate herself to the Goddess of Love by living in the temple until the first visitor engaged sexually with her. This statement by Herodotus may be misleading, in that he may have heard this from people who referred to women of lower morals who would concentrate around the temple practicing their profession.*

one to believe that they were of Semitic ethnicity. **King Hamurabi,** a well-known figure in Babylon, ruled from approximately 2123 to 2081 B.C., and established laws and regulations for trade--as well as codes of conduct for his people. The **Code of Hamurabi** was famous in antiquity; it was a set of laws, supposedly a gift from Heaven, similar to the **Laws of Moses.** The tablets on which the laws were written were discovered in 1902 in **Susa,** and they are preserved today at the **Louvre Museum in Paris.** Besides the secular quality of these laws, Hamurabi was clever enough to link his authority with the approval of the gods. He built temples as well as forts, and convinced the clergy to construct a gigantic sanctuary for **MARDUCK** and his wife (the national deities) at Babylon. The same theocratic power structure that we encountered in **Egypt** and **Sumer** appears here as well--strong and omnipotent.[2] After the death of Hamurabi, Babylon was subdued by northern tribes and did not recover until 500 years later under **King NEBUCHADNEZZAR,** who re-established the power of Babylon--which lasted until its final demise around the 6th century B.C.

One of the greatest achievements of the Babylonians, and for which they became renowned throughout antiquity, is the **Suspended Gardens of Babylon.** These gardens were built by

Clay Walls of Assyrian Capital

Nebuchadnezzar as a gift to his wife, who longed for her homeland, shortly before their final subjugation by the Assyrians. On top of this structure, which was 75 feet tall and supported by columns, the builders deposited a great amount of fresh soil and planted marvelous gardens with a variety of birds, trees, and vegetation. Through a sophisticated hydraulic system, powered by human-slave labor, water was pumped up from the Euphrates for irrigation. These gardens were known by the Greeks as one of the **Seven Wonders** of the ancient world.[3] The language of the Babylonians was a mixture of the Sumerian language and other tribal dialects. Their writing consisted of the syllabic form, which evolved from **pictographs** and **hieroglyphics.** They did not develop an alphabet, but were close to developing one. In the 1930's, the deciphering code of the Babylonian language was discovered, in a fashion similar to the **Rosetta Stone.** In the mountains of Mesopotamia, the King of Persian, **Darius I,** had recorded the victories of his army engraved in stone—in Farsi, Babylonian, and Akkadian. These writings enabled researchers to decipher the Babylonian, as well as the Assyrian language. The method of Babylonian writing consisted of inscribing the text on fresh clay tablets, in symbols and in syllabic sound

---

[2] *See Reference, #6. For the city of Babylon, and the people in general, Herodotus devotes several pages in his Book A (75-206).*

[3] The other six were: (1) The **Pyramid of Cheops** in Egypt; (2) The **Pharos (lighthouse) at Alexandria;** (3) The **Colossus of Rhodes;** (4) The **Temple of Artemis at Ephesus;** (5) The **Mausoleum at Halikarnassus;** (6) The **Statue of Zeus (by Phidias) at Olympia.**

representations. After these tablets dried, they were fired and glazed if necessary. In reference to **Babylonian art,** nothing remains to witness the style or quality. But judging from some structures remaining today, archaeological findings, and descriptions by Herodotus, we can infer that they excelled in building and architecture. The ancient **Code of Hamurabi** was *the first official code of laws*; even though the Sumerians, as mentioned earlier, had developed a code of their own concerning trade, as well as civil and criminal statutes, prior to the Babylonians.

Babylon

The **Babylonians** excelled more in science than in art. They promoted mathematics, astronomy (akin to astrology today) and geometry. These developments were advanced by the priests and inspired by the gods; not for the sake of science and research, but only for the purpose of solving daily problems--and were considered the gifts and the will of the gods. They subdivided time in a fashion similar to today: the weeks for the phases of the moon; the months for the orbits of the moon around the Earth; and the year for the sun's orbit. In the area of medicine there was nothing more than witch doctor practices, supernatural diagnoses, and magical cures. The **Babylonians** made important contributions to the development of human civilization. In the area of science they contributed extensively; for, along with the Egyptians, they took the first steps in astronomy and geometry, and set the first code of Law; even though that contribution was constrained by religious dogma and could have advanced further without such a hindrance. In the area of philosophy they contributed little, because it was difficult to draw a distinction between religion and philosophy during this period. The gods and the priests were the predominant force that governed the will and the destiny of man. This was true for all pre-Greek civilizations. [4]

THE ASSYRIANS

The Assyrians were the **warriors** of ancient times. They lived in the same area of Mesopotamia as the Sumerians and the Babylonians, along the banks of the rivers Tigris and Euphrates, but further north near the area where **Mosul** is today. They were considered the barbarians of the Middle East and succeeded, in the span of a little over 300 years (9th century B.C to 7th century B.C), in conquering the then known world. Their conquests were slow and methodical, but by the turn of the first millennium B.C., they were the masters of the Middle East region. They never managed to conquer Egypt, however, even though they attempted to several times. The **Assyrians** inherited a civilization from the Babylonians and others to whom they were

---

[4] See references #4 and #5 for a further detailed exposition of the Babylonian and other Middle Eastern cultures. We know from **Diogenes Laertius,** that Thales (the first Greek philosopher) and **Pythagoras,** as well as **Democritus** and **Plato,** visited Babylon and Egypt extensively--and were acquainted with the achievements of these two cultures.

paying tribute in previous centuries. Not only did they add little, but because of their continuous wars, conquests, and terror inflicted on the people in the region, progress was actually retarded for several centuries. When the **Persians** defeated the Assyrians and took control of the area in 746 B.C., a similar climate prevailed until the time of Alexander. The god **Ashur** gave his name to a city where the Assyrians worshipped him and all other deities--and finally, from the name of this city, the nation assumed its name. The capital eventually changed to **NINEVEH**--which had a better climate. The entire history of this society encompassed a litany of kings and slaves; wars and conquests; bloody victories and sudden defeat. Several kings were infamous in the history of this nation; but one of them, in particular, was unusually cruel. His name was **Ashurbipal** (**Sardanapalus** for the Greeks), who lived from 884 to 859 B.C., and came to be known as the "Brutal King." An example of the ferocity of the Assyrian kings is found in the following passage, which describes practices during warfare:

"In my fierce valor I marched against the people of Qumuch and conquered them. I carried off the booty from their cities; and their goods and property were taken without reckoning. I burned their cities with fire; destroyed and devastated them. The people left their mountains and came to embrace my feet. I imposed taxes upon them." [5]

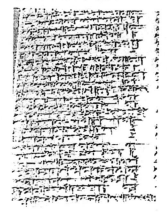

Cuneiform Writing

Next to the army, the monarchs relied heavily on religion and paid lavishly for the support of the priests. The formal head of state was, by consensus, god **Ashur** himself. The people, as subjects of the King and the Priests, had little to say about the government. They were drafted to fight in continuous wars while morality and ethics declined considerably; far below that of the Babylonians. Theirs was a life of barbaric and cruel executions, tortures, slaves, prostitution, and harems: all directed by the will of their "god."

There is little to be said about **Assyrian art.** There are certain columns at NINEHEV which indicate meager architectural effort, but either as a result of wars at the time of the **Persian** subjugation or by Babylonian revolts--there is nothing left of substance. The Babylonians united with the Medes, Scyths, and other northern tribes to revolt against Assyria, and destroyed the great city of NINEVEH near Mosul. The Assyrians developed, however, certain methods of **provincial administration,** necessitated by their extensive conquests that were passed down to the Persians, the Greeks, and eventually the Romans--who made use of these methods in their conquests as well.

---

[5] *See Reference #5, which contains detailed information about the Assyrians, their practices, and the impact that they had on Middle Eastern civilization.*

THE PHOENICIANS

The **Phoenicians,** of unknown origin, appeared in the Near East region by the beginning of the 3rd millennium B.C. They excelled in trade and sailed to the shores of the Mediterranean and established colonies--leaving names of places from their language. With the advent of the Assyrians they lost their independence and subsequently were conquered by the Persians, Greeks and Romans. They were of Semitic background and lived along the shores of the eastern Mediterranean, in the area where Lebanon, Syria, and Palestine are today. They were known to have an excellent navy. When the Persians claimed the eastern Mediterranean, as they had no navy of their own, they seized the Phoenician navy-- which provided the naval force necessary to invade Greece and capture the Ionian cities in Asia Minor. The Phoenicians strongly resisted **Alexander's** efforts to conquer their cities, **Tyre** and **Sidon,** and it took extraordinary efforts by the Macedonians to subdue them. The **Phoenicians** established the city of **Carthage**, in North Africa, where Tunis is today, which presented a considerable obstacle to the Romans in their effort to expand eastward in the first and second centuries B.C. They worshiped a deity taken from the Egyptian divinity tree, and it is said that this divinity was extremely cruel at times. The Phoenician civilization was an advanced civilization in the region, and because of their colonies in all areas of the eastern and western Mediterranean, they derived great benefits from their association with other cultures [particularly the Greeks--who were then (800 B.C.) rapidly developing into a strong competing force in trade]. The Phoenicians developed the maritime arts and were successful shipbuilders--using timber from the cedar mountains. They also excelled in agriculture--successfully cultivating: cereal, vines, olives, dates and other crops—using extensive irrigation systems in the fertile hills cascading to the sea to improve production. They were artisans in metal work, ivory carving, quarrying, masonry, and carpentry--as well as art and architecture. Even though they carried the traditions of earlier civilizations-- Sumeria, Babylon, and Egypt--their artists and artisans contributed a great deal beyond their original prototypes. As pointed out earlier, the position of Phoenicia on the map is located at the crossroad from east to west and north to south, which resulted in continuous pressure from invaders who often demanded tribute and taxes.

The Phoenicians deserve credit for the advancement of human civilization. They were the ones who, from the Egyptian syllabic writing, developed the first 22 all-consonant letter alphabet. The Greeks later modified and improved it by adding vowels, and passed it on to the Etruscans who developed the Latin alphabet. Phoenician merchants probably employed use of the alphabet: a great departure and significant deviation from the hieroglyphics and symbolic characters of earlier civilizations. Another important contribution of the Phoenicians was the spread of the papyrus trade. Papyrus originated in Egypt and was used as a means of writing: a great improvement over older methods using animal skins, clay tablets, and rocks.

THE PERSIANS

Northeast of Mesopotamia, where Iran is today, the **Medes,** a group of Indo-European stock, descended from the shores of the Caspian Sea and established themselves around the turn of the first millennium. They were strong warriors who invaded their neighbors, engaging in warfare that lasted for several decades. Around the 9th century B.C., another fearsome tribe, also of Indo-European stock, subjugated the **Medes** and took possession of their country. The **Persians**--also fierce warriors--destroyed the Assyrians, conquered Babylon, subjugated Egypt, and established an Empire that extended from the western shores of Asia Minor to the western banks of the Indus River. (See Map 5). They contributed modestly in art, architecture, or in the sciences; but they adopted the Babylonian writing and left some tablets that inform us of their predecessors' life. The Persians, however, made significant contributions to the **art of administration,** because they showed how effectively one can rule an empire, extending over 3,000 miles, through the establishment of semi-autonomous administrative subdivisions **(satrapies).** As was true with other groups mentioned so far, the priests played an important role in the affairs of state. The king was the absolute monarch, and was believed to be inspired in his decisions by the gods; therefore, disobeying the king meant disobeying the gods: and that meant death. The cruelty of the kings was feared and the obedience of the population guaranteed. Of interest, is a passage by Herodotus relating the case of a father who, after having witnessed his son's execution, praised the king for his **"archery."**[6] **ZOROASTER (ZARATUSTRA for the Greeks)**--(6th or 7th century B.C.), the Persians' major religious prophet and reformer, founded Zoroastrianism (known as Parseeism in India). The Persians believed that there is a continuous struggle between **"good"** and **"evil;"** and **ZOROASTER** represented the power that came to assist man in this struggle. **ZOROASTER** advised his people to exercise free will; act independently, and fight evil. The **Magi** (Priests) were the ruling party and exercised great power. The Persian Empire was dissolved by **Alexander** in 329 B.C.

THE INDIANS

The **Indians** played an important role in the development of world history, and it is appropriate to present a summary of their influence; as the Indian philosophy probably affected some of the Hellenistic philosophers: particularly the Stoics. The Indians were very influential in the development of the sciences, and one might say that they preserved the achievements of prior cultures and developed a multifaceted civilization that provided doctrines and practices that remain almost intact today. Before we describe their contributions, we present the impact that the **Indo-Europeans** had on the region. We already have alluded to their influence--following the **Mede** and **Persian** invasions--but in the case of India, the **Indo-Europeans,** otherwise known as the **Aryans,** had a particularly strong impact. They appeared (approximately 950 B.C.) near the northern

---

[6] *See Reference #6, Book II.*

provinces of the Assyrian State, and affected the affairs of the people in the region significantly. The Indo-Europeans originated on the shores of the Caspian Sea, and migrated eastward and westward around the middle of the second millennium B.C. (ca. 1500 B.C.). These were the **Mitannians,** the **Hittites,** the **Armenians,** the **Scythians,** *et al.* Of these, the Hittites settled in the area of Asia Minor, where they left very little behind of cultural significance. We do know, however, that they encountered some difficulties with the Egyptians and were recognized as strong warriors. Their language closely resembled Greek, Sanskrit, and Latin. Some examples of the similarities of these languages follow:

ENGLISH	SANSKRIT	LATIN	GREEK
one	ek	uno	en
two	dwee	duo	duo
three	tree	tres	tria
four	chatoor	quattar	tettara
five	panch	quinque	pente
father	pitar	pater	pater
mother	matar	mater	meter
foot	pad	ped	pod
I	aham	ego	ego
me	mam	me	eme
cow	gav	bos	bous

The Armenians and Scythians stayed further north around the shores of the Black Sea, near the Caucasus Mountains. The **Indians** were also affected by the invasion of the **Indo-Europeans,** resulting in significant changes to their lifestyles and customs. The **caste system,** pervasive even today in India, was established to distinguish the fair colored Aryans from darker native Indians, and originated at the time of the Aryan invasion. It is also true that the Indians developed successful trade and prospered materially after the invasion of the Indo-Europeans. In order to establish a time perspective of the events that took place in India, the following chart chronicles events up until the time of **Alexander.**

Prior to ca. 1600 B.C.	Period of Neolithic culture
c. 1600 B.C.	Indo-European invasion of India
c. 1000 to 500 B.C.	Formation of the Vedas.
c. 800 to 500 B.C.,	The theocratic system of Upanishads
599-527 B.C.	Mahariva: founder of Jainism
563-483 B.C.	The Buddha
329 B.C.	The Greek invasion of India

From Alexander the Great to the Christian Era, various kings ruled successfully and productively. The natives who lived in the sub-continent prior to the invasion of the Aryans had led a passive, peaceful, and religious life; associating closely with the civilizations of the Sumerians, the Babylonians, and the Egyptians. Trade flourished extensively between these groups, and the Indians contributed to the development of the civilization in the general area at the time. It is also true, that the native **Indians** had progressed rapidly prior to the invasions of the Aryans. They lived along the banks of the Indus River, which originates in the **Himalayas and Hindu Kush** and runs into the Indian Ocean. But for the rest of India--from **New Delhi to Ceylon**--the dominant factor is **"heat"**; not the dry heat of Mesopotamia and Egypt, but the humid heat that makes life insufferable.

Initially, the Aryans did not assimilate with the local people, but instead developed a system that separated them from the natives on the basis of skin color: the word "color" was the word characterizing this distinction. Later the Portuguese used the word **caste,** which originated from the Latin "pure" (**castus),** to distinguish the difference between the two groups. From the time of the Aryans until the advent of **Jainism and Buddhism** (1500 B.C. to 600 B.C.), considerable progress was achieved, and during this period these religions (or philosophies) came to be known as **Unorthodox Hinduism.** Jainism transformed some of the fundamental tenets of Hinduism and, prior to its appearance, **materialism** and **agnosticism** flourished. The fundamental tenets of **Hinduism** as a religion, and as a philosophy, can be found in the "Vedas"--which were developed at this time and had a significant impact on the lives of the people.

HINDUISM AND THE VEDAS.

The basic scriptures of Hinduism are the **"Vedas";** secret books of unknown authorship. These books were inspired by **BRAHMAN** (the **Creator),** who is eternal in time and omnipresent in space. The **Vedas**--through hymns, chants, and secret formulas--impart knowledge about the world and life and death, as well as what is to be done on the path to salvation: in order to reach **Ultimate Reality.** The authority of the Vedas cannot be contradicted by any empirical evidence. **Hinduism** was, and is, a highly **polytheistic religion** that developed over centuries of evolution. It was not recorded until around the 3rd century B.C., in an alphabet similar to that of the **Phoenicians.** The language of the **VEDAS** was ancient **Sanskrit,** of Aryan origin, very similar to **Latin** and **Greek.** The word VEDA means "knowledge," and the Vedas are four: The **Rigveda;** the **Sambaed;** the **Yajurveda,** and the **Atharvaveda.** Each of the Vedas was further subdivided into four categories: **The Mantras, The Brahmanas, The Aranyakas** and **The Upanishads.** This Indian religion has been classified chronologically into the following periods: **(1) The Pre-Logical Period** (also known as **Orthodox Hinduism).** This period extended until the time of Jainism and Buddhism; **(2) The Logical Period** (also known as the **Unorthodox System),** which extended from the Christian Era to the 11th century A.D; **(3) The Ultra-Logical Period,** which extended to the 18th century A.D. Of concern to us in this discussion is the period known as the **Orthodox**

Religion (the **Pre-Logical Period**)--the period of Jainism and Buddhism. As we have noted, the theocratic systems of the people along the Tigris and Euphrates rivers, as well as the Nile, did not extend beyond strict religious interpretations of life or address questions of formal logic, origin of the world, ethics, and morality. Also, in the case of the Indians prior to the first millennium B.C., the situation did not differ substantially from that of the eastern Mediterranean people. They followed the Vedas and the austere Hindu principles of religious life: Brahman was the Creator— god; and all had to be interpreted through the Vedas.

THE HERETICS AND THE REVOLUTION

In a fashion similar to the revolution of **KING IKHNATON (or AKHENATON)** of Egypt, Indian heretics during the early centuries of the 1st millennium B.C., introduced changes that had a serious impact on the religious doctrines of the **Hindus.** The heretics expressed concern on matters that had not been addressed before; such as: the nature of the world (cosmology); the nature of reality (metaphysics); the nature of knowledge (epistemology); logic, ethics, and morality. This heretical philosophy diminished the effect that the **VEDAS** and **UPANISHADS** had on the people. It undermined everything that the Vedic mysticism had brought forth, and created an environment similar to one brought on by developments during Hellenistic and Roman times. Specifically, they taught that all phenomena in Nature are natural; only simpletons attribute them to **gods or demons. Matter is the only reality;** the body is a combination of matter: the mind is merely matter *thinking*. The body--not the soul--thinks, sees, hears, and feels. There is neither immortality nor rebirth. Religion is an aberration, a disease, or a chicanery. The hypothesis of a God is useless for understanding or explaining the world. Men think religion is necessary only because, being accustomed to it, they feel a sense of loss--an uncomfortable void-- when the growth of knowledge destroys faith. **Morality** is a social convention and convenience: not a Divine Command. Nature is indifferent to good or bad, virtue or vice, and lets the sun shine indiscriminately upon saints and sinners alike. There is no need to control instinct and passion, for these are Nature's instructions to man. **Virtue** is subjective; and the purpose of life is living: **Only wisdom equals happiness.** There were a number of proponents who formulated this doctrine, **"CHARVAKAS,"** named after some early **Hindu materialists.**

This revolutionary thinking in India was probably brought about by striking changes that took place at the turn of the millennium. It could be argued that prosperity always brings a re-examination of the status quo in religion, economics, social standards, morality, ethics, and politics. In the past, most critical changes have occurred during times of prosperity and growth. India is rich in natural resources, and quite a number of products--such as: spices, cereals, fruits, and vegetables were traded with impoverished people of the Middle East and Mediterranean shores. Overall, the Aryan impact was beneficial. The highly materialistic system of the **Charvakas** brought change. But the extreme nature of some of its tenets was repressive, and eventually the heretics embraced religion and the notion of "God." Around the middle of the 6th century B.C., new doctrines were developed. Hinduism continued to have an impact, but the introduction of **Buddhism and Jainism** altered the life of India and all of Asia: even though they were **godless religions.** They offered a new solution to the question that Socrates attempted to answer throughout his life: **"What is the best way that one should choose to conduct his life."**

JAINISM

Jainism, as a religion or doctrine, was introduced during the 6th century B.C., by a man known as **MAHAVIRA,** who lived from 599 to 527 B.C. At the age of 30, he left home and wandered around India practicing an ascetic way of life; eventually developing an agnostic doctrine that espoused complete denial of all sensual pleasures: similar to the **Greek Stoics.** Gradually this sect formed some strange ideas for its time. It advanced the principle that logic is relative and temporal--and that nothing is true except from one point of view. The Jains relate the story of seven blind men who were touching different parts of an elephant's body and giving various interpretations of what they were holding.[7] They claimed that the **Vedas** are useless because they cannot be inspired by **God:** for **there is no God.** It is not necessary to assume a Creator or a **First Cause,** because any child can refute this argument by showing that an Uncreated Creator or a Causeless Cause is just as nonsensical as an uncaused or uncreated world. It is more logical to believe that the universe existed from all eternity; its changes and mysteries due to the inherent powers of Nature and the inability of man to perceive them--rather than to the intervention of a deity. This model of life developed an attitude that all creatures are entitled to an undisturbed existence. The honey belongs to the bee and the soil to the worms. The soil should not be disturbed because the worms would die. You are entitled to take own your life--and nothing more. Some of the leaders of India, such as **Mahatma Ghandi** and **Jawaharlal Nehru,** were influenced by this **"religion."** The Jains eventually became a minority, but are still influential in the life of India today. In the year 79 A.D., they split into two groups. The reason for the schism was a disagreement over what the proper attire of a true Jain should be. Jainism approves of suicide--especially by denial and slow starvation. In a similar fashion, the parents of Mahavira, the creator of Jainism, committed suicide when he was 33. The ultimate objective of a good Jain is to achieve understanding and purification through: asceticism, purity of life, and meditation. The good Jain takes five vows: **Not to kill anything** (even a fly); **Not to lie; Not to take what is not given; To preserve chastity,** and **To renounce pleasure** *of all external things.*

THE LIFE OF THE BUDDHA

It was only a few years after the birth of Mahavira (599 B.C.) that the Buddha (the Enlightened One) was born in 563 B.C. The Buddha lived a full life and died at the age of 80 in 483

---

[7] Compare this concept of the **Jains** with similar convictions that the Greek **Skeptics** embraced during Hellenistic times.

B.C., at the beginning of the **Golden Age of Athens.** It is interesting how two powerful doctrines developed in India simultaneously, and how both followed similar paths and exerted such a profound influence, not only in India but throughout Asia--including China and Japan. The effect that the Hindu heretics had on the people paved the way for **Jainism** and **Buddhism.** During the prosperous years, at the turn of the millennium, an environment developed conducive to liberation from pious restraints and rigid philosophies. **China's Confucius, Greece's Protagoras,** and **India's Buddha** have something in common. The Buddha wrote nothing himself, similar to **Christ** and **Socrates,** and what was written about him was recorded by his followers: and he had many. He would wander throughout the country, followed by his disciples. His birth and life are shrouded in mystery--just as Homer's and Shakespeare's. Legend has it that he was born of a queen by *"Immaculate Conception,"* and that kings came to offer tribute when a light appeared in the sky.[8] He married and had children, abandoned his family to his parent's care, and for six years wandered alone--surviving on seeds and grains until he became a skeleton seeking release from his tortured senses. However, he soon abandoned asceticism and decided to preach on how to achieve emancipation from human misery. He taught that happiness is never possible; neither here--as pagans think--nor after death--as some religions profess. **Only peace is possible,** and that can be achieved when one reaches **NIRVANA.** The Buddha preached benevolence, forgiveness, returning love for hatred *(the Christian ethic of turning the other cheek),* and spoke in parables. The **Four Noble Truths** suggested by the Buddha (comparable to the **Ten Commandments** of **Moses)** are:

1. *Birth, sickness, old age, sorrow, lamentation, dejection, and despair are painful (Odukkha).*
2. *the cause of pain is the craving for: rebirth, lust, pleasure, passion, existence and non-existence (Tanha).*
3. *The cessation of pain can be achieved by: abandonment, forsaking, release and non-attachment, and cessation of craving (Nirvana).*
4. *The Noble Truth that leads to the cessation of pain is to have: the right views; right intentions; right speech; right action; right living; right effort; right mindfulness, and right concentration (The Noble Eightfold Path).*

In spite of the fact that in all Buddhist doctrine there is no deity of any kind, the Buddha believed in and preached reincarnation. He had an Epicurean view of God and offered a philosophy free of dogma and priests: suggesting a means to salvation open to infidels and believers alike. **Reincarnation** was accepted by the Indians and those who followed Buddhist doctrine as axiomatic. The ultimate objective of the Buddha was: achieving complete emancipation of the human mind and body in order to reach the state known as **NIRVANA.** The word **nirvana** has a **Sanskrit** origin and literally means **"extinguished."** It has been difficult to interpret and many definitions have been advanced. But in summary, it can be stated that nirvana means: *(1) emancipation from selfish desires; (2) liberation of the individual from the desire for rebirth*

---

[8]Note *similar Christian accounts in the New Testament, describing the birth of Christ.*

(sexual desire); (3) annihilation of individual consciousness; (4) the inclusion of the individual with a Super Power, and (5) a Heaven of happiness after death. **Buddhist doctrines** differ substantially from those developed by the **Greek philosophers,** and later by **Jesus Christ,** but it is acknowledged that the Buddha's influence on the development of subsequent religions was profound.

This concludes the discussion of the basic principles and tenets embraced by Greek philosophers: from the beginning of the Greek Era until the time of the Romans. With the inclusion of civilizations prior to the Greeks, in the last two chapters, one has the opportunity to compare various efforts made throughout the centuries to achieve the elusive concept of *Happiness*, and ponder questions pertaining to: *the secrets of Nature; quality of life; the origin of creation, and the mystery of birth and death.* Let us conclude with an admonition by Aristotle that exemplifies the Greek spirit:

> *"Habituate the self to the Humanities; for from them and in them are seen the wonders of thought and the subtleties of reflection."*

INDEX

REFERENCES AND BIBLIOGRAPHY

A. REFERENCES.

For information concerning the private lives and philosophy of the various Greek thinkers mentioned in this work, the following material can be recommended for further study. In the text, we often cite these references with a footnote.

l. Amos, H.D. and Lang, A.G.D., **These Were the Greeks,** (1979: Chester Springs, Penna, Dufour Editions, Inc.)

2. Aristotle, **Nckomachean Ethics**, **Meta Ta Physika**, (2 volumes) **Physica**, **Athenian Republic**, **Poetics**, **Eudemia Ethics, Minor Physica, On the Psyche**, **Physiognome**, **Rhetoric**, **Politics**, (1935-1975: Athens, Papyros Publishing Co, 8 volumes) (in Greek).

3. Clagget, Marshall, **Greek Science in Antiquity** (1994: New York, Barnes and Noble).

4. Frederick Copplestone, S. J., History **of Philosophy**, Vol. l. (Greece and Rome). (1962: New York, Doubleday Publishing Co.)

5. Will Durant, **The Story of Civilization, Vol. l. Our Oriental Heritage.** (Chapters XII to XV), (1942: New York, Simon and Schuster, Publishing Co

6. Herodotus, **Histories**, (1955: Athens, Papypos Publishing Co,)
There are three volumes of Herodotus **Histories**. For this work, of interest are: **Book I, 6-94, Book II, Book III (1-160),** (in Greek)

7. Hamilton Edith, **The Greek Way** (1930: New York, Book of the Month Club)

8. Hicks, R.D. Diogenes Laertius, **Lives of Eminent Philosophers** (1925: Cambridge, Mass. Harvard University Press), 2 volumes.

9. Laertius, Diogenes, **The Lives of Eminent Philosophers** (1940: Athens, Papyros Publishing Co.), in Greek, one volume.

10. Plutarch, **The Lives of Famous Men** (in Greek) Papyros Publishing Co., Athens, 1940, (5 volumes).

11. Plato, **Dialogues,** (1935-1975: Athens, Papyros Publishing Co.)
    (There are in total 6 Volumes of the Dialogues, and separately, **The Republic, The Laws.**)

12. **Suidas Lexicon, Lives of Prominent Men of Antiquity.**

13. Taylor, A.E, **Plato, The Man and His Work** (1927: New York, The Humanities Press).

B. <u>ADDITIONAL REFERENCES AND BIBLIOGRAPHY.</u>

The following are references pertaining to all subjects of this work, and are recommended for reader interested in pursuing further study.

14. Adler, M.J.J. **Aristotle for Everyone** (1978: New York, MacMillan Publishing Co.).

15. Atherton, Katherine, **The Stoics on Ambiguity** (1993: Cambridge, Cambridge University Press,)

16. Asmis, Elizabeth, **Epicurus' Scientific Method** (1984: Ithaca, N.Y., Cornell University Press.)

Barnes, Jonathan (editor), **Aristotle** (1995: Cambridge, England, Cambridge University Press)

17. Baird R.M., et al. (editors), **Contemporary Essays on Greek Ideas, The Kilgore Festschrift** (1987: Waco, Texas, Baylor University Press)

18. Bloom, Allan, **The Republic of Plato** (1968: New York, Basic Books, Harper Collins)

19. Charles, David, **Aristotle's Philosophy of Action** (1984: Ithaca N.Y., Cornell University Press).

20. Cornford, F.M., **Before and After Socrates** (1950: Cambridge, Cambridge University Press),

21. Dannhauser, W. J. **Nietzsche's View of Socrates** (1974: Ithaca, N.Y., Cornell University Press),

22. Dudley, Donald R. **A History of Cynicism** (1937: London, Methuen and Company),

23. Freeman, Kathleen, **The Pre-Socratic Philosophers** (1946: Oxford, England, Oxford University Press),

24. Fuller, B.A.G. **History of Greek Philosophy** (1923: New York, N.Y, Henry Holt),

25. Furley David, J. **Two Studies in The Greek Atomists** (1976: Princeton, N.J., Princeton University Press.)

26. Gadamner, Hans, Georg, **The Idea of Good in Platonic- Aristotelian Philosophy** (1986: New Haven Conn., Yale University Press)

27. Giovanni, Reqle, **A History of Ancient Philosophy: From the Origins to Socrates** (1987: New York, The State University of New York Press),

28 Groissant, Jeanne, **Etudes de Philosophie Ancienne, Cahier de Philosophie Ancienne** (1986: Bruxelles, Belgium, Ousia Editors, S.C),

29 Guthrie, W.K.C., **A History of Greek Philosophy**, Six Volumes (1965: Cambridge, England, Cambridge University Press),

30. Hardie, W.F.R., **Aristotle's Ethical Theory** (1980: Oxford, Clarendon Press,)

31. Harris, R. Baine, **Neoplatonism and Indian Thought** (1982: Albany N.Y., State University of New York Press,)

32. Hankinson, R.J., **The Skeptics** (1995: London, Rontledge Press.)

33. Heidegger, M. and Fink, E., **Heraclitus Seminars 1960/1967** (1970: University, Alabama, The University of Alabama Press),

34. Huffman, Carl A., **Philolaus of Croton: Pythagorean and Pre- Socratic** (1993: Cambridge, England, Cambridge University Press),

35. Huson, Hobart, Pythagoras, **The Religion Moral and Ethical Teachings of the Pythagoreans** (1947: Robert Husson, N.Y)

36. Ingle. William R., **The Philosophy of Plotinus** (1918: London, Longman's Green and Co.)

37. Jordan, William, **Ancient Concepts of Philosophy,** (1990: New York, Rontledge Press),

38. Jowett, B., **The Dialogues of Plato** (1953: Oxford, England, Oxford University Press).

39. Kerterd, G.D., **The Sophist Movement** (1981: Cambridge, England, Press Syndicate of the University of Cambridge),

40. Jones, Howard, **The Epicurean Tradition** (1989: New York, Rontledge Press,)

41. Long, A.A. and Sedley, D.N., **The Hellenistic Philosophers** (1987: Cambridge, Cambridge

University Press,)

42. McKeon, Richard, **The Basic Works of Aristotle** (2001: New York, The Modern Library)

43. Moline, Jon, **Plato's Theory of Understanding** (1981: Madison, Wins. The University of Wisconsin Press.).

44. O'Brien D., **Empedocles' Cosmic Cycle** (1969: Cambridge, England, Cambridge University Press),

45. Oates, W.J., (editor), **The Stoic and Epicurean Philosophers** (1940: New York, Random House,).

46. Copleston, **Frederick, Medieval Philosophy** (1952: London, Methuen and Co.)

47. O'Brien, J. Michael, **The Socratic Paradoxes, and The Greek Mind** (1967: Chapel Hill, The University of North Carolina Press,)

48. Salis, John, et al. (editors), **Heraclitan Fragments** (1980: University, Alabama, The University of Alabama Press)

49. Kroner, Richard, **Speculation in Pre-Christian Philosophy** (Philadelphia, The Westminster Press)

50. Romilly, J., **The Great Sophists in Periclean Athens** (1992: Oxford, Clarendon Press),

51. Sciappa, Ed., **Protagoras and Logos, A Study in Greek Philosophy and Rhetoric** (1991: Columbia, S.C., University of South Carolina Press),

52. Reesor, Margaret E., **The Nature of Man in Early Stoic Philosophy** (1989: New York, St. Martin's Press)

53. Shorey, Paul, **What Plato Said** (1933: Chicago, University of Chicago Press,)

54. Stokes, M.C., **Plato's Socratic Conversations** (1986: Baltimore, The Johns Hopkins University Press,)

55. Strodach, George, **The Philosophy of Epicurus** (1963: Evanston, Ill., Northwestern University Press,)

56. Terrence, Irwin, **Plato's Ethics** (1995: Oxford/New York, Oxford University Press,)

57. Teran, Leonardo, **Parmenides Commentary and Critical Essays** (1965: Princeton, N.J.,

Princeton University Press).

58. Van Doren, Charles, **A History of Knowledge** (1991: New York, Balantine Books)

59. Vlastos, Gregory, **Socrates, Ironist and Moral Philosopher** (1991: Ithaca, N.Y., Cornell University Press,)

60. Wedin, Michael V., **Mind and Imagination in Aristotle** (1988: New Haven, Yale University Press,)